SHIFTING CULTIVATION IN
SOUTHEASTERN ASIA

SHIFTING CULTIVATION IN SOUTHEASTERN ASIA

BY

J. E. SPENCER

UNIVERSITY OF CALIFORNIA PRESS
BERKELEY, LOS ANGELES, LONDON

University of California Publications in Geography
Advisory Editors: H. P. Bailey, C. J. Glacken, J. J. Parsons, J. E. Spencer,
Kenneth Thompson

Volume 19

University of California Press
Berkeley and Los Angeles
California

University of California Press, Ltd.
London, England

❖

ISBN: 0-520-03517-8

Printed in the United States of America

PREFACE

On reflecting as to how this study came about, it is possible to suggest that my concern with shifting cultivation really began in 1934 in the higher hill country marginal to the Yangtze River of central west China, where I first saw fire being used to clear a field. Other contacts with fire-cleared fields came casually during the years until, one day in 1948 in the southern Philippines, I wandered through one fresh *caingin* after another. Since 1948 I have spent a lot of time intellectually tending field-clearing fires, and pondering over the associated technologies and related culture habits. The continued concern for the origins of what so often is termed "Oriental hoe culture" has led back toward the beginnings of crop growing by any simple system, arriving quite naturally at shifting cultivation as one of the very early systems. This study forms one segment of a long-term project; in a later monograph I will deal with the evolution of permanent-field cropping and the rise of rice growing as a specific cropping system.

An enormous number of people have contributed in some way to this study. Graduate students enrolled in seminars over the years have had a part in it. Many oriental families have contributed to it by engaging in various of the activities of shifting cultivation, while I naïvely watched. Numerous hosts, guides, interpreters, and translators have helped in almost every country in the Orient. A far larger number of authors than are named in the bibliography have contributed to my understanding. As the footnotes indicate, Harold Conklin, J. D. Freeman, the von Fürer-Haimendorfs, and R. F. Watters have played notable parts in back-stopping my own notions through their critical studies. My wife, Kathryn, has tolerated a great deal of absentminded cogitation, and has cheerfully suffered the manipulation of travel itineraries off regular routes while accompanying me in the pursuit of shifting cultivators. The wrong notions, misinterpretations, and mistakes must devolve upon me, alone.

The help of several different institutions combined to make this study possible. A sabbatical leave from the University of California permitted acceptance of a Fulbright Lectureship at the University of Malaya for the academic year 1957–58, a combination that located me at a central point in southeastern Asia. A travel grant from the Wenner-Gren Foundation made possible local travel and field observation in the Philippines, Thailand, British Borneo, Ceylon, and India during vacation intervals. Grateful acknowledgment is given, separately and in combination, to the University of California, Los Angeles; the University of Malaya, Singapore; the Conference Board of Associated Research Councils; and the Wenner-Gren Foundation for Anthropological Research for the courtesies, leave, appointment, facilities, and financial assistance.

J. E. S.

CONTENTS

I. Introduction 1

II. Distribution and Overall Structure 13

III. Relationships to Physical Environment 26

IV. Relationships to Cultural Environment 53

V. Land Systems and Their Territorial Administration 84

VI. Crops, Crop Systems, and Complementary Economies 110

VII. Technologies, Tools, and Specific Typologies 136

VIII. Summary and Conclusions 166

Appendixes
A. Families and Land Areas Utilized in Shifting Cultivation 174
B. Terminology Employed in the Description of Shifting Cultivation . . 175
C. Diagnostic Criteria Significant to an Analysis of Shifting Cultivation 181
D. Distribution and Usage Patterns of Crop Plants 187
E. Distribution and Usage Patterns of Faunal Elements 201
F. Suggestive Classification of Hierarchies of Shifting Cultivation . . . 204

Bibliography 215

Index 241

FIGURES

1. Present practice of shifting cultivation 12

2. Persistence of early ethnic elements 18

3. Generalized landform patterns 28

4. Distribution and retreat of taros 112

5. Distribution and retreat of yams 113

6. Field-shift patterns 144

CHAPTER I

INTRODUCTION

ONE OF THE THEMES in the wide-ranging study of tropical agriculture has to do with a historic and early technological phase of the subject, the theme that commonly goes under the heading of shifting cultivation or one of its many synonyms. This study is wholly devoted to an examination of this one element of tropical agriculture in southeastern Asia and in a part of the island world of the southwest Pacific. The present analysis attempts to bring together the work of many scholars in many disciplines using as background understanding my personal observations on shifting cultivation in most parts of the rural scene in southern and eastern Asia and the western sector of the island realm. My chief concern is to present the common features of the cropping system in an orderly and comparative manner in an effort to distinguish the critical characteristics of this particular segment of tropical agriculture. This work is not a study of cultures or peoples as such, although it deals with many different culture groups.

Studies of a general subject for a large part of the earth employ many different approaches, and studies concerned with how man lives in a region utilize any one of several approaches. At least seven broad systems of attack can be isolated and summarized:

1. *Area.* Studies using physical attributes and regional patterns of landscape, fields, roads, houses, soils, crops, and related visible attributes.
2. *Commodity.* Studies using variety and volume of crops, animals, minerals, forest products, and exotic commodities.
3. *Economy.* Studies using production output, energy input, labor force, capital resources, balance of payments, and trends in development.
4. *Culture.* Studies using population numbers, groups, organization, customs, language, religion, way of life, and acculturation or deculturation.
5. *Technology.* Studies using tools, techniques, methods, power, artifacts, typologies, and systems.
6. *History.* Studies using chronology of occupance, with sequential development of aspects of varying thematic specialization.
7. *Government.* Studies using evolving political organization, the patterns of structure, institutions, power, and control.

The first two approaches, either separately or in combination, frequently are employed by the geographer to produce a regional or land-use study. The economist normally uses primarily the third approach, incorporating aspects of the second, at least. The anthropologist customarily utilizes the fourth method, including something of the fifth, or, using the archaeologic chronology, operates from the sixth method. The agronomist or student of agriculture often starts with the second concept, bringing in elements of the first and fifth systems. These generalizations are somewhat too broad, but in dealing with aspects of tropical agriculture it is clear that many of the workers placing sketches or drawings on the canvas of tropical agriculture do so from many different conceptual systems.

It is quite normal for the student of one discipline, working with one concept, to use the materials of another discipline and approach, yet almost to ignore the methodology and conceptual framework of the other discipline and its approaches.

[1]

This monograph attempts to combine several disciplinary approaches in a comparative analysis of one sector of tropical agriculture, but it is not organized to present each of the above approaches independently. In this chapter I broadly review certain preliminary aspects of the subject, and deal with issues not germane to the technological aspects considered in later chapters.

WHO PRACTICES SHIFTING CULTIVATION?

If one reads the anthropologists, it may appear that shifting cultivation is chiefly carried on by peoples of simple cultures, perhaps small and fragmented groups living in splendid isolation in some mountainous or far-off region. If one reads the foresters, the peoples practicing the cultures of the past are rapidly destroying the tropical resources of the world of the future. One may read the suggestive conclusion that shifting cultivation is an ancient, primitive system, today but a remnant of the past, not followed by civilized peoples. One may get the impression that shifting cultivation is a narrow system unto itself, totally unrelated to a general way of life, casually and totally discarded by all who learn of a more productive system of crop growing.

It seems nearer the truth to state that shifting cultivation is the assemblage of techniques of living followed by those for whom it is a practical procedure, at any time, in any place, for any of innumerable reasons and purposes. It cannot possibly be considered a single system, a single device, or a single trait that can be altered by a single simple stimulus. To a given practicer of shifting cultivation, the practice always involves some multiple complex of motivations, factors, aims, culture traits, habits, political pressures, and causal forces. It is true that shifting cultivation is practiced by peoples in interior New Guinea, just coming out of the Stone Age, as an integral aspect of their total culture, peoples to whom no other example of total culture has been easily available. But it is equally true that shifting cultivation is utilized by graduates of agricultural and forestry colleges who have been exposed to the best of modern agricultural science teaching, when an easy opportunity or a cause makes it practical. It sometimes is a subsistence economy practiced by peoples who have almost no opportunity to trade or to sell their produce. But it is also a system followed by crop growers whose sole aim is to produce a crop for sale to a distant market. Shifting cultivation often is a technology of expediency, used because it will work better under a given set of conditions than will any other system available to the practitioner.

Throughout the area of concern to this study people of every race practice shifting cultivation, and it is followed by people of every level of culture. It is practiced against the will of government, and with the sanction of government. It is utilized by the seeker after quick profits, unmindful of destruction, waste, or problems created for the future, just as it is practiced by the careful occupant who thinks of the long-term good of the land. It is discarded when conditions and circumstances suggest; it is given up also by the occupants of a region only when subjected to the strong and compulsory pressures of government. Appendix A suggests possible total numbers of families currently practicing shifting cultivation, and the possible acreage of land involved, in the several political regions under review. That in the neighborhood of 12 million families practice shifting cultivation suggests that the system is a significant element in the economy of the southern Orient.

CONTEMPORARY REACTIONS TO SHIFTING CULTIVATION

It is popular in many quarters to express concern, distress, and even horror over the destruction and waste resulting from shifting cultivation. Almost a priori the modern forester uses a standard vocabulary on the subject, whether he is a commercial timberman, a government civil servant, or a member of an international organization. Many soils men use a somewhat similar vocabulary. Geographers often casually contribute similar conclusions. Agronomists normally stress the low productivity rather than the waste and destruction. Conservationists normally decry the destruction of flora, fauna, and wild landscapes, but express less concern for the economic problems of the peoples involved. Anthropologists sometimes tend to apologize for the alleged destruction, if they acknowledge it at all; but they sometimes appear to resent the organized attempts to alter the economy of the simpler cultures described by others as their social laboratory. In recent years some anthropologists have carried out studies of shifting cultivation which view the system from the inside, that is, from the point of view of the culture itself, rather than from the viewpoint of Western concepts of land use. Studies by Conklin, Freeman, Geertz, and others mark a strong advance in the organized analysis of shifting cultivation as a system of land use.

Colonial government administrators formerly tried to stabilize mobile agricultural populations, the better to count, tax, and pacify them, and the better to control land and forest resources for exploitive purposes. More recently a few such civil servants have sought to teach a more productive agriculture when it could be carried out, recognizing that attempts at eradication of the traditional system must be accompanied by some replacement system.

Newly independent governments recently have discarded the alien rules and permitted freedom of action to now independent populations. Courts have followed a humanistic legal philosophy, declining to punish persons following a traditional cultural practice made illegal by an alien concept of land and its use.

Here and there a dissenting voice has been raised to suggest that shifting agriculture is not axiomatically destructive of plant growth, soil, and other resources. Such opinion suggests that shifting cultivation is really a long-range rotation of land use, ecologically in balance with tropical environments. There has been recognition of the fact that when local populations possess adequate land ranges, their shift cycles usually are ecologically sound and constructive rather than destructive. Such opinion does also recognize that shifting cultivation may become destructive when local populations become too crowded, or when commercial aims strongly enter into the practice.

Currently occidental alarms over population growth in particular parts of the world, and alarms over the statistical indexes produced by projecting population growth against land areas, are producing a new wave of opinion that shifting cultivation must go, or the world will go hungry and stand in want of many resources. It is a bit difficult to restrain a reaction to the most recent surge of emotion against shifting cultivation; now that the tropics are passing out of the hands of the mid-latitude nations, something must be done to save the productivity of the tropics for the world as a whole, but specifically for the occidental world. I would enter the plea that not all aspects of shifting cultivation are destructive, that we must know what it is we seek to improve, that we can so far present no alternative use concept for many mountainous areas, and that the total replacement of shifting cultivation by traditional, unplanned sedentary agriculture will bring more ills than it will cure.

Particular aspects of the destructiveness of shifting cultivation are dealt with in particular chapters. In general, however, it would appear that when local populations have their own way, when a whole culture is relatively in balance, and when the pressures of exploitation by outsiders do not rest too heavily upon a given region, shifting cultivation is not destructive of resources of value. Shifting cultivation often utilizes landscapes that contemporary advanced agricultural systems find difficult to exploit without engaging local populations at relatively low return.

THE GENERAL IMPORTANCE OF SHIFTING CULTIVATION

Shifting cultivation is the most widespread type of cropping system employed in the Orient, though no longer is it the primary one. Its importance lies less in the productivity inherent in the system than in the total area of territory it covers, and in that it is a technique engaged in by all kinds of people. Its importance lies also in the fact that at present it cannot possibly be abolished in a few short years, for it is critical to the continuing livelihood of people in all parts of the Orient. Elements of importance lie also in the fact that the nature, purposes, methods, and results of shifting cultivation are but poorly understood by much of the world. Because it has remained throughout the world's tropics as a common system, it has inherent values under conditions as they have existed. It is important to understand what many would try to abolish, important to learn what changes must be made throughout the tropics *before* it is, or can be, abolished.

THE HISTORICAL ROLE OF SHIFTING CULTIVATION

It perhaps is a fair preliminary judgment to suggest that shifting cultivation, in broad terms, was the elementary and pioneering cropping system used by the early agricultural occupants of many forested regions all over the world. It does not seem to have been widely used in grasslands or in truly arid regions, though it is applicable in many of the drier margins. There is evidence to suggest that it spread progressively across almost the whole of southern and eastern Asia, Europe, and humid Africa in the early stages of settlement of these regions by agricultural folk. Certainly it was widespread in the pre-Columbian Americas, and it was the basic system by which the earliest Europeans occupied much of eastern North America, though the term seldom has been used directly in American colonial agriculture. The substitution of a better and more advanced cropping system has been slow, gradual, and related to the rest of group culture. The critical factors in this substitution are the development of group culture in general, and the development of the environment in respect to cultural landscapes. Shifting cultivation, therefore, has disappeared from large parts of the world through the substitution of better systems of agriculture in balance with culture in general, and in balance with landscapes as modified by continued occupance and development.

Where group cultures have not advanced, shifting cultivation remains the standard practice. Where development of the cultural landscape has not sufficiently modified the early landscapes and produced developed cultural landscapes, shifting cultivation has remained in practice long after its initial establishment. And, where groups of people have been subject to disrupting influences and exploited by other peoples, they may continue to employ shifting cultivation as the only possible system.

Currently shifting cultivation still is a pioneering system, employed on the frontier of settlement of forested landscapes in the tropics and subtropics. Many of those who become landless in regions of permanent agricultural settlement and are unable to find other economic support gravitate to the frontiers, the reserves, and the empty regions. Lacking capital resources, and facing life in an undeveloped region, they employ shifting cultivation as a beginning system. Once they begin to gain control of their landscapes, their agriculture takes on various manifestations of permanence, provided they are not again subjected to pressures that render them once more landless. Every country included in this study possesses an agricultural frontier that is being advanced by the shifting cultivator.

The shifting cultivator has been, and is, a primary agent in the development of mature cultural landscapes of forested regions. By his own efforts he begins the process of transforming the forested landscape, and he is followed by other settlers who complete the job. Historically, therefore, shifting cultivation has been one of the processes of transforming wild, forested landscapes into developed cultural landscapes.

There have always been culture groups that appear tenaciously to hold to the system of shifting cultivation. It is today characteristic to consider shifting cultivation so integral a part of their whole cultures that it cannot easily be changed. This is historically true, and it remains true today. In many contemporary situations such peoples have a long tradition of being subject peoples, of being displaced, and of being shoved into less valuable territorial ranges. For them the continuance of shifting cultivation in some further underdeveloped range of territory is a matter of economic expediency as much as it is a matter of prevailing and continuing culture.

There also have been populations in relatively isolated regions into which the advancing cultures of other regions have not penetrated, so that cultural and economic pressures upon them have not been strong. Such is interior New Guinea, a region that only now is having pressures placed upon it. In earlier times there were several similar regions, but perhaps New Guinea was the last of these.

Last, there is the role of shifting cultivation as an economic auxiliary to a more advanced system of agricultural life. In regions of difficult environment the stable resources are too few to support the populations that have accumulated in them. In such situations the retention of a historical practice as a marginal and auxiliary resource is a defensive tactic against the occasional extradifficult period and against the pressure of overpopulation.

THE FUTURE OF SHIFTING CULTIVATION

In the long-term future it is likely that shifting cultivation will become an unimportant, marginal cropping technique. The process of creating permanent agricultural landscapes of a mature degree of development will work toward the end of eliminating shifting cultivation from most of the rest of the forested parts of the world which can become mature agricultural regions.

The replacement of shifting cultivation by other agricultural systems cannot be merely a process of formulating legal statutes, penalizing transgressors, and establishing formal forest preserves. The whole economic and social culture of all populations now using the system must be upgraded before shifting cultivation will disappear or before it will decline to insignificant proportions. Implicit in this upgrading is the development of such permanent elements of the cultural landscape as transportation lines, marketing facilities, manufacturing facilities, settlements, educational facilities, and other facilities giving populations economic alternatives to the practice of shifting cultivation. Implicit in this upgrading of economic culture must also be the upgrading of the whole of the social and political culture, for one sector alone cannot be altered without altering others.

Even in today's world of rapid change, the total development of all areas of the world tropics in which shifting cultivation continues will not be accomplished within a short period. Only recently have programs been deemed holistically applicable to the problems of the tropical regions of the world; their full development still requires considerable time. In the political world of today, when independence is coming to tropical regions, reaction against the kinds of economic and political controls imposed in the past will require time for populations to live down their animosities before more progressive developments can be put into effect.

Shifting cultivation will be a continuing practice, but on a declining level. The less able and undeveloped sectors of a population will continue shifting cultivation longest, as will those parts of a regional population less affected by cultural development, and those localities less developed by the processes that mature a cultural landscape. As these populations are hardest to reach, and as forested uplands are the most costly to develop fully, the eradication and replacement of shifting cultivation will be both slow and costly.

TERMINOLOGICAL CONSIDERATIONS

In this study I employ the terms "shifting cultivation" and "shifting cultivator" as the general labels applicable to all forms and to all practicers of the general system in use in the Orient. These basic terms are simple, the most direct, and the broadest in frame of reference. Because there are many types and subtypes of shifting cultivation, the generic label should be broad, inclusive, and as nearly self-explanatory as possible. In specific discussion of particular subtypes, special terms and names are applied; Appendix F attempts a classification of the types found in the Orient.

A large number of terms surround the many categories of impermanent cropping systems found throughout the world, particularly in the tropics, and there is active discussion as to the term that should be used as the general name. Most such discussion seems to follow the thought that all shifting cultivation is almost totally alike, and that it can be effectively described by one highly defined term, which at once can be made a noun, a verb, and an adjective. It is my conviction that no single, highly defined term can serve adequately as the generic label for the mobile techniques of crop growing which do not use systems of permanently sited fields under specified legal tenure. In the same way no single, highly defined term can effectively cover all the varieties and forms of permanent-field agriculture the world over.

Shifting, as a term, carries implications not only of the actual change of the site cultivated in a particular crop season, but it implies something with regard to the system of land tenure. I have used the term "cultivation" in one of its early English meanings to indicate a simpler form of crop growing than is normally implied by the term "agriculture" in the modern world, wherein agriculture has become highly complex, variably mechanized, considerably commercialized, and surrounded by differing degrees of scientific control and procedure. It is clear that the term "cultivation" is applicable, for most followers of the general system do some preparation of the soil for planting, and few are those who do not disturb the soil at all in their land clearing and site preparation prior to planting.

Clearly there must be effective recognition of the evolutionary elements in the systems of crop growing, from the earliest possible description of conscious planting to the level of our modern highly scientific agriculture; and the seeking of category names which neglects this issue will prove faulty. Practically all shifting cultivation, except for a few subtypes of modern application, is a relatively simple form of plant growing, a kind of gardening. One may question whether the very early and simple varieties of crop growing ought to be called agriculture at all, except in the very broadest terms of reference. There is ground for distinguishing between the varieties of gardening and the varieties of developed agriculture. Terminologically, and functionally, it would be fitting to place the distinction at the point of introduction of nonhuman powered tools, integration of the larger domestic animals into the economy, introduction of different field systems made possible by power tools, addition of new crops and cropping combinations, and the differing procedures introduced to handle the quantitatively larger yields.

In view of the above distinction it is preferable to think of shifting cultivation as a kind of protoagriculture, in the evolutionary sense, thereby necessitating care in terminological discussion. My own personal preference for a single, short, generic term for shifting cultivation would be "jungle gardening" as closer to the practical operation normally carried out, at least in the tropics, but, as there is ground for declaring the term not self-explanatory and not fully inclusive, I neither propose nor use the term.

In the historical development of the world's cropping systems, it is clear that shifting cultivation was one of the very earliest; whether its simplest subtype was actually the earliest cropping system is still quite uncertain. Historically it is clear that some variant of shifting cultivation was a part of early Neolithic forest clearing and crop growing in most forested parts of the world. So long as this form remained the general type of crop growing, it is likely that no differentiated language terms became very complex. I believe it true today that among most of those cultures in which shifting cultivation is the only form of crop growing known, specific and definitive language terms are lacking by which to describe either shifting cultivation as such, or a quite different cropping system. Many cultures using shifting cultivation, of course, had multiple terminology by which they described differing stages of procedure, different kinds of lands, and different kinds of crop plots. As soon as a system of crop production basically different from shifting cultivation evolved, however, language terms were devised to distinguish among different systems. I believe it true also that every culture group knowing both shifting cultivation and permanent-field agricultures has some term or group of terms for shifting cultivation.

Thus there are literally hundreds of terms and variants in use around the world which refer to shifting cultivation in some way. As various kinds of vegetatively covered lands are used, there are terms that refer to shifting cultivation on lands covered with mature forest, secondary forest, brush, brush and grass, scrub, and grass. As various methods of clearing fields have been employed, many of the terms originally had specific connotations. Grubbing and burning, in many languages, involved variant terminology from felling and burning. A common early language development apparently was to apply a specific term to classes of lands cropped in different ways; these terms are often used today to refer to the system of cropping rather than to the classes of lands. The long-term change in meaning of many terms today often involves use of terms as general rather than specific applications. The evolution of the modern Ceylon term *chena* and of the Burma term *ya* clearly illustrates this development. The three-term series *ijran* (sometimes *komon*), *upraon,* and *talaon* used in the Garwhal and Kumaon Himalayas for lands worked in different ways shows careful terminological distinction and development.

Appendix B lists language terms in some way applicable to shifting cultivation, including native languages, non-English European languages, and common English terms that are applicable. No effort has been made to make any of the lists complete by linguistic research, nor to make each term etymologically accurate within its own linguistic framework, for the tables were simply compiled from the literature surveyed, as the terms were actually used, and few of the authors were expert linguists. It is obvious that strict grammatical reference does not always obtain, and I have made no effort to find linguistic origins of terms. The appendixes are presented merely as an indication of the variety of linguistic reference to shifting cultivation. Appendix B-1 lists all the terms used in the Orient which I found, but, as no search was made, terms from other parts of the world are fewer in number. Because no Slavic-language literature was used, Appendix B-2 contains no Slavic terms, though they obviously exist.

It appears quite normal among occidental scholars that individuals come to prefer certain terms, both in English and in non–English-language reference, to defend them heatedly, and occasionally to deride most other terms. Gourou, in recent writing at least, seems to prefer the term *ladang* when referring to shifting cultivation in any part of the world. *Milpa* has become the most commonly used term among scholars working in the American realm, and *chitemene* seems to be gaining preference among African scholars. My own preference is the Filipino term *caingin* for any and all types of shifting cultivation anywhere in the world, because I first gained reasonable field familiarity with the workings of the system in the Philippines.

Recently a few scholars have made precise efforts to define shifting cultivation, and to promote a new general term to cover it which can be used as noun, verb, and adjective. Such efforts use highly specific definitions applicable to only a few sub-types of shifting cultivation, and generally seem to place it as a kind of crop growing used only by the simpler cultures. These attempts merely confuse the problem of dealing with the broad range of shifting cultivation. The selection of the old Scandinavian verb root from which to take the obsolete English word "swidden" is a case in point, as is the effort to promote the French word *brûlis*. Swidden, in its old English frame of reference, concerned the burning of heather, brush, scrub, and peat off moors or tracts of unenclosed wasteland which often were wet to boggy. Because it is now obsolete, it has some virture, but it carries as much a regional and situational connotation as does *hena,* from Ceylon, or *marram erka,* from central India.

The term "swidden" is, in a sense, totally alien to modern language, to the vocabulary, and to the literature, without intrinsic connotations by which to understand it.[1] I can, of course, be charged with an emotional response similar to that ascribed to others, but I do not think the term "swidden" suitable as the generic term applicable to all forms of shifting cultivation. We do not have one term, usable as a noun, a verb, and an adjective, for all contemporary American techniques of crop growing, and indeed there seems no serious reason why we should have. Similarly, there seems no strong reason why we should try to set up a single term into which we tightly press all forms of shifting cultivation.

Shifting cultivation, on the other hand, already has a degree of familiarity among botanists, agronomists, pedologists, foresters, economists, geographers, naturalists, conservationists, and anthropologists. Its very looseness is, in a sense, useful, for the generic term used to apply to a series of categories should be broad and general. The chief objection—that the term is used vaguely and carelessly—is somewhat invalid. The difficulty has not lain with the term itself, but with the scholars who have written casually on the subject without carefully describing and analyzing the specific category with which they were dealing. Such references as "the usual bush fallowing" and "practice normal shifting cultivation or migratory horticulture," without a careful description of what is under discussion, are not scientific observations, and the attempt to substitute a single precise term, such as "swidden," will receive the same kind of careless treatment. The solution lies not in a single, narrow, new name, but in careful study, observation, and writing about multityped patterns of crop production (see Appendix B-3).

Beyond the names that are applied to shifting cultivation, other items of vo-

---

[1]The term "swidden," in the contemporary linguistic context, derives from a 1955 contribution by Ekwall, who considered it a clarification of the terminology of anthropology. Were anthropologists the only people concerned with the subject, the matter could remain a subject for argument; the series of short notes in the journal *Man* (Ekwall, 1955; Greenaway, 1956; Bushnell, 1956; Fautereau, 1956; and Ehrenfels, 1957) show that there are advocates for the French term *brûlis,* and for some form of the German term *Brandwirtschaft.* Far more disciplines than anthropology, however, are concerned with the practice of some of the simpler forms of crop growing, as argued in my textual paragraphs.

cabulary need comment. The word "abandon," applied to the shift of cropping from one plot of land to another, is perhaps the most misused word in all the literature on the subject. It derives from application by nineteenth-century Europeans who, misconstruing the functioning of shifting cultivation, applied an erroneous term to the change of plots and to the reversion to regeneration of plots once cropped.[2] The phrase "temporary abandonment" is equally incorrect, in addition to being grammatically in error. The function of moving from one plot to another among all but a very few practicers of shifting cultivation implicitly carries the concept of reuse at some later time by someone. The meaning of the word "abandon" given in most dictionaries is "give up with the intent of never again resuming one's rights or interests in." The great majority of shifting cultivators think in terms of the future group use of once-cropped land, including use by descendants, and the return of land to the regenerative process is integrally a part of the developed concept of shifting cultivation.

Another term that is misused is "cultivation," again implying a whole concept. From the mid-latitudes the European has come almost automatically to consider failure to turn the soil vigorously at frequent intervals as an attribute of laziness, slovenliness, unproductiveness, poor skills, or primitiveness in respect to crop growing, and the generalization is too often reached that no cultivation is done. Most tropical soils that have been under forest cover are loose, soft, permeable, and croppable when cleared of their wild cover, and very little formal tillage is required to prepare them for planting. Most tropical soils should not be turned too often or too deeply by cultivation. In these circumstances a very little disturbing of the surface soil constitutes cultivation adequate to the edaphic requirements, and it is normally achieved by clearing, planting, weeding, and harvesting. Where insufficient regeneration of plant growth has not yet fully reconditioned the soil, where grassland must be cropped, or where overwet soils must be aerated and provided with drainage, the specific problems to be dealt with are different from those of well-grown and well-drained forest lands. In such instances shifting cultivators do turn the soil, drain it, aerate it, compost it, or otherwise manipulate it.

DISCIPLINARY AND BIBLIOGRAPHIC

The subject of shifting cultivation contains aspects of interest and concern to a wide range of disciplines, and a large number of scholars are therefore in some way concerned with some part of it. Most students dealing with a phase of the subject have been interested primarily in something else, and have dealt with their major concerns more carefully and more fully than with the nature and system of crop growing. Within recent years the subject has begun to attract more attention, and the literature is reflecting the increased study of the subject. Several recent studies by anthropologists and geographers have turned full-scale and critical attention upon shifting cultivation, and there is a growing list of very sound publications.

---

[2]Many authors use an almost standard sentence to describe the field shift involved in shifting cultivation. It is often stated: "After one or two years the plot is abandoned to forest for some years before being used again for a crop." Most dictionaries do not permit this usage of the word "abandon."

Although the distribution of shifting cultivation is worldwide for the tropics and subtropics, much of the literature has specific reference to a particular region or sector. This study, likewise, is restricted in its purview, and concerns only the Asiatic tropics and subtropics. For that region, however, it does concentrate on the whole system of shifting cultivation, to the exclusion both of other forms of agriculture and of other aspects of human activity. I hope that this study will provide a better understanding of shifting cultivation as a form of crop growing historically practiced in specific geographic landscapes of southern and eastern Asia.

I have made no attempt to review the whole of world literature dealing with shifting cultivation, nor to exhaust fully the literature dealing with the Asiatic sector of the tropics and subtropics. Rather, I have tried to sample the literature for representative and descriptive commentaries on all the regions under review. The formal bibliography, rather than the works specifically footnoted, lists the studies I examined which provided something of value. Studies examined but found to have no value for my purposes are omitted from the bibliography, even though they contain useful material on many fields close to the subject.

My use of the literature was subject to my own lack of ability in certain lines. But my understanding of the subject through the literature was handicapped by the fact that many writers have been far too casual, fragmentary, and even contradictory in their writing on things pertaining to crop growing. In part these inadequacies result from the fact that the study of shifting cultivation to date has largely been simple description of things casually noticed, with little attempt to compare, analyze, and classify, and with but slight effort to understand shifting cultivation as a whole system of deriving a living from a particular environment.

One specific problem—the comparability of information of different dates during a period in which technological change has been rapid—requires examination and comment. Many writers often use the present tense when reporting something from a previously published study, though the study may be decades old. I have tried to keep in mind the dates of all statements about specific practices of a given people, in order to note the patterns of change, but this sometimes is difficult to do accurately. Such dating is enormously important in the present assessment of shifting cultivation. For example, Forsyth's *The Highlands of Central India* contains excellent descriptions of shifting cultivation as the standard practice in all the hill country of central India in the period 1850–1875. By the late 1950's, however, shifting cultivation was all but gone from most of this region. I spent days in 1958 in the northern Chota Nagpur hill country, amid industrial landscapes of coal and iron-ore mines, steel plants, and a commercial agricultural economy, without once finding the shifting cultivation that was common before 1900. In the Agusan Valley of northern Mindanao, in the Philippines, Christian Filipinos have almost completed the establishment of a permanent-field agricultural landscape in some of the areas where John Garvan's *The Manobos of Mindanao* depicted the simplest of migratory shifting cultivation in the early 1930's. Both in the use of specific data and in framing generalizations and conclusions, I have made every effort to handle dated information as accurately as possible.

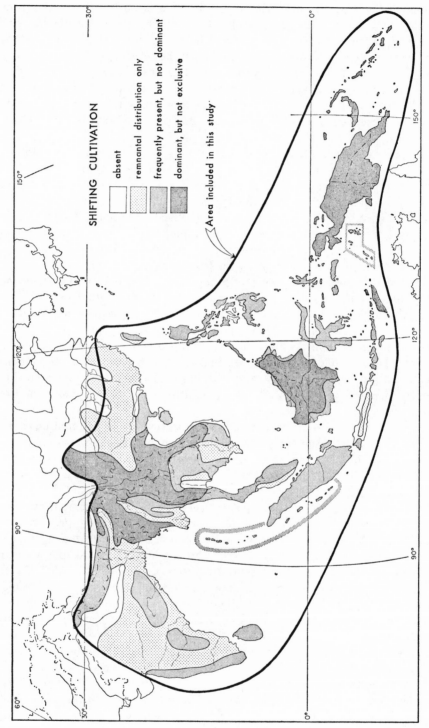

Fig. 1. Present practice of shifting cultivation.

CHAPTER II

DISTRIBUTION AND OVERALL STRUCTURE

REGIONAL DISTRIBUTION

SHIFTING CULTIVATION is practiced in all the humid regions of southern and southeastern Asia, from the tidal coasts to the upper limits of crop growth in the higher mountains.[1] Only India and West Pakistan contain areas too arid for the normal practice of shifting cultivation; parts of the Deccan, the northwest of India, and most of West Pakistan lie outside the zone of active shifting cultivation. The map in figure 1 indicates the generalized areal distribution of the system at the present time.

Many of the best descriptions of shifting cultivation refer to the steep slopes and rugged hill country chosen by followers of the system, but equally good ones exist for peoples using shifting cultivation on the flat lowlands.[2] Many of the descriptions that come from the hill country pertain to ethnic groups whose residence there was fixed by conditions other than those of the agricultural system they follow, in that they retreated to such areas under pressure.[3] Because anthropologists have often studied smaller culture groups in remote mountain environments undue emphasis has been placed upon the rough, steep, and mountain locational situations.

It is, of course, true that many of the lowlands today show little shifting cultivation, for it is chiefly in the lowlands that more advanced systems of agriculture have taken over the land—the best land.[4] The map of the present distribution of shifting cultivation (fig. 1) is therefore dated. It is not the map of a century ago, and it will not be the map of two or three decades hence. This characteristic of change in the location and distribution of shifting cultivation was native to the pre-European agriculture of southern and eastern Asia, for the making of permanent agricultural landscapes has been a long-continuing process. The arrival of the European, together with the launching of European-controlled agriculture,

---

[1] I have observed shifting cultivation practiced from sea level to 12,000 feet elevation; in parts of southeastern Tibet and the upper mainland of Southeast Asia it can be found above this level. See Pelzer (1945, p. 17) for one statement of the matter of hill versus flatland preferences, and see chapter iii of this study for a more specific consideration of the issue of sloping terrain versus flatlands.

[2] Pelzer, 1945, p. 17. Chaudhuri (1903, pp. 507–508) describes extensive shifting cultivation in upper Bengal, India, on flat lowlands in 1903, but also says that the demand for land was increasing year by year, and that the whole area would soon come under permanent settlement. Here Bengalis either encouraged Mech and Garo tribesmen to clear farms for them by their traditional techniques, or followed in their wake to acquire cleared lands. See Geertz, 1963, for a discussion of the sequence in Java. On Wogeo Island, off eastern New Guinea, cultivators use only sloping land when flatlands do not suffice (Hogbin, 1938, pp. 127–128; 1939a, pp. 117–149). For Malaya see Ooi, 1959, p. 92; for the Solomon Islands see Blackwood, 1931, p. 201.

[3] There are many references to the effect of pressure upon shifting-cultivator peoples, causing them to retreat into poorer areas not of their own free choice. See Forsyth, 1889, pp. 125–161, Rahman and Maceda, 1958, pp. 866–869, Wiens, 1954, pp. 283–287, C. and E. von Fürer-Haimendorf, 1945, pp. 282–308, and Groves, 1932, pp. 342–350, for the results of general cultural pressures; Nag, 1958, pp. 62–75, Chattopadhyay, 1949, p. 15, and C. and E. von Fürer-Haimendorf, 1948, p. 83, for the impact of the forester; Stebbing, 1926, for a full discussion of problems in regard to forestry methods; Hodson, 1911, p. 114, for an illustration of deliberate harassment; and Bower, 1950b, for the result of government action in awarding lands of one tribal group to another tribe. There are many other sources of pressure, historically.

[4] See Chaudhuri, 1903, pp. 506–508, as an example.

was a second and very potent factor in further changing the distribution and location of shifting cultivation. In the preceding four centuries many large areas have been added to the permanent agricultural landscape, and shifting cultivation has been displaced from many regions.

It should be remembered, however, that shifting cultivation can be found close to large cities, political capitals, and international ports.[5] As an expression of complex ecologic balance among physical landscape value, economic land value, cultivator economic technology, and cultural tradition, shifting cultivation turns up in many different situations distributed throughout many parts of the Orient. It may remain as a remnant, regional-use technique in areas passing into other systems of land development. But it also turns up as an initial system of land development in regions previously unsettled.[6] It should also be noted that shifting cultivation is used in many localities where land is now privately controlled, and in many regions from which the aboriginal forest cover has long been cleared.

QUANTITATIVE REGIONAL DISTRIBUTION

Appendix A gives a quantitative estimate of the land embraced in some phase of the shifting cultivation cycle in the region considered in this study. The total area actively cropped by shifting cultivation in any one year may amount to 35–40 million acres, a large part of which will have been cleared for cropping during the year. Cleared land once or twice cropped, but not to be planted again, from which some harvests still are being taken, may add another 10–12 million acres. Land in crop, in the harvest-gleaning stage, and in various stages of fallow, including all land that is required to maintain the annual cropping sequence, may reach the figure of 250–275 million acres. The annual crop area may amount to about 55,000 square miles, whereas the total land needed to maintain the annual crop area may perhaps be as much as 400,000 square miles.

The above figures are slightly deceptive, as a certain amount of land every year passes from usage in shifting cultivation into the permanent agricultural landscape of sedentary crop agriculture. With few data to go on, my own estimate is that at the present time between 1 and 2 million acres per year are being added to the permanent agricultural landscape from lands formerly used for shifting cultivation. Additionally, some lands each year revert to regrowth and will not again be cleared for agriculural crops prior to the time they may be cleared by the commercial timberman in the future. Thus a certain share of mature forest (not virgin forest by any means) is being cleared each year by the shifting cultivator. But not all the land put into the annual cropping cycle is mature forest by any means, for much of it has been used at a recent date by a cropping cycle six, ten, twenty, or thirty years previously. As the commercial timberman today is an active cutter of mature forests in many areas of the Orient, he often precedes the shifting cultivator, so that some of the new land taken into the cycle

---

[5] I have seen shifting cultivation within a few miles of Hanoi in Indochina, Colombo in Ceylon, Cebu and Manila in the Philippines, and Kuala Lumpur in Malaya.

[6] In the Philippines, British Borneo, and Thailand I have seen shifting cultivators following the timber cutters, and in most areas of south and eastern Asia settlers are pushing into newly opened areas and using shifting cutivation as their initial cropping system, quickly switching to permanent-field cultivation on the cleared lands. Such people do not traditionally practice an integral system of cultivation. (On integral and partial systems of shifting cultivation, see p. 23).

of shifting cultivation is cutover land to start with, containing little but malformed, immature, or less valuable timber.

DISTRIBUTION BY POPULATION PATTERNS

It is customary to regard shifting cultivation as a system that will support only a very low density of population, and to think of the system as operative only in areas of sparse population. There are but few regions in southern Asia, however, in which shifting-cultivator peoples have been allowed the economic and political freedom, over a long period of time, necessary to fully test the issue of the maximum carrying capacity of shifting cultivation as a system. Constant encroachment upon the lands of shifting cultivators, coupled with economic exploitation, backed by superior political and economic power, historically has been driving shifting cultivators from their lands, upsetting the stability of their cultures, and promoting the decline of whole societies. Population densities for shifting cultivators in such circumstances seldom have been able to reach potential maximums in particular environments. Highland interior New Guinea may be one region not heretofore subjected to such pressures, so that population densities there may express the possible maximum densities that could be supported by shifting cultivation.[7] That population densities of close to 500 per square mile, supported by a very complex and efficient form of shifting cultivation, do actually occur in highland New Guinea at least indicates that most shifting-cultivator societies are operating at less than maximum potential so far as their agricultural system is concerned.

Declining population patterns have been characteristic for many of the shifting-cultivator societies in many of the regions taken under European colonial administration in the past four centuries. In part this decline relates to land areas available for use by the shifting cultivators, but it also reflects the impact of epidemics of disease and the deterioration of autochthonous culture.[8]

Light areal density patterns of population are naturally associated with many groups following shifting cultivation because of their intrinsic social system. Among many such groups there is a continuous splintering off of new "villages,"

[7] Population data for strictly shifting-cultivation cultures are limited, and not fully accurate in the sense of applicability. Gross figures for the Assam Plateau range from 6 to 66 per square mile, but these involve more than shifting cultivation (Chaturvedi and Uppal, 1953, p. 12). Freeman (1955, p. 320) notes Iban density figures of about 11 to 16 people per square mile in western Borneo as against a shifting-cultivation maximum potential (which could live without damaging the landscape) of about 50 per square mile. The arithmetic density figure of 130 people per square mile, as a long-run carrying capacity, worked out by van Beukering (1947, p. 249) for Indonesia, is widely quoted as an upper limit. Conklin (1957, pp. 146–147) has figures very close to this total. Recent data for highland New Guinea, specifically the Chimbu area, indicate density patterns of almost 500 people per square mile (Brown and Brookfield, 1959, pp. 25–32), but this may be a special case. See also Brookfield, 1962.

[8] In almost every place where the Europeans established colonial administrative patterns, the issue of land control became a sore point. New legal patterns of land control deprived native cultivators of reserve land that had long been part of the rotational system of shifting cultivation. Restrictions that European administrators placed upon hunting and gathering also played a role in depriving native populations of traditionally complementary food supplies. For India, see Majumdar, 1944, 1950, Bower, 1950a,b, and Stebbing, 1926; for Ceylon, see Ceylon, Government of, 1951, and Farmer, 1957; for Burma, see Stebbing, 1926, Scott and Hardiman, 1900, vol. 2, and Furnivall, 1948; for Indochina, see Chemin-Dupontes, 1909; for Malaya, see Ooi, 1959, Allen and Donnithorne, 1957, and Ginsburg and Roberts, 1958; for Indonesia, see Furnivall, 1948, and Pelzer, 1945; for eastern New Guinea, see Reed, 1943; for the Philippines, see Pelzer, 1945, and Spencer, 1952; for similar problems in China, see Wiens, 1954. For the effect of disease in New Britain, see Todd, 1934.

living groups, and working communities.[9] The insistence upon living in small family groups at widely separated space intervals is an old tendency which makes for low area densities of population. This cultural tradition cannot be interpreted in terms of carrying capacity of the land, so that the social phenomenon, rather than the literal carrying capacity of the land itself, has assumed the dynamic role of controlling population density.

Traditionally, throughout much of the Orient, people have been drifting down out of the hills into the lowlands, thus abandoning their former living systems. This locational shift involves the taking on of new cultures, including the acceptance of permanent agriculture. The long-term population dynamics of the lowlands has involved the slow, cyclic, or rapid, but almost continuous, increase in population densities. There has been areal expansion of permanent settlement, but much of the recent increase has been absorbed on existing lands, rather than splintered off to distant lands, as among the shifting cultivators, until in a few regions the densities have been built up to the point of diminishing returns by permanent agriculture. Here high density is no virtue, for the level of living has been declining. Many permanent agriculturists of the lowlands have shown extreme reluctance to move to new areas at a distance, and their very sedentary state itself is in sharp contrast with the dynamics of shifting cultivators, who often have moved long distances, willfully.

In consequence of the long-term trend, many areas of permanent agriculture have densities that are far too high, whereas many areas of shifting cultivation have densities that are low but will continue to support existing populations for long periods. It is true today that by far the greater volume of the total population lives by permanent agriculture, or in semiurban and urban situations by secondary economic activities, since the traditional trends have been for the expansion of the permanent agricultural landscape against the shifting cultivation landscape, making for the accumulation of high densities in ever larger areas. The total share of the population which lives by shifting cultivation, therefore, seems a small one, perhaps 6 to 7 per cent. My estimate of the total population living by shifting cultivation reaches 50 million, against perhaps 675 million living by permanent agriculture.[10] The latter must provide the great bulk of the food supply going to feed the nonagricultural population, possibly 200 million, making up the balance of the perhaps 925 million people residing in the area covered by this study. The 675

---

[9] The Manobo of Mindanao in the Philippines in the early 1930's showed a preference for isolated family locations, often miles from a neighbor. The Manobo then used chiefly annual clearings, had movable houses, and felt no land pressure (Garvan, 1941, pp. 37, 73, 159–164). On Tanga, in the Bismarck Archipelago, people prefer to live in loosely scattered family units, with their houses located in their garden plots. Gardens are cropped a second time, and then new ones are located, the cycle seldom requiring reuse of a plot during a lifetime, meaning that a population chooses to live a rural life (Bell, 1946, 1954). In many areas peoples formerly thinly scattered have been persuaded by European administrations to live in large, central villages. The Garia of northern New Guinea complied in form, but in the 1950's still spent much of their time in scattered hamlets near their gardens (Lawrence, 1955, pp. 2–3). The Orokaiva of eastern New Guinea formerly lived in large villages owing to defense needs, but under the peaceful conditions of the 1920's preferred to splinter-settle in hamlets near the gardens (Williams, 1928, p. 155).

[10] This rough approximation is arrived at by taking available population estimates for all countries south of China, and then adding 250 million as an estimate for the area of south and central China where shifting cultivation was an active system in the nineteenth century. Communist Chinese pressure upon national minorities and upon Han Chinese in China has almost obliterated traditional shifting cultivation since 1950 (Wien, 1962; Winnington, 1959).

million have at their disposal 560–580 million acres of permanent cropland (the best agricultural land available). The 50 million shifting cultivators have some 250–275 million acres in their total land resource (the poor elements of the landscape for agriculture), but cultivate only some 45–52 million acres in any one year.

This kind of regional imbalance cannot continue peacefully. There is a real rationale behind the urge to replace shifting cultivation with a system of land use which will prove more productive of human support, square mile for square mile; this would ease the burden upon the too densely settled lands that no longer can support their dependents. But a campaign that merely aims at producing more from the less productive lands, without acting to restrict population growth, can be only a short-term palliative, postponing for perhaps a century the problem of overpopulation in all parts of the Orient. The Orient is filling up, and the shifting-cultivation lands provide, in themselves, no permanent solution. An effort to prohibit the practice of shifting cultivation among those now carrying on this system, without concurrently and effectively teaching them some other means of livelihood, will create a large population element of cultural misfits. To force shifting cultivators to become permanent farmers, as has been done in the past, without teaching them all the practices of permanent farming and sedentary social and economic living, can result only in the ruination of large areas of cropland, and in depressing the level of living of still more millions of people.

ETHNIC DISTRIBUTION

It is commonplace to consider that the practicers of shifting cultivation must be possessed of primitive culture, and must be what frequently are termed tribal peoples, sometimes termed indigenous peoples, or often called hill peoples.[11] In terms of ethnic structure, then, the areal distribution of shifting cultivation ought to be synonymous with the areal distribution of tribal groups or groups of relatively simple culture. The ethnic map (fig. 2) may be compared with the map (fig. 1) showing areal distribution of shifting cultivation. Maps of this scale do not clearly distinguish small localities, but it is evident that shifting cultivation is far more widespread than are ethnic groups of relatively simple cultures.[12]

Nor is it at all clear today that all members of all tribal groups do practice shifting cultivation. Probably for centuries some members of tribal groups have been changing to permanent-field crop production. Within the past century certainly, and within the past half century increasingly, the system of crop production used by individual members of some tribal and simpler cultures has become diversified, so that it is no longer possible to type a system of agriculture as

---

[11] The following is not unexpected in this connection: "However, since the Wa carry on shifting seasonal cultivation, there appears to be little doubt as to their primitive condition" (Intenational Labour Office, 1953, p. 73). The Wa are a tribal people of the China-Burma border zone. It is true, of course, that when whole culture groups do carry on shifting cultivation they are apt to be politically subject peoples, nonindustrial, nonurban, and otherwise lacking in the more sophisticated aspects of "modern civilization." It does not follow, however, that all members of the so-called civilized culture groups must refrain from using shifting cultivation.

[12] No finite definition of simple culture is attempted for this study, and no argument is sought on the matter. In general, a population that differentiates its own culture from those of surrounding populations, adheres to its own mores, language, religious practices, marriage customs, and other culture traits, and cannot maintain its own political administration in territorial terms, may roughly be termed a population of relatively simple culture, taking a generalized concept from anthropology and political economy. See chapter iv for a discussion of culture.

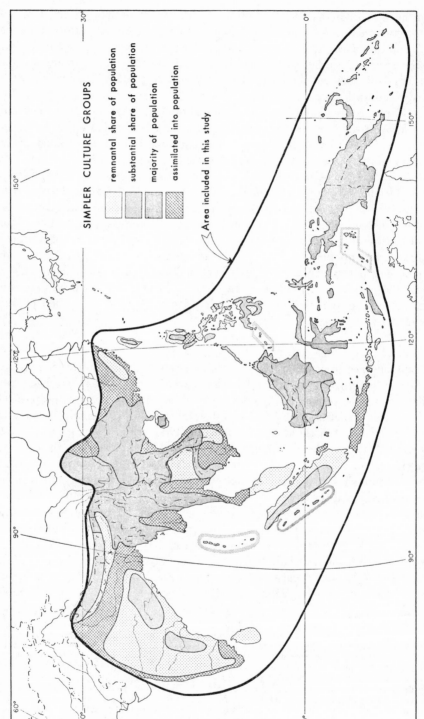

Fig. 2. Persistence of early ethnic elements.

synonymous in distribution with the area occupied by the particular group.[13] Almost everywhere throughout the Orient, members of ethnic groups normally distinguished as tribal or primitive are taking on forms of permanent-field crop growing. This is a part of the type of regular change noted earlier, and it affects the actual distribution of shifting cultivation in any one decade.

It is, of course, possible to isolated certain tribal groups as engaging only in shifting cultivation, and such groups are scattered all over the Orient. Some groups are still relatively monolithic in their practice of a given cropping system, but these form a minority, both in numerical total and by ethnic grouping. In general, such groups demonstrate an earlier evolutionary form of shifting cultivation.

The practice of shifting cultivation is not a measure of the level of culture of a population group, but a measure of practical crop-growing techniques in a given situation. Were one to label as "primitive" all peoples who do practice shifting cultivation, one would so label every ethnic group in the Orient, including many Occidentals who engage in crop production.

LEVELS OF ECONOMIC OPERATION

The generalization that shifting cultivation must produce low yields because it is a simple system is too easy and too broad. Naturally a low yield accompanies shifting cultivation when it is characterized by the planting of too little seed stock on poor soils that have been overworked, or when it is accompanied by little care, or when planting is heavily raided by numerous predators. It may be added, however, that sedentary farmers also secure very low yields when, through poverty and through ignorance of truly advanced agriculture, they crop the same poor soils in marginal climatic situations year after year.

For the really primitive practice of shifting cultivation, in what may have been one of its earliest and simplest forms, final yields are very small, though the predators may have secured a goodly yield for themselves. Such yields resulted from the casually cleared, casually planted, unfenced, and unwatched patches operated by simple migrant groups such as the Rajis of the Kumaon Himalayas. The Rajis were not really farmers, but itinerant hunter-gatherer-woodcarver folk whose crop-growing endeavor was largely subsidiary. A dying remnant of an ancient tribe, at least as late as 1932 they roamed the forests of the middle Himalayan ranges for food and for forest products, watching for likely patch sites.[14]

[13] Although the precise date is not clear, the following statement, for India, is typical of many comments: ". . . among the Kolam in Madhya Pradesh the practice of *podu* [shifting] agriculture is disappearing. Only those near the hills still practice it" (International Labour Office, 1953, p. 276). Many Indian ethnic groups are settling down as poor, depressed, tenant farming peoples (Rao, 1949, 1952). The Santals (Santhals) of western Bengal, formerly famous as shifting cultivators and sought after by would-be sedentary farmers as forest clearers, now range from shifting cultivation through several forms of sedentary agriculture to Assam agricultural laborers on tea plantations and to urban industrial labor (Majumdar, 1958, pp. 138–139). As early as 1880 Gond tribal peoples in central India were being Hinduized and were becoming sedentary farmers, but frequently they were also becoming landless laborers after being fleeced of their lands by Hindu moneylenders (see Forsyth, 1889, p. 161, and C. and E. von Fürer-Haimendorf, 1948, for notes on the Kolam, Naikpods, and Raj Gonds). Although citations are not given for each country, the phenomena of diversification of agricultural systems is general.

[14] Majumdar (1958) uses the present tense in describing the Rajis, but this is a common practice in anthropological literature. Pant (1935) also uses the present tense, but in the substantive sense of reporting results of field surveys completed in 1932. I have no later factual ethnographic data.

These patches were cleared and planted in the right season, but left unfenced and untended while the main business was carried on. Toward harvest time the opera-tors returned to glean what was left of the harvest after the local fauna had taken their toll.

Shifting cultivation as practiced by the Rajis, however, was a far cry from that practiced about the same time on Wogeo Island, off the north coast of New Guinea. The Wogeo were farmers through and through, with a love for their land, a pride in their gardens, and a long tradition of living off the land, which they handled carefully and productively in a long-term rotational sequence. A year-round eco-nomic cycle of production incorporated a variety of pursuits and a comprehensive utilization of their environment.[15] It is highly doubtful if forcing the Wogeo to become routine sedentary farmers would improve their lot, or provide the world with a larger return. Granted that they cannot, within the confines of their little island, expand in population at the rate found in Ceylon or Malaya and maintain their present level of living; granted that they do not live in sheer luxury; granted that there are problems. But here shifting cultivation was productive, thoroughly practical, stable, and in tune with the physical environment, and was not ruining its landscape.

In north Cachar, Assam, a disintegrating Zemi (Sema, Zema) Naga community illustrates an economic dilemma found repeatedly in many of the rougher parts of the Orient. For several centuries the community of Asalu had maintained an equilibrium in an extremely rugged and broken terrain, possessing only small bits of land that could be cultivated. These units were widely scattered, and this com-munity was the only Zemi Naga group practicing a cycle migration around its cultivable range. The British and migratory shifting-cultivator Kuki tribesmen arrived at about the same time, the British to maintain the peace under the banner of Pax Britannica and prevent the Zemi Naga from driving the infiltrating Kuki out of their territorial range. Thus the Kuki took over sectors of Naga fallow lands undergoing regeneration. "Only the Zemi knew that two tribes were now living on land enough for one."[16]

The arrival of one British official, knowledgeable and experienced, led to at-tempts to introduce terracing, but the official was transferred, the terrace-culture demonstrators were poor, and the attempt failed. In an already poor environment, and on less than the needed range, restricted by government but also unaided by government, the people of Asalu could but shorten their fallow term and too rapidly recrop their remaining range. The grass cover increased, fire hazards grew, yields lessened, soil erosion developed where it had not previously occurred, productivity declined, and poverty ensued. In 1950 the community was in the throes of economic depression and was disintegrating through emigration, throw-ing upon other areas people quite unprepared for life elsewhere. Presumably the Kuki were in relatively similar straits. This kind of pattern represents a minimal economy and poor use of a landscape, but the rugged and broken terrain far from highly developed regions probably cannot be utilized today in any highly produc-tive way by any people.

In northeastern Mindanao, of the southern Philippines, Christian Filipinos from

---

[15] Data are from Hogbin (1934*a*,*b*; 1938; and 1939).
[16] Bower, 1950*b*, p. 150.

northwest Luzon and the Visayan Islands are following the timber concessionaires and, at the same time, moving ahead of them.[17] The Filipinos pick out sites and make several annual clearings as shifting cultivators, but plant a variety of fruiting trees, chiefly coconuts. Their subsistence pattern resembles that of most normal shifting cultivators until the tree crops begin to produce. Coming from areas of sedentary permanent agriculture, they know what must be done in the long run, but often they possess few economic resources and cannot afford to develop simultaneously whole farms of the permanent agriculturist's variety. Often they lease a sector of uncleared land to an itinerant occupant, who clears and crops it as a shifting cultivator, on the requirement that he plant crop trees. Many such itinerants move on in a year, perhaps hunting for their own sites. The first occupant pays taxes regularly, but cannot afford the private survey by which to secure the land title he needs in order to borrow cheaply the funds to develop his land; he has little hope from the government surveyor, who is years behind his backlog of work.[18] Many of these beginnings through shifting cultivation become the permanent farms of a generation hence, and as an economic operation they are productive.

In the dry zone of Ceylon a crowded permanent village possessing a small area of land that can be irrigated and cropped annually uses shifting cultivation to augment its slender economic resources. A group of villagers may cooperatively clear an acreage (about an acre per participant) of low jungle which has not been cropped for some years, and plant cotton, aiming at a cash crop to bolster their annual income. In a good year a return of about one bale per acre (and about one bale per participant), a reasonably good return in productivity terms, may well ensue.[19] As the land has no water supply available, it cannot be cropped annually; the economic return to the villagers helps them just about to maintain their level of living. In economic terms such shifting cultivation is rather productive, and it cannot be abolished without penalizing the level of living of the village.[20]

In many parts of the Orient mature forest growth is being cleared for cropping by shifting cultivators, who reap rice returns of 1,500–2,500 pounds per acre the first year, with a continuing yield of such items as bananas, tubers, and vegetables for two or three years longer. By continued practice of shifting cultivation, they continue to reap these crop yields. The forest is destroyed, but in many such areas it was not being used anyway. In some of these areas sedentary settlers are also coming in, clearing the forest by similar burning techniques, and starting permanent farms. Their first yields are bountiful, like those of the shifting cultivator. They do not rest the soil, nor do they fertilize it; neither do they practice organic farming techniques to return plant materials to the soil in adequate amounts. By the third cropping the yields are half those of the first year; by the tenth year they are down to a third or a quarter the initial yields, and a population is facing eco-

---

[17] Observed in personal field reconnaissance, July, 1957.

[18] Recent reports from the Philippines claim all backlogs of basic survey are now cleared up, but this applied only to a small area of Luzon Island by 1962.

[19] Observed and checked in personal field reconnaissance in May, 1958, as an actual happening of the year before. For general observations on Ceylon shifting cultivation see Farmer (1954, 1957).

[20] Ceylon chena cultivation, in the dry zone, might be claimed as a special case in which the shifting cultivation complements the permanent wet-field and permanent garden-cultivation acreage below a tank on a line of water seepage, but this fact is seldom pointed out by those who generalize upon the evils of primitive shifting cultivation among primitive peoples. Ceylon chena cultivators, with few exceptions, cannot be described as primitives.

nomic depression.[21] Undoubtedly the population-carrying capacity of the permanently farmed lands is higher than that of the forest zones remaining, but the economic status of the people living there is not high enough to recommend permanent farming to many of those still engaged in shifting cultivation.

These six examples of the economic operation of shifting cultivation, ranging in levels of productivity from the very low to the reasonably high, illustrate the widely varying range of shifting cultivation as an element in an economic system. Though different ethnic groups have been used, the concern is economic. The patterns indicate multiple variation in the functioning of the system.

OVERALL STRUCTURE OF SHIFTING CULTIVATION

As a consequence of more intensive study in recent years, definitions of shifting cultivation have been progressively reduced in preciseness in order to include exceptions formerly ruled out by the specific listing of characteristics. A recent minimal definition has described shifting cultivation as "any agricultural system in which fields are cleared by firing and are cropped discontinuously."[22] According to a longer definition, "Shifting-field agriculture may be defined as an agricultural system which is characterized by a rotation of fields rather than of crops, by short periods of cropping (one to three years) alternating with long fallow periods (up to twenty and more years, but often as short as six to eight years); and by clearing by means of slash and burn."[23]

Probably no good English definition that includes all the variety existing can

---

[21] Observed and checked in personal reconnaissance in the Cotabato Valley of southern Mindanao, Philippines, in 1948, and here itemized as an illustration. On the matter of yields by shifting cultivation, there are very few data that can approximate the data for permanent-field cropping in the United States, where data collection is a matter of culture habit. Few anthropologists have been interested in the comparative economics of cultures practicing shifting cultivation, but the simple problems of estimating crop returns among shifting cultivators are formidable. In field reconnaissance I have been given figures for rice yields on first-year cropping of mature forest lands which I interpolate at rates ranging from 1,000 to 2,500 pounds per acre in good years. However, I have also had answers from cultivators for bad years, on good land, that ran as low as 400 pounds. For yams and sweet potatoes the returns ranged, in good years, from 3,500 to 7,000 pounds per acre of harvested tubers, with many being left in the ground for the pigs, as they were surplus and not needed. Data on taro yields suggest up to 8 tons per acre after seven to twelve months in the ground (Barrau, 1953, pp. 31–32). Shifting cultivators can grow this large a yield but often do not, for they cannot consume it all. Salisbury (1962, pp 78–82) notes production estimates of 4 tons of sweet potatoes per acre for highland new Guinea. Among the Angami Naga of northeast India, some groups, prior to 1920, grew irrigated rice on manured wet terraces, whereas others held plenty of land and preferred shifting cultivation and here "good jhum land, cleared once in twelve or fifteen years, say, is said to produce a better crop than the 'panikhets' or terraced fields" (Hutton, 1921b, p. 72). For Sarawak, rice yields of 780–960 pounds per acre "as typical of the sort of return generally achieved under worse than average conditions" has to be balanced against a better than normal return that totaled 2,600 pounds per acre on the basis of small test plot (Freeman, 1955, p. 96). Freeman (*ibid.*, pp. 96–99) also mentions rice yields ranging from 750–1850 pounds per acre. Izikowitz (1951) has calculated that the Lamet averaged a rice yield of 1258 pounds per acre the year he observed them, and that they sold a little more than half of their total yield. Yield-per-acre figures are not highly meaningful in ascertaining the preference of a people for a system of cultivation at this level; man-days of labor are more significant, along with the average timing of labor in the yearly cycle. There are many judgments that good shifting cultivation does as well as, and requires less annual labor than, converting landscapes to permanent cultivation, maintaining them, and doing the work required in permanent-field agriculture (see Leach, 1949). Data from one detailed study in the Philippines suggest that the labor cost of rice grown by shifting cultivation there compares favorably with labor-cost figures for the best of rice production elsewhere in the tropics (Conklin, 1957, p. 152).

[22] Conklin, 1957, p. 1.

[23] Pelzer, 1958, p. 126. Both Conklin and Pelzer have used more complex definitions (cf. Pelzer, 1945, p. 17).

be composed. The effort to formulate a brief inclusive definition must therefore necessarily limit itself to the key characteristics. The two features mentioned above —clearing of fields by fire and discontinuous cropping—are by far the most significant and useful diagnostic elements.[24] They are present in an overwhelming majority of cases and, taken as a pair, are critical. Other elements of the system are subject to tremendous variation according to landscape, biotic assemblage, population total, culture patterns, history of application, and patterns of pressure exerted upon the practicing group.

Until quite recently discussions of shifting cultivation were confined to descriptive elements, and did not attempt to list the effective distinguishing characteristics or to describe an order of types. Recently both Conklin and Watters have made efforts in this direction. Pelzer, though recognizing the wide variety of shifting cultivation, has not expressed in writing a classification of major types and subtypes. Conklin distinguishes what he conceived as *partial* systems of shifting cultivation, indicating the use of the technique as a technological expedient for a given purpose, and *integral* systems, indicating that the whole of the practicer's way of life and his system of crop growing are inseparable.[25] His full listing of types and subtypes follows:

A. *Partial systems* of at least two major subtypes:
   1. *Supplementary* swidden farming (where a permanent-field cultivator, through necessity [poverty, insufficient lowland or terraced grain fields] or as a tenant, devotes part of his agricultural efforts to the cultivation of a swidden which may be at some distance from his residence).
   2. *Incipient* swidden farming (where the cultivator, often with little prior knowledge of swidden techniques and usually from a crowded permanent-field agricultural region, moves into an upland area as a homesteader, squatter, or resettler, and devotes all his agricultural efforts to the swidden in or near which he makes his home).
B. *Integral systems* of at least two subtypes:
   1. *Pioneer* swidden farming (where significant portions of climax vegetation are customarily cleared each year).
   2. *Established* swidden farming (where tree crops are plentiful and relatively little or no climax vegetation is cleared annually; including an unknown number of subtypes such as the Hanunóo system described in this report).

Conklin also suggests that the subtypes may be distinguished on the basis of the following ten criteria: (1) principal crops raised; (2) crop associations and suc-

---

[24] The effort to set up criteria that distinguish agricultural systems probably can never become totally exclusive. A few areas are so lacking in dry periods that fire cannot be used in preparation of a field for planting, and discontinuous cropping is found in many areas within the United States in a commercial agricultural system. I have seen fire used to clear sugarcane fields of their cane rubble in commercial agriculture in the Philippines. Sometimes sugarcane fields are burned before cutting, to remove the leaves and make the job of cutting easier (see photograph in *Saturday Evening Post*, Dec. 2, 1961, p. 15). To the purist, then, no definition can be set up for which some singular human practice in crop growing may not provide an exception.

[25] Conklin, 1957, pp. 2–3. The term "partial," as employed by Conklin and accepted here, refers to that form of shifting cultivation used by persons who operate as individuals or families, who are concerned with the system as a simple means of producing a crop. Such persons or families usually are members of a culture group that normally practices permanent-field, sedentary agriculture. Such persons or families may not always, themselves, have been agriculturists, but may be employing shifting cultivation as a secondary economic pursuit. They may also, however, be agriculturists originally practicing sedentary agriculture who now have moved to localities where the practice of some type of shifting cultivation is purely expedient. The term "integral," in Conklin's words, reflects the "traditional, year-round, community-wide, largely self-contained, and ritually-sanctioned way of life." Integral shifting cultivation is thus the only form of agricultural practice known to members of such groups.

cessions; (3) crop-fallow time ratios; (4) dispersal of swiddens; (5) use of livestock; (6) use of specified tools and techniques; (7) treatment of soil; (8) vegetational cover of land cleared; (9) climatic conditions; and (10 edaphic conditions.[26]

Watters, on the basis of his own field studies and the writings of others, particularly Pelzer and Conklin, suggests eight major types of shifting cultivation:

1. Predominantly hunters and gatherers, but practising shifting cultivation to a small extent.
2. Depending mainly on shifting cultivation, although indulging in some hunting, fishing or gathering.
3. Depending almost entirely on shifting cultivation, with almost no other source of food production.
4. Predominantly pastoralists, but also practising some shifting cultivation.
5. Depending mainly on shifting cultivation with some pastoralism.
6. Depending mainly on shifting cultivation but with some permanent form of cultivation.
7. Some shifting cultivation, some permanent cultivation, and also some pastoralism.
8. Depending mainly on some permanent form of agriculture with some shifting cultivation.[27]

At this point I prefer to refrain from setting down my own concept of classification, though I would agree with all the points made by both Conklin and Watters.[28] In examining shifting cultivation in the field and through the literature, it is evident that variation may occur in a large number of features, but at this stage of our knowledge it is not clear how many features are critical. I have finally come to the theoretical principle that, to fully assess and distinguish the shifting cultivation of two given groups, data are needed on at least twenty-six different specific aspects of the workings of the agricultural system as a part of a culture system. Only when authors publish the results of careful full-scale studies of peoples is anything like this full range of data provided. There well may be more criteria of importance rather than fewer than the number suggested, and some groups here put together may need to be separated. Appendix C itemizes the twenty-six categories of data suggested, supported by detailed and specific items in each instance.[29]

SUMMARY

Although the minimal definition of shifting cultivation is of real value, it must be clear that no one-sentence definition can be totally satisfactory. The gross morphologic criteria are centered on the use of fire in readying land for planting and

---

[26] *Ibid.*, p. 2.

[27] Watters, 1960, p. 65. I have purposely omitted mention of briefer classifications set up by others working in Middle America and in Africa as being incomplete.

[28] See pp. 162–165 and Appendix F, discussing classifications.

[29] The appendix tabulation is offered tentatively, with full recognition that it may not meet all conditions found. Many students of agriculture will, at first, regard the tabulation as needlessly complex and overlong, and as raising many elements that are unimportant to the level of major factors. When dealing with integral systems of shifting cultivation, however, it often is not the planting practice per se that distinguishes the agriculture economy of a given group, but some other aspect of total culture. It seems fair to state that the very casual way in which many such feaures have been considered is what has produced the stumbling blocks to a better understanding of the nature of shifting cultivation as it is actually practiced in the tropics. Perhaps, eventually, the truly critical elements can be isolated, and insignificant elements omitted. As this study seeks to expose all aspects of culture which have a real bearing on the subject, the list has purposely been kept long and detailed. Conklin (1961) has set down a numerically categorized index-topic list that is far more detailed than mine and far more cross-patterned by a six-digit system whose numbers are: 0, general (which covers the whole range of culture as such); 1, site selection; 2, cutting; 3, burning; 4, cropping; 5, fallowing. The permutations of Conklin's system are far greater than those of the list in my appendix. His manner of indexing may be considered a fieldworking, note-indexing system, whereas mine was formulated only to illustrate the variety of choices, activities, and factors that need to be considered in a discussion of shifting cultivation.

the shift from one field to another in cropping, but there are many variations in these basic elements and many critically important elements that pertain to other phases of the crop-production cycle. They cannot be ignored if we are fully to understand the system employed by so many different peoples throughout the tropics.

In any attempt to distinguish briefly the gross characteristics of shifting cultivation, the following features and qualitative elements may be helpful:

1. Practiced chiefly by simpler cultures of small total population, but occasionally used by almost anyone to whom the cropping system appears expedient.
2. Human labor chiefly operative, using a few hand tools primarily, but power tools occasionally.
3. Labor patterns frequently cooperative, but involving many variations in working-group structure.
4. Clearing of fields primarily by felling, cutting, slashing, and burning, and using fire to dispose of the vegetative debris after drying; in special situations fire may not be used.
5. Frequent shifting of cropped fields, normally in some kind of sequence, with land control resting in specified social groupings under customary law, but sometimes occurring under other legal institutions of land control.
6. Many different systems of crop planting in given fields, but both multiple cropping and specialized cropping present.
7. Use of annual and short-term food crops predominant, but important use of long-term shrub and tree crops common.
8. Use of crops primarily for subsistence, but admitting that exchange patterns may reach total sale of whole product.
9. Use of permanent dooryard, village, or near-homestead gardens frequent among groups using permanent or near-permanent settlement sites.
10. Yields per acre and per man-hour normally compare with those of permanent-field agriculture within regions in which comparison is properly made, but yields are often below those of mechanically powered permanent-field agriculture.
11. Small annual cropped area per capita, but comparable to that of other nonpowered sedentary cropping systems.
12. Use of vegetative cover as soil conditioner and source of plant nutrients for cropping cycle.
13. When system is efficiently operated, soil erosion no greater than soil erosion under other systems that are being efficiently operated.
14. Soil depletion no more serious than that under other systems of agriculture, when operated efficiently.
15. Details of practice vary greatly, depending upon the physical environment and the cultural milieu.
16. Transiency of residence common but not universal, with many patterns of residence according to evolutionary level of detailed system employed and preference of culture group.
17. Operative chiefly in regions where more technologically advanced systems of agriculture have not yet become economically or culturally possible, or in regions where the land has not yet been appropriated by people with greater political or cultural power.
18. Destructive of natural resources only when operated inefficiently, and not more inherently destructive than other systems of agriculture when these are operated inefficiently.
19. A residual system of agriculture largely replaced by other systems, except where retention or practice is expedient.

It is obvious that the above gross characteristics do not conform to the list of features frequently set down as characteristic of shifting cultivation. The criticisms of the systems, however, are directed against practice almost always at less than the operative maximum, practice that frequently cannot be made to operate at the maximum because of interference by forces beyond the control of the practitioners.

Chapter III

RELATIONSHIPS TO
THE PHYSICAL ENVIRONMENT

Shifting cultivation is a cropping system that permits a wide choice of the physical sites to be utilized, in terms both of the major choice of the physical attributes of the environmental region, and with respect to the precise choices of garden sites. Shifting cultivators are essentially pedestrians at the simpler levels of operation, and can walk or climb to almost any variety of surface site. Their simple tools can be transported to, and their crops removed from, virtually any sort of garden location. When free choice obtained in the past, in broad terms, the selection of the environmental region often did make the choice of smooth to open regional environments, as the occupance history of many culture groups indicates. Precise choice of garden site, on the other hand, has long been a matter of applying many criteria. These have varied from group to group, but almost always practical physical considerations and subjective cultural rules have been involved.[1] For centuries, however, many culture groups have not had free choice of the environmental regions they have occupied. Many such groups live where they do because of the competitive cultural, political, or military pressures put upon them by neighboring culture groups.

There is a long history of regional competition for environmental regions in the territory covered in this study, and many of the shifting-cultivator cultures have become tied to rough and hilly environments through their inability to occupy and hold less rugged and more attractive open to smooth environmental regions. As their broad choices have been restricted, they have had to apply their garden-site criteria to environments less than optimum.

Landform Factors

Nothing in the systems of shifting cultivation demands the selection of steep slopes. The nearest such an apparent factor is indicated, by frequent comment in the literature, is the choice of steep slopes because felling trees is easier there. Although felling large trees can be done more easily on certain kinds of sloping lands than on flatlands, this factor alone would not prohibit the choice of flatlands, whether they contained large trees or were covered only by a lesser vegetative cover. Tree-felling systems have been worked out by many shifting cultivators who do use lands of marked slope covered by mature forest growth. These systems have been described by such terms as "domino," "wedge," "inverted V," or "key-tree," and are commonly employed throughout the Orient when the plant cover includes many large trees.[2]

---

[1] Normally the older men of a working group, with memory and experience behind them, lead in site selection when there are alternative choices. Soil quality, conditions of moisture drainage, vegetative regeneration, physical exposure, and uniformity of surface are among the physical factors considered. Practical considerations that are cultural in nature include such items as distance from residence sites, placement with regard to other sites, the crops to be grown, omens interpreted in particular ways, and purely subjective impressions about sites. In this chapter I discuss the physical factors as related to the physical environment.

[2] The system, somewhat variably employed, involves partial cutting of large trees all over the

Integrated felling systems are absent among the simplest groups, whatever the cover, and are not required by sites lacking many large trees. Clearing systems on lands carrying less than mature vegetation often involve simple directional clearing from top to bottom, bottom to top, or side to side, and employ varying detailed patterns of dealing with different kinds of plant growth, regardless of the degree of slope. Occasional larger trees may be handled by lopping their more massive branches or by girdling or burning their lower trunks. There is so much variety in the detail of clearing procedures, with so close a correlation to the nature of the vegetative cover, that the factor of easier felling of mature cover on slopes cannot be regarded as truly causal in the choice of sites.

As shifting cultivators can get to any kind of physical site and carry out their operations, it is necessary to examine physical conditions in varying site situations for an analysis of relevant factors. The flat bottoms of the great river valleys have always been subject to heavy flooding during and after the peak rainy sasons. In some regions the period of flooding has extended throughout the main part of the growing season, or into the annual period during which clearing and burning should be done. Very early practicers of crop growing were both too few in number and too limited in technological skill and power to cope with floodable lowlands.[3] Obviously floodable flatlands in large river valleys could not have become primary environments in which shifting cultivation could be carried on. Short-season cropping of such lands during the dry parts of the year could be done provided clearing and planting could be carried out. Within the historic period there is evidence that flatlands have been used by shifting cultivators in a seasonal pattern to complement their crop growing on other sites or to complement their alternative economy. Shifting cultivation along riverbanks, on exposed mud flats, or on higher bits of ground not actually flooded, as a seasonal operation, is extensively practiced at the present time.

On flatlands and smoother slopes marginal to the great floodplains, primary physical conditions did not prevent the practice of shifting cultivation. Historically these lands were open to selection by shifting cultivators, as were those smooth to flat lands well away from the river channels. These regions have been the areas most attractive to culture groups that early took on and developed more complex systems of crop growing. By the nineteenth century a significant share of the larger regions, the more attractive territories, and the areas adjacent to population centers had been preempted by the practicers of complex permanent-field agriculture. Nineteenth-century references indicate the declining practice of shifting cultivation in such regions.[4] The present continuance of shifting cultivation

site. Then a particular tree in a favorable position at the upper margin of a site is fully felled so that its fall carries down partially felled trees lower on the slope. This system, though seldom completely effective, saves considerable labor in clearing mature forest on sites with many varieties of angular slope and configuration. The pattern of tree fall is also important in burning, for a smoothly layered fall burns more evenly than one in which trees lie at all angles. Cleanup after the burn may also be easier in a layered fall than in an irregular one (see Steinberg *et al.*, 1957).

[3] It is notable that no significant occupation under any agricultural system took place in the lowland floodplains and deltas of the lower Ganges, Irrawaddy, Menam, and Mekong rivers until flood control and drainage systems could be developed. Older systems of control achieved only partial occupance, and full-scale regional occupance became effective only in the nineteenth century, when modern technology and power became applicable.

[4] See Dalton, 1872, pp. 26–29; Baden-Powell, 1892, 3:397; and Chaudhuri, 1903, pp. 504–508, for reference to the decline of shifting cultivation in the Ganges-Brahmaputra valley lands owing

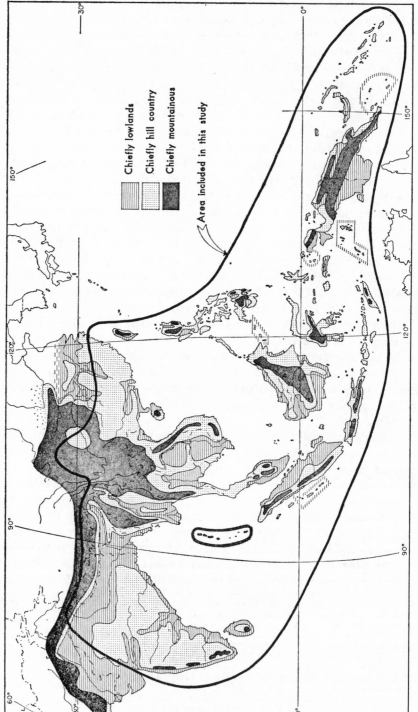

Fig. 3. Generalized landform patterns.

Chiefly lowlands

Chiefly hill country

Chiefly mountainous

Area included in this study

in many open to flat areas in regions and localities of small total size indicates that shifting cultivators, when permitted the opportunity, can practice their system on such lands as effectively as on sites of steeply sloping surface (compare fig. 1 with fig. 3).

Physical conditions affecting flat to steeply sloping surfaces in regions small in area may show the same variety of annual problems as is found in the great river valleys. Such conditions may well affect the practice of crop growing during a given year, but will not prohibit it in the long term. Heavy rains produce floods even on small areas of flatlands surrounded by slopes. But in such situations alternative practices often are quickly applicable when the crop-growing group decides upon an alternative. Smoother lands may remain the preferred choice during years in which no physical problem presents itself.[5]

It is culture and culture history, rather than physiography, which dictates the broad environmental location of shifting cultivation as a cropping system. When free choice of any landform situation has been available, and when the group has not been culture-bound, the choice has been for open to smoother areas, with the choice of precise sites depending on the physical and cultural criteria of soil, exposure, drainage, distance, locational relationships, and animistic omens. When all such territory has been preempted by more powerful groups, the choice is no longer free, and groups have had either to take less favorable situations or to fight for the space they deemed desirable. Many shifting cultivators have been shoved into environmental regions of lesser quality, generally rougher in landform, and chiefly made up of acutely sloping surfaces. An alternative, of course has been the adoption of some form of permanent-field cropping. What we see in the past century is not the optimum and logical operation of the system of shifting cultivation but its declining practice in regions and on lands that as yet no one else really wants.

Historically, a culture group that has long had to live in hill country has become accustomed to working with slopes.[6] It has often developed a wide range of tech-

---

to the preemption of such lands by the practicers of permanent-field agricultural systems. Appendix B suggests that many India-Pakistan terms carry an earlier meaning relating to flatlands, and that others refer specifically to sloping lands. That terminological differentiation of the class of lands employed in shifting cultivation did exist indicates that flatlands must formerly have been in common use by shifting cultivators and that such cultivators also had access to sloping lands.

[5] Hogbin (1951, p. 38), writing about coastal eastern New Guinea, notes what often must have happened on relatively small areas of flat lowland. The rains of 1947 continued right through the dry season, and the lowland flat surfaces became both waterlogged and insect-ridden. Before it was too late in the season, hillside plots were cleared at a distance from the village and were planted to enough taro to carry the group through to the next crop season. The sites were chosen at a distance so as not to disturb the rotation sequence of vegetative regeneration on lands near the residential sites, sites that would be used in later years. Note that this happened among a group normally planting taro, for which moist sites are preferable to well-drained sites.

[6] For example, the Miao peoples of southwest China, northern Indochina, and northern Thailand have been moving southward out of China for several centuries. Many of the Miao from China were shoved into the rougher hill country centuries ago, and since then, as they have moved southward, they have tried to retain about the same relative position in the vertical layering of peoples in the hill and mountain country of Thailand, Laos, and Tonking which they occupied in China in recent centuries.

Miao culture in many respects appears tradition-bound today, accommodated to the customs and procedures that fit the upland environments of the Miao peoples. Other groups, like the Burmans and the Thailand Tai, either were originally hill-country peoples or evolved a facility for living in the hill country. But when they had penetrated sufficiently far southward in Burma and Thailand, repectively, to force their way down into the lowlands, they did so. Some of their

niques adapted to slopes, of which the clearing system is only one. Techniques of living become adapted to environments among a people lacking a powerful and able technology that could rebuild their landscape. These techniques, customs, and habits all become traditional elements of culture patterns that constitute the whole living system of such a group.

Today many of these culture groups regard the hill country as their preferred environment. They have come to love it, and hill-country living has become so much a way of life that they do not seek to alter it. The causal factors that made them take to the hill country originally lie long buried in their past. Such a group may well assure contemporary investigators of cropping practices that they prefer steep slopes on which trees can be felled easily because such have become their traditional choices.

A point often overlooked in the generalization that shifting cultivators prefer steep slopes is the configuration of the slope. The configuration of a plot or garden site appears more critical than the angle of slope. Several elements, such as irregularity, rockiness, and the presence of drainage lines down or across the slope, are involved in configuration. What Conklin translates, from a Hanunóo definition, as "regular" (meaning that the whole plot is all in one plane) is for the advanced seed-grain planter a more critical aspect of the site than is the angle of slope.[7] For the simplest type of shifting cultivation, employing only vegetatively reproduced plants, this issue may not have been so critical. Little comparative investigation of this issue has been undertaken, and only a general statement can be made here. The earliest planters may not have concerned themselves with the physical details of the site itself. Yams, bananas, taro, and other such vegetatively planted crop plants can be put into prepared planting holes on almost any kind of surface, whether it is regular or irregular, steep or level. Planters of seed-grain crops, on the other hand, find the all-in-one-plane regularity of the surface a marked advantage in planting, weeding, and harvesting of the crop, and its actual angle of slope is not highly critical.

SOIL CONSIDERATIONS

SOILS OF THE ASIAN TROPICS

The illusion of the rich soils of the tropics dies slowly among those who have not closely followed the modern study of soils and agriculture. In this section I review certain concepts that all soil scientists and agronomists, most geographers, and a few others consider quite elementary.

In the Asian tropics areas of really rich soils are relatively uncommon. They are found chiefly on recent stream terraces, on recent alluvial plains, in the newer sectors of deltas, or on surfaces covered by the basic volcanic materials of relatively recent geologic age. In few other situations are there highly productive soils that are not man-made. It is an illusion that the large areas formerly covered by mature forests possessed soils of high quality.

---

agricultural practices changed as they occupied different physical environments, just as other features of their cultures changed. In moving down onto the open plains and the lower country both culture groups progressively altered their crop-growing economies, until now both are, for the most part, lowland permanent-field crop growers.

[7] See Conklin, 1957, p. 38.

The clearing and cropping of a plot carrying a mature vegetative cover often produces relatively large returns the first two or three years, regardless of the essentially low soil fertility, the system of clearing, the nature of the crop, or the technique of growing the crop. Such initial production is based upon a small store of nutrients present in the surface soil itself, reinforced by the remaining organic matter left over at the time of clearing, and upon the ashes and decaying organic matter resulting from clearing. Without replenishment of that organic matter, or without some other supplied volume of nutrients, continuous cropping beyond the initial period results in a steady decline in the crop yield on most of the soils of the Asian tropics and subtropics. Almost everywhere this is the record of permanent-field agriculture that does not practice some specific technique of fertility replenishment.

Another illusion concerns cultivation practices. The too-active cultivation of Asian tropical soils only hastens the complex group of processes that deplete the stocks of soluble nutrients and minerals and reduce the organic matter present. The mid-latitude cultivation concept involves getting surface organic matter into the soil, aerating the soil, preventing moisture evaporation, and, in spring, hastening the warming of soils made cold by low winter temperatures. The hastening of the breakdown of organic matter is a significant element in the traditional concept of mid-latitude cultivation practice. Such practices are both out of place and not needed in the tropics and subtropics for normal cropping on ordinary soils. Under normal conditions, the tropical cultivator traditionally has disturbed his soil as little as possible. The judgment that Asian shifting cultivators are primitive, inefficient, or lazy because they do not fully turn the soil at every break in the cropping cycle is misinformed.

Soils that have been under ground-covering jungle or forest, when first cleared, normally are loose and permeable, so that planting can be done without cultivation in the mid-latitude sense. Such soils have been protected from undue oxidation, from baking hard through drying out in full sun exposure, and from direct packing by heavy rains. Exposure to sun and rain rapidly tends to compact such soils so that they become hard and dense in physical structure, and in a very few years such exposure can make them into difficult surfaces in which to plant crops with simple hand tools.

Actually, most shifting cultivators do disturb, loosen, and move small amounts of surface soil. The very procedures used in good site clearing do some of this. Many people rake ashes over the planting surface or lightly scarify it in some way. Planting procedures normally involve variable amounts of soil movement, whether it is the small amount resulting from the use of the digging stick in seed-grain planting or the larger holes required for vegetable planting. The planting of taro, yams, and bananas frequently requires the digging of holes up to a foot deep, and the earth is often kept loose around the young plants as they start their growth. Probably the crudest and simplest type of shifting cultivation does not involve appreviable soil movement in clearing and planting, but certainly advanced shifting cultivators do sufficient moving of the soil to achieve good growth conditions.

It should be noted here that the highlands of New Guinea and of the Himalayan border are not ecologically within the tropics, as their higher elevations give them temperature regimes akin to those in mid-latitudes. In such areas the turning of cold soil, the composting of vegetation, and the provision of drainage for regions of high rainfall is ecologically sound practice.

The zonal, mature soils of many of the smoother to flat areas today are quite stable and very low in fertility. High in pure clays, they often are rather strongly leached and contain few mineral compounds whose further breakdown can contribute soluble mineral nutrients to crop plants grown upon them. The regrowth of thick jungle may be rather rapid on such soils, but the final accumulation of the heavy canopied forest is a slow process.

Some intrazonal soils also are very low in fertility because their parent materials, formation processes, or drainage conditions were peculiar or irregular. The unstable and immature azonal soils of the Asian tropics normally are less leached, bear lower percentages of pure clays, and contain mineral compounds still partially unweathered and incompletely broken down. Structurally these unstable soils also differ from the zonal, mature soils, and often are more easily handled by the simple tools of the shifting cultivator. Such soils in the mid-latitudes would be described as easily cultivable. They occur on stream margins, on young stream terraces, in the changeable sectors of river floodplains, in the newer sectors of river deltas, and on other smoother to flat sectors subject to relatively steady transport and to mixing of alluvial materials. Unstable azonal soils occur on almost all areas of distinctly sloping surface, ranging from slopes of rather low angle in some places to slopes of high angle in others.

Unstable soils, normally azonal in nature, also occur on all surfaces built out of recent to relatively young volcanic materials. Where these materials are chemically basic in nature, as in many sectors of the island archipelagos, they correspond to other azonal soils. A few areas are composed of chemically acidic materials, and their soils correspond more to intrazonal soils in respect to fertility. Most of the azonal soils, wherever they are located, stand somewhat higher in fertility ranking than zonal and intrazonal soils because they contain reserves of unconverted chemical nutrients in variable quantity.

Too little of the Asian tropics has been mapped by soil scientists on scales that permit detailed examination of the relation between soil and shifting cultivation. Most of the areas in which shifting cultivation is the common agricultural practice have not been mapped at all. As a later section indicates, shifting cultivators are often well aware of variations in soil fertility and productivity, but the available evidence does not permit definitive comment on possible causal relations between soils and the locational situation of shifting cultivation.

A speculative conclusion might be advanced that such shifting cultivators as had come clearly to appreciate variations in soil quality may have been attracted to locations affording azonal soils. Sloping surfaces most commonly provide such soils, but azonal soils occur on many kinds of surfaces, including flat ones. At this point about as far as such a statement can go is to say that knowledgeable shifting cultivators should avoid smooth to flat surfaces having highly mature and nearly sterile soils.

The burning of the vegetative cover on prospective garden sites by shifting cultivators has a direct effect upon the soil. There has been much argument as to the effect of burning, citing both helpful and destructive results. The excellent synthesis by Watters, describing both the good and the bad effects, is worth quoting in full:

> The close dependence of shifting cultivation on soil fertility is clearly evident in analyses of changes in the soil following burning. The advantages of the burn, expressed empirically in the traditional practices of various systems, can be demonstrated. Burning leads to an accumulation of potash (probably the most prized by-product of burning) and valuable phosphates are often released at just the right time—immediately prior to planting the crops that will need them. Burning produces, moreover, a marked decrease in potential acidity, which is especially important in the more senile lateritic soils; it often performs a function similar to that of frost in the temperate countries in preparing a friable surface that is often ideal for the germination of seeds. In view of these facts, it can be seen that burning is not only part of the shifting cultivator's technology—a device for clearing away vegetation—but also leads to an improvement in certain properties of the soil which in some areas makes cultivation possible and generally leads to increased yields during the period of cultivation.
>
> On the other hand, burning has been shown to be on the whole a disadvantageous practice in view of the destruction of humus and consequent decreased nitrification. Valuable micro-fauna and flora are destroyed and valuable organic matter is oxidized. The most detrimental effects, however, accrue from colloidal transformation, and where burning is common (or dry conditions commonly prevail) significant changes in composition and structure favor fallow growth of slower growing species that are more xerophytic and pyrophylous, tolerant of high light conditions, and able to withstand extremes of drought and moisture. If burning is excessive and end result will ultimately be the replacement of high forest by a degenerate savannah flora.[8]

SOIL EROSION

The whole of the Asian tropics cannot be covered by a single generalization on soil erosion, for the variety of conditions is extreme. One of the serious problems of the Asiatic tropics, however, is the existence of extensive areas where there has been too little erosion.[9] Large areas of mature laterite, old red earths, and hard-baked, bare surfaces would be improved could sheet erosion effectively strip off all such materials to expose newer soil materials below, which have not deteriorated so sharply as have the existing surface soils. Parts of Cambodia, Thailand, India, and Borneo have too long lain stable without significant erosion, producing large expanses of mature and near-mature laterites (or materials similar to them in soil quality) which are almost useless for cropping.

On the other hand, large areas of low hill country and higher, rough hill country are suffering seriously from active and deep soil erosion. Parts of the southeast Asian mainland, the upland Philippines, and parts of the upland of Indonesia today show the serious impact of soil erosion. Particularly the semiarid regions, such as upland Timor Island, have been seriously affected.

Many agencies are responsible for causing soil erosion. Among these the shifting cultivator is one, but it is doubtful that shifting-cultivator culture groups (if they can still practice integral shifting cultivation of the traditional variety) have caused as much soil erosion as is laid at their door. A large share of blame must rest

---

[8] Watters, 1960, pp. 81–82. Sources quoted by Watters, supporting his statement are: Dundas, 1944, p. 124; Joachim and Kandiah, 1948, pp. 3–11; Kivekas, 1941, p. 44; Gourou, 1947 (Eng. trans.), pp. 16–17; Masefield, 1949, pp. 135–138. See also Birch, 1960. The section on soils had been written by the time I came upon the little volume by Nye and Greenland, 1960, which is an excellent review of soils under shifting cultivation.

[9] Pendleton (1940, 1954) has repeatedly made this point with regard to many local regions, most specifically for Thailand.

with those who burn off grasslands on which to graze cattle, buffalo, horses, or goats, and some must lie with those who carelessly build or later neglect terrace systems. Significant are the lumbermen who often leave behind them a torn and bared earth in which local drainage is disturbed and erosion channels are created by log transport. Important are permanent-field agriculturists who encroached too closely upon active floodplain margins and interrupt natural drainage, or who cultivate slope lands by permanent-field technologies inefficiently and without constructing terraces. And occasionally responsible are engineers who build modern road systems without regard for the initiation of erosion or for local drainage patterns. Small shares of blame for soil erosion must be laid to those (other than shifting cultivators) who burn off grasslands and light jungle in game hunting, and to partial shifting cultivators who settle on the frontiers to begin the process of becoming permanent-field agriculturists. In the recent past Europeans who laid out plantations and tried to maintain clean field surfaces by constant cultivation and weed removal have caused some soil erosion. A full listing of the agencies promoting soil erosion would include numerous other elements. An example is the rooting for tubers and other edibles on the part of the wild pig; in some areas the wild-pig population is a significant initator of serious erosion.

There is considerable evidence that advanced shifting cultivators are aware of the dangers of soil erosion and take measures to prevent or reduce serious impairment of their cropland ranges. The simplest of all shifting cultivators, who have not yet learned the critical techniques of handling soils, probably have been unaware of the dangers. Usually, however, these simple groups move their fields annually, carry on poor clearing and weeding operations, and are so inefficient as crop growers that they probably have not contributed markedly to soil erosion. Between these hierarchical extremes it is probable that some shifting cultivators have produced considerable soil erosion.

Shifting cultivation has resulted in serious soil erosion when those who employ it can no longer maintain their traditional practices at full scale. Where culture groups have been forced to shorten their rotational cycles of land use to the point that vegetative regrowth has been scanty, soil erosion may become serious. These conditions obtain when neighboring culture groups invade territorial ranges and restrict original occupants to cropland ranges too small in total area. Such conditions also have often obtained when colonial governments took over areas of land for forest reserves, declared unoccupied lands public domain, or otherwise restricted the freedom of the original occupying population without providing alternative ranges or alternative economic opportunities. It is likely that the pressures of European colonial governments upon shifting-cultivator societies have been significant in the production of some of the most serious regional occurrences of soil erosion. It is also clear, however, that the same kind of restrictive pressure was sometimes applied by Asiatic political agencies in regionally competitive patterns.

It may be considered heresy to state that when and where advanced, integral shifting cultivators have been able to practice their system as they knew it should be practiced, as little soil erosion has resulted as from any other cropping system that man has so far devised. This statement cannot be documented in the usual manner, but it is the conclusion I have reached. A corollary follows: when an integral shifting-cultivator culture group is forced in some way to curtail the full practice of shifting cultivation, then soil erosion on the lands cropped by the group is only one of several manifestations that the whole living system of the group is in serious danger of breaking down.

ATTITUDES OF SHIFTING CULTIVATORS TOWARD SOILS

There is ample evidence in the literature that shifting cultivators recognize many characteristics about soils.[10] In general the shifting cultivator seeks out areas with the best soil available or the soil most suitable to the particular crop he wishes to grow. Among shifting cultivators who grow many different crops, planting is done, so far as possible, to utilize varying qualities of soil. Even in small patch clearing, microvariations in soil quality are recognized and utilized. Planting of a few units of a particular crop may utilize a very small area, and sometimes what looks like an unplanned garden may be quite precisely planted. Thus, Thai shifting cultivators may put a few tobacco and tomato plants in the soil of a demolished termite mound, whereas rice is planted over much of the rest of the field.[11] Most peoples in New Guinea clearly distinguish between soil, including other edaphic features, for taro and soil for yams and sweet potatoes. In the 1930's, the shifting cultivator of Wogeo Island, off eastern New Guinea, when looking for a new garden site, avoided stony ridges, sandy patches, swamps, and white and black clay patches, and chose the spot with a dark-brown soil. If he could find such a patch on which a particular indicator shrub grew, he knew that both bananas and taro would do well there.[12]

The Lamet, of northwest Laos, considered black soils the best, red soils good, heavy clayey soils only fair, and sandy soils poor for their main crop of rice. They maintained a crude soil memory map of the characteristics of areas formerly cleared, so that the next rotational clearing could avoid the poorer spots. Millet and Job's tears were planted in the same soils as rice, but maize normally was put into little patches of stream-bank soil, and a sweet reed crop into a wet spot. Manioc, yams, sweet potatoes, and taro were put in selected patches, but the evidence does not indicate whether this was merely selective grouping in terms of microvariations in soils. Green vegetables were grown in mulched beds in gardens; vegetables, bananas, and newly acquired experimental plants were grown near the permanent villages in crudely terraced beds filled with soil.[13]

Obviously not all shifting cultivators are so skillful and knowledgeable about soils as the Wogeo Islanders or the Lamet. Between Finschhafen and Salamaua on the Huon Gulf coast of New Guinea distinctions in soils appeared less important to shifting cultivators than soil moisture. About a dozen varieties of taro were planted during the year, but the chief element in the selection of planting sites was

---

[10] It is quite true that some culture groups today seem to pay little attention to the issue of soil, but some of these have been restricted to the point that they now have little alternative other than cultivating the ground with the longest fallow. Such patterns should not be made the qualitative standard for all shifting cultivation. Other groups have not learned enough about soils to make preferential judgments. Most experienced shifting cultivators retaining freedom of choice do show by their site selections a strong appreciation of differences in soils (see Watters, 1960, pp. 77–86; Izikowitz, 1951, pp. 207–210). Conklin (1957, pp. 20–44, esp. p. 37) points out that Hanunóo fertility ratings correlate with both pH ratings and with chemical analyses for mineral consituents.

[11] Personal observation.

[12] Hogbin, 1938, pp. 143–144.

[13] Izikowitz, 1951, pp. 57–58, 207–210, 240–241, 257–260.

soil moisture; marshy flats were preferred in the dry season, and well-drained stream-bank sites were chosen in the wet season. Manioc, amaranthus, sugar cane, and bananas were inserted as minor crops into the plantings, apparently without worrying about their soil preferences, for taro was the basic crop.[14]

Shifting cultivators who had barely grasped the concepts of planting obviously had not fully learned all the many implications of soil, exposure, edaphic variety, and operating procedures which go with successful crop growing. As described in 1904, the Negrito of Zambales, western Luzon Island, cannot long have been growing crops, nor can they have ranked very high in the scale as crop growers.[15] Like the Rajis of the Indian Himalayas, they must be deemed elementary shifting cultivators in terms of their slight comprehension of the relationships between soils and crop production. More careful study of the understanding of this relationship would undoubtedly aid in the classification of varied technologic ratings of shifting cultivators.

VEGETATION AND FIRE

It is rather obvious that the modern forester and the shifting cultivator view the twin subjects of vegetation and fire from rather different points of view. These two factors are inextricably interdependent in the discussion of shifting cultivation. It is first necessary, however, to review the value judgments placed upon vegetation by different cultural groups before other issues can be discussed.

VALUES OF VEGETATION TO CULTURE GROUPS

Wild vegetation presents different qualities to different cultures and to different economies. Its aspect as a part of the physical environment is significantly affected by this variation in human outlook. Depending upon outlook and aim, culture groups and individuals formulate, vaguely or specifically, mystical notions, points of view, or crassly utilitarian concepts about plant assemblages and their preservation in, or eradication from, the landscape. Culture groups may continue to hold the same predominant views for long periods of time or, as their culture changes, may drastically alter them. Some of these viewpoints may be framed into specific programs, whereas others will remain unspecific leanings. In a large and complex society such as that of the United States many different viewpoints are held, but they are less divergent than those of so vast and varied a society as that of India. A smaller and more uniform society, like that of Cambodia, or a simpler culture group, like the Kachin of Burma, show less divergence in viewpoint as well as a different emphasis of outlook toward wild vegetation.

The major points of view hold that wild vegetation has value as:

1. A resource range from which to mine a major item, such as timber.
2. A continuing resource of economic value, such as a forest reserve to be operated as a type of tree farm.
3. A protective agent against soil erosion of future farmland.

---

[14] Hogbin, 1951, pp. 42–62.

[15] Around 1900 their cropping included girdling trees, cutting brush, burning once, making crude brush fences, and planting tobacco, maize, a few vegetables and, infrequently, rice. Men did the cutting, but there was no other division of labor. The only tools were digging sticks and knives. As nonpermanent residents, they cropped a patch once only, and depended for their support chiefly on hunting, gathering, and fishing (Reed, 1904, pp. 42–43). Fox (1952, pp. 245–247), writing about one group of these Negrito, remarked that they still were not really crop producers, but that about half their subsistence came from the sweet potato.

4. A protective agent against the filling up of rivers of value in inland navigation.
5. A protective agent against the silting up of streams, to preserve fish life.
6. A scenic area, not only as part of the general landscape, but also in parks and botanical gardens.
7. A recreational area and playground.
8. A watershed control, serving to augment water supplies in purer form.
9. A wild-plant reservoir from which to cull interesting decorative and utilitarian plant stocks.
10. A wilderness area, to be preserved as a phenomenon of the past physical environment not elsewhere remaining.
11. A game preserve and wildlife sanctuary.
12. An experimental plant preserve where manipulation, trials, propagation, and experiments may be tried.
13. Simply an aspect of the physical environment, with no clearer or more concrete concept of its value.
14. A problem element in the landscape, whose removal would permit productive use of the land.
15. A confusing mask over the earth's surface, preventing recognition of structure and rock content by those seeking mineral deposits, for example.
16. A free and productive range on which to graze domestic animals.
17. A simple habitation shelter and source of support for animal and bird life, which may then be hunted.
18. A simple screen, ensuring domestic privacy.
19. A protective screen or zone in terms of military defense.
20. A source of danger in military terms, from which human attackers may threaten.
21. A source of danger from predatory wild animal life.
22. A refuge from persecution, into which to withdraw from enemies.
23. A religious and mystical symbolism, with sacred trees, groves, and forests, and the home of gods, both good and evil.
24. A resource range from which to extract food and items of value in everyday life or for trade.
25. A repository of "fertilizer," a supply of organic material, and a conditioner of soils, acting as a regenerative agent.

The list begins with values familiar to American culture, and perhaps the first seventeen are of contemporary significance.[16] In earlier American culture history the problem element (item 14) was extremely important in the eastern half of the country. The game shelter (item 17) was meaningful, and the human military threat and the predatory-animal danger (items 20 and 21) were significant. In the western part of the United States the grazing-range concept (item 16) has been of paramount importance. In the contemporary period the scenic-park aspect, the playground, the watershed, the wilderness, the wildlife sanctuary, and the experiment range (items 6, 7, 8, 10, 11, and 12, respectively) are being stressed, and are of great concern to many Americans. The American viewpoint pattern reflects, in general, the advanced culture of the occidental world of today.

It is significant that the outlook of many peoples in the tropics and subtropics still is more fully reflected by items 16 through 25 than by any of the first fifteen items. Many who practice shifting cultivation as an integral part of their whole culture are entirely concerned with items 17 through 25, whereas some of the

---

[16] Readers may feel that these viewpoints could be grouped in some way to express oriental and occidental patterns of outlook, or tropical and mid-latitude patterns. Consideration of the historical trends for any one region reveals that the changing outlook is a complex matter of culture, economy, and technology, coupled with the threat of the disappearance of the wild landscape. The changing outlook is behind the whole of the conservationist and nature-lover viewpoints being expressed in the United States today. Thus the scale of values attached by any people to vegetation is essentially a matter of cultural evolution, and not a matter of East versus West, or tropics versus mid-latitudes.

simpler culture groups think in terms of the last three only. A few culture groups, almost entirely nonagricultural, regard vegetation as a combination of the refuge and the appropriative resource range (items 22 and 24), but we are not here concerned with such limited views. A considerable number of groups have taken on the cattle-grazing outlook expressed in item 16 through their adoption of animal economies.

It is clear that, in general, the attitudes expressed by items 1 through 11 increasingly were put forward by colonial administrators during the late nineteenth and early twentieth centuries as these points of view came to the fore in the respective home countries. Many European peoples looked to the tropics as a timber resource (item 1), even though in their homelands the tree-farm concept (item 2) had already replaced the concept of "mining" timber

While such attitudes were being stressed by colonial administrations, much of the local population in each country was reacting in terms of the problem element and the cattle range (items 14 and 16), steadily reducing the forests to make way for permanent-field agriculture and the extension of animal-grazing grounds. With the increases in population in all of the Orient, there was a marked growth in the desire to "mine" timber resources (item 1) to provide the necessary supplies of lumber. Increasing emphasis upon these points brought colonial administrators and one sector of the population into direct conflict with another sector of the population—the shifting cultivators—in the forested areas of the country. With the power of government and the changing views of a large part of the population behind them, colonial administrators succeeded in creating forest reserves and in reducing the freedom of shifting cultivators in most parts of the Orient.

At the present time occidental influence is pushing hard for worldwide extension of the attitudes expressed by items 2 through 12. Newly independent political states in the Orient find adherents for these same attitudes, and both continuing and new programs working in the same direction foster them. But the weight of popular expression in many areas is strongly conditioned by the traditional concepts of sectors of the populations, and by culture groups within the populations, so that in some countries the emphasis upon protective, conservational, and long-term attitudes, as in items 2 through 12, has been relaxed in favor of the satisfaction of more immediate needs.

In such regions as the Himalaya foothills, Laos, Mindanao Island in the Philippines, Borneo, and New Guinea, the practical possibilities of putting into effect administrative patterns representing items 2 through 12 are seriously handicapped by the pressing needs of populations already overcrowding their territories or by the sheer inability of the various governments to carry out the programs.

FIRE, FOREST, GRASSLAND, AND CULTURE PRACTICE

It is still a moot point whether all tropical grasslands are man-made; there are vigorous arguments on both sides of the issue.[17] Although no firm answer to the question can yet be given, it is certain that man is responsible for much of the relatively recent extension of tropical grasslands. It is now conventional to ascribe

---

[17] See bibliography in Bartlett, 1956, and annotated bibliographies in Bartlett, 1955, 1957. See also Fosberg, 1958; Conklin, 1959.

most of this extension to the shifting cultivator, but the truth of such assertions is open to question.

The nature of existing patterns of shifting cultivation suggests that the shifting cultivator, when he has a free choice, often selects well-grown forest plots for new cropping endeavors. The literature often refers to this choice as the selection of virgin forest. Virgin forest, in the sense that it has never been cleared by human or natural agency, may actually exist in numerous small areas. It is likely, however, that most of the mature forests of the Orient today are not virgin forests in the proper sense, but merely old forests that have reached a fairly stable equilibrium of ecological succession after some earlier clearing by human or natural means. In some areas it is possible that old forests are not secondary forests or even tertiary forests, but forests of some number well above three.

Old forests contain in their very volume of vegetative material a considerable store of plant nutrients, which, when reduced by organic decay and by burning, afford a free source of "fertilizer" that enables any cultivator to reap one or more good crops of his choice. On good or fair soils the yield will be larger than that produced on soils of low fertility, for the vegetative material cannot supply the needed volume of nutrients. This is the regular system of the shifting cultivator, who then returns the land to the regenerative processes by which wild plant growth accumulates from depth a new store of nutrients, which through the dynamics of living plant life provides another later store of nutrients available to the next clearer of the land.

This process also physically reconditions the soil so that it is soft and permeable at the next clearing. Tree and shrub growth accomplishes the renewal more rapidly than does grassy growth, because tree and shrub roots work at greater depths and have larger expanses of top growth than grasses. Trees, shrubs, scrub, bamboo, and grass, however, all work toward the same end. The longer the period of restoration and the heavier the growth, in general, the greater is the store of nutrients accumulated and the better is the condition of the soil itself, to the point where age and deterioration of the vegetal cover set in.

Plant growth serves in two ways, therefore: as an accumulator of nutrients and as a conditioner of soils. Plant growth, however, can do only so much in this direction. Once real deterioration of the soil has set in strongly, wild plant growth may require an inordinately long period to restore any semblance of fertility to soil materials. This is seen in some areas where heavy forests have been found growing over lands cultivated for a considerable period at some time in the past. The luxurience of the cover suggests fertility, but once such an old forest is cleared and its small quota of accumulated fertility dissipated, the land proves so barren that for decades nothing but poor scrub will grow again. Many shifting cultivators are aware that not all heavy forest lands are good lands for clearing and cropping.[18]

Despite much study of the role of fire, the durability of pyrophylous tree and shrub species, and the spread of grasses, great uncertainty remains about the succession of species in tropical vegetation after cultural clearing and the return of land to regenerative status. In general, it does appear that in forested zones where little clearing has been done, the succession of vegetation after one clearing pro-

---

[18] See Conklin (1957, pp. 39–44) for a discussion of Hanunóo appreciation of vegetation.

duces shrub and tree growth that is rapid, vigorous, and full-covering, with soft-wood species of trees maturing rapidly.[19] Competitive growth eventually introduces slower-growing hardwoods which seem to require nurse-crop forest cover for their introduction.

As the degree of regional clearing increases, marked patterns of change appear in the sequences of succession of plant-shrub-tree species. Fire is a significant element in changing this pattern of succession, but the precise patterns of change are unclear and the role of selective cutting of various tree species for timber, tools, and other uses is inadequately known. When we look at grasslands or grassy parklands we see dominant grass covers dotted thinly or thickly with shrubby trees and shrubs in which frequent firing prevents the return of forest. But we do not always know how old these grasslands are, nor what succession of clearings produced them. We do not know what range of cropping, selective wood extraction, and firing accompanied the clearing process. Some grasslands seem to have appeared abruptly, but other grassy parklands seem to be the products of a long and slow process of deterioration from heavy forest through light forest to tree-dominant parkland to grass-dominant conditions.

In general, fire appears to inhibit the regeneration of many of the less common hardwood large tree species, but I am unable from the literature to distinguish the role of fire from that of selective cutting of some of these species. It does appear that with continued cutting—second-, third-, fourth-, and up to tenth- or twentieth-round clearing—certain tree species disappear, others thrive, and grass or pyrophylous species tend to increase. But the known data do not permit real generalization, and regional patterns do not all follow the same sequence. The simple generalization that grasses become dominant where clearing is repeated does not stand up in many areas where shifting cultivators have been clearing and regenerating vegetative cover for long periods. Grass is not the automatic result of carefully maintained shifting cultivation itself.[20] Intermingled with the role of fire are the roles of grazing animals, selective timber extraction, preferential preservation of selected trees when clearing, selective planting of particular tree species before returning land to vegetative regeneration, avoidance practices from taboos and religious beliefs which tend to perpetuate certain species, and perhaps other factors.

In addition to shifting cultivation as a cropping system, numerous other patterns of economy or patterns of cultural practice contribute to the spread of grasslands in the tropics and subtropics. The practice of grazing animals, involving the annually repeated burning off of mature old grass growth to permit animals easily to get at the new tender growth, is a very significant factor; it may actually be more important in the failure of forest regeneration than is clearing for crop growing. The very grazing of animals in parkland and forest margins, where the animals indiscriminately eat new tree seedlings and recurrent regrowth parts

[19] In the forest areas of eastern Mindanao, timbermen interested in extracting softwood logs of tree species suitable for manufacturing matches hunt up old Manobo clearings, knowing that some of the desired trees are among the first full forest-cover patterns. Because the Manobo spot-cleared at remote location intervals, forest reproduction on old Manobo clearings would be rapid and complete. See Richards, 1952, for a general discussion of successional trends.

[20] In many places the tall heavy grasses, so hated elsewhere, are actually grown as a crop, because of their very scarcity. I have seen this crop grown for thatching in northern Thailand (cf. Hutton, 1921b, pp. 76–78).

of shrubs and trees, tends to prevent the reestablishment of forest growth and to allow the extension of grass. The burning of parkland in hunting operations, when group hunting parties set fires to drive animals toward zones in which the hunters concentrate, may be a significant factor if regularly practiced. The careless use of fire in burning off crop clearings in zones where grasses, bamboos, and certain other plant associations are significant does result in escape fires that extend the areas of grasses.[21] It is obvious that not all groups or individuals practicing shifting cultivation are equally careful in their use of fire as a clearing agent. But it is equally obvious that not all escape fires can be laid at the door of the shifting cultivator.

In areas still well forested, and among certain other plant associations, the extent of escape fires or uncontrolled burning is slight and damage is extremely light. Toward the forest margins, the danger of escaping fire varies from serious to ruinous in areas where bamboos are naturally numerous, in heavily logged-off areas where good stock for reproduction may be somewhat lacking, and in areas where animals may retard the reproduction of forest. Such burning results in the steady advance of grassland and the elimination of nonpyrophytic species. Where shifting cultivators do not also graze animals in numbers, do not repeatedly employ fire in hunting operations, and do not burn carelessly, they cannot often be held responsible for the serious decline of forests.

Conversely, when shifting cultivators employ fire in certain other ways, their contribution to the decline of the forests is a major one. The same general result may occur when shifting cultivators are forced to an abnormally rapid rotation cycle in cropping.

In many localities of the Orient, economy patterns are opposed to each other by virtue of social and economic stratification, each making inroads upon the forests. Many crop growers who employ shifting cultivation as their cropping system do not themselves keep animals in large herds, use fire in hunting, or permit serious escapes of fire. They sometimes form the mass of the population. Above them in social, economic, and political position are small numbers of landed and well-to-do aristocracy and of rulers who, as a mark of their status and as an element in their own economy, keep large herds of animals. The employment of fire by these groups to provide grazing, the damage done by the animals themselves, and the impact of uncontrolled burning compound the effect of the shifting cultivator's use of fire. On occasion, such ruling groups also put on "hunts" which have little economic value, but may also employ fire. Where such compounding of practices occurs, the spread of grass or of other poor plant species, the serious lowering of

---

[21] The literature supports a tentative generalization that most groups practicing an integral form of advanced shifting cultivation are both conscious of, and careful about, the escapement of fire from their clearings (see Conklin, 1957, pp. 64–72, for an example). Many groups clear firebreaks, use backfiring, and avoid burning under wind conditions that would promote spreading of fire beyond the desired areas. Below this advanced level, of course, are those peoples who have not yet learned such control practices, and doubtless suffer escapes.

Escape fires in heavy tropical forest rarely go far or do much damage. Escapes in secondary forests of good growth in a climatic zone lacking a long dry season similarly do little real damage. Escapes in parkland, including both humid climatic areas and those with a prolonged, seasonal dry period, are more common and more damaging. The great sky-filling conflagrations mentioned in the literature may sometimes include the firings by strictly crop-growing shifting clutivators, but are often associated with hunters and grazers. Some of the most advanced shifting-cultivator groups show an increasing continuity of field use. Among such groups firing is not the primary clearing agent, but has become a complementary one. Groups that manipulate the soil by turning or composting it have almost stopped using fire as a land-clearing agent.

the value of the plant cover, and the possible entry of serious soil erosion may have grave consequences for a landscape and for a people.[22]

ATTITUDES OF SHIFTING CULTIVATORS TOWARD VEGETATION FACTORS

That primitive peoples often know more about plants and their uses than do highly civilized peoples is now fairly well accepted. Urban Americans, long divorced from close contact with other than decorative plants, frequently know almost nothing about the ecologic world in which wild plant communities are at home. In this sense most advanced practitioners of an integral form of shifting cultivation are keenly sensitive to many different aspects of the plants that make up the vegetation cover of their home regions.[23] In deciding when regeneration of vegetation of a given tract has proceeded far enough to be cropped successfully without lasting damage to either vegetation or soil, many are quite skillful. The Wogeo Islander who hunts for his indicator plant, the Hanunóo native who is sensitive to the shadings of change in vegetation, and the highland New Guinea Kuman who watches the diameter of casuarina plantings have sound experience behind them in their native scenes, enabling them to use vegetational evidence to its practical utmost.[24]

The presence of indicator plants, the thickness of tree growth stands, the luxuriance of growth, the volume of vegetative material that will produce the best volume of chemical-yielding ash, the centering of certain plants either in very poor or in the best possible soils, the size of trees in relation to the cutting labor required—these and many other evidences have long been known to experienced shifting cultivators. Other groups, less advanced in the technical practice of shifting cultivation, often have known only particular things about site selection and the vegetative relationship to productive cropping. Toward the bottom of the scale have been the practicers of a very elementary form of shifting cultivation. Among the whole variety of shifting cultivators have been those who could not use what they knew because of a wide variety of pressures upon them. Sedentary agriculturists who moved to the frontiers to practice shifting cultivation in some form have had some general knowledge, but have lacked the finely adjusted skills of the long resident.

FACTORS OF CLIMATE AND SEASONALITY

There seems to be no permanently causal relationship between tropical climate and shifting cultivation. It may be that shifting cultivation did originate in a climatically stable, humid zone near the outer margin of the tropics or in a favorable sector of the humid subtropics. At present the world distribution of shifting cultivation as a cropping system falls chiefly into the tropics and subtropics.

---

[22] Timor Island is a classic illustration of the compounding of the factors mentioned in which all elements of deterioration are well advanced (see Ormeling, 1956).

[23] Fox (1952, p. 188) has noted that the Pinatubo Negritos of western Luzon were acquainted in detail with about 450 plants, though they were then not yet really an agricultural people. The Hanunóo utilize about 1,600 different plant types from about 1,200 species, more than 430 of them being cultigens (Conklin, 1957, pp. 39–44). The Hanunóo also distinguish six major and ten minor vegetative "associations," the former being regional cover types. Their recognition of these six involves the distinction of gross composition, species groups, rates of growth, maturity, significance as a regenerative agent, and other diagnostic elements.

[24] Hogbin, 1938, p. 144; Conklin, 1957, pp. 39–44; Nilles, 1943, pp. 118–121; Brown and Brookfield, 1959, p. 18.

Unfortunately, many observers are thereby led to assume that shifting cultivation is inherently a tropical system, and that it does stand in cause-and-effect relation to the climate of the tropics. If, however, shifting cultivation did originate within, or on the margins of, the tropics, it has been carried to far regions lying well outside the tropics in the period since the Neolithic era began. Shifting cultivation is still practiced in Korea and Japan; it was commonly employed during the nineteenth century clear across northern Eurasia; and the last crop of grain rye grown in Sweden by shifting cultivation was harvested in 1918.[25] There is abundant evidence that shifting cultivation was employed as a cropping system by early man in almost all the forested regions of the earth where cropping was carried on at an early date.[26] The culturally inventive abilities of crop-growing peoples in the period since the early Neolithic have led to the devising of many other cropping systems better suited to physical environments and ecologic situations of high quality than was shifting cultivation.

Shifting cultivation has been replaced in much of nontropical Asia, in Europe, and in most of North America through the processes of cultural invention, evolution, and diffusion of crops and cropping practices. These processes have also replaced shifting cultivation by permanent-field systems of crop growing in large sectors of the Asian tropics, though these systems have differed from those devised in nontropical climatic regions. The view is here taken that shifting cultivation is still practiced in sections of the Asian tropics because there has been developed no other system of greater efficiency, effectively suited to the rather poor physical environments and specific ecologic situations in which shifting cultivation is still employed. When such a system is developed and the practicers of shifting cultivation learn it effectively, shifting cultivation will disappear.

Although the region of this study lies within the major confines of the tropical climates in horizontal lowland distribution, in highland regions of sufficient elevation any kind of crop growing is restricted by low temperatures and a seasonal frost period. The Indian, Burmese, and Chinese borders of the Tibetan highlands form one such region. In numerous small localities throughout the island sector the upward limit of any kind of crop growing is set by low temperatures and a frost period. Shifting cultivation has pushed to the upper limits of crop growing in a long strip through the center of New Guinea. In the upland regions of microthermal climatic conditions, crops, as well as some techniques of handling soils, vary from those of the lowlands, but the gross controls over crop growing do not significantly alter shifting cultivation so as to make it essentially different from the systems practiced on the lowlands.

Some aspects of regional variation in the practice of shifting cultivation are produced by regional climatic differences. On the one hand, broad regional variation is caused by gross differences in climate. On the other hand, detailed variations from locality to locality are produced by specific variations in some aspect of

---

[25] For the last item noted see Darby, 1956, p. 210.

[26] No really full bibliography is cited at this point, for the subject has been given slight attention in most regions of the earth and the literatures often are inconclusive. For Europe see Narr, 1956, Darby, 1956, and Evans, 1956, and the sources they cite for the role of shifting cultivation in very early Europe. It is my belief that in the early period both Chinese and Indian agriculture included the practice of shifting cultivation. Today, in the mountain country of the Middle East, westward from the area I am concerned with, shifting cultivation is still in use, though little attention has been paid to the practice.

climate. In the following sections, the nature of such climatic variations and the resulting regional differences in the practice of shifting cultivation are considered.

MAJOR REGIONAL VARIATIONS IN CLIMATE AND CROPPING PRACTICE

The gross seasonal shift of the solar cycle, with its variations in temperature and insolation values, produces a distinct seasonality in the agricultural calendar in areas of the Northern Hemisphere which lie beyond the equatorial zone. In northern India, Burma, Thailand, Indochina, southern China, and the northernmost island sector, primary cropping practices are distinctly seasonal, with a "spring" planting season and an "autumn" harvest season. Toward the equator the climatic seasonality lessens, of course, and the southernmost regions, south of the equator, included in this study do not show a marked increase in seasonality patterns traceable to the solar cycle alone, as they lie relatively close to the equator.

The gross variations in seasonal distribution of precipitation also produce patterns of regional variation which are essentially seasonal. In almost continuously humid regions the seasonal timing of clearing and burning must be fitted to whatever dry period is long enough to permit the drying out of vegetation. Dry periods do occur even close to the equator. In the broad region covered by this study clearing and burning are practiced in some locality in every month of the year. Planting normally follows quickly upon burning, so that the planting calendar becomes a function of the timing of the local dry season. A very few localities are so continuously humid that the culture groups resident there do no burning at all, but practice a slash-and-mulch cropping pattern.[27] At the other extreme are the dry margins, with a very long dry season, in which clearing and burning may be timed over a long period. Here planting need not follow burning so closely in time. In the dry-margin localities, the onset of the rainy season initiates planting and following agricultural calendar. The onset of the rainy season occurs in almost every month of the year in some region within the area of this study.

Although all peoples who practice shifting cultivation realize that annual variation in seasonal weather does occur, they also recognize the broad seasonality needed for the agricultural calendar. Every people for whom there are adequate data recognize the annual cycle, use some systematic diagnosis of this cycle, and base that diagnosis upon some specific criterion.[28] In the more poleward regions

[27] In Southeast Asia I know of only two specific areas so continuously moist that burning is not used, though further examination might reveal more local regions where mulching is employed because fire cannot be used. Conklin (1961, pp. 27–28) notes a report (in Maass, 1902, included in bibliography but not available to me for Mentawei Island, off Sumatra, of taro cropping by shifting cultivation with mulching only. On the upper hill country of the Mindanao east coast a pattern of mulching of cleared vegetation has been seen, but has not been reported in writing (Yengoyan, personal communication). West (1957) has reported a slash-mulch cultivation of maize from Colombia, and there may well be other examples in other parts of the tropics.

[28] Many of the nonliterate ethnic groups in Asian and Pacific low latitudes reckon their annual work calendar by the Pleiades. In western Borneo the planting season correlated with the appearance of the Pleiades above the eastern horizon at the break of daylight (when reported by Roth, 1896, 2:239). According to Freeman (1955, pp. 40–41) the Iban of Sarawak used the Pleiades, Orion, and Sirius in calendar reference: clearing of sites began when the Pleiades were rising near dawn; planting started when the Pleiades were at zenith just before dawn and continued until Orion was at zenith at dawn. The Iban reckoned that rice would not mature if sown after Sirius was more than 5 degrees past zenith at dawn.

Farther east, on Dobu of the D'Entrecasteaux Islands, clearing for gardens was timed when the Pleiades had risen to 15 degrees above the horizon at dawn (Fortune, 1932, p. 127). In the past some groups, from the Bismarck to the Solomon Islands, used the flower-to-harvest cycle of

the annual calendar is rather emphatic. Close to the equator the broad climatic factors are less emphatic, but the detailed climatic factors of seasonality are delicate matters often obscured by elements of agricultural practice which are essentially cultural factors. Some shifting cultivators, however, are rather expert at handling agricultural practices that correlate closely with delicate factors in seasonality.

Geographic literature, perhaps because of the lack of marked variation in the temperature and precipitation records of tropical rain-forest climatic stations, has made too much of the nonseasonality of life in the tropics. The delicate and detailed nature of tropical seasonality has been little studied in general, and has been even less studied in relation to the practices of crop growing. The detailed factors of climatic seasonality in themselves need careful study. There is an acute need for studying the reactions of crop plants to the detailed climatic patterns of change. This is true both for crop plants that belong essentially to the tropics and for crop plants that have been introduced into the tropics from more poleward margins where particular seasonality reactions were native to wild plants and perhaps further induced by the processes of domestication.[29]

SPECIFIC AND DETAILED REGIONAL VARIATIONS IN CLIMATE AND CROPPING PRACTICE

There are few effective data to indicate the impact of minor temperature variations on cropping systems within the tropics and humid subtropics because of the casual generalization that temperature variations are so slight that they are not effective. Precipitation is the obvious effective agent in causing variation in regional cropping practices. The many hundreds of localities within the region under study possess distinctive precipitation regimes. Each locality has its own seasonal calendar for the agricultural cycle. This situation has developed from the whole climatic complex, in which the particular aspect of the solar cycle, the major wind systems, and the precipitation mechanisms produce the specific result of climatic regionalism. The factors contributing to this regionalism are, of course, geographical location with regard to windward or leeward coasts and littoral or inland position; general exposure in terms of exposed situation or rain shadow; elevation; and detailed orographic position.

Viewed as manifestations of seasonality or of regional weather calendars, the important components of such regionalism are the length and timing of the dry season, the timing of the onset of the rainy season, and the length of the primary rainy season. Among folk cultures, the onset of the local rainy season appears to be the most important item; it is the subject of popular concern, and is the aspect of climate and weather around which magic, ritual, rites, and the appeals to the gods are focused.[30] These calendar manifestations express themselves to the shifting cultivator as questions: (1) Will the dry season be long enough for cleared vegetation to dry out sufficiently for a good burn, and will it come at the proper time? (2)

---

the nut-bearing tree, canarium almond, as their basic calendar criterion in cropping activities (Bogesi, 1947, p. 221). The Kelabit of Borneo, who are rather new at crop growing, base their crop-year calendar on the arrival of migratory birds, not a very efficient criterion (Tom Harrison, Sarawak Museum, unpublished data, 1957).

[29] See the first part of Spencer, 1959*b*, for an illustration of the problems involved.

[30] See Freeman, 1955, pp. 44–46, for an example.

Will good rains come soon after what has been interpreted as the proper burning period? (3) Will the rainy season be normal and good, will it be too wet, or will it be too dry to produce good crops?

These regional variations in the agricultural calendar show direct relationships to the annual weather cycle, and to this degree there is clearly a climatic influence upon cropping practices. Calendric correlations, however, are to be found in all systems of crop growing. Shifting cultivators however, maintain lower efficiency in their patterns of correlations than do users of other cropping systems because many of them do not use sound criteria in studying the annual calendar.

Another element of regional variation, the microclimatic relationships between the solar cycle and crop varieties as regionally acclimatized, enters into the detailing of such patterns. As the effective data are extremely scant, however, only a suggestion can be made here. Shifting-cultivator populations are often as acquisitive as more advanced agriculturists in securing new varieties of crop plants, a trait particularly marked among the seed-grain crop cultivators. The spread of the rice plant toward the equator from its subtropical homeland presents numerous puzzles with regard to local regional success or failure. Among the many thousands of local varieties are innumerable variations in the length of the growing season required to mature grain. Many of these varieties have been bred in regional environments where they become delicately attuned to local insolation values, to variable length of light and dark periods, and perhaps to rather minor shifts in temperature values at critical times.

We really know very little of the effective microclimatic impacts produced by moving crops within a broad zone in which gross similarities are marked. Rice is not the only crop thus affected, for we also know that many of the fruits are acutely subject to minor climatic changes. What the facts are with regard to root crops, tubers, and other vegetatively reproduced plants is not at all clear. Regional variations in crop varieties are a factor in creating specific differences in the details of shifting cultivation, but they are not features that produce shifting cultivation as a cropping system, any more than are the major regional variations in climate.

It is customary to suggest casually that nonseasonal planting is the rule in equatorial latitudes, as there are no prohibitions or marked seasonal ranges that discourage it, but there has been little investigation of the localized or detailed aspect of the problem. On Bougainville in the Solomon Islands, at about 7° S. latitude, taro was planted every two or three weeks the year around, for it was a point of honor among the inhabitants never to have to borrow or buy taro. Taro may well be a plant that is chiefly at home in the lowland low-latitude tropics and is amenable to such planting sequences; but how far poleward or into higher altitudes does such nonseasonality extend? And what are the precise factors that begin to create seasonality of crop maturity in different species and different varieties of vegetatively reproduced plants? How much alteration in maturity patterns can plant breeding accomplish, either in different latitudes or in different regions in the same general latitude? For example, on Malaita in the Solomon Islands, at about 9° S. latitude, yams were planted in April, whereas on Ulawa, very close by, they were planted in January or February and seemed adjusted to this variation in timing. The taros, on the other hand, were planted on and off all during the year.

In the Trobriand Islands off eastern New Guinea, at about 8° 30′ S. latitude, there were two yam-planting periods, an early one in May–June and a major one in July–August. Taros could be planted at various times during the year, but plantings were peaked in October–November and January–February so as to provide large taro yields at intervals between yam harvests.[31] Are these planting patterns cultural in timing, or are they related to microclimatic controls with respect to crop varieties long grown in precise regional situations? Without having precise data about the history of regional varieties or about maturity rates for specific varieties, it is hard to distinguish climatically determined seasonality from culturally determined seasonality. Vague notations suggest that many varieties of vegetatively reproduced tropical plants, such as taros, yams, bananas, and others, do have specific variations in maturity periods, but very little is really known about the relations between maturity periods and the precise microclimatic controls over plant growth in specific tropical and subtropical localities.

Rice, as a plant from the more poleward subtropics, is distinctly a seasonal plant in its maturity patterns, whatever the variety, regardless of whether it is long-season or short-season rice. The planting calendar is apparently much more critical for rice than for taro. Although rice fields in all stages of growth pattern may be seen at any one time in the tropics and subtropics, it appears that in most regions each variety of rice is planted only once during a calendar year. The closer to the tropics rice is planted, the more critical the precise timing becomes for many varieties to take advantage of microclimatic factors that cause the grain to mature. Hence the Iban pay close attention to the solar-cycle calendar (see n. 28, above). Close to the equator, it has been reported, rice plantings have failed to produce mature grain in one growing season, but it is unclear whether the timing was bad or whether the reports referred to new varieties not yet adjusted to local microclimatic factors. I cannot solidly document this whole subject as yet, for the data are inadequate in precise terms. The known data are sufficient to make suspect the broad generalization that all planting of all crops in the tropics is nonseasonal, but far closer observation is required to distinguish clearly the true nature of seasonality and nonseasonality.

The microclimatic factors controlling plant growth and maturity include the length of light and dark periods; the cyclic occurrence of changing length in such periods; the timing and amounts of moisture; the factors promoting transpiration of moisture, such as effective plant temperature and the sunshine-cloudiness ratios; insolation values in several different kinds of measures; and the critical values of temperatures at different stages of plant growth. These frequently are summed up under the heading of photosynthetic processes of plant growth. Only recently has the study of photosynthesis advanced sufficiently to make possible critical examination of the relative regional impact of climate upon plant growth. To date little such work has been done in the tropics.

FACTORS OF BIOTIC ECOLOGY

Almost none of the specific versions of shifting cultivation are operated as plant-

---

[31] For taro planting on Bougainville see Thurnwald, 1934, p. 120, referring to the years 1908–1909; for Malaita in the Solomon Islands and yam planting see Ivens, 1927, pp. 355–363; for the yam-planting seasons in the Trobriand Islands see Malinowski, 1935, 1:60–63.

cropping systems alone, wherein the sole support of the population is the produce of the gardens. The complementary economies of shifting cultivators take many forms, some being directly related to the biotic environment in which the people live, and some being of an entirely different nature and related to social, economic, or political environment. This section deals with the biotic forms that are significant to the whole economy of shifting cultivation by serving as complementary sources of economic support. The biotic environments of the Asian tropics and subtropics are extremely variable in several different ways, and the variations have much to do with the specific system of shifting cultivation employed by a specific people.

Several different aspects of the biotic environment as a whole must be considered in a full survey. These include the natural distribution of plants and animals by floral and faunistic life zones; the present degree of abundance or exhaustion of wildlife patterns, both plant and animal; the cultural-historic impact upon the original biotic assemblage through domestication and adoption into the crop-live-stock assemblage; and the impact upon the original assemblage of life forms through cultural extermination, religious taboos, cultural refusal-acceptances, and other similar process relationships. Each of these aspects may have much to do with the specific economy of shifting cultivation as it actually is practiced today in the various regions here under consideration. This section, although not including a full survey of each of the above subjects, suggests, the range of conditions and outlines some of the obvious aspects of the subject needing attention in regional, culture-group, and whole-economy studies.

The written record on shifting cultivation clearly indicates that all groups who carry on shifting cultivation also engage in a certain amount of collateral and complementary activity contributing to economic support. Such operations may take the form of simple gathering of wild vegetables by which to provide variety and flavoring agents in the daily dietary, or they may aim to provide fruits, nuts, and miscellaneous items to be used as snack foods. They take the form of hunting for wild game that provides the only meat foods eaten, or they may consist of trapping animal predators that invade gardens, some of which will be eaten. The complementary economic activities may be daily or seasonal performances, or they may be operations resorted to only in the so-called starvation period occurring between the end of the last harvest of one annual crop cycle and the first harvest of a new crop cycle. In simpler versions of shifting cultivation, these appropriative activities may not be complementary at all, but may be the main economic operation to which crop growing is properly distinguished as the complement. In any version that has been carefully described it is clear that a close relationship exists between the activities of crop-animal production by shifting cultivation and the activities that utilize resources of the wild biotic environment.

Typical of a good commentary is that on the Lamet of northern Laos, applicable to 1950.[32] Primarily rice growers by shifting cultivation, they do have permanent gardens around their permanent villages and do grow plots of tea on permanent sites. They also raise buffalo and zebu cattle, pigs, chickens, dogs, and bees. Cloth, iron tools, salt, pottery, blankets, bottles, and old clothing are purchased; beeswax,

---

[32] Izikowitz, 1951; data are from scattered references but the calendar review is summarized from pp. 166–169.

honey, rice brandy, fermented tea leaves, deer horn, bear gallbladders, baskets, wild animal hides, and rice are sold. Deer, wild buffalo, bear, monkeys, wild pig, wild chickens, wild pheasant, and many other birds are hunted. Bamboo, rattan, fibers, pandanus leaves (for hats, capes, and basket covers), tool wood, and wood for house construction, traps, and weapons are gathered. The Lamet live too high for much fishing, but do some in local streams. Bamboo and rattan shoots, varied green leafy vegetables, and many fruits are gathered. Gathering is at a low ebb from late September through February.

The annual calendar review follows. In March food becomes scarcer and fish are caught from pools in streams. In April and May old garden sites are combed for anything edible, domestic or wild. Gathering of bamboo shoots and other plant foods from wild ranges becomes serious in May, but animal hunting is still poor. In June rice is running low, families have moved to garden clearings, and the gathering season is in full swing. Fishing and hunting begin in earnest. Some early wild fruit is now ripe. By July many families are out of rice (having sold too much, perhaps); the first cultivated vegetables can be harvested, but gathering of wild plant food continues, as do fishing and hunting, and now fish and wild meat provide an adequate diet. In August the rice supply is exhausted for everyone, but garden vegetables provide a good supply of food, augmented by the major wild fruit ripening period and by wild meat from hunting. In September the early rice harvest again provides rice, but hunting and gathering go on late into the month. From late September through November trapping of birds and animal predators raiding ripe fields provide meat supply, but harvest labor precludes range hunting, gathering, and fishing. In December late harvesting, curing, and transporting to village preclude hunting, gathering, and fishing. In January traps for scavenging animal predators in old gardens yield some meat, but hunting, fishing, and gathering are not done. In February the root-crop harvest terminates, new clearing begins, and gathering may be incidental but not purposeful. No hunting or fishing is done now.

What may one conclude from this calendar sequence? Hunting, gathering, and fishing are important to the economy, but the share they contribute to the annual group food intake is impossible to determine; the author himself was unable to put a percentage to the total. I intend no reproof to the author, who has provided a better than normal commentary; the measurement of proportionate production among an ill-omen–conscious and nonstatistical-minded population is exceedingly difficult. Even subjective estimates would be useful, however, in determining the share of the economy provided by appropriative activities.

Although the above remarks would seem more applicable to the integral variety of shifting cultivation, the issue is present also among those who carry on a partial system of shifting cultivation and among frontier settlers whose shifting cultivation is preliminary to sedentary occupation. Among the frontier varieties in particular, appropriative activities are significant because the wild landscape is often near at hand.

NATURAL WILD BIOTIC ECOLOGY

At any date a good many centuries back, when fewer areas were occupied by sedentary cultivators and when less lumbering for export or domestic consumption was carried on, it is a fair assumption that wild game, wild birds, and stream and lake fish were more common than they are now. At that time shifting cultivators who normally derived part of their food economy from appropriative activities had relatively easy access both to wild plant resources and to game, bird, and fish resources. In more recent centuries this accessibility has been greatly reduced. This section, however, considers only the natural distributions of biotic resources with a view toward the historic orientation of shifting cultivators toward appropriation.

In general, the life-zone patterns in the whole of the area under consideration provided an extremely varied set of faunal resources, rather abundant in volume. Wild pigs probably were the most ubiquitous single faunal form, for in the eastern islands the domesticated pig had long ago gone wild. Some forms of deer and antelope were present throughout most of the mainland and into the western islands of Indonesia.[33] Although many of the mainland faunal forms are not found east of either Wallace's or Weber's line, faunal forms from the Australian life zone replace them, and wallabies and rat bandicoots were widely distributed. Shifting cultivators everywhere had to fence against wild animal predators, and many of them incorporated trapping or hunting procedures into their crop-protective activities. Almost every shifting-cultivator group has a background of animal hunting as a part of the economy. In some areas it was specialized or seasonal, and in some the sporting aspect was significant, but it is clear that the faunal resources provided good hunting for those who chose to employ it as a form of economic endeavor.

Similarly the life-zone patterns for bird life and aquatic life were rich and varied. Many distinct regionalisms were apparent in the detailed zoning of birds and aquatic resources, but everywhere many forms were available. Even mountain-dwelling peoples were able to carry on fishing activities extensive enough to permit the conclusion that fishing is a historic culture trait among almost every ethnic group practicing shifting cultivation. In the island realm, among some groups on small islands fishing was naturally much more important than hunting either land animals or birds.

Plant resources are extremely rich throughout the whole of the region under discussion.[34] Every people practicing shifting cultivation, because of their intimate contact with the plant world, knew a wide variety of plants that could be utilized in some aspect of the food economy.[35] The saving of choice items, such as fern tips, edible roots, and many tuberous forms, at the time of clearing land for new gardens was widely practiced. The ability to cull edible items from either forest undergrowth or regenerated cutover land was well developed. The scavenging of edible items from garden plots, returned to regeneration but still not well regenerated by natural cover, often presented a considerable resource, and the purposeful planting of cultivable items able to maintain themselves during vegetative regen-

[33] No full effort is here made to describe faunal distributions. For a more detailed assessment see Spencer, 1954, pp. 90–93, with a bibliography on p. 426. Also see Laurie and Hill, 1954; Raven, 1935; Tate, 1947; Troughton, 1957.

[34] Here also no full plant survey is made (see Spencer, 1954, pp. 78–84, and the bibliography on pp. 425–426).

[35] See n. 23, above, for an applicable comment.

eration provided significant amounts of fruits, berries, nuts, tubers, buds, and leafy materials.[36]

The natural distribution of regional floras by life-zone subregions and the natural endemism of plant families, effective both horizontally and vertically, meant that there was both variety in kind and variety in economic utility in the plant resources upon which shifting cultivators could depend. The degree to which plant succession maintained species patterns in some areas of long occupance, or the degree to which repeated cropping of the landscape eliminated some useful wild plants, varied greatly throughout the whole of the region. But in general it is a fair inference that, despite the variety to be found, plant resources were always available for appropriation by shifting cultivators who wished or needed to draw on them.

Without going fully into the subject, many other biotic resources were utilized by particular groups in all sectors of the region. Omnivorousness is a characteristic ascribed to many ethnic groups, particularly those whose shifting cultivation was not highly advanced. Omnivorousness, however, is a trait long retained by many groups who had no literal need for some of the simpler edible resources. One finds widespread comment on the eating of snakes, grubs, lizards, rats, rodents of all sorts, and many forms of food not widely consumed by so-called civilized peoples.

To knowledgeable groups of shifting cultivators, the natural biotic ecology provided a wide range and a large volume of resources that could be tapped regularly or in times of need. Many groups engaged in regular gathering activities all year long, but it is equally true that many groups either drew on such resources for occasional variety in the dietary, or resorted to them only as starvation-period resources.

CONTEMPORARY SUPPLY LEVEL OF BIOTIC RESOURCES

As large areas of lowland have been put under sedentary cultivation, as population densities have increased in many parts of the hill country, and as commercial lumbering has thinned out much of the remaining forested areas, the variety and the abundance of biotic resources have been reduced. In many regions where exotic faunal forms have been pushed toward extinction by big-game hunters, zoo collectors, commercial buyers, or the local population itself, faunal forms can no longer supply the food resource they formerly did. This is true both of the Asian mainland and of the larger islands. With the expansion of forest-reserve concepts has come the restriction on hunting or the actual elimination of items formerly used in the food economy.

Through restrictions on territory that can be utilized as hunting and gathering ranges, as well as on the practice of shifting cultivation itself, some groups have had to draw on the limited territory at too heavy a rate, so that the actual volume of resources is lower now than in an earlier period. There are many reports that the hunting is poorer than it was formerly, or that groups no longer engage in hunting because there is nothing significant left to hunt. In localities where stream fishing formerly was a significant complementary element in the economy, fishing practices have declined in importance. In many such regions fishing no longer is effec-

---

[36] See Conklin, 1957, pp. 86–87, 123–126.

tive in the economic support of a culture group. Elsewhere the gradual increase in the density of population has raised the level of appropriation of resources, with consequent depletion of the complementary support that can be drawn from hunting.

Apparently fewer plant resources can be drawn upon than formerly, but it may be inferred that the lessening of rare woods, rattans, gums, extracts, and other quasi-exotic products is to be measured more by its impact upon exchange economy than by its effect on food resources. Only in localities where large areas of grassland have replaced former jungle or forest cover, or where restriction of appropriative ranges has markedly increased, has there been a significant reduction in the amount, type, or variety of plant resources usable as food.[37]

It is impossible in this section to comment with much accuracy on the variety and relative abundance of faunal and floral resources still available to shifting cultivators in the areas they still occupy, for reports on the subject are both casual and fragmentary. The above remarks, resting upon a few reports only, must be taken only as general inferences for the whole region. Not only is the factual commentary on the presence and utilization of faunal and floral resources incomplete, but there have been very few attempts to determine what share of the dietary or of the total economy these resources constitute. Although interest in ethnobotany has been growing fairly rapidly little equivalent concern with ethnozoology has been shown. Studies in both cultural plant geography and cultural animal geography are very badly needed, not only in the area here under discussion, but throughout the tropics. They are needed not only for the more accurate assessment of the total economy of shifting cultivation, but for the assessment of the economy of sedentary agriculturists, many of whom also depend upon a variety of appropriative activities of economic significance.

[37] See comment about reduction in the range of plant varieties in chapter iv.

RELATIONSHIPS TO
THE CULTURAL ENVIRONMENT

In the last chapter the point was made that shifting cultivation has remained in practice on many southeastern Asian landscapes because no other cropping system became available which was sufficiently superior and more attractive to particular peoples to replace shifting cultivation on the landscapes they occupied. This statement refers to a historical process that has a long background, and to southeastern Asia at a particular stage in the process of changing agricultural systems. A map of the comparative distribution of shifting cultivation and permanent-field cropping a thousand years ago would be far different from the map depicting the distributions of the two systems today, for the areas under shifting cultivation then would have been far larger. The map for the year 2166 will undoubtedly show a reduced distribution from the pattern of 1966, for change is occurring more rapidly now than it did in past centuries. In time, shifting cultivation may well totally disappear from all Asian landscapes through the cultural process of substitution by other cropping systems.

Shifting cultivation appears to be the oldest cropping system now used in southern Asia. Whether it originated in the area or was brought in from outside cannot be determined, but this issue need not concern us. Any younger and perhaps better systems, either evolving in southern Asia or brought in from the outside, would have competed with the oldest system for acceptance and application on any lands cropped. The newer systems, if better, would have created regional cropping patterns which would have tended to expand at the expense of the older system.

The historical processes making for improvement in cropping systems employed in Europe and North America have led to the disappearance of shifting cultivation, for practical purposes, in those areas. In Europe those processes operated upon a particular chronological sequence and contained an element of inventive cultural dynamics. In North America, though the same end was achieved, the chronology and the cultural dynamics differed from those of Europe. In southern Asia the chronological processes have not yet brought the practice of shifting cultivation to an end. The chronology has been far slower than in Europe, and the cultural dynamics behind the processes have not generated the power for change in southern Asia which was generated either in Europe or in North America.

In this chapter I am concerned in part with the cultural processes that brought about the widespread acceptance of shifting cultivation as a cropping system quite satisfactory to the tropical and subtropical lands of southern Asia. I am also concerned with the chronology involved in the evolution of cropping systems as such. In order to discuss cultural processes, it is necessary to state operative principles about the development of shifting cultivation. Hence it will be useful briefly to examine some concepts of the nature of culture and its spread and growth.

Culture as an Active Agent

Crop growing and systems of crop growing are procedures devised by man through time. These procedures are the result of men working in groups, and constitute but a single set of the total cultural procedures devised by men working and living in groups. Concepts from the disciplines of anthropology and historiography are pertinent.

Culture is defined in varied specific ways, and the following is a combination of such definitions: "Culture is the historical sum total of learned and regularized modes of behavior, modes of thinking, and designs for living, rational and non-rational, which exist at any given time as potential guides and which are characteristic of the members of a society of human beings."[1] History, somewhat more variably defined and limited in different phrasings, is often distinguished by the qualifying terms "a" and "the." One of the earlier meanings of "a history" still currently in use is "a written account of events involving or affecting the past of a large number of people"; a somewhat later meaning of "the history" often employed is "events of the past occurring among a people or peoples."[2] It is with concepts of culture and "the history" that I am concerned in this chapter.

Three basic "axioms" of anthropology are pertinent to the discussion of shifting cultivation.[3] First is the axiom that each separate society possesses a distinctive and distinguishable culture. Culture traits may exist in the behavior habits of individuals, and the same may be said of culture complexes, but culture becomes the generalized behavior pattern of a group of people. A first corollary to the axiom is that the composition, size, and form of the society depend upon elements of social organization. A second corollary is that continuity of culture among a group depends upon the kinds, amounts, and nature of the processes of change to which a culture group is exposed, but it also depends upon the inherent strength of the culture of the group as a whole. (There are many other corollaries of the basic axiom.)

A second axiom is that material culture (tools, artifacts, houses, monuments, toys, and clothing) always results from nonmaterial culture (ideas, concepts, mores, person-habits, and techniques), and that every object of material culture has specifically designed uses, functions, and utilities in line with the concepts of the nonmaterial culture of which it is a part. Only when the controls (nonmaterial culture ideas and concepts) alter themselves will there be successful change in material culture (artifacts), though it is true that the acquisition of, or the exposure to, a new kind of artifact very different from the artifacts already possessed or created may stimulate the changing of the control to permit institutionalization of the new item. The relations between material and nonmaterial culture are complex, interfunctional, and, properly speaking, inseparable, and their distinction in the above manner seldom is made by the competent contemporary anthropologist.

---

[1] This summary definition is compounded from several sources, but a definition may be found in any basic anthropology textbook. For an extended discussion of the implications and concepts involved in the definition of culture, see Bagby, 1959, chaps. 4, 5.

[2] See *ibid.*, chaps. 2, 3.

[3] No detailed references for each statement are given. Comment on these matters may be found in any textbook in anthropology, though not all are explicitly presented in any one volume (but see Kroeber, 1948; Beals and Hoijer, 1959; Linton, 1955; Hoebel, 1958; Herskovits, 1960; Montagu, 1957; White, 1949; and Childe, 1951). I have spelled out some points that are obvious to anthropologists, and I have grouped together some statements in a way that anthropologists do not commonly employ.

A third axiom is that culture change for mankind as a whole, in terms of originating cultural enrichment, has always been the product of a very small part of the total population. Implicit in this statement are the ideas that volitional enrichment is rare in primitive society and was a slow matter of incidental and accidental accretion in early human prehistory, and that only very recently has volitional enrichment or inventiveness become at all common, effective, or willful as a functioning human process.

A corollary follows that in early human time the chance was extremely small that any small single human group would contribute a significant discovery, invention, or improvement in technique or procedure. Another corollary is that most advances in the culture of specific groups, particularly small groups, are achieved by the practice of borrowing, or diffusion. Items of culture (either single traits, partial complexes, or full trait complexes) tend to diffuse in terms of form only, without an equivalent or comprehensive transfer of concepts, ideas, significances, or contexts surrounding the item. Such transfers require the development by the recipient group of some kind of contextual comprehension by which the new item may take on value and become integrated into the culture. A following corollary is that acceptance of some new trait or complex normally requires the subordination, partial elimination, or total discard of some older trait or complex for which the new feature is a substitution. Total elimination is seldom required, because the new item seldom serves functionally every single purpose served by the older item. The acceptance of new items serves to broaden, enrich, or make more complex the culture receiving them. A further corollary is that, despite broad-spreading diffusion of many items of culture, acceptance is seldom uniform among the varied cultures located within the limits of diffusion. The prehistorian, the historian, and the anthropologist all record variations in the spread of aspects of culture which amount to regionalisms of a broad sort or regional specializations of a far more specific sort.

From the studies of sites and artifacts the prehistorian sees long-continued runs of time during which similarities prove continuity of culture, with evidences of change making themselves noticed only in gradual degree within some simple range of artifacts, or by the appearance of trade goods at some horizon. But the prehistorian also sees the drastic results of change in the sudden appearance of a totally new sequence of artifact patterns, sometimes accompanied by evidences of the expression of brutal power. He can see the rise, flowering, and decline of levels of culture in the changing craftmanship by which his artifacts were manufactured. In similarities of artifacts which transcend all major regionalisms the prehistorian sees the ancient impact of widespread diffusion. In highly localized patterns of regionalism in artifacts he sees the results of local origination which never spread by diffusion. The former similarities are greater than the latter among the general range of materials that become artifacts.

The historian also depicts long runs of time during which particular continuities of culture clearly emerge, but just as often he works with materials whose time sequences are replete with sudden, brutal, or sweeping changes. Sometimes he deals in evolutionary successions which indicate clearly the importation of dynamic factors of change which remold cultures in wholesale fashion. At other times he deals in long continuities in which the gradual enrichment of regional culture is notable but is lacking in dynamic and revolutionary remoldings.

From the above fields, and from others whose axioms are not here extrapolated, come somewhat the same general implications regarding human processes in the occupation of regions of the earth.[4] These implications suggest that, once a society has acquired an effective working body of culture, the way in which it lives in any region is decided more fully by man than by environment.[5] It is perfectly clear that earliest man had to operate extremely close to the level of animal existence, but at that level man had not yet developed an effective working body of culture. Even then man lived his life in groups whose particular patterns distinguished one from the other. Progress was slow at first, but a daring leader could guide a migration toward another environmental region. Discovery and invention were then applicable in small sequential steps. Because the early population of all mankind was small, progress was slow; it depended upon the insights and advances of a very few, and even the opportunities for borrowing were slight. Perhaps it was the best borrowers, at certain times and places, who made the most progress.

In the course of time the population grew, insights sharpened, and opportunities for borrowing increased. Groups or societies that set store by improvement of their culture through borrowing and integration made contact with other human groups to improve these changes; such groups steadily acquired new devices of culture by which to make their environment produce more for them. Their cultures changed, grew complex, advanced in level, and gained competence. Some cultures, both willingly and unwillingly, became dynamically remolded by visionary concepts which transformed them rapidly into far more complex cultures of much higher level. Such cultures often became the agents of culture spread and culture change in regions and among more traditional cultures around their borders.

Groups that clung tenaciously to their old ways and saw threats to change continued their old patterns; they became traditionalized cultures which preserved ancient procedures and techniques. Sometimes these cultures fell by the wayside, overwhelmed by expanding cultures or by expanding neighbors.

Some cultures, on the other hand, arrived at a point of ecological equilibrium with their environment so that population remained relatively stable. Visionaries were incapable of instituting significant change, interregional population movement in historic patterns remained slight, and processes of diffusion brought so little that was new and different that no changes took place which could not be integrated into the culture systems without disruption.[6] When such groups occupied territory not vigorously contested by other groups, a static situation could be maintained for long periods of time.

In the society whose population grew large, ecologic stability was hard to maintain, for visionary producers of new tools, techniques, and concepts were born in

---

[4] See Wagner, 1960, for a general statement in the field of geography.

[5] The phrase "effective working body of culture" is open to argument, but I do not feel able to pinpoint what constitutes such a minimum. In the past the problem has often been obscured by conclusions arrived at prior to examination of the data, or by hunting for a photo that would illustrate a summary statement about an issue not studied at all. Conclusions about land occupance in ignorance of the culture of the occupying group have been particularly common among geographers, so that there are few reliable guideposts at present.

[6] The paragraph states essentially what I believe has happened to many small ethnic and culture groups scattered all over Southeast Asia.

sufficient numbers so that change could not be stayed. The patterns of progress, historically at least, have lain with relatively large societies or with sizable societies whose cultures have been amenable to the efforts of dynamic and effective innovators. Only occasionally has a small group of simple culture been able to upgrade its culture so markedly that it rose to outstanding power. It is only in very recent time that volitional change has become recognized in value and has been sought after by giving commendation to those who suggested procedures leading to change. It is only in modern society that the individual has had the freedom to work for willful change, and it is only in modern society that problem sectors can be so identified that specific solutions may be sought in new procedures.[7]

Citizens of modern societies, often resident in the purely artificial environments of cities, frequently prove unable to maintain themselves when set down in jungles, bleak mountain terrain, or deserts, as witnessed by occasional notes of inexperienced travelers who perish and by the rise of survival training. From our vantage point, many a bleak regional environment seems so formidable that we wonder how early man ever survived in it at all. From this same vantage point a few other environments seem so ample, provident, and trouble-free that one can dream of peaceful existence there without any labor at all; to escape to that mythical South Sea isle and let coconuts and hibiscus blossoms fall into one's lap forever is the secret idle wish of many an urban Amercan. Survival training was what early man received in plenty in any environment into which he ventured all over the earth. There can be no question whatever that every environment on our earth has its trials, dangers, obstacles, problems, secrets, and resources for untutored man, singly or in groups, or for man tutored in the wrong body of knowledge.

The tutoring of early man was a long, slow process, as witnessed by the common characterization of the Old Stone Age—when man lived simply by depending upon nature's bounty to very large degree—as spanning about 900,000 years. But to man equipped with regularized designs for living (culture), any environment presents opportunities and resources, limited only by man's own abilities to recognize opportunities and to put resources to work. In these terms it is as much the dynamics of the group (band, tribe, society, nation) and the forward-thinkingness of the culture which determine how man will live in an environment as it is the influence of the environment upon man.

The above paragraphs suggest the necessity of stating a position on the old but recurrent problem of environmental determinism. I am not, for all people at all times, an environmental determinist, a possibilist, a probabilist, or a cultural determinist. I view earliest man, almost without culture, as being very strongly influenced by his environment. I view culture as a means of freeing man from some of the influences of his environment. Highly cultured societies have acquired and devised powerful cultural tools by which to alter environments and reduce the influences of environments upon themselves. Even highly cultured societies today do not constantly, and for every member of a society, alter or negate all environmental influences. The foreseeable potential power of "science in the service of man" suggests the possibility of creating environments to human order. Until that

---

[7] Volitional change and its commendation refer to the rise to respectability of the job specification "inventor," and to the practice of granting patents to protect inventors.

day arrives environment will have some influence on all mankind, but essentially my position envisages a sliding scale of judgment in which the growing quality, strength, and purposeful operation of culture may increasingly alleviate, alter, counter, or downgrade the influence of environment over the life of man.

THE ORIGIN AND EVOLUTION OF SHIFTING CULTIVATION

There should be relatively little question that shifting cultivation is an early system of crop growing. But how early is it, and what were its relations to the very beginnings of crop growing, that is, plant domestication? In order properly to orient the discussion of the possible origins of shifting cultivation it is necessary to set down the basic concepts that enter into my present thinking about plant domestication and the initial orgins of crop growing as predecessors to the formulation of any agricultural system. The following section, though generally applicable to the beginnings of all domestication, is set down from the base point that domestication could have begun in the tropics and that it was a process necessary to the beginning of shifting cultivation.

THE IDEA COMPLEX AROUND PLANT DOMESTICATION

My basic concepts of plant domestication include the following points, few of which can yet be proved.[8]

1. Plant domestication may have begun with vegetative reproduction rather than with seed planting of grainlike plants (but see point 16).
2. Plant domestication through vegetative reproduction began in a rather equable environment, in which the local ecology, edaphic conditions, floristic variety, and local environment variation were such that ignorant and unskilled early man could achieve minimal initial successes in making plants grow without facing too many obstacles.
3. Plant domestication was not achieved by half-starving migratory gatherers or animal hunters who eked out minimal biological survival while warding off predators at every turn.
4. Plant domestication was not the result of a hungry man sitting in a cave mouth deliberately pondering some wonderful new way of filling his stomach by suddenly enlarging the size, nutrient value, and seasonal timing of the edible parts of such wild plants as he saw from the cave mouth; he did not one evening suddenly invent agriculture.[9]
5. Plant domestication was first accomplished by human groups who already had access to, and some site-occupational control over effectively sustaining, sources of food supply in one general locality and who therefore had sufficient time, leisure, and localization of residence to observe, learn about, and "experiment" (through extended trial-and-error operations) with the multiple processes involved in working with wild plants, from initial selection to harvesting.

[8] Many of these concepts have been stated by others, most specifically by Sauer, 1948, 1952, 1961, and by von Wissmann, 1957. The listing here is a tabulation designed to help orient the reader and clarify my own position. My position, although in general agreement with that of Sauer and von Wissmann, is of many years' standing, maturing out of study and observation of landscapes of southern and eastern Asia since the early 1930's.

[9] There is far more thinking of this kind than one might presume. As an example of what primitive invention is not, Hoebel (1949, pp. 472–473) cites the following, taken from F. C. Hibben, "Corn," *Atlantic Monthly*, 175 (1945), 121, which is worth setting down in full: "What vision some ancient fellow must have had to start this process [the domestication of corn]! Can you imagine some primitive hunter of long ago as he sat in the mouth of his cave after an unsuccessful hunt? This man's empty stomach had stimulated his mind and he began to reason, which is the process that distinguished this man from the animal he hunted. A bird was eating grass seeds before him. If only those seeds were as large in relation to the man as they were to the bird! Could they be made larger? Possibly by picking out the very largest seeds and those which tasted best, and planting them next year, he might have a larger plant with larger seeds. The process was started."

6. The beginnings of plant domestication lie much further back in time than the dates customarily given for the beginnings of agriculture.[10]

7. Plant domestication may well have begun with plants not then utilized as food supply.[11]

8. What is termed "plant domestication" did not occur all at once, but over a lengthy period of the Mesolithic during which numerous peoples acquired and shared bits of experience pertaining both to different aspects of the basic process complex and to different plants in different localities and ecological niches, within the broad limits of the equable environment mentioned in point 2.

9. The beginnings per se of learning and achievement about plant domestication may not be traceable to what are now frequently termed "centers of plant domestication," but possibly to the margins of such areas.

10. Plant domestication may have had its simplest beginnings in several specific localities within the broad environment mentioned in point 2, but before plant domestication could be declared effective, there had to have been a merging of process patterns through diffusion of knowledge and experience.

11. Because of the higher proportion of domesticables found in certain floristic regions, inviting greater experimentation, the largest numbers of semidomesticates and domesticates occurred in regional concentrations, both for initial domestication and for secondary domestication, once the process had become effective. That is, a regional center of plant domestication is an indication both of primeval floristic richness and of a volume of experimental activity.

12. As knowledge, experience, and plant-growing operations spread widely from the initial centers into environmental localities less equable and less suitable, ecologically and edaphically, there was further trial-and-error manipulation of processes involved in growing some of the first cultivates in nonideal environments.

13. Diffusion of plant growing beyond the equable environment evoked further experimentation with other plants that were ecologically at home in the particular environmental locality, producing secondary domestications and variations in the basic processes.

14. Plant growers often transported cultivates relatively long distances from the environmental locality where they were originally domesticated. The resulting change in both procedures and uses tended to produce varietal changes in plants prior to conscious varietal manipulation or hybridization.

---

[10] Beals and Hoijer (1959, p. 263) place the Mesolithic epoch as being from 6,000 to 10,000 years in length for Europe and the Near East, date that of northern Europe as starting about 8,300 B.C., and, without giving dates, suggest that the timing for southern Europe is earlier. Braidwood (1960, p. 133) puts the Near Eastern threshold of food production at between 11,000 and 9,000 years ago, and adds (p. 134): "Around 8,000 B.C. the inhabitants of the hills around the fertile crescent had come to know their habitat so well that they were beginning to domesticate the plants and animals they had been collecting and hunting." I have no quarrel with this date, but feel that the "threshold" of plant domestication must be placed well before 8,000 B.C., in order to have the "threshold" of crop production come at about that date. Barring good evidence to the contrary about the tropical aspects of lowland climate during the end of the mid-latitude and polar glacial climate transition to that of the present, a date of about 12,000–11,000 B.C. for the starting sequence of the Mesolithic epoch in tropical regions seems preferable. Human knowledge about plant utilities must be carried ever further back in the sense that man had to learn much about the plant world before he could start much in the way of plant manipulation. I believe that a long, slow background prepared the way for the final Neolithic "revolution" to which many of the advanced cropping systems of agriculture properly belong.

Braidwood continues to sweep aside as speculative and unproved the suggestion that vegetative reproduction may have had a role in plant domestication and the early initiating of cropping activities. But Braidwood and Howe (1960) make constrained statements that leave ground for speculation along other lines. An example is this passage (p. 181): "Our way out of this difficulty is to postulate an era of incipient cultivation as an ideal type. We do this in the face of the impossibility of conceiving of its subsistence activities as other than still largely food-collecting (even as an ideal type) and in the face of our extreme difficulties in abducing and demonstrating artifactual evidence for incipient cultivation." A similar statement (p. 182) admits of no evidence for incipient cultivation. As I point out in a later chapter, the evidence suggests that the southeastward spread of grain-seeded cropping replaced rather than initiated cropping by vegetative reproduction. This replacement does not prove that vegetative cropping is older than seed planting, but at least it suggests that there must have been an alternative origin to cropping other than grain planting.

[11] Reference here is to the use of plants having exotic properties (colors, poisons, cathartic, sedative, healing), magic connotations, string-making qualities, and so on.

15. Some plant domestication was accomplished at a fairly late date (well into the Neolithic), in a few instances at long distances from the original centers of process development and plant accumulation (in the category of domesticates) by experienced crop growers.

16. Domestication of the first seed-producing, grainlike plants may have come secondarily in broad environmental regions varying ecologically a good deal from the initial areas of vegetative reproduction. This domestication may have developed slowly from the general inapplicability of continuing to work with the old vegetatively produced plant stocks.[12] It is also possible that plant domestication occurred more than once, in independent terms.

17. If domestication of grain-seed plants is to be construed as independent of the development of vegetatively reproduced plants, then domestication of grainlike plants, in conjunction with an animal economy, slowly evolved an essentially new set of procedures and processes terminating in agricultural systems quite different from the simple cropping systems developed in the initial areas of vegetative reproduction.[13]

18. If domestication occurred in more than one kind of ecological environment and involved different sets of plants, the diffusion into the areas of vegetative reproduction of ideas about and processes of seed planting of grainlike plants resulted in additional domestications and in the same transfer in the other direction.

19. Therefore seed planting of annuals of all sorts (not restricted here to grainlike plants, but including them) in the areas of vegetative reproduction is a secondary and accessory form of crop growing. At first it was subordinate to vegetative crop-growing patterns (possibly even introduced from different environments), but eventually it had a secondary effect upon the agricultural system, even to the point at which seed-grain planting replaced vegetative-reproduction planting.[14]

20. Seed planting of bush, shrub, and tree-crop plantings is a relatively late development in the areas of initial vegetative reproduction, and has some secondary effect upon the agricultural system.

21. The growing of semidomesticates and of wild plants in fields, patches, clearings, or dooryard gardens by so-called primitive cultivators is an accessory element in plant domestication, probably at many levels of proficiency in agriculture, and is a factor in evaluating agricultural systems, for it is still practiced.[15]

22. Many accessory activities had an accelerating impact upon the domestication of semidomesticates and wild plants and upon varietal improvement of domesticates, once the initial agricultural system was in operation. I am thinking of such things as weeding, hilling the earth, providing poles for climbers, mulching, fertilizing, draining excess water, providing needed water, spacing plantings, storing planting stock, and other activities not originally included in the processes of plant domestication. The more obvious aspects, such as simple varietal selection, stimulation of natural hybridization, and conscious hybridization, may or may not have been significant in the early stages of domestication, though there is no question of their becoming operative once crop-growing systems were functioning.

23. Hybridization, evolution of weeds into crops, varietal proliferation, and varietal selection for particular environmental localities marginal to original areas where domestication was initiated are fairly late phenomena.

---

[12] Here I am suggesting that seed-plant domestication in the drier margins of the subtropics could have been an outgrowth of existing knowledge, but I am not insisting that it must be.

[13] Reference here is to field systems, tool systems, power-application systems, planting systems, crop-combination systems, and other aspects of true agriculture, as opposed to the older systems of jungle gardening, which worked with other kinds of plants.

[14] Applicable to points 18, 19, and 20 is considerable evidence that grain planting is later than tuber planting in southern and eastern Asia in the more nonseasonal regions. There is little question that rice has been replacing yams and taro. I cannot yet prove that the millets were an agent earlier in this same replacement pattern, preceding rice, but there is some tentative evidence that millet did precede rice among some peoples. The millets, like rice, are at home on the savanna margins of the tropics, and, ecologically, perhaps were at home in a different niche or local environment from the majority of vegetatively reproducing plants when both groups were merely wild flora.

[15] There are many references to the planting of semidomesticates and wild plants by shifting cultivators today. Often the observers could not identify such plants and failed to collect samples for purposes of taxonomic checking; on the general subject, Conklin (1957, pp. 44, 86–87, 94, 138) has shown careful observation.

24. Many processes of change in all kinds of plants that eventually became domesticated ante-dated domestication itself. In general, botanists believe that the notable evolutionary change in many economic and decorative plants is about as old as man himself. Such change is related to man's use of fire in hunting and other activities in the Old Stone Age. The heliophilous tendency of many economic plants increased during that age, thus rendering them more useful to man, producing new varieties of plants, increasing the annual habit, and the like.

THE BEGINNINGS OF TROPICAL CROP-GROWING SYSTEMS

The enunciation of any system of procedures that began with the planting of semi-domesticated plants and ended with conscious harvesting of a purposeful yield can be only theoretical, but assuredly the beginnings must have been uncertainly made with no firm set of procedures in mind. They can only have been spasmodic, lacking in order and neatness, desultory in follow-up, producing a bare variant of the ecological situation that obtained when nature initiated the growth cycle of the plants involved.

Particularly is this true of tropical growth patterns which are best described by the word "jungle." It is notable that planting patterns in the tropics, when not motivated by modern mid-latitude concepts, still achieve something often best described physically as a jungle. Ecologically such patterns are nearest to the natural balance of things, and are actually to be preferred in regard to plant health and productivity. This may, in fact, have been one of the earliest lessons learned in tropical vegetative-planting patterns. The above speculation is not restricted to the Asian tropics, but is generally applicable throughout the world's tropics.

If a group with a relatively localized residence situation (not the modern fixed and formal village settlement pattern), and with a relatively good source of sustaining food supply, were to begin to work with plants that could be labeled initial domesticates, their first clearings for plants could not have been either large or clean.[16] They may have been mere patches of ground around a campsite, hacked out and cleaned by campfires and by the burning of the occupants' shelters. Such people must already have possessed cutting and pounding tools for other purposes, but we cannot assume that they had specialized planting tools as well, though not many would have been needed.[17] Certainly wild plant growth would have reasserted itself relatively quickly to fill in such plant clearings before more than one cropping season would have gone by. Would waning soil fertility have then been very evident?[18] Would a later trial in another already cleared patch be more natural at this level of operation than deliberately clearing a new space for planting?

[16]The question of sustaining food supply is pertinent in itself, but lies outside my specific subject. I agree with and follow Sauer (1952, pp. 12, 22–24; 1956, p. 56) in his suggestion that lowland freshwater sites yielding all forms of aquatic resources and easy access to nearby land resources provided an ideal situation.

[17] The digging stick, thought of as a planting tool, had a long prior history as a crowbar for levering logs to get at grubs, as a digging and prying tool for uprooting tubers and edible roots, and as a knocking stick for bringing down fruit and nuts, as well as being a staff, a beating stick, or a spear for protective use. It may have been the first agricultural implement used as a tool for digging a hole in the ground in which to plant a bit of vegetative material, but its use in such advanced forms as an implement for making holes for planting rice came late.

[18] Although experienced shifting cultivators appreciate the need to rest soils in the tropics (see Hogbin, 1938, p. 143, for an example), the first growers of crops would not have known about soil depletion, but would have been more oppressed by the exuberant regeneration of wild plant growth. Whereas the Wogeo Islanders (*ibid.*) felt strongly about weeds, primordial crop growers would have been faced with few true weeds as we know them today in our gardens and fields.

What might have been planted in such patches? Plants for magic, for dyes, for ritual use, for exotic properties connected with the group's cultural mores? Who did the actual planting, and who kept a planted patch from being trampled or consumed by predators? Was the patch a "field" or a composite "dooryard garden"? Did the women or the men perform the tasks? Planting as a process of working with vegetatively reproduced plants would have been extremely simple. No large hole had to be dug; no real cultivation was required; the bare hands, an axe, a stick, or a cutting or scraping tool would have been sufficient to get the appropriate part of a plant into or next to the moist earth, with or without a little cover over it.

One must be wary of advancing the whole sequence too rapidly, as in one description of the invention of maize farming.[19] The suggestion of humble trial-and-error origins implies further that a small-patch jungle garden near the living shelter may well have been the first agricultural system, utilizing fire, an occasional change in planting site, vegetatively reproduced plants, and the simplest tools to produce very small yields which were complements to culture materials or the dietary rather than sustaining portions of the dietary. Is it not possible that in time something crudely resembling shifting cultivation on a very small scale came into being for a population beginning to work with domesticated plants, but kept locally resident because of their main source of food supply? For a group having no control over a sustaining food supply, another admittedly theoretical construct suggests that observation of a going planting pattern could lead to similar planting around campsites, which, because they were not permanent enough, had to be left untended for periods of time.[20]

Still another variant may be suggested. With a population expanding around an area of sustaining food supply, the splintering-off of families, working groups, lineage groups, or living groups might well have removed some units to a position marginal to the sustaining food supply, and these units may have begun to assume

---

[19] See n. 9, above. When early man began the domestication of plants, he still derived most of his food, clothing, housing, and tool economy by appropriation from the plant, animal, and mineral environment around him. The matters that have followed in the wake of plant domestication have been the results of cultural processes developed by man to make the environment produce for him more plentifully than did primeval nature, particularly in places where nature did not seem to provide bountifully.

As man's research improved and accumulated, the agricultural system became more complex, but at first man took his simple system with him wherever he happened to go and applied it to whatever environment he happened to be in. Only slowly did agricultural systems mature which worked better in one broad region of the earth than another. Any one system, however, is merely a set of procedures applied by man, and it can be applied to production in any part of the earth where plants will grow to maturity, for it depends upon man's own efforts, and not upon the permission of the environment.

[20] Sauer (1952, p. 22) remarks that crop growing requires constant attention and that he has "never seen primitive plantings that are not closely watched over until the crop is secured. A planted clearing anywhere is a feast set for all manner of wild creatures" (see also Sauer, 1956, p. 56). This is perfectly true of peoples who have come to depend on their planting for their sustaining dietary, but it cannot have been true of the most elementary beginnings. There are records of plantings by proto–crop growers who neither watched over their plantings nor practiced any of the numerous other protective measures. Many of the Negrito groups, originally practicing what was essentially a gathering economy, when first starting to grow crops, did very little crop protecting; the previously noted Raji people of the Himalayas did nothing to protect their crops. Crop watching, like fencing, construction of scarecrows, setting of traps around fields, and crop-season residence in the fields, is a culture trait developed as an integral part of an evolving system of crop growing. The better the system became the more such traits came to be part of it. Such traits become integral morphologic elements in a version, or typology, of shifting cultivation.

importance for the total dietary. With going patterns, the evolution of a kind of shifting cultivation may be envisaged.

DIFFERENTIATION OF SHIFTING CULTIVATION

Whether the simplest version of shifting cultivation is typologically close to the first cropping system that emerged from plant domestication none can say for certain. That the first system was in the ancestral line of present systems appears likely. From the history of cultural advancement in other fields it also seems likely that the very first typology of crop growing did not interminably remain unaltered.

How much differentiation is required in the detail of a primitive system of crop growing to justify the differentiation of typologies? In contemporary American agriculture, "tobacco and general farming" is commonly differentiated from "general farming" by the presence of the tobacco-cropping complex, and the "hard, red spring wheat" belt is differentiated from the "hard, red winter wheat" belt. In primitive cultivation, slight changes in the cropping complex would apparently be sufficient to indicate typologies, if these could be reliably determined.

As we cannot be certain just when and where the first cropping typology was practiced, we can be no more certain about the second, third, fourth, and later typologies, as to time and place. It cannot be presumed that fully definitive ethnic, social, economic, living-place, occupational, or political structuring had evolved by the time crop growing first began. Nor can it be presumed that every crop now domesticated was then available to some group or other. The effects of environmental factoring on primordial man cannot be presumed to be fully causal, once man had acquired procedures for changing his local environment and providing a food supply of his own ordering.

The increase in the volume, range, and competence of culture began to alter conditions. Through diffusion, the abilities to change the environment and provide a food supply were spread around among those who chose to use them. But with changes in food-producing ability there came the structurings of culture which formulate and codify its traits, trait complexes, and institutional elements. Anthropologists have used various concepts in discussing the patternings of culture which create group norms, styles, or configurations by which a given group develops and adheres to one pattern, whereas another group develops and adheres to another pattern.[21] Once this process is well started, elders pass on to younger members the "proper" ways of doing things until these become codified into traditional patterns.

The geographer cannot erect hierarchies of cropping typologies in a vacuum, looking only at concordance with environment. The patternings of crop growing are integrated into other patterning sectors of a culture, such as form and permanence of settlement, system of land control, and social structure, and are vitally dependent upon them. It is for this reason that the large number of diagnostic elements has been suggested as an index of morphology. The pattern of a cropping

---

[21] "Configuration" denotes a concept stated by Benedict and "theme" is a principle mentioned by Opler; for a convenient comparison, see Beals and Hoijer (1959, pp. 230–238), who used the concept of pattern. Kroeber (1948, pp. 311–343), in a chapter on patterns, employed the term "style"; he (p. 313) spelled out the connotations of the "pattern of plow agriculture." Honigman (1959) dealt with a whole group of concepts of this sort.

system (in orthodox geographical language, the method of combining fields, crops, and cultivation practices) must be viewed from the perspective of the whole culture, and its hierarchical position must take into account many more elements than the basic technology employed in raising the crops.

THE ROLE OF THE CULTURE GROUP

We cannot proceed far in the discussion of shifting cultivation before running into the distinctions that appear among population groups as culture groups. The differences that show up in the cropping systems of the many Naga groups of the Assam-Burma border, for example, have less to do with the ecology of the environmental region than with the fact that these groups distinguish among themselves as peoples and as culture groups.[22] Such distinctions are based on many definitive and long-standing criteria. Cropping systems among the Naga and other tribes in the same area range all the way from a very simple, crude shifting cultivation (meaning heavier dependence upon appropriative techniques than upon crop growing) to almost complete dependence upon wet rice cultivation on excellently terraced, privately owned landscapes, and from major dependence upon taro to almost complete dependence upon rice. Some groups who use shifting cultivation alone crop a site one year only, whereas others have complex clear-and-recrop cycles. Some groups sow rice by broadcasting it, whereas others do it by dibbling.

Similar variations are to be found in New Guinea, with perhaps greater complexity of permutations though with a narrower range of cropping systems. Laos and the southwestern borders of China are other areas of great ethnic complexity, where extreme variation in cropping systems may be found. Elsewhere the range today is narrower, though a few centuries ago many of the hilly parts of peninsular India had extreme ranges of cropping systems correlating closely with ethnic variation.

THE ROLE OF SETTLEMENT PATTERNS

The normal tendency of human beings to form groups of some kind extends to the locating of campsites and homesites. The size of the group varies tremendously, however, and the number of houses and the manner of grouping them vary to the same degree. There appears no real scaling of size in group living or group residence by the level of culture attained so long as the discussion is confined to peoples who have not evolved the sophisticated political structuring that goes with the concept of the state.[23] Among noncultivators the relative amounts of foodstuffs available for appropriation probably restricted groupings of early man to rather small numbers in some environments, for which the anthropologist long has used the term "band." In more productive environments and resource ranges the band still might have remained small, but several bands would have operated in contiguity. Campsites or more permanent homesites at such levels tended to remain small, and were composed of a few shelters only. In situations providing plentiful

[22] There is an extensive literature on the Naga peoples; many studies survey a single ethnic group, and numerous bibliographic items listed pertain to the Naga. In discussions of different cropping systems employed among different groups, two studies (Smith, 1925, pp. 147–149; Hutton, 1922, pp. xxvii–xxix) point out many distinctions.

[23] I believe that towns and cities belong to societies whose political organization has matured sufficiently so that something approaching the territorial state has been institutionalized, thereby permitting institutionalizing of economic funcions, which in turn support settlement patterns of large size carrying on multiple forms of organized activity.

appropriative resources and more advanced levels of culture, clusters of housing units sometimes were rather large.

What happened to patterns of campsites and homesite grouping with the introduction of cropping? It is the normal inference in most writing that groupings increased in size among most peoples with the advent of food production, but there seems very little evidence to bear this theory out with regard to simpler cropping systems. It is my suggestion that tendencies to social structuring inherent in an ethnic unit continued to determine the size of residential groupings long after crop growing had become a sustaining pattern. The cropping system that evolved among a particular ethnic unit did not of itself produce inherently new forms and sizes of settlement. I suggest, further, that the patterns of group mobility were not altered intrinsically; that is, the introduction of crop growing did not alter the frequency of homesite moving.

It is impossible to state that a given social structure produced a particular settlement pattern, for there is too much variation among the peoples of southeastern Asia. It does seem true that very loose social structuring permits dispersed settlement or loosely articulated hamlet groupings, and that highly developed and closely integrated social structuring makes for compact village settlement. But a closely integrated social structure also makes for closely integrated cropping practices, which in turn favor village settlement. Such interrelationships are common features.

The literature refers to the permanence of villages as coming with the Neolithic, but the meaning of the word "permanence," is open to question, as are the implications of the lack of sedentariness in earlier times or for nonagricultural peoples.[24] The term "abandoned village" is to be found in all literatures, and specific inquiry attests that many a village reputed to be millenia old has had several different sites within the neighborhood. This is a matter of principle rather than of fact during a given century, however, and the literature of today properly speaks of permanent village settlement patterns among many shifting cultivators.[25]

THE SITING OF VILLAGES

The siting of villages, hamlets, housing clusters, or homes is in part affected by the cropping system, but intrinsically the siting of a residence comes first by other specific criteria whenever relative permanence is involved. If protection is not the primary criterion, then siting either by sources of domestic water or by stream transport seems primary; also considered are exposure to climatic elements, material convenience, sense of privacy, and other similar criteria. If protection is the primary criterion, then siting on ridge tops or spurs, against cliff lines, on islands in lakes away from the shore, or in similarly protected and defensive places be-

[24] Mumford (1956, p. 382), for example, says that "permanent villages date only from Neolithic times." Although many of the great kitchen middens were work sites where shellfish were shucked, surely people must have lived sedentarily on, beside, or near them to have accumulated such volumes. The salmon-fishing Indians of the Pacific Northwest were fairly sedentary village dwellers. What was to prevent fishing folk with a permanent resource from having been rather sedentary, even in late Paleolithic time?

[25] "Permanence," as used here, indicates continued occupance of the same general location for a matter of decades, as opposed to occupance of radically new locations selected annually or for two or three years at a time. The impermanence of early housing often necessitated the building of new structures on different sites in the same general location.

comes the rule, with other criteria taking secondary position. Cropping-system considerations are important for the gross locational elements of residence among groups that live in permanent villages, but among peoples to whom village life is unimportant, cropping-system considerations become the critical factor and housing tends to go where the crop site is located.

THE MORPHOLOGY OF VILLAGES

The formal morphology of the settlement pattern varies widely, but the causal relationship of this variation to cropping patterns in a narrow sense seems doubtful. Cropping did raise the storage problem after annual sustaining yields became normal; the harvest had to be concentrated in a specific period, with storage for the rest of a time period. This specific problem, however, was associated with certain crops only, and many shifting cultivators do not have storage problems. The location of storage shelters varies from a room within the housing shelter to separate structures outside the immediate zone of residence, and reflects many considerations. When protection was important, compact settlements surrounded by protective devices were common, but the lessened need for rural protection in the modern era has caused many shifts in settlement patterns devised originally for protection. When village settlement is involved, villages range from very formal to completely helter-skelter ones.

In the 1930's the Kiriwina people in the Trobriand Islands still were using a very formal pattern, with a dancing square in the center. Here also was the chief's house and his food-storage house. In a ring around the square were yam storehouses for village families, and beyond them in a second ring were family residences. The inner location of the yam storehouses has no protective function, at least in modern times, but it does facilitate public display of the size of individual yams and of the yield achieved by each family. Before final storage the yams are stacked in the square in front of each house in public display, and it would seem that pride in husbandry and the wish to display family achievements were more important than protection.[26]

In contrast are the straggling, formless collections of buildings in the villages of some of the Gond peoples of peninsular India. Scattered clusters of from one to five houses each, each cluster at some little distance from another, constituted a village. Such village locations were moved at intervals of years to more appropriate sites, with the same straggling form again resulting.[27]

The long-house type of village is another morphologic expression of social pattern, rather than of other specific factors. There are varied types of long houses, but the essential feature is that there is one continuous building for the whole living group.[28]

Settlement patterns are affected, morphologically and otherwise, by the social

---

[26] Malinowski, 1935, pp. 24–26, 179–180.

[27] C. and E. von Fürer-Haimendorf, 1948, pp. 67–81. I may be misinterpreting in part, for the statements on which my comment is based are somewhat general. Apparently some Gond groups formerly used a regular village form, and perhaps this straggling tendency is a result of governmental restriction and is expressive of deculturation.

[28] The best single reference on the subject is Loeb and Broek, 1947. The origin of the long house is in modes of postnuptial residence related to patterns of clan descent, rather than in environmental, protective, or cropping-system factors.

structural elements of grouping systems. Such influences upon grouping, siting, and morphology includes separate houses in which men and women sleep, regardless of family system; special houses for age-groups; the issue of whether the chief's house is bigger and specially sited; the presence or absence of a dancing ground or village common; and many other similar customs.

When village settlement is not involved, housing is sited by a variety of preference patterns which may have more or less specific utility. Considerations are location in the middle of a clearing. above it, below it, or slightly away from it, midway between two clearings, or at a water source near a trail. Nonvillage settlement location can hardly be discussed in terms of morphologic characteristics.

In areas where European influence is in some way expressed, changing settlement morphology is characteristic of many shifting-cultivator peoples. Most obvious is the lessened need for protection, but also significant is the European tendency to concentrate peoples into more formal settlement sites for many different reasons. Another element is changing religion, and many now-Christian peoples have altered their forms of settlement.[29]

GREGARIOUSNESS AND SIZE OF RESIDENTIAL UNITS

Although the tendency to travel, work, eat, sleep, fight, and play in groups is most frequently found, nuclear families and individuals have long shown tendencies toward separateness. Residence patterns among shifting cultivators therefore display every range of size up to the large, compact village. Some nuclear families are scattered singly at remote points from one another,[30] but it is more common to find groups living in a kind of extended contiguity, each family in its own house set apart, but the group as a whole constituting a formal unit in terms of social, work, lineage, clan, or "people" patterns.[31] Sometimes clusters of homes or hamlets within a local regional pattern form such units, each hamlet containing neighbors, yet possessing a degree of privacy.[32] Small-village patterns are common to some peoples, with an undelimited but recognized concept of what constitutes a maximum size. When such limits are reached, new village cores splinter, or hive, off to start new settlements. Among the patterns described above, the need for protection or

---

[29] See, for example, Williams (1928, pp. 155–156; 1944, p. 94) on the effect of government pacification of tribal groups, and Lawrence (1955, pp. 2–3) and Hobgin (1937, pp. 69–70) on European administrative attempts to concentrate people in larger, central villages. Durrad (1939, p. 392) pointed out that a village of earlier type had two rows of houses facing a dancing-festival floor, but that upon becoming Christians the villagers had given up their former festival-dance patterns and changed the shape of the village. Numerous other reports attest to the impact of Christianity upon settlement morphology.

[30] Describing the Subanu of Mindanao, Finley (1913, p. 25) wrote: "The Subanu dearly cherish the independence and freedom of the family unit and look with suspicion and even fear upon the many restrictions that must of necessity be imposed upon people when they are closely associated in communities. As soon as the young men take to themselves wives they break away from the old family home and establish new family units at remote points, where they can enjoy all the freedom of their peculiar nomadic life."

Most Subanu then practiced annual cropping, sometimes with very short moves between sites, and houses might be occupied for two or three years or moved annually, according to the site location. Finley (p. 6) mentioned long-continued raiding and slaving by Moros against the Subanu and the Subanu habit, in areas exposed to raiding, of hiding single homes in protected spots. One wonders if isolated residence may not have been a partial response to persecution. In more recent time the pressure of immigrating Christian Filipinos taking up land have begun to force some of the group to supplement their shifting cultivation by taking up permanent field cropping (Frake, 1960, p. 51).

[31] Goodenough, 1953, p. 33; Gusinde, 1958, p. 562; Bell, 1946, p. 140.

[32] C. and E. von Fürer-Haimerdorf, 1948, p. 67; Blackwood, 1931, pp. 210–211.

defense appears minimal. Some peoples prefer to live in large villages, sometimes having several hundred houses and often very compact; there is a question as to whether these have always been based on preference, or whether a history of warfare and defense is involved.[33] Subjectively judged, the height of group living is to be found in the communal long-house villages. On the other hand, some peoples appear to have no single standard, and several patterns are found contemporaneously within the same region.[34]

Every variant of size, form, shape, location, motivation, and influencing factor appears to exist, and the patterns of settlement seem to depend largely on cultural preference by social procedures which fit adequately into other patterns of the whole culture of the group. From a survey of the literature it would appear that village residence is the more common in the contemporary period, but perhaps European pressures on native habits account for a considerable share of this. From the literature it is difficult to ascertain whether some groups follow only one pattern, or whether multiple patterns are not in fact the more common.

Among frontier settlers who carry on incipient shifting cultivation, residence usually tends to be on the individual lands occupied rather than in villages, but for such peoples there is no generally applicable rule. In the Philippines many caingins are claimed and operated by people holding jobs or carrying on other occupations. Residence is thus not determined primarily by the occupation of crop growing, and residence at the field plot itself may be more in the nature of weekend camping.

SEASONAL RESIDENCE FOR CROP PROTECTION

Among shifting cultivators who prefer to live in compact villages, one kind of seasonal rhythm in living patterns does owe its characteristics to the necessities of crop protection. Village-dwelling shifting cultivators often locate their current clearings for the main crop at some distance from the village. The total number of clearings is often three or four per family. Though some peoples who are village-resident clear one large tract for all gardens, it appears more common that either nuclear familes or several families forming one working group clear individual plots. Soon after the planting season the village population must move to their field locations for the growing season, and thus becomes widely scattered. Temporary housing is erected, scarecrow devices are installed, fences are maintained (having been built prior to planting in most instances), and fence and path trapping devices are set and kept functional. Weeding, late planting, tool repairing, some

---

[33] Mills, 1922, pp. 21–24; Smith, 1925, pp. 1–6, 27; Hutton, 1921*b*, pp. 43–49. The Angami Naga of Assam, described by Hutton, had some villages with up to 400 houses, practiced both wet rice cultivation and shifting cultivation, and had occupied their villages for long periods. The Zemi Naga, resident in very rough country with small areas of cultivable land in widely separated localities, preferring to live in sizable villages owing to the continual state of war in Nagaland and the need for protected group residence, practiced shifting cultivation by cycle migration. A whole village population moved to a village site occupied years before, wherein each family had a recognized house plot. New houses were built, and annual clearing plus two-year cropping of available lands went on until all land had been worked over. The village group then moved to another old village site and repeated the process, working each set of lands from each site in a regular cycle. The Zemi had lived well for more than 200 years until the British upset the whole system by awarding Zemi land to Kuki tribes (Bower, 1950*a*, *b*).

[34] The Massim of southeastern Papua illustrate this trend; their residence patterns range from single homes in gardens through other distributions up to villages of 50 houses (Belshaw, 1955, p. 1).

hunting, and food-gathering activities round out occupational patterns, and village dwellers thus enjoy a season of rural privacy.[35]

Crop watching is a continuous operation that must be carried on from well before the first harvest dates for the earliest plantings until very late in the harvest season. Its critical period is dependent upon the crops planted and upon the number of bird and animal predators, but its peak falls at the main harvest season. The necessity for crop watching among rice planters is much more serious than among among taro planters, and there are other variations, but almost everyone practicing shifting cultivation must protect against varying kinds and numbers of predators. Human thievery from within village, ethnic, or kinship groups appears to be minimal, but thievery in terms of raiding parties from another culture group is serious in some areas; it is part of one form of tribal warfare which has been particularly notable in the Assam-Burma border country and in interior New Guinea. European administrative police control in the past has lessened intertribal difficulties in accessible areas, but the troubles continue in regions where traditional intertribal mores obtain.

Peoples carrying on partial systems of shifting cultivation are less affected by the issue of seasonal residence, and no fully definitive statement can be made about them. Ceylon chena cultivators, for example, who practice a partial system of shifting cultivation, must still engage in crop watching. Normally whole families do not move to the field locations, but a single member will spend time there.

The issue of seasonal residence introduces a fluctuating element into the residence pattern. The social systems of people preferentially using village residence long ago made the adjustments required to carry on their lives in this manner, crop watching is not among the primary issues that affect residence patterns. When administrative pressures were invoked to induce village residence among shifting cultivators using scatter-clearing of crop lands, a tug-of-war between administrative officers and the citizenry has followed, but this purely secondary issue has not affected the original basic cultural choice.

THE ROLE OF RELIGION, RITUAL, AND MAGIC

Religious beliefs, behavior patterns, and reaction systems are universal elements of human culture. Among the simpler cultures these elements bring both the plant and animal worlds into active relationships with man. The supernaturalism of some religious systems, particularly the simple ones that are close to animism, blends magic and religion together in setting up both positive necessities in specific action and taboos upon certain patterns of action. Particularly at the simpler level, the nonperformance of the positive commands of religious belief, and the violation of

---

[35] This commentary, too brief and too generalized, on the variety of patterns that may be followed by a particular people is not intended as a fully descriptive statement. It merely calls attention to the impact of crop watching on the annual residence of village dwellers. Freeman (1955, pp. 33–39) has described for the Iban of western Borneo a system by which the population of a permanent long-house village seasonally occupies several multiple-family field houses for several years in succession while their cropping activities are concentrated in a given locality. Conklin (1957, pp. 100–102) has described a different pattern for the Hanunóo of Mindoro: the village is never completely deserted but individual family field shelters are variably occupied during the required season. Crop watching with field shelters is employed not only by shifting cultivators, but also by many sedentary populations practicing permanent-field agriculture. The crop-watching shelter is one of the common structures on cultivated landscapes throughout the Orient, where village settlement patterns are the norm.

taboos as well, brings disaster. Among crop cultivators using the simpler systems these commands and injunctions upon the activity of man, both positive and negative, have emphatic effects upon the practice of crop growing in almost all its aspects.[36]

The significance of religious behavior patterns to crop-growing systems is that, particularly at the simpler levels, many of the actions taken are directly accounted for by the religious beliefs of the particular culture group. The frequency of field shifting, the planting of particular crops, the timing of essential steps in the annual cycle, the planting and harvest routines, the shifting of homesites and village sites, and many other elements that are implicit parts of the system are controlled by religious beliefs. Though each of these may be shrewdly interpreted by a shaman, chief, or group elder from some sound environmental motivation, they often find everyday expression in practices that may, in particular instances, be quite illogical.

The tendency for religious behavior patterns to freeze into patterns of inviolate practice obscures whatever rationale the behavior trait may originally have had. To give up a cleared and burned planting site because a particular species of bird was seen near the site the day before planting was scheduled to begin may make no sense to an agnostic Occidental observer no longer close to nature; in the specific instance it may well have lacked sound reason. At some point in earlier history, however, cropping disasters may well have resulted from an irregular environmental anomaly, for which the undue appearance of the bird species was the only tangible observation that could be noted and interpreted by the ancestral group. The interpretation of clues of the seasonal weather cycle, the maturing of cyclic generations of plant pests, and the productivity of crops planted are hazardous in all parts of the world, including the highly scientific world of American crop planters. The simpler cultures used far more clues from nature itself, and developed far more positive commands and negative injunctions based on omens, signs, and portents in their agricultural activities, than are common among the practicers of advanced systems of agriculture. The latter have sucessfully learned more objective ways of reaching decisions, and have a more powerful technology at their command by which to do what they choose to do in increasing proportions.

THE ROLE OF THE ECONOMIC FACTOR

There can be no argument that the early cultivators of crops undoubtedly grew the crops to supply plant materials for their own use. Perhaps the same might also be asserted about crop growers who had devised a slightly improved system, but

---

[36] For an excellent discussion of these matters among two shifting cultivator peoples, see Conklin, 1957, and Freeman, 1955. For an excellent rendering of the role of ritual, religion, and magic throughout the annual crop cycle recited by a Sarawak Dyak see Howes, 1960, pp. 448–493. Too long to reproduce here, it clearly indicates how many items of ritual or magic have sound rationale behind them. The ritual of the trial fire (*ibid.*, p. 489) illustrates the point. Some weeks after clearing has been finished, the village priest on a morning selected by him goes through the ritual of preparing a sacrificial meal at the clearing and scattering portions of it as an offering to the spirits. He then tries burning a selected piece of material in the sacrificial fire. It it burns properly it is a sign that the clearing is ready to burn; the village assembles and the clearing is burned that afternoon. A compulsory rest of one day follows. Final clearing comes next and the Dyaks comment was: "Unburnt wood is piled together and burned. If the burn has been a poor one this work may be very heavy, and run into two weeks. A good burn should leave not more than two or three days' work to do. Hence the interest in the 'trial by fire.'"

how far up the scale can this be taken as implicit and total? The judgment that all shifting cultivation is entirely a subsistence economy is untrue, but how untrue is it? When did minor barter of surpluses or specific exotics become sufficiently major so that certain crops were planted only for barter or sale? At what point can any early system of crop growing be declared no longer a subsistence system? Only when metal coinage is exchanged between grower and buyer of a given product? Only when 100 per cent of a given crop is sold away from the producing group? Only when 100 per cent of all crops grown are removed from the producing locality and sold to noncrop-growing consumers?

Likewise there can be no denying that the very first cultivators of crops did not produce a large economic return from their cropping activities. This statement is also true of the second typology of primitive cultivation to develop. But, again, how far up the scale of development can the term "unproductive" be applied? And unproductive as compared with what? Evidence has been presented earlier to show that per acre, per man-year, and per unit volume-in-cost returns from good shifting-cultivation practices compare very favorably with the unit returns for crop production elsewhere in the Orient (chap. ii, section on Levels of Economic Operation).

It has frequently been said that the problem of the shifting cultivator lies in the difficulty of conserving wealth and making it cumulative, in the necessity of starting over in each new clearing cycle, and in the inability of the shifting cultivator to produce more than perishable goods which are seasonally consumed. Here there are obvious truths, though the last point is often found not to be true of some of the more advanced shifting cultivators. At this point the cropping system itself no longer is under discussion; the discussion centers on the whole economic system.

The economic systems that go with shifting cultivation frequently have built into them various social-system, obligational-exchange elements that serve the economic function of trade. These elements both achieve forms of exchange and prevent the accumulation of surpluses by distributing produced commodities among varying sectors of culture-group populations. The function of exchange here is basic and primary, disposing of commodities before they spoil. The economic systems place no value on the kinds of surplus considered meritorious in occidental economic theory.

Modern economic analysis cannot deal with the kind of economic system in which social custom prescribed a great postharvest feast, after which a tribal chief proudly remarked that all the able-bodied men had gone hunting because there is "nothing left to eat. They have gone into the forest to hunt and fish. . . . It was a fine feast, wasn't it? Word of truth, there isn't even a single yam left!"[37] The social pride and the elevated status of a culture group or a whole village that used its accumulated harvest of crops and carefully matured stock of pigs to feed a neighboring village for days on end cannot be translated into the economic symbols conventionally employed in the occidental socioeconomic system. The economic function of the social obligation on the part of the group thus fed to return the favor after a later harvest period is equally bewildering. American culture does retain

---

[37] Dupeyrat, 1955, p. 156, pertaining to the Fuyughe tribe of Papuans north of Port Moresby, Papua. The resulting shortage is not properly a "hunger period" of the seasonal type.

many elements of obligational economics, but they have been sublimated into personal and family matters.

It is particularly true of societies practicing an integral form of shifting cultivation that crop production and jungle appropriation are the only important production systems that can create wealth. Any other potential production systems are kept entirely latent through culture custom, or are so underdeveloped that they are utilized only for the satisfaction of domestic economic needs. There is no question that shifting cultivation and jungle gathering, as operated in the context of the economic systems normally present, cannot match the agriculture, handicraft manufacturing, cash sale of minor surpluses, and off-the-farm labor that go with the economic system of sedentary village dwellers who are members of a higher society in other parts of the Orient. But it does not follow that no forms of shifting cultivation can produce surpluses, or that no economic system of a shifting-cultivator society can develop exchange patterns or value systems for the accumulation of surpluses, or establish patterns of wealth accumulation. In this respect shifting cultivation as a cropping system must be separated from economic concepts. When a shifting cultivator chooses to sell either a crop or jungle produce for money with which to buy occidental manufactured goods, he has made such a separation.

Societies practicing integral shifting cultivation may not use their crop produce as materials of economic exchange, but they do have other sources of economic production which can be so utilized. The products of jungle appropriation form one such resource. It is true that these sources yield small volumes of products which still contribute, even if only slightly, to a pattern of wealth accumulation because they are treated by economic principles not fully akin to the principles of modern economic theory. When the Lamet of Indochina sell bear gallbladders, deerhorn, wild animal hides, beeswax, honey, rice brandy, fermented tea leaves, and baskets, they do so within the context of an economic system not greatly modified from that of the providers of obligational feast.[38] Even the much simpler Raji people of Himalayan India produced and "sold" wood carvings, but the whole social, political, and economic structure of the controlling society was rigged against them, and their own society contained no effective means of changing the economic tide and learning a new economic system.

Societies practicing integral shifting cultivation do possess accumulated volumes of wealth, though these are not to be judged by occidental norms in the full sense. The large pottery jars that are common among Iban families of west Borneo are of great value to these people, and constitute a form of wealth, but they are neither manufacturing implements nor objects that can be lent out at interest. They can be sold in time of need and thus do represent wealth. The culture groups that keep certain forms of cattle possess a potential productive source of wealth which rarely is utilized for economic purposes. Rather, cattle keeping among such peoples is for religious sacrifices; the cattle are considered a form of wealth, but such wealth is thought of in terms different from those used in American society. A Mindanao tribesman once refused to sell me his hat because it was a symbol of wealth and status among his peers. An extremely fine hat, admired by his

---

[38] See chap. iii, n. 32, derived from Izikowitz, 1951.

peers, made by his own hands, it constituted a form of wealth considered unproductive in occidental theory. It was not within range of the tribesman's economic thinking that he could have made another for himself, or that he could have made additional hats to sell at prices that would have brought him other forms of wealth.

In the past, integral shifting cultivators possessed a valuable form of wealth in the lands to which their culture group could maintain a claim against their neighbors. The political-administrative actions of ninetenth-century colonial administrations, which deprived many shifting-cultivator societies of their reserve lands undergoing regeneration, constituted a kind of confiscation of wealth. At the very least it was a confiscation of the means of producing wealth. The more enlightened policies followed by more recent governments have recognized the vested economic interests of culture groups in lands to which continued shifting cultivation could be applied. This policy has recognized and institutionalized a form of wealth, as well as a means of producing wealth.

If shifting cultivation is to be upgraded into a more productive agriculture, there must be an accompanying upgrading of whole economic systems. The abolishment of shifting cultivation in favor of hand labor-operated permanent-field cultivation, without upgrading the economic culture, can only increase the density of the population, which becomes poorer as the density increases. Is the small Indian cultivator family better off when it is tied to permanent fields and to a tax burden that can never be removed from its shoulders? Many such Indian families have been converted from shifting cultivation to permanent-field farming in the past century by the simple prohibition of shifting cultivation.

It possibly is true that the economics of shifting cultivation, regarded simply as a cropping system and considered acre for acre, are fully as good as the economics of permanent-field cultivation carried on in many parts of southeastern Asia today. There is ground for believing that shifting cultivation as a cropping system, combined with an economic system that values surpluses for their creative worth in occidental terms, would yield a larger accumulation of wealth, acre for acre, than permanent-field farming of producing land in some parts of the rough country where it now operates. I am unable suitably to document so heretical an idea, but it does suggest the possibility of maintaining shifting cultivation as a cropping system while upgrading the economic system to the point that surplus accumulation could be devoted to improvement of the cropping system. Such a pattern of reform would necessitate the upgrading of the whole culture as the route to the upgrading of the cropping system. The agencies of agricultural reform, on the contrary, merely campaign for abolition of shifting cultivation. Yet there are grounds for believing that upgrading would work better than simple prohibition.

The term "upgrade" is here used to denote the processes of improving, advancing, and developing the patterns of life that now obtain in the so-called underdeveloped world, as spoken of by the Western world. In respect to shifting cultivation, upgrading would involve the introduction of permanent-field cultivation. But it would also involve the introduction of an economic theory that thinks in terms of investment of surpluses in land, tools, and procedures of further improving production patterns, to the end that added surpluses could be sold off the farm to provide monetary returns usable in other directions. Upgrading would also substitute known agronomic principles of production for the folk customs customarily controlled by magic and animistic ritualism, and it would initiate the use of labor-saving devices in crop production. Such upgrading would suggests the planting of crops known to have marketability in an outside economic realm, as well as the utilization of spare labor in some forms of secondary economic activity.

These introductions and improvements, however, would require the education of the whole culture group along many lines. Its members would have to understand (1) the legal principles and economic theory behind permanent-field systems; (2) the economic theory behind production for monetary exchange, development of capital resources, and the use of credit as a tool of production; (3) the agronomic principles of advanced agricultural practice properly articulated to the local environmental ecology; and (4) religious philosophy as a code of moral principles instead of a primary system of propitiation of the elements of nature controlling crop production. Also prerequisite would be adoption of the technologies of advanced tools and equipment and the technologies concerned with secondary varieties of economic production; the reorganization of labor routines; and the effective utilization of a labor force. This listing is but a bare outline of the changes that would have to take place in the culture of a particular population group. The requisite educational processes would include wholesale changes in all aspects of the culture of the group.

Enough has been said to point up the problem. Economic production of crops by shifting cultivation is only one institutionalized element in the great complex of the economic system of the integral shifting cultivator. The failure of his level of living to advance cannot be reversed, and the economic problems he faces cannot be solved, simply by abolishing the cropping-system element of his economic complex and by tying him down to one small part of the land he now uses. This restrictive policy was employed in large part by the early European colonial administrators who were more concerned with the exploitation of the forests than with the future level of living of the shifting cultivators. It brought some degree of peace to warring tribes and secured remaining timber for the good of others, but it failed to teach a better agricultural system and to elevate many other facets of culture which have a strong impact upon the whole of the economic system of the peoples involved.

The Political Factor

There can be no certainty as to precisely how the finite groupings of early human beings were formed, though I suggested earlier that a food-appropriative motivation lay behind the sizing of such groups. Rapidly developed, however, was a sense of territoriality. It is doubtful whether this development may be ascribed to political motivation at the start; the psychological elements of simple fear of predators, recognition of familiar haunts, the sense of being "at home," and the knowledge of the location of simple food resources were probably more operative among primitive cultures. Whatever its basic origin, a developed sense of territoriality must be reckoned a political factor because it involves the "organized" control of a portion of earth space. Infractions of territoriality result in counterexactions, expiatory actions, and wars, leading to external political relationships between groups. Within groups and inside group territory political systems of division of resources, rights, sites, and locational patterns also have developed.

The evolution of patterns of territoriality, in connection with external relationships, has taken different directions in late time, though there is no certainty as to the kinds of patterns in early time. Sometimes groups developed a mystic sense of ownership which prevented them from leaving a given territory, though the sense of "owning" the land never developed. Other groups developed neither, but used their group power to determine the rights of appropriation of resources on the land in a certain area. Still other groups developed almost nothing of an organized concept in these matters, but they are the exceptions. Sedentariness, continuity of residence within a territorial range, and the form of resources appropriated probably were factors in motivating such systems and patterns of territoriality.

The evolution of patterns of internal territoriality—that is, the subdivision of the whole territory among nuclear families, lineage groups, age groups, and the like, and the bases for such division—has also shown considerable variation. Such patterns have had both areal distribution and qualitative distribution; that is, chiefs and elders had first choice of sites, areas, particular kinds of resources, and related patterns.

The addition of cropping practices to economic systems may well have increased the sense and the strength of external territoriality, and probably motivated the origination of different ways of recognizing and dividing internal landrights for cropping, thus adding another level of significance to the concept of territoriality. The object of this section is not to trace the full evolution of systems of political organization, but to point out that the variations and competitive decisions arrived at by early peoples were factors in the occupance of particular landscapes.

As more sophisticated political organization did mature, "imperialistic" expansion undoubtedly occurred among some peoples, with the result that less ably led and organized peoples were shoved around. The active competition among simpler groups, resulting in wars, squabbles, invasions, evictions, retreats from pressures, and the like, expressed land-occupance and territorial patterns that had much to do with distributions of ethnic, political, and cultural groupings of peoples as they existed when the Europeans came upon the scene in southern and eastern Asia, as well as in recent time. The effort of European colonial administrators to pacify such regions, though reducing tribal competition, often stacked the deck in favor of one group against another.

The addition of cropping practices to economic systems produced marked changes in internal territoriality and political administration. Land became a productive site rather than an appropriative range. Systems of site allocation had to be much more specific than formerly. Specific rights to sites replaced general rights to areas or specific resources. As patterns of this sort gradually evolved, many different variations in internal systems developed, according to the needs of the group in question. The full evolution of patterns and systems, both internal and external, is beyond the scope of this study, but three aspects of the subject call for specific comment.

CONTROLS OVER TERRITORIALITY IN THE EXTERNAL SENSE

The literature on the subject suggests that most culture groups that practiced shifting cultivation had clear concepts of land areas that "belonged" exclusively to the group in question. In the frame of reference of their own level of culture, the group "owned" such areas without question. Many groups made no effort to go beyond their own boundaries, which could be descriptively delimited with considerable exactness. Group reaction to invasion, infringement, territorial conquest, or other form of transgression upon the "owned" area was as clear as is the contemporary reaction to transgression across boundaries by modern political states. When possible, transgressors were driven out by force; if strength did not permit repulsion, the yielding of territory was inevitable. Whether every part of the owned territory was used for cropping each year within any given time period was not an issue. Such areas formed the productive territory of the group either for cropping or for appropriative activities. Traditional occupance of such areas was the chief basis for the concept of territorial ownership.

The history (rather than "a history") of many groups, on the other hand, suggests a progressive pattern of movement by slow extension on one boundary and retraction on another, suggesting the definition of territoriality by "zone of occupation" at a given time.[39] The history would similarly indicate expansionist patterns on the part of groups growing in population, sometimes accompanied by military force, to produce additional *Lebensraum*. It is also possible that some groups of simple culture had concepts of territoriality only weakly developed in the specific sense, amounting to an accustomed range of area through which bands, lineage groups, or working groups ranged periodically. Such territorial ranges apparently were not always exclusive to the group, and a group of simple culture did not always recognize the exclusive territoriality of a different culture group. Thus the total loss of a territorial range might well occur in time by the assertion of exclusive territoriality on the part of stronger groups. Many Negrito groups of island interiors within recent centuries appear to have had this weak form of territoriality, and earlier the Rajis of the Kumaon Himalayas must have followed a similar pattern.

CONTROL OVER TERRITORIALITY IN THE INTERNAL SENSE

Within the territory of a given culture group, there are many different patterns by which subarea and sector divisions are defined and systems of rights are established. In almost all instances where a formal political state has not yet matured, these patterns and systems do not properly constitute political arrangements, but social custom and kinship organization are the bases for decision making regarding districting, usage, and inheritance of land. In effect, these social-custom and kinship-system rules take on the strength of civil law. They operate in lieu of formal political institutions.

The kinship structure, the agency that controls the public domain, administers the allotment or selection process in taking up new garden sites, adjudicates disputes over specific sites, and establishes the patterns of inheritance of rights. Among groups whose kinship systems are complex, the body of custom and rules becomes bewilderingly complex. Among simpler groups, which have not yet developed precise patterns of territoriality, the body of custom and rules is less com-

---

[39] For example, Hutton (1921*b*, pp. 6–14, with map) suggests that all the Naga tribes have been moving slowly northward, as all the northern tribes indicate an ancestral home to the south. The Kuki tribes, south of the Naga region, also were pushing steadily northward, exerting pressure on the Naga.

plex, often seeming to operate with very few controls. When population pressures begin to build up and cultivable lands become scarce, the process of formulating a body of custom comes into active operation.

Among most shifting-cultivator societies in southern Asia, internal territorial control seems amorphous and uncodified. The systems operate themselves with few precise institutions and agencies. Few native informants can succinctly describe the theoretical bases of the systems. Such informants can be precise, however, about the boundaries of land belonging to a given kin group, and often they can relate the precise history governing the rights to, the claiming of, and inheritance of particular plots of ground. This aspect of territorial control, to be considered specifically in chapter V, is part of the functional land system.

OUTSIDE IMPACTS UPON NATIVE TERRITORIALITY

The above two sections refer to territoriality patterns operative when all peoples, culture groups, legal institutions, and concepts of territoriality are roughly on an equal plane, as in New Guinea prior to the coming of the European.

When higher civilizations have come into contact with culture groups practicing an integral shifting cultivation, new political and administrative factors with regard to land have come into operation. The concept of the organized state for the higher culture has legal institutions that are not present among the politically simpler cultures using shifting cultivation.[40] Rather than being a territorial unit operated and administered by the population itself, a state is an entity administered by a bureaucracy which to some extent stands aside from the population as a whole.[41] A state has a formal system of controlling lands, and collects taxes on them.[42] Lands may belong to a ruler who may bequeath them to members of the population, or they may be part of an impersonal public domain. Rights to land, when bequeathed or claimed, become personal rights to the land itself, with the privilege of alienation in perpetuity at the choice of the one who holds the rights. Failure to pay taxes, or to render services demanded by the bureaucracy, results in forfeiture in perpetuity. A state normally asserts hegemony over territory, population, and resources of any lesser political structure. Resistance to such hegemony normally results in punitive conquest, carrying with it the cancellation of all existing elements and systems of political administration of the area in-

---

[40] Here one must bear in mind not only two contrasting bodies of custom, as opposed to law and legal codes, but also the two contrasting types of institutions by which each body of law is administered and executed. First, there is a difference in the law itself, i.e., the right of tenure by usufruct as opposed to the right of tenure by private ownership. Second, however, there is a difference in the administration of the respective laws. The simple culture employs only the collective memory of the group and/or its elders, chiefs, shamans, or "peacemakers." The higher culture employs the written deed, the office and archives of the county recorder (in the United States), and the legal agents and officers who administer the whole institutional pattern. This topic is more fully discussed in chapter v.

[41] Political administration of the territories of simpler cultures was in the hands of chiefs, elders, village leaders, or groups of some kind, but control over decisions rested so directly with the local population, with so much participation in the decisions by the leaders themselves, that the accompanying distinction between a state and a tribal territory is essentially accurate.

[42] Leaders, chiefs, shamans, and other select members of tribal cultural groups exert some control on the choice of land for cropping, though they do not control it as do formal states. Such persons receive gifts, contributions, tribute, first choices, and the like. But these exactions from a populace, which are in kind, are dependent upon productivity and prosperity and seldom have the inexorability of taxes as exacted in a formal political state. See C. and E. von Fürer-Haimendorf (1945, pp. 284–290) for the impact upon one culture group.

volved, and in a sense canceling out all lesser bodies of law, custom, or adat and the accompanying institutions.

The above analysis, though broad and somewhat overgeneralized, expresses the maximum of what may occur as a result of contact. During the many centuries prior to the arrival of the European in southern Asia, numerous states had arisen, had expanded against lesser culture groups, and had established varying patterns of political and cultural hegemony and territorialism. For all the despotism theoretically accompanying oriental political statehood, rarely did an adminstration try to carry out fully the code of law regarding land, particularly when a simpler culture was surrounded or engulfed. Rarely were taxes so finite and inevitable, rarely were theoretical rights to land so severely administered, and rarely were the lands of a simpler culture preempted so fully or so destructively as after the European came upon the scene.

After the coming of the European, an interest in land was slow to develop, and effective political administration by political state patterns came gradually. Through time, however, European principles have replaced oriental principles in political administration, and have been carried to ends they never reached under oriental political states.[43] Interest in timber resources developed roughly contemporaneously with interest in land and with the final reachings out of new bureaucracies. The European concept of the political state replaced the oriental concept, with new types of written title to land, more efficiently inevitable taxation, and a concept of a public domain that belonged to those who could exercise a right to it under appropriate legal institutions. Shifting cultivators in all the simpler societies, lacking written documentation and permanent-field systems of crop production by which to establish effective claim to lands, were simply thought of as abandoning land in perpetuity when they no longer cropped it. All uncropped lands were to be considered as public domain.

This development seems less a matter of purposeful, vicious imperialistic exploitation than of imposition of the legal institutions of an alien concept of the state by bureaucrats unaware of the conditions they faced. Europeans were ignorant of the principles by which integral shifting cultivation worked, and in some localities they did not seem to learn until it was almost too late. The establishment of large reserved forests, which could be cut only by those granted concessions and permits by the state, was perfectly in line with European concepts of the forest as a resource, but the policy wreaked havoc with many shifting-cultivator cultures. As the political state was an impersonal entity administered by bureaucrats, the political factor operated to kill off, at the worst, or to cause economic deprivation to, at the least, many cultural groups of integral shifting cultivators.

The Role of the Social System—Labor Factor

Early man lived and worked in groups. He devised innumerable ways of organizing

---

[43] Throughout the whole of the Orient and the island zone there was wide variation in the timing of many of the aspects of these developments. Nagaland in the eastern India-Burma border country, sectors of north Burma, parts of Laos, small sections of Mindano, and the interior of Borneo still had not been brought within the effective reach of European colonial administration at the time independence came to the several political states in the area, and much of interior New Guinea still lies outside effective political administration in terms of the institutionalisms of the modern political state.

groups, but in all of them individuals were dependent upon other individuals. Earlier societies were societies of groups; in a sense, United States society is one of individuals. Early societies stressed membership in a group; United States society places extraordinary emphasis upon individualism. Historically, group organization for the activities of living was far more normal than individual organization. In cultures that based their economies on appropriative techniques, all able-bodied members helped to procure the products needed, but each member received support and sustenance. Ideally, the procedures of social organization prevented the accumulation of lazy drones in a group, and kept the strongest or the greediest from hogging the necessities of life while letting weak or incapable members go without them.

The beginnings of cropping did not alter the basic premise of social organization. Participation by all members of the group was still required, once the initial tasks of domesticating plants and evolving systems for planting and harvesting were in effect. As cropping became the dominant production element in the economic system, and as the use of land became more regular and normal, social organization and systems of labor must have been adjusted to fit the basically altered conditions of living.

It is not the aim of this section to follow these complex convolutions of social systems and labor systems, nor to suggest that social organization is a factor in present areal distribution of shifting cultivation. The basic aim here is to suggest that, because of the intricate combinations and cross-linkage among social organization, system of labor, and shifting cultivation as a cropping system, the final abolition of shifting cultivation does not depend simply on teaching people to grow crops by a different technical system. Shifting cultivation can be successfully eradicated only by wholesale processes of culture change. To do anything less is to create misfits in large numbers who will only be a drag on the rest of the world society at large. The processes of culture change must transform all aspects of group culture so that the populations in question are enabled to live their lives at improved levels compatible with the altered agricultural systems they are taught to use.

Among integral shifting cultivators, shifting cultivation is a way of life. All elements in social living are geared to, and integrated into, the continued operation of culture on this particular level. The basic organizational structure of a shifting-cultivator culture group is utilized to control and manage the land, to carry out the technical procedures in cropping the land, to provide labor forces when and where they are needed, and to divide among the population the fruits of labor."

44 When the Dyak quoted in note 36 was asked why he could not become a Christian, he answered in these words (Howes, 1960, pp. 493–494): "I have not become a Christian because I *can't*. You see for yourself that our *adat* is bound up with our work. Our worship goes with our work. We don't worship unless it has something to do with our work. We don't work unless it has something to do with our worship. You Christians are different. Your worship has to do with the heart, and it does not touch your work as our's does. I have not become a Christian because I cannot. I need help on my farm, for planting, weeding, harvesting, and to get help I must give it in return. I can only get it and give it if I farm with others, and observe the same periods of work and rest as they do. It is not what I believe, but the way I have to live that keeps me from becoming a Christian. Perhaps you think I ought to move out of the village and set up house on my own like So-and-So. But he had land next door to Padawan. I haven't any land there, and I can't go off and set up house in the middle of nowhere. Added to that, I don't want other people to hate me. It seems to us that the man who separates himself leaves all his debts behind and

There are many different ways of doing this, but the end product is the same: the production and distribution of economic goods among the whole population within the context of a whole culture.[45] Another way of growing crops may be taught to people, but it will be unsuccessful in the long run unless their whole culture is sufficiently altered so that the new cropping system can operate within its context.

Partial Systems of Shifting Cultivation

In this chapter I have discussed mainly the culture groups that practice an integral system of shifting cultivation because they make up the large majority of shifting cultivators. I have made only oblique reference to situations in which the practice of shifting cultivation is not the way of life to a culture group as a whole. Obviously the discussion in earlier sections does not apply fully to the practicers of partial systems of shifting cultivation, for they come chiefly from areas of more complex culture and already are members of a population that carries on a different and more advanced system of cultivation.

There are, in general, three partial systems of shifting cultivation; two of these have been described by Conklin.[46] Conklin labels as *supplementary* the pattern followed by people who already have an established system of agriculture, generally high in level and in complexity, and who practice a regular system of shifting cultivation as a complementary aspect of the primary economy. He labels as *incipient* the pattern carried on by people who, having been primarily agriculturalists in a region of established agriculture of a permanent nature, move to a frontier zone with available land and practice a variant form of shifting cultivation. There is a third situation, perhaps best described by the term *opportunistic*, in which individuals of many callings and primary occupational patterns temporarily or regularly carry on a varient form or version of shifting cultivation for any of several different reasons whenever the opportunity presents itself.

The supplementary system, as specified by Conklin, is a program of economic necessity. Although he does not enlarge upon the description, the inference is that the system will be carried on year after year, on about the same plane of operations,

---

lives as he pleases without any obligations to anyone else. When he lived in the village, many families helped him build his house. Now he will not help others to build in the village. He no longer has to give his pigs for sacrifice, whether he wants to or not. He no longer lends a hand with the repair of the Guest House, or joins with the rest of us in making the verandah. It is true he gets no help from us, but we get none from him. We cannot, because he will not associate with us. He won't accept our way of finding a farm; he won't observe our times of 'taboo.' So he cannot live with us. And yet the older men do not like to see him go because his going weakens the only way we know of ordering our lives. In the village as you know, people can be difficult enough and want their own way. But in the end we have to form into groups for farming. We all have to help. We are all certain to receive help, and if we lost the *adat* we are afraid we should lose the discipline that goes with it. That is why we all say that our children may become Christian. They will grow up as a new generation, and together will be able to make a new way of living, but so far as we older people are concerned we are tied to that old *adat*."

[45] Nothing said here is meant to imply that social organization does not also serve other ends than direct economic ones in any culture. One of the important side issues of land control in a society in which land is a free good is the pattern of inheritance of rights to land. Rights to cultivate land could still be manipulated so that one family might acquire most of the rights to a whole territory, were there not some organizational procedure designed to prevent it. Patterns of inheritance through organized manipulations of social organization tend to equalize and cancel out over a period of time, to prevent undue accumulation of rights. In many situations land rights revert to the common pool. For varied detailed patterns see Hogbin, 1939a; Fortune, 1932; Lawrence, 1955; Baden-Powell, 1892; Freeman, 1955; and Conklin, 1957.

[46] See p. 23, above, and Conklin, 1957, pp. 2–3.

at some distance from the area where the permanent-field system of cultivation is in operation. Another inference is that the individuals carrying on supplementary cropping are knowledgeable as to the minimal practices and operations of the system being employed, and that they utilize some of the techniques and practices that go with their primary agricultural economy. It is also possible to infer that they are less careful in their practice of shifting cultivation away from the area of primary activity.

The incipient system, as specified by Conklin, is a program both of necessity and of opportunity, in that the participants are frozen out of the region of former residence and are seeking opportunity in a zone where pressure upon the land is less. Conklin suggests that they know little about the practice of shifting cultivation. We may infer, then, that they achieve little in the way of results, and possibly damage the landscape in their new residence area. The use of the term "incipient" suggests that their newly adopted practice of cropping is to be permanent.

Both supplementary and incipient systems of shifting cultivation, by classification, are thought of as systems carried on by individuals. The total number of individuals may be large. As shifting cultivators they are operating, not in a whole culture context, but merely as individuals making a living for themselves. As such they are out of context and do not participate in a full realm of culture. They are individuals who have diverged or departed from the full context of culture in which they formerly operated.

The opportunistic system also is operative among individuals who are equally out of context with a unified pattern of culture. But it is likely that they are far more out of context, and that they form a random series of anomalous cases rather than a composite series. The variety among them and the range of applications are very wide; the skills they bring to the practice they follow differ greatly. As the purposes they have in mind vary enormously, their impacts on the bits and pieces of landscape they use are quite different.

Here the object is to consider the influence the practitioners of partial systems may have on the system of shifting cultivation as a whole, and how they may affect the larger body of shifting cultivators who follow integral systems. Conklin, Watters, Pelzer, and other students of shifting cultivation in southern Asia, like myself, are observing partial systems as we find them operative at the present time.

It is inconceivable that partial systems are a product of the modern era only, during which we have some historic documentation in substantive descriptions. From the present data it is clear that supplementary shifting cultivation has been going on in the dry zone of Ceylon since at least the seventeenth century, at which time the stylized concept was well in force that chena land was an economic complement to the wet rice land lying below the tank (reservoir) and to the village garden land.[47] It is most likely that several types of partial shifting cultivation have been operative for a great many centuries in varying situations throughout the Orient.

The practicer of a higher form of agriculture migrating to a frontier becomes

---

[47] Pieris (1956, pp. 41–47, 241–244) discusses the traditional patterns of supplementary chena as already being an integral part of the village economy of Ceylon in the seventeenth century. Wikkramatileke 1963, stresses the traditional linkage between the tank, the wet rice fields below it, the *gangoda* (village site on high ground with gardens), and the forest pastureland where chena was practiced and whence came timber and firewood.

an agent in the diffusion of knowledge. In the practice of crop growing he becomes the spearhead of change. It often has been remarked that the migrant to the frontier adopts the practices of the frontier, but it has not been documented that, as a practitioner of crop growing, he drops every shred of his former practices. He is most likely to take with him specific crop plants, some knowledge of tool uses and tool making, some consumption habits, and a few techniques. He may utilize the clearings of previous practitioners, or he may clear land anew. He trades with, often intermarries with, and otherwise mixes with peoples of other cultures who were there before he was. When his kind becomes numerous enough, his former method of agriculture begins to reassert itself, both as a system and on the landscape. The practicers of earlier agricultural systems may retreat before him, until little more retreat is possible. The historic pattern has been that the migrant to the frontier has followed close behind the retreating groups. And along the fringes of the zone, on the landscape, and in human practice there evolves a transitional practice in which the two systems are mixed. The end result can be only the eventual breakdown of the more elementary early system, though the time required may be long. Either the group using the simpler system becomes assimilated as a group, or its members lose their own group integrity and disappear as an entity of population. The only alternative is fully evasive removal, migration away from the zone of cultural danger.[48]

The label "incipient," given to the second of Conklin's partial systems of shifting cultivation, implies the long-term adoption of shifting cultivation as a permanent practice. Observation throughout the Orient suggests that this inference is wrong. As the migrant frequently is poor, he can adopt only the simplest of cropping systems, with subsistent economic existence the aim, until he can bring a large tract of land into production by a pattern he knew earlier. This is the aim of almost every migrant to a frontier. He begins with a primitive system and ends with a permanent system which has altered the basic landscape.[49]

The above paragraphs oversimplify the process of cultural change introduced by the practicer of partial systems of shifting cultivation on the frontiers, in the hill country, near to and in contact with the practicers of integral shifting cultivation. They omit other culture processes, not specifically related to agriculture, which help to accomplish the same result in the long run. But, to cite an extreme application, it is the agricultural colonists from northwest Luzon, from Panay, Cebu, Bohol, and Leyte, who, by initiating shifting cultivation in the Agusan Valley of Mindanao, and then by degrees turning their shifting cultivation into permanent-field agriculture with a commercial component, have driven out most of the former Manobo shifting cultivators and caused those who did remain to take on new prac-

[48] C. and E. von Fürer-Haimendorf (1945) discuss the processes of culture change among the Reddis of southeastern India, and (1948) the changes among the Hyderabad Gonds. Chaudhuri (1903) noted the processes affecting the Mech and Garo of the upper Bengal Delta-Brahamaputra valley region. Gorer (1938) recorded the effects in Sikkim among the Lepcha, and Majumdar (1950) did the same for the effects on the Ho of Chota Nagpur. See Williams (1944) for changes among the Keveri of southeast Papua, and Nilles (1953) for changes among the Kuman of the central New Guinea highlands. See Austen (1945) for changes in the gardening of the Trobriand Islanders. Many other sources could be cited, but the above are representative of patterns of change. Earlier reference has been made to the evasive migration of the non-Chinese peoples out of southern China (see Wiens, 1954).

[49] I have seen this happening in many parts of the Philippines.

tices in crop growing. The land scarcity created by the same migrants around the fringes of the Zamboanga peninsula of Mindanao is now causing the solitary Subanun to feel pressure and to copy from the colonists the permanent-field cultivation practices they are beginning to use.[50]

Throughout the Orient the same story can be read today, just as it must have been readable in the long patterns of the past. Partial-system practicers of shifting cultivation on the frontiers have been the agents of change among the integral-system cultivators who preceded them. That the patterns of frontier expansion have not yet spread over the whole of the remaining hill country merely indicates that the process is not yet complete.

---

[50] Frake (1960, p. 51) comments: "In recent years, population pressure and deforestation caused by the immigration of Christian Filipinos have forced the Subanun in a number of areas to supplement or replace swidden farming by permanent-field agriculture."

CHAPTER V

LAND SYSTEMS AND THEIR TERRITORIAL ADMINISTRATION

THIS CHAPTER tentatively reviews the concepts of control and administration of land among those southeastern Asian culture groups that employ shifting cultivation and jungle appropriation in the operation of their economies. The chapter also deals with the institutional changes that take place in the control and administration of land when the formal political state replaces simpler systems of territorial organization. Control and administration of land is an aspect of the internal territoriality dealt with briefly in the preceding chapter. The variety and complexity of shifting-cultivator land control need to be considered in greater detail. It must be emphasized, however, that this chapter is but a tentative treatment of the basic conceptual and operating principles, not a specific distillation from detailed concrete case studies.[1] In the almost infinite variety of specific systems there are many exceptions in detail to the basic principles here set down, and the land system of a specific culture group ordinarily will exhibit numerous departures from the minimal norm that is here generalized.

Since the onset of the Neolithic era and the beginning of production economies, an important group of culture complexes has developed around the concept of land as property in the simple economic sense. Almost every human society has formulated a conceptual system for controlling the land that supports its economy. The few exceptions to this rule may have preserved conceptual systems for territorial ranges which are essentially Paleolithic in context.[2] Ignoring the remnants of such Paleolithic systems, it appears that in southeastern Asia there exist two categories of conceptual systems for land control and administration. Each category contains a series of specific systems. These systems contain some similarities but also contain numerous variations, because each category applies to many culture groups. One of these categories, chronologically the older, pertains to land systems of peoples who have territorial organization but no formal concept of the organized political state. The second category, younger in age, includes land systems that employ the agencies and institutions of control and administration which developed out of the formal organization of the political state.

The older category, which pertains to patterns of territorial organization less developed than the organized political state, is the category of land systems employed by shifting cultivators. On its earliest and simplest margin this category includes conceptual systems that display little development beyond the vague territoriality and vague identification of specific rights that are characteristic of

---

[1] The modern literature on land and land systems is rather inadequate for the simpler cultures in general, though there are effective studies of a few specific groups. Hallowell (1943) deals with the subject, and Herskovits (1960) has a chapter on property in general. Hoebel (1958, chap. 25) has a brief but succinct treatment of property and land tenure among simpler food growers.

[2] See Hoebel, 1958, pp. 433–437. Many American Indian groups of the Great Plains had rough concepts of territoriality, but no concepts on land itself, for buffalo herds could be found anywhere. Territoriality, however, is not restricted to man, but is common to most terrestrial vertebrates; certainly the concept of territoriality among human societies was present all during the Paleolithic.

purely appropriative Paleolithic cultures. On its most complex margin this category includes conceptual systems in which there is an approximation of the detailed and specific control over land which begins to make it the private property of persons; on this margin the older category shades into the category that pertains to land systems of the formal political state. Between these two margins there is considerable range, both in the conceptual principles and in the specific operation of the individual land system. The specific land system, conceptually and in day-to-day operation, has close relationships to many aspects of the total group culture. Perhaps the most basic relationship is that between the land system and the social organization. A land system and a form of social organization are interlocking, though it is unclear in many cases which of these dominates the other.

The younger category, pertaining to territorial organization formulated into the political state, also shows a wide range of variation. On its simplest margin are land systems in which very few agencies and institutions of land control have been developed. In such a system there may be a duality of conceptual principles, those applicable to land operated under shifting cultivation and those applicable to land considered to be either private property or the property of the state. On its most complex margin this category includes land systems introduced and administered by Europeans in their colonial territories. Between these two margins also there is considerable range, both in the conceptual principles and in the administration of the specific systems. Included here are the land systems of political "states" ranging from petty sultanates, created by one man and lasting only during his lifetime, to the highly institutionalized modern political state, organized to operate in perpetuity.

Land Control and Administration Among Shifting Cultivators

In the discussion of the older category of land systems, that of shifting cultivators, three aspects must be considered separately. First are the basic conceptual principles that control all land within the territorial range belonging to a single culture group. Second are the specific operational and administrative procedures that put the conceptual principles into effect. Third are those changing concepts and procedural alterations that characterize the land system that is beginning to develop principles of land management leading to private ownership. These procedures normally are labeled systems of tenure among advanced cultures, and the term "land tenure" is also widely used to cover the procedures of shifting cultivators. The conceptual principles of all specific systems are roughly similar among almost all groups practicing shifting cultivation, but the specific procedures that characterize the operation of individual systems may vary considerably. A group without a well-developed culture has comparatively few procedures for administering its land system. If such a group is relatively small in numbers but has a relatively large territorial range, there will be little difficulty in administering the cyclic operation of the land system. More complex cultures have more numerous procedures; the administration of these procedures can become rather intricate. A culture group with a well-developed culture, a large population, and little surplus good land may have an intricate set of procedures for administering its lands. Among such a group there may be relatively frequent disputes over land. Groups with highly developed cultures and populations that can be described as large in relation to the territorial range may devise procedures of land administration which alter the basic conceptual principles. There are instances in which the conceptual principles and the administrative procedures are undergoing changes that make the land systems begin to resemble those of the category normally belonging with the formal political state.

It should be emphasized that the following three subsections are tentative in their generalizations and attempt to state only the normal principles and procedures.

CONCEPTUAL PRINCIPALS OF LAND CONTROL AMONG SHIFTING CULTIVATORS

It is not customary to analyze land systems of simple cultures in the full terms applicable to the modern Occident, but this can be done conceptually in such a way as to clarify these simple systems. The lack of such analysis has resulted in confusion in descriptive commentary on the land systems of shifting cultivators. The following statements attempt to put these conceptual principles in terms commensurate with the terms employed in our own systems in order to clarify the subject.[3]

1. *The acquisition of ownership.*—Occupation of a territorial range constitutes ownership by occupancy. Ownership is here used in the proper and full sense; occupants of a given territory clearly consider they hold a possessory right of ownership to real property. The first generation taking over a new territory may determine areal division of occupance by formal or informal means according to the structure of their social organization. Once these divisions of the new territorial range are accepted they become precedential subdivisions. To later generations born in the territory, or its subdivisions, ownership accrues by right of birth.

2. *The repository of ownership.*—The repository of ownership to land rests in oral tradition and group memory. Such tradition and memory are normally good for societies that are not breaking down and becoming relict, and they provide clear distinctions of ownership so that the basic issue is seldom in serious doubt. Oral tradition and group memory must function as the repository of ownership because there usually is no institutionalized agency or archive for the recording, storage, and guarantee of written title. Oral tradition and group memory form a sound guarantee for several generations; beyond about six or seven generations (roughly 175 to 250 years), the guarantee loses distinction among most cultures and merges into the hoary tradition of antiquity.[4] Disputes over ownership in the extraterritorial sense turn into "tribal wars"; such disputes within the territorial subranges become civil disputes and are aired in public hearings, during which claims and counterclaims usually are recited orally and adjudicated in a manner common to the society. Occasionally such internal disputes may also turn into "tribal wars."

---

[3] This section contains my own synthesis of what seem the basic principles to be extracted from the literature on southern and eastern Asia. As the literature often comments very briefly on land tenure, my formulation of principles may be incomplete, incorrect, or weighted in one or another direction. Ter Haar (1948) deals broadly with the subject in Indonesia, but his volume, written as an introduction to the study of customary law for law students, intermixes concepts of private ownership and right of usufruct because in the modern period the two concepts are widely overlapping in most parts of Indonesia.

[4] Oral tradition with regard to territorial boundaries of culture groups, clan divisions of territory, and similar issues, is better than oral tradition with regard to individual or family rights of inheritance of specific plots. On the latter issue a comment on a later page suggests that oral tradition beyond the third generation becomes faulty (see Hogbin, 1939*a*).

3. *The holding of ownership.*—Ownership of the whole area of land claimed rests in common among all individuals, living and yet unborn, who are acknowledged as members by the rest of the group. Ownership is conceived as applying to all lands in the territorial unit, whatever their utility, and ownership is held in perpetuity, without reference to the frequency of specific land use. When subdivisions of the whole territory are made internally, ownership in common applies only to the territorial subdivision recognized as the home territory of a social unit.

4. *Inheritance of ownership.*—The inheritance of ownership normally accrues to those persons born into a social unit that holds ownership to lands, whatever this pattern may be. The lineage group is the most common unit of population holding ownership, although it is often stated that landownership rests in the clan. Clan, however, has a technical definition in anthropology, and the use of the term "lineage group" aims at more general application. No single individual can acquire sole ownership of land, nor can he inherit sole ownership. Frequently, references to inheritance of land do not clearly distinguish between inheritance of landownership, as such, and inheritance of right of tenure (the right to cultivate land). The right of tenure (discussed later) can be privately inherited.

5. *The territorial division of land.*—When a culture group occupies a territorial range as a group in common, each individual shares ownership of the whole range. If a culture group possesses a social structure that divides the whole group in some particular way, the ownership applies only to land belonging to a particular organizational subgroup. The wide range of social organization found among shifting cultivators means that there are many different patterns by which clans, lineage groups, extended families, and other groupings divide the total territorial range. Division may result either in contiguous or in noncontiguous holdings.[5]

6. *The concept of taxation.*—Nothing conceptually equivalent to periodic taxation of land is found in the system used by shifting cultivators. There are neither procedures nor agencies for assessing or collecting taxes. Among some groups there are concepts and procedures by which a share of the fruits of cultivation are levied from certain classes, groups, or persons, but such levies do not constitute a tax on land; they constitute a "tax" on the exercise of the right of tenure. Levies are not collected on unused land, but the exercise of the tenure right on any piece of land may result in the obligation to share its products.

7. *The loss of land.*—When culture groups continue to occupy a given territorial range no land can ever be lost in the sense that ownership is forfeited. Land can be lost in this sense only by being taken over by aggressors who are not members of the culture group. So long as a culture group continues to occupy a given territorial range *no land is ever abandoned.* Land can revert from a private right of usage only to the common pool of land held in ownership by a given group or subgroup.[6] Only when a culture group emigrates permanently from a portion of, or the whole of, its previously held territorial range does the group give up ownership of lands within the range.

---

[5] Malinowski, 1935, 1:345–348; Williams, 1928, pp. 124–128; Bell, 1954.

[6] This is one aspect of the European failure to understand the native land systems. The European reaction to the reversion of land from private tenure (next section, par. 4) was that it had been "abandoned" in the full meaning of the term. The failure to distinguish between ownership and the tenure system, in regard to land, constituted one of the primary grievances against the imperialism of the sixteenth to the early nineteenth century.

8. *Alienation of land.*—The concept of a territorial range for a whole culture group is a concept of contiguous territory, subject only to subdivision as stated in principle 5. Since ownership in common of land is held in perpetuity by a group, there is no conceptual principle by which any land within the claimed territorial range may be transferred to outsiders, either temporarily or permanently.[7]

9. *Rights of appropriation.*—All land not occupied by specific private tenure is free public domain for all purposes of appropriation, except as modified by principle 12. Included under rights of appropriation are all wood, stone, and mineral products, all the usual plant products, all normally hunted birds and animals, and all aquatic products within the territorial range. Subdivisions of the territorial range which apply to ownership of cropland also apply to ownership of land used for all forms of appropriation.[8]

10. *Land used for secondary purposes.*—There are no completely separate sets of principles that govern control of land devoted to uses other than cropping and appropriation, and the basic principles extend to control over land used for residence, storage, and other such private patterns of occupance. Possibly, control over ancestral grave sites approaches such a separate occupance principle when customs provide ancestral sites.[9] Details of practice are discussed in the following subsection.

11. *Land tenure.*—Among shifting cultivators the principle of land tenure is the principle of usufruct. "Land is a free good: tenure is by usufruct only."[10] This may be termed a possessory right of usufruct.[11] Tenure involves the concept of a private right to the use of land to produce crops during a recognized cropping cycle only. By extension of this principle, rights of appropriation and rights to use land for secondary purposes are included, as itemized in principles 9 and 10. Tenure does not extend to the land itself. However, the concept of tenure is an important accessory agent in the establishment of landownership for a culture group. First occupance of unclaimed land, in terms of use during one cropping cycle, establishes ownership in perpetuity of such land for the group occupying the territorial range. Aggressor occupance of land formerly claimed by a different culture group establishes ownership for the aggressor group. First occupance by a group peacefully immigrating into a territorial range previously given up by an emigrating group is the same as first occupance of unclaimed land. Whereas ownership and control of land belong to the group, tenure is private and follows specific rules and procedures which are dealt with in the following subsection. One specific exception to the operation of land tenure is stated here in the following primary principle.

12. *Ownership of perennial trees.*—Perennial trees of utilitarian varieties are controlled by a principle that cuts across the principle of land tenure by usufruct only. Utilitarian and productive trees planted by the occupant of a plot of ground during his occupational tenure become the private property of the planter by right

[7] Here lay another grievance against the imperial overlord. The responsibility for alienation in perpetuity was thrust upon chiefs, headmen, and elders by Europeans demanding private or state ownership of land, without consideration of the native land systems.
[8] Williamson, 1912, pp. 117–121; Bell, 1954; Hodson, 1911, pp. 73–74.
[9] Fortune, 1932, pp. 1–2; Bell, 1954; Hogbin, 1939*a;* Reay, 1959*a.*
[10] Conklin, 1957, p. 35.
[11] See Hoebel, 1958.

of planting. Successive occupants of the same plot of ground may neither destroy the trees nor harvest the produce. The produce remains the private property of the planter during the life of the tree, and trees may be inherited should they outlive the planter.[12]

ADMINISTRATIVE PRACTICE OF LAND CONTROL AMONG SHIFTING CULTIVATORS

The workings of the system of tenure can best be expressed through a series of statements that follow the cycle of occupance, characterizing the operational rules of the tenure systems. The procedures for a group having a median tenure system are stated first; then statements for simpler groups and for groups suffering from land shortage are given. The procedures for the most complex patterns are considered in the following subsection.

1. *Initiation of rights to land.*—Every head of a household is entitled to a crop plot during every growing season, and every person old enough to clear and plant his own plot is also so entitled. Group practice determines whether plots are operated by an individual or by working groups sometimes composed of several households. The area of the plot depends upon the number of persons to be fed, upon the industry of the persons involved, and upon the crop staples. The choice of specific land to be cropped during a given season may be made by the individual, the family, the working group, the lineage group, the village, or by mass caucus, depending on the social organization of the group. Chiefs, shamans, and land masters may make these choices, or such agents of control may be entirely lacking. Choices of sites will have taken into account the total amount of cropland available, state of regeneration of the vegetative cover and the intended cropping cycle. Marking the plot or publicly declaring the intention to crop a specific piece of land establishes the private right of occupance. Among very simple culture groups the practice involves only the simpler elements suggested above, and group activity is more normal. Among groups short of land there may be more careful adjudication of plots, so that each household receives a proper share. The state of regeneration of the land normally is the maximum that can be afforded under the circumstances.

2. *The occupance cycle.*—The length of the occupance cycle and the duration of private rights to specific plots depend upon the cropping cycle in general use among the culture group. What may be termed "current practice" among the group determines both of these time sequences. In southern and eastern Asia current practice varies from a single planting of a single crop that matures in less than a calendar year to a repetitive cycle in which several successive crops are planted during several cropping seasons. The last harvest may thus extend to a date four or five years from the establishment of a tenure right. Very simple culture groups usually do not employ successional planting on the same ground, but have shorter cycles of occupance. Groups short of land continue the occupance cycle to its practical maximums, taking into account vegetative regeneration and cropping systems.

3. *Privacy of land held in tenure by occupance.*—Land appropriated for a cycle

---

[12] Ownership of trees varies with the culture group. Among some groups only men can own and inherit, whereas in other groups trees are owned by women only. Not all groups follow this principle of considering trees privately owned, but it is a general rule. For an exception see Hogbin (1934*b*, p. 319).

of occupance becomes strictly private from the moment of marking or public notice of the intention to clear. Among many of the culture groups who employ crop magic the strictness of private occupance is far greater than that among occidental landowners. So strictly private is the tenure that the simple act of setting foot within the garden of another may constitute a major "crime." Among almost all groups specific permission to enter crop plots is mandatory once the planting magic has been performed, and the "borrowing" of produce from the garden of another constitutes a breach of law more serious than a misdemeanor; among some groups such transgression is equivalent to our concept of a felony.[13] Among very simple culture groups this privacy of tenure often has not developed; its very development is an indication of the maturity of a specific land system. Among groups short of land, there may be some sharing of produce during periods of shortage, and some relaxation of the rules of transgression, particularly late in harvest periods.

4. *The reversion of private tenure and the regeneration cycle.*—Conklin has stated the duration of private tenure: ". . . all cultivates are privately owned as long as they remain productive."[14] This means that the duration of the tenure depends upon the continued harvest of planted crops; when commonly recognized harvest procedures are terminated the tenure has ended and the land is considered as returned to the regenerative cycle. Such land has then reverted to the common pool of land owned by the group. Land on which private tenure has ended becomes public domain open to all forms of appropriation, and the holder of former tenure has no more right to the products of appropriation than do other members of the group. The regeneration cycle lasts until it is generally agreed that the vegetation on the plot has matured sufficiently to warrant another occupance cycle. Among very simple groups that are somewhat mobile the cessation of tenure on a given plot may involve moving one's residence a considerable distance. Among groups short of land the regeneration cycle may last only long enough to put all other lands through occupance cycles.

5. *Inheritance and transfer of rights to land.*—The rules governing inheritance of rights to land show close relationships to the forms of social organization, but the correlation is not perfect. A given system of tenure, with its rules governing inheritance, makes sense only in relation to the social system to which it applies.[15] Whether the social organization or the system of tenure has been the dominant element of the pair in the evolutionary history of crop-growing cultures is quite uncertain.

There is a common assumption that gardening in early Neolithic times was women's work, and that matrilineal social organization resulted therefrom, with inheritance of rights to land running from mother to daughter. This assumption has a corollary that working with animals was men's work; social organization

---

[13] Among culture groups with a pattern of hostility toward one another there is a recurrent pattern of raiding and stealing by members of one group from gardens of another group as an act of aggression or reprisal (see Berndt, 1962, p. 259). The statements made here concerning the principle of privacy apply, generally, within one culture group.

[14] Conklin, 1957, p. 35.

[15] Lawrence (1955, pp. 8–11) makes this point explicitly in his study of the land system of the Garia of northern New Guinea, but the generalization is implicit in every study dealing with control of land.

among animal herders became patrilineal, with inheritance running from father to son.[16] If this was the beginning pattern it is clear that some crop-growing societies either copied their social organization from animal-raising societies, or switched over from matrilineal organization at a late date, because many shifting-cultivator societies now follow patrilineal systems. Another possibility is that some animal-raising, patrilineal societies altered their economies to crop growing after their primary formation of social structure had matured. Throughout the area of this study the rules governing inheritance of rights to land show mixed relations to patrilineal and matrilineal forms of social structure, to patrilocal and matrilocal patterns of residence, to bilateral structure, to lineage-group structure, to clan delineation, to tribal organization, to relative permanence of residence, and to other elements of social organization.[17]

A general rule is that husband and wife do not inherit rights to land from each other among shifting-cultivator societies. Patterns of inheritance through manipulations of social organization tend to equalize and cancel out over a period of time, thus working to prevent undue accumulations of rights in the hands of any one person, family, or group. Provision for reversion of rights to the "public domain" ensures that there normally is land available to those who need it but who do not already hold such rights. Energetic individuals and large families can and do clear more land than indolent persons or small families. First clearing of a productive site or an ancestral clearing long ago establishes a right of preference to general or specific sites among many culture groups. Many families may inherit and hold more rights than they can exercise in localities with plenty of land. Cultivation rights may be borrowed or lent; they may be exchanged, given as gifts, bequeathed, shared, granted for a lifetime, fractionated, or accumulated. Oral tradition and group memory serve as the repository of record, as well as of title, and public hearings serve to keep the record alive and to adjudicate disputes. Group memory concerning tenure rights normally is effective for only about four generations, and many disputes over tenure rights result from the faultiness of the oral record beyond the third generation. The oral record for rights is less efficient than that for ownership, because the complexity of social relations within a group is greater than that between groups.

Among very simple culture groups the rules of inheritance show very little development, perhaps because mobility among such remaining simple societies as can be observed today makes systems of inheritance unnecessary. Societies short of land, on the other hand, specify detailed patterns of inheritance and, in many respects, show procedures quite atypical of median-level shifting cultivators.

6. *Rights of appropriation.*—Within a territorial range occupied in common by a single unit of the social organization there is normally no subdivision of the territory, and all land not held in private tenure is "public domain" available to anyone as a range for appropriating plants, game, extracts, and so forth. Similarly, water surfaces form a domain in common. But within a territorial range that is subdivided into clan territories or into similar areal units the domain open to

---

[16] See Hoebel (1958) for a general statement of these relationships.

[17] See Frake and Goodenough, 1956, for a statement and a reply on the subject. Terra (1949, 1950, 1953) tried to sort out these relationships for nearly a hundred culture groups in southeastern Asia, but was disappointed to find no clear-cut patterns. He did find many anomalies, cross mixtures, and contradictions.

appropriative activities by members of one social unit consists only of that land and water owned by the particular social unit. Trespass upon the appropriative ranges of other groups may be a serious matter. When such subdivisions control a riverbank, a lakefront, or a section of seashore, they hold ownership of all aquatic resources and possess the rights of appropriation. Such territories are often considered more valuable than hinterland territories lacking such frontage. Conversely, good upland hinterland ranges sometimes possess more value as animal-hunting ranges than do lowland or shore-front ranges. When private tenure of a crop plot has reverted to the domain of appropriation, gleaning, scavenging, hunting, or free passage is the normal right of all members of the group. Presuming friendly relations among such subunits of a larger group, permission to appropriate from lands of another subunit usually must be requested, and under normal circumstances such permission is freely given.

Among simple cultures the rights of appropriation seldom have finite territorial limits. There is usually greater mobility, less developed concepts of territoriality, and the general concept that all territory is open to appropriation. Culture groups short of land often possess too little domain for appropriation, and may do relatively little in the way of appropriating. If they possess particular resource ranges of significant value, the rules governing the use of such ranges may be acutely developed.

7. *Rights to land for secondary usage.*—As previously suggested, there are no separate principles covering plots of ground used for housing sites, storage sites, working sites, or other secondary quasi-private uses. The primary principles are extended to cover such usage, and the rules regulating practices also are extended. Every family unit is entitled to a plot of ground which serves as a house site, whether it be in a village, in a hamlet, or in a crop garden. During the period of occupance the ground is in private tenure and is subject to such rules of privacy as are common to the group. The same rules normally apply to seasonally occupied houses built in gardens by village dwellers. In villages often described as permanent the duration of tenure may be a matter of some years, decades, or even a century or more. If another house is built on a different site in the settlement, and if it is occupied, private tenure attaches to the new site, but is relinquished for the old site. The same general rules apply to ground sites for storage shelters, for working sites, and for sites of club houses, men's houses, women's houses, and other such structures.

The literature does not yield very specific information concerning grave sites. It would appear that when culture groups use specific plots of ground for grave sites such plots are held in title by clans, lineage groups, territorial units, or by whole culture groups. Right of burial derives from membership in the particular unit, and the whole areal unit is sacred to the whole social unit. It would appear that nothing corresponding to strictly private ownership of grave sites by families or persons has developed, but I am uncertain of the facts on this whole subject. Many groups do not dispose of the dead in a manner that requires permanent sites, so the subject has only limited application to land tenure.

Among very simple cultures the rules for tenure of housing sites and other forms of land use are very slightly developed, since residence patterns resemble camping patterns rather than seasonal or permanent occupance. Among groups short of land for cropping purposes, there often seems to be an extension to dwelling site rules of the more acutely developed practice for cropland.

8. *Levies upon the exercise of tenure.*—The presence or absence of a levy upon the production of crops in gardens or upon extracts appropriated from the public domain appears to depend upon the degree of political organization within the society. If a society possesses the institutionalized system of the chief, the headman, the shaman, the land master, or a similar form of sociopolitical leadership, there is apt to be some form of levy upon the cyclic production of the crop garden, of the appropriative range, and upon labor service of the society's rank and file population. If there is a generally recognized class structure, the levy may rest differentially upon various classes. Such a levy serves the same purpose as the application of the formal tax in politically organized states, since it provides the leadership with goods and services that may be dispensed in the discharge of duties and obligations by the leadership. Societies lacking such institutionalized leadership may lack specific forms of the levy.

Related to the levy, however, are other forms of exaction which either supplement or take the place of the levy. In societies possessing a developed pattern of obligational hospitality among villages, subgroups, or other socioeconomic units of the population, there is usually some form of mass levy or mass contribution which serves the economic function of supporting the obligational expenditure; this mass levy serves the same purpose as the "appropriation of public funds" in more formally organized societies. In some situations there is what amounts to the payment of tribute by a politically inferior society to a superior society; the accumulation of goods included in this tributary payment usually involves some form of levy. Within a single unit of a society there is also a variable pattern, somewhat akin to a levy, which is properly a function of intrafamilial or interfamilial economics and sometimes becomes confused with the levy as such. Often ambitious heads of households attempt to manipulate inheritances of tenure rights, labor services, and accumulations of garden and appropriative products in order to gain personal wealth, status, power, and privilege. Such status constitutes leadership, although the status may not be institutionalized in the true sense.[18]

EVOLUTIONARY ASPECTS OF LAND CONTROL SYSTEMS

The previous subsections have dealt chiefly with what may be termed contemporary median-level concepts and practices. Toward the complex margin of the conceptual category of land use among present-day shifting cultivators there begin to emerge procedures that result in changes in systems of tenure. There are relatively few

---

[18] Reay, 1959*a*, p. 82, remarks: "A man who wishes to be renowned has to contribute lavishly to feasts and provide food for a constant stream of visitors as well as for a domestic group which is likely to be a large one. He has to have many gardens in all stages of production. The relationship between wealth and landholding is thus fairly complex. Some of the largest landholders among the Kuma are the least wealthy. That is, if we mean by 'landholders' those who have a prior right to cultivate and occupy land. It is more important to exercise such rights as can be acquired, and only 'big men' who have sons and followers can do so.... Clearing land is hard work, and sons are the only kin a man can always call upon to help. Such help is one of the concrete advantages of achieving the common ambition to have many sons. A man may use his sons' labour to fulfill obligations to others." The Kuma occupy the southern Wahgi Valley of highland central New Guinea.

societies that demonstrate this direction of change, and the data concerning both the conceptual principles and the procedures employed are not well marshaled. Here it must suffice to point out trends and lines of development; the subject is well worth field research among specific societies in order to evaluate more critically the patterns of evolution. In general, these trends appear to lead toward land management, permanent-field cropping practices, and systems of private ownership. Most such developments are among areas of relatively high population density, and perhaps such systems themselves help account for such densities. It is notable that all culture groups exhibiting these changing trends occupy territories that have been cropped over many times; the systems of shifting cultivation employed are, in general, high-level systems.

Among the situations leading to changing land control, that of the New Guinea highlands is outstanding. Some of the culture groups occupying the highlands have developed agricultural practices that lead to changing concepts of land control. Practices such as trenching, draining, composting, replanting of casuarina trees on land between cropping cycles, and other lesser procedures have led to concepts akin to what may be termed "soil management."[19] Greater care in handling soils has led to longer cropping cycles, with shortened regenerative cycles that leave less to natural processes. Reoccupation of crop plots often involves returning to the same plot as previously occupied. In some instances soil management has been controlled to the end that almost perennial planting takes place on some plots. The closer identification of families and individuals with particular plots of ground as productive cropping sites leads to changing concepts regarding control of these sites. Identification of families with specific plots approaches that identification of persons with land found in private ownership. Land control, of course, has been but one facet of the evolutionary growth of agricultural economy among some of the culture groups of the New Guinea highlands. Interlinked and interacting have been cropping systems, tools, soil managment, productivity, population density, labor volume, social structure as related to land and cropping, and the conceptual control of croplands. The material economy of some of the New Guinea highland culture groups is quite atypical of the shifting cultivation that so often has been described.

In northeastern India, various Naga peoples illustrate other evolutionary patterns of change that point in the same direction, although some of the features that characterize the New Guinea highlands are lacking.[20] The reoccupance of old sites among some Naga groups has involved a return to particular plots of ground which have been carefully marked out. Identification of the cultivator with a particular plot developed over a period of time, not with the very first clearing. This practice may actually have begun as the identification of a person with an inherited right that gradually became more precedential until the right and the plot were specific.

[19] Numerous studies of highland New Guinea indicate some aspect of the high-level practices followed by certain culture groups. Brown and Brookfield (1959) are more explicit than most observers in a critical assessment of the level of cultivation and its implications in respect to land control (see also Brookfield and Brown, 1963, pp. 38–42). But see Lawrence (1955) and Pospisil (1958b) for other cases in which the tenure system is changing. Ter Haar (1948) describes for Indonesia a general process of evolution of concepts of private ownership, with the preservation of many of the rules for alienation of land by clan and village groups. See also the scattered comments on evolution of tenure in Geertz (1963).

[20] Bower, 1950a, b; Godden, 1898; Hodson, 1911; Hutton, 1921b; Smith, 1925.

Such specific plots come under individual control. Yet among these same groups, other lands have remained under the control of clans and lineage groups, to which rights are general rather than specific. Shifting cultivation is practiced on both classes of lands, with fairly long intervals for regeneration, and with no real development of soil management. Among some of these Naga culture groups the development of wet-field rice growing introduced other elements of change with regard to land control. The adoption of terracing and water control for wet-field cropping led to the growth of new concepts about the precise plots, the control of water, and the systematic cropping of a whole range of land in wet-field rice. This was a direct adoption of permanent-field cropping, and it necessarily required the formulation of new concepts of land control. Among some Naga groups wet-rice land is not only private but can be bought and sold. The Naga have also developed patterns of village residence which sometimes have become almost truly permanent. In a village located in the same spot for more than a century, residents repair, renovate, and rebuild their houses from time to time, rather than erecting a new house on a different plot of ground at some other location in a settlement. The personal identification of house and residents with precise site is another element in the changing concept of land control.

Many of the hill country peoples of northeast India have not retreated at the approach of immigrant culture from the Indian lowlands. Such hill peoples as the Khasi, the Kachari, and many of the Naga groups have had considerable exposure to the Indian land control system as a result of competitive meetings of the two culture patterns.[21] Such competitive contact has led to the exposure of the hill peoples to alternate concepts of land control and to their adoption of certain of these principles in self-defense, even though they alter their older systems. There is evidence of this same reaction pattern in parts of New Guinea in relatively recent times as a response to the penetration of European influence.[22]

There is also a limited amount of evidence that the concept of the private ownership of trees has been employed to gain control over land in a way counter to the traditional patterns.[23] The original concept of private ownership of one tree, or a very few trees, purposefully planted during a cropping occupance, was the accural to the planter of the products of the tree. When, however, sufficient trees are planted on specific plots so that the resulting groves or orchards decrease the utility of the plots as garden sites in other cropping patterns, a change is evident in the concept of control over the land as land.

In all these kinds of cases the evolutionary change in land control has not yet been sufficient to transform the total land systems. Both in New Guinea and among the Naga the identification of individual control over precise plots of land lies in the realm of procedure and practice, that is, a modification of the system of tenure. It would appear from the evidence that ownership of the land remained in the hands of the original group holding original ownership, that is, the clans and lineage groups. Alienation of land in perpetuity by the individual still remains

---

[21] See Gurdon, 1914, for the Hinduized Khasi of Assam.

[22] Berndt, 1962, p. 20; Department of External Affairs, Australia, 1958.

[23] Williams, 1936, pp. 207–213. Coconut plantings in the islands east and north of New Guinea may reflect this same motivation, or may reflect relatively recent urgings by Europeans interested in the copra trade (see Hogbin, 1937; Groves, 1934). See Millon (1955) for a statement of the effect of tree cultivation on the development of private landownership.

impossible, and the conceptual principle of ownership in fee simple has not yet evolved.[24] The traditional system of land control, as applicable to normal shifting cultivation, is being altered, nevertheless, in the direction of the system of land control normal to the organized political state.

THE POLITICAL STATE AND ITS IMPACTS

It is normal to consider that the formal political state exercises relatively complete control over the lands that compose it. Most political states distinguish between public land and private land, and most states have a system of taxation by which private lands pay revenue to the state. It is quite likely that in very early political states there was no narrow and tight concept of public domain as it has been conceived in modern time. It is equally likely that in early political states the two concepts of privately owned lands and lands held by right of usufruct existed side by side perhaps for long periods of time. How totally free of claim such public lands may have been would have depended upon the number of simpler culture groups occupying lands within the bounds of the state and the scope of their own patterns of territoriality.

Along with the elaboration of the concept of the political state as a territory there evolved the concept of "kingship," personifying in a ruler something of military might, something of the supernatural, and something of secular administration. The origins and scope of kingship aside, the aspect of secular administration came to involve, among other thing, some control over land.

In southern and eastern Asia the concept of kingship, in the earliest periods, did not make all land the private domain of the king, but it did make the power of the king absolute over people as individuals, and it did evolve the concept that the king was entitled to a share of the products of the land.[25] The king, therefore, very early obtained the power to grant individuals and groups the right to cultivate land upon the payment of a share of the produce or some other form of tribute. Very early, also, the king practiced the right of awarding individuals the right to collect the kingly share of products or tribute. These rights of cultivation were rights of usufruct only, and lands acknowledged to be truly abandoned reverted to the category of lands that could again be granted to other persons. Just when and how the institution of private landownership came into operation in southern and eastern Asia is not at all clear, but it did become operative in those political entities that could be termed political states.

In southern and eastern Asia the political territoriality of a culture group, as well as the political administration of some area by a self-styled king, presents the historically unanswerable query: Did this group and its territory, or this ruler and his area, constitute a political state? In some cases the answer categorically is yes, and in others it is no. But among the innumerable principalities and private domains of aspiring pirates, traders, princelings, and self-styled rulers, there is difficulty in answering the question. Among those culture groups having the institution of chief, there existed some rule that a share of the products of land

---

[24] That some of the Naga do buy and sell their wet-field rice lands is a step beyond what is here suggested. How old this practice is, and to what it owes its introduction, is not clear. Lehman (1963) notes that buying and selling of house sites is now followed by the northern Chin.

[25] See Brown (1953) for a general consideration of kingship in India, and see Majumdar and Pusalker (1951, chaps. 17, and 21) for a more specific discussion of the role of the king in India.

cultivated by right of usufruct went to the chief, whereas this was not the case among culture groups lacking chiefs. When did a "chief" become a "king"? When did the role of "chief," in supervising the allotment of land claimed by right of usufruct, become the role of "king," in awarding land either by right of usufruct or by right of private ownership? When did land claimed as privately owned by grant from one "king" become recognized as privately owned by a later "king"? When and how did culture groups previously using the right of usufruct principle begin to consider house-plot land or terraced wet-field land as privately owned without ever claiming to constitute a political state? Although such questions largely are unanswerable for much of the region, they are questions that affect the issue of land systems.

Long before the coming of the European to the East there were in operation systems of private ownership of land, systems of right of usufruct of land, systems of controlling land donated to temples and monasteries, systems of considering unclaimed land as open public domain or public domain within the control of the ruler, systems of royal lands, and varying categories of land under dispute with different patterns of settlement of such disputes.[26] There were varying degrees and conditions of political territoriality, ranging from the simplest concept of rights of appropriation from land to the fairly strict definition of the domain of a sophisticated political state. Among these variables there existed almost endless possible permutations of conditions affecting any single piece of land. Indian concepts and their applications differed considerably from those of China, and the old native Burmese Kingdom's concepts differed from those of both China and India, tracing back to the early tribal patterns of the Burman peoples before their arrival in lowland Burma.

Of most concern to this study is the fact that as political states matured and multiplied, in terms of sophistication and territorial spread, the concept of private landownership grew steadily, with an increasing encroachment upon the realm of

---

[26] There is no one source for data on land systems within the area covered by this study. For a short commentary on Khmer law and pre-European Cambodian practice see Steinberg *et al.* (1957, pp. 203–205), who also noted the confusion created by the French after 1884 and the fact that most cropland is still not registered. For a brief note on Cambodian land law see Norodom (1956). For Thailand, an inheritor of many Khmer institutions, see de Young (1955, pp. 185–186), who notes that in Thailand, the only country to escape colonialism, squatters' rights still are recognized on public lands, and that the first modern land titles were issued in 1901. See also Wales (1934) and Ingram (1955). Buttinger (1958), in numerous short notes, briefly discusses the history of land tenure for Indochina.

Scott (1910, *passim*) discusses tenure practices in traditional Burma, and Baden-Powell (1892, 3:490–494) notes that Burmese kingdom law recognized seven different methods of acquiring control over land: allotment by government officers, gift of the king, inheritance, gift of person to person, purchase, clearing virgin forest, and unchallenged possession for ten years. He says further (*ibid.*, p. 490): "It can hardly be doubted that the idea of proprietary right in land has long existed in Burma, and it is dependent upon the fact of clearing the jungle.... The right of a sovereign to a tithe is also recognized." The quotation does not distinguish privately owned land from land held by right of usufruct, since both constitute proprietary rights. The Land Act of 1876 set for British control of Burma the modern definition of right in land, in Baden-Powell's words (*ibid.*, p. 494): "The landholder's right is only recognized in permanently-occupied land. Where toungya cutters are still found to practice their destructive method of shifting cultivation in the hill ranges, it is only on sufferance; they have no recognized right, and the practice is regulated under the Act." Thus the British refused to recognize the traditional operation of the sixth method of securing control over land, which was operative among many of the poor, the hill peoples, and the simpler cultures, and defined control of land in respect to private ownership only.

Ter Haar (1948) discusses the subject at length for much of Indonesia, and Pelzer, (1945) provides detailed material for both Indonesia and the Philippines.

land control by right of usufruct only. It is of little consequence whether this oc-curred through the territorial enlargement of a particular state, or whether the concept of private ownership diffused to peoples not operating a political state but permanently cropping individual fields. The patterns of encroachment began on the flatlands, near coasts, or along rivers, and spread toward, into, and across the hill country. The patterns of cultivation often changed as the concepts of land control, taxation, and ownership changed. Shifting cultivation and the control of land by right of usufruct have retreated together to rougher country, to the more isolated reaches of inland territories, and to more remote locations off the main routes of political and cultural encroachment. Systems of land control by private ownership and systems of permanent-field cultivation have proceeded in the same patterns of directional expansion and territorial replacement, though there has not always been a strict parallelism between them.

This gradual replacement of land systems was an old historic process long before the coming of the European, but the European added another and more formal dimension to it. In the process, systems of land control through right of usufruct generally were replaced by systems of control through private ownership, with variations dependent upon the specific political institutions developed in the par-ticular political state. In the system of private ownership the chief elements were private ownership of land as land, the right of alienation of land by individuals, a method of taxation of the land as land, a method of making grants of land to individuals by a political ruler, the concept that all land belonged to the political ruler, and the concept that the ruler could confiscate the land of individuals. Our factual knowledge of the precise operations and variations from state to state, the total amounts of land privately granted and claimed, and the precise workings of other aspects of the general system is very scanty for the whole region. There certainly were variations in it among the different states, and within the long time span involved.

In India the development of private land tenure for certain sectors of the popu-lation had begun by the Mauryan Empire of the fourth century B.C., although there were preservations of the systems of control by right of usufruct in which villages, culture groups, and other groupings continued the older patterns. Indian references to early land system operations are quite unspecific. The spread of Indian culture into southeastern Asia and parts of the island realm carried with it the establishment of principalities and kingdoms in lower Burma, Cambodia, and the western Indonesian islands in the early centuries of the Christian era. Consequently, it is only fair to surmise that in those localities in which sedentary settlement and permanent-field cultivation became the rule, political institutions developed through which the system of land control was altered toward the system of private ownership. Although we are quite unclear as to the precise political institutions that developed for the control of land under the Khmer Empire, it seems almost inevitable that sedentary cultivation and permanent-field cropping systems were accompanied to some extent by land systems involving private owner-ship.

Similarly, the extension of Chinese influence into upper Indochina during the early centuries of the Christian era must have introduced some of the political institutions by which the Chinese had developed a land system centering on private ownership. These political and agricultural institutions, spreading southward through Annam, must have carried with them both the institutions and the practices of land control. The development of the concept of private landownership in north China long predates the beginning of the Christian era, but its maturation took several centuries; and its first introduction into Indochina must have been less complete than it became in the course of time.

Because sedentary agricultural settlement and the development of permanent-field cropping systems took place first on the open lowlands and around centers of urban influence, the development of patterns of private land ownership had to appear in such regions first. Everywhere in south and southeastern Asia the extension of permanent settlement and permanent-field cropping systems normally enveloped the lowlands and the lower hill margins first, but in the early periods it is doubtful whether they extended very deeply into the higher hill and mountain country, or whether they extended very deeply into the island realm of the southwest Pacific. Accompanying such development must have been systems of land control by private ownership, so that the replacement of land systems was extended but never fully achieved in the higher hill and mountain country, in the deeper portions of the island realm, or in those sectors not effectively reached by basic changes in agricultural economies and political institutions.

In the repeated rise and fall of Indianized and Sinicized states in mainland southeastern Asia and in the western Indies there must have been periodic replacement of land control systems. The decline of political states must have meant the decline of administration of land systems, but not necessarily the total abandonment of the systems of private landownership. Certainly the Thai continued some of the practices they took over from the Khmer. Certainly on Java, at least, some of these institutions and practices were continued. It is evident, however, that in Cambodia itself the Khmer institutions and practices relating to land control had degenerated considerably by the time the French stumbled onto Angkor in the nineteenth century.

Changes in the local political institutions and practices relating to land control certainly were initiated by the fourteenth-century spread of Moslem influence which resulted in the setting up of numerous political states and principalities from Malaya to the southern Philippines. European influence caught up with the spread of Mohammedism before these political institutions had matured, so that no full development of land control institutions based on a Moslem pattern took place.

Certainly it must be clear that between about 400 B.C. and A.D. 1600 the processes of agricultural settlement on the open lowlands, along accessible coasts, and in other selected localities had produced sedentary occupation of the land and the development of agricultural landscapes worked by some variation of the permanent-field system, and that there also had developed political institutions based on some version of the political state. With the development of political systems more complex than those of tribal systems, the institutions surrounding the private ownership of land were extended. Such an extension took land out of a public domain and made it inaccessible to those culture groups employing simpler political systems in which the political institutions concerning land were focused upon systems of land control based on concepts of usufruct. The two avenues of recourse open to such culture groups were retreat into territory not yet controlled by the evolving political states or conversion to some pattern of the younger and more highly developed system. Both avenues led to the same place: the decline of land control by the system of usufruct and the expansion of land control by some version of the system of private ownership, with all that this entailed.

When the European arrived in southern and eastern Asia the map of land system distribution was extremely complex. Europeans knew only their own particular national systems, which retained only minor elements of the traditional system of control by right of usufruct. Europeans came chiefly as traders rather than as territorial administrators; but when they did begin to administer territory, the general tendency was to apply the political, administrative, and institutional patterns of the homeland, for they operated as political superiors and not as scholars examining patterns, or as civil servants applying the law of the land. Only slowly did the control of land through right of usufruct enter the comprehension and adaptive practice of the modern European. The resulting European practices differed markedly by political nationality within the regions that were separately administered. In the earlier period, the British often disallowed all previous claims to land not accompanied by literal cultivation with permanent-field practices. They proclaimed all unoccupied land as crown land and began "land settlement" projects by which claimants would be recognized in terms of annual tax payments.[27] The Spanish used different procedures, as did the Dutch. Throughout all the colonial lands of southern and eastern Asia administrators worked from coastal points inland and up river valleys, establishing some variant of their European system of land control in such areas as could be brought under administrative supervision. Never did they complete the job of installing their own systems of land control, never were the untouched hinterland systems fully codified and adjusted to the basic administrative system, and never was the concept of public domain made fully effective in all remaining territories

In simple fact it remains true today in southern and eastern Asia that no political state exercises full legal control over all the lands of its territory in the sense that the legal concepts and the legal institutions by which the state is organized can be made to apply to every part of its land. Private ownership of land is the basic legal concept pertaining to land in every state of southern and eastern Asia except those states that recently have gone over to the Soviet Communist pattern of land control. Each state has specific concepts of the public domain, and of the legal procedures by which land in the public domain may be secured for private use and private ownership, but no state so far is able to enforce the legal institutions of private landownership over the whole of its territory.

---

[27] Baden-Powell (1892, 3:417) tells how Kachari tribesmen of Assam, after the British introduction of land settlement systems and regular taxation, would file a claim on a piece of land, crop part of it for a year, and give up the claim to escape taxation, and the next year would renew the claim for the same piece, crop a different section of it, and again give up the claim. Baden-Powell (1892) and Stebbing (1926) describe the changes that came in land systems in India and Burma as a result of the British introduction of forest reserves, formal claiming, and entitlement of privately owned lands, and the general introduction of the concepts of private ownership to peoples who had previously held the older concepts of rights of usage in land systems. Ter Haar (1948) contains similar data for Indonesia, and Phelan (1959) discusses the changes brought about in land systems in the Philippines by the Spanish.

Some states have inherited a mixed bag of legal practices and legal institutions, compounded over many centuries, which pertain to and govern the control of land. In some there are quasi-legal practices that, as a rule of thumb, permit both control of land by right of usufruct and simple appropriative activities within the lands constituting the public domain. In others such practice is sufficiently governed by administrative rules that it has the full protection of the law of the state. In some states the civil servants merely shut their eyes to a situation they are powerless to control because there has been made no conscious effort to rationalize the two conflicting conceptual systems of public domain and private ownership of land as opposed to control by right of usufruct.[28]

Almost every new political state in southern and eastern Asia, upon gaining its independence, preserved the conceptual principles that go with sophisticated political statehood in matters of control over land, but almost every state yielded to the urgent pressures of men upon the land and relaxed such strictures, prohibitions, and penalties as had been even partially effective under the previous colonial administration. Not only were the peoples of simple culture involved, but many other citizens apparently had not completely given up the old concepts of land control by right of usufruct. The postindependence increase in the amount and distribution of shifting cultivation in terms of practice of partial systems has not been spectacular, but it has been present. The modern European concept of the inviolability of the public domain is violated both by the integral shifting cultivators and by the landless poor who practice some form of partial shifting cultivation on the frontiers. Every state in southern and eastern Asia faces the necessity of compromise between the conceptual principles of land control accompanying the occidental political state and the traditional conceptual principles accompanying lesser patterns of territoriality. Thus no state, at present, is able to put into full and effective practice over its whole territory one single and uniform set of procedures governing the control of land.

No state in southern and eastern Asia today possesses a clear and ordered conceptual system of land control which will fit present-day administrative problems. No state possesses the administrative power and effective machinery by which to renovate totally the infinitely complex systems of control over land in order to assure all its citizens honest, fair, and equal treatment, unfettered by the residue of historic exploitation, and unfettered by the vindictive urge to get even which is felt by the exploited. No state, at present, can effectively provide land in the public domain for all the citizens who want land. Every state has passed laws governing the control of land, has set up organizations to administer land reform, has varied conceptual principles about the compromises needed, but none is in a position to carry out these concepts to the full letter of the conceptual principles. Every state in southern Asia faces the specter of violent revolutionary action that will entirely upset all systems of conceptual principle and administrative procedure which have obtained in recent centuries.

It is here, one may note, that the whole program to abolish shifting cultivation in a great hurry becomes a harzardous tactic. In waging their vigorous campaign that "shifting cultivation must go" (with the slogan that better productivity of

---

[28] Pelzer, 1945, pp. 27–28, 88–114; Spencer, 1952, pp. 112–149.

land is needed to feed future generations), silviculturists, pedologists, agronomists, and geographers do not recognize the complexity of the problem.[29] The campaign to abolish shifting cultivation looks at timber and soil, forgetting that such abolition would turn present shifting cultivators into permanent-field farmers without the provision of all those cultural trait complexes that go with permanent-field systems. The administration of land must guarantee to shifting cultivators honest ownership of the lands to which they are to be restricted in some manner that will make up for the loss of lands they now utilize. The technological procedures employed by permanent-field farmers to preserve fertility must be taught and financed. Sources of power must be provided to carry out cultivation. The great tracts of land to be freed from shifting cultivation must not fall into the hands of the privileged and highly placed few who understand the intricacies of acquiring land for private ownership. There must be effective provision made so that the permanent-field cultivators do not become debt-ridden peasantry, unhappy with their lot but having no recourse.

In the past the power of the political state has often been utilized by the privileged and the well placed. Through the institution of private landownership backed by the administrative organs of the political state, many great landlords have been created, and the holders of land by right of usufruct have been unceremoniously shoved aside. Although the nationals of the new states accuse Occidentals of being the chief profiteers in such matters, every state in southern and eastern Asia possesses many nationals who have become landed lords through the introduction of the system of private landownership. There are already many people throughout southern and eastern Asia who view the institution of private landownership as very bad for the masses and who urge revolutionary procedures to correct the injustices of the past. The too-rapid pushing of a total ban on shifting cultivation could create added numbers of landless poor and debt-ridden, who could be recruited to the ranks of those who wish to forcibly abolish great landlords and the entire system of private landownership. The specter of Communist revolution, with its total and brutal abolition of all traditional and institutionalized systems of land control, haunts every country of southern and eastern Asia. Integral shifting cultivators are not, now, active agents in advancing such a revolution. Such cultivators, unceremoniously turned into underprivileged permanent cultivators of small patches of soil degenerating under exploitive cropping every year, might well become active agents of revolution.

PROBLEMS OF SURVEY, TITLE, CREDIT, AND IMPROVEMENT

Everywhere that the principle of land control by private ownership has been effectively adopted, there have been initiated other institutional procedures by which the productive capacity of the land cultivated by permanent-field systems

---

[29] Not all advocates of the prohibition of shifting cultivation take the extreme position suggested by the above slogan. But the urgency of the plea by Watterson (1958, p. 17) suggests a trend in this direction: "The day of primitive agriculture in the jungle is drawing to a close.... Deterioration of the soil in the tropical forests has not yet reached a very serious stage. But unless early action is taken to counter it, it will be serious within a very few years. Now is the time for moderately simple action to avoid the necessity for very drastic measures in, say, ten or twenty years' time." There is little in this recommendation of "moderately simple action" to suggest the far-reaching program of reform, financing, education, and technological acculturation which will be needed over a period of decades to accomplish the desired termination of shifting cultivation.

could gradually be increased. In addition to the inevitable taxation systems there have been procedures for definition of a piece of land as an area plot, for registering a record of ownership, for mortgaging land for credit, for the redemption of such credit mortgages, and for the individual or collective improvement of farmlands. Perhaps it has been in lands colonized and developed by Occidentals since 1820 that the most comprehensive and effective institutional procedures are to be found, but the basic elements are almost as old as private landownership itself. It seldom is recognized, even today, that the increasing prosperity of permanent-field agriculture is dependent upon the whole complex of these institutions, and that the omission of any one of them prejudices the long-term operation of permanent-field agriculture, as such, and private landownership as a land system. The actual history of private landownership in many countries of the world clearly indicates that the entire complex has not been available to the whole of a regional population much of the time, making for a long series of agarian crises in country after country.

When one examines the situation in which land control by right of usufruct has been the operational system, it appears at first glance that the institutional features that complement private landownership have no corresponding elaboration. Obviously they do not, in terms of such specific institutions as survey plats, recorders of deeds, title companies, banks that lend money, and government bond issues that finance land improvement. The corresponding elements are there, however, insofar as one can effectively compare Neolithic cultural institutions with the institutions of the twentieth-century mechanized era. The common memory of the collective culture group served to identifiy specific lands and as the repository for title. Collective lending of labor, normally counted in working days, served the purpose of the credit facility, and it could be collected in return when credit was needed. To many integral shifting-cultivator societies the first cutting of virgin forest (a costly development in terms of labor) constituted an investment in productive development of the land, since dealing with regenerated secondary vegetative growth in later reclearings would involve much less labor cost. If monetary credits were not available, neither were heavy annual tax burdens. The cooperative sharing of costs and the same sharing of resources in time of real need supplied a credit bulwark not common in our pattern of individual family economies. Within the framework of their general cultural level, the institutional complements to the control of land by right of usufruct were often as highly developed as are the institutional complements to our patterns of land control. Among integral shifting cultivators, those who did not operate their system at its peak are matched in our culture by those societies whose system of permanent-field agriculture is poorly developed and involved in crisis.

The above comparison is a theoretical construct of equivalence because the two basic systems and their complementary institutions really are as different as the Neolithic age and the twentieth century. But it should serve the real purpose of this section, which is to point out clearly that one cannot transform a Neolithic-system crop grower into a twentieth-century mechanized farmer merely by passing a law that abolishes the right of Neolithic-system crop growers to continue their operations.

It is very easy to assert that the shifting cultivator can never prosper because "Man is never induced to intensify his agriculture, nor to proceed with long term improvements of his land. Having to move away periodically, he does not accumulate any permanent material wealth."[30] The statement is not literally true, as has been indicated in previous sections, but it may be true relative to the activity of some of the better agriculturists in our more successful modern societies. But simply turning a shifting cultivator into a cropper of a permanent field does not produce improvement in land nor does it accumulate permanent material wealth. The reading of many an economic survey of an overcrowded region of permanent-field cultivators will yield the following sequence of generalizations:

1. Many rural peasants do not hold deeds or titles to their permanently cultivated fields, though these have been farmed for decades, and land taxes have been paid on them regularly.
2. Deeds and titles can be secured only after an approved land survey and after filing records with legal offices.
3. Governments do not provide land surveys, and the costs of survey through private sources are high and must be borne by the claimants to land.
4. Lacking the money to secure a private survey, the permanent cultivator is therefore at a dead end.
5. Since the cultivator, and taxpayer, has no title to his land he has no access to nonusurious financial credit facilities, for tax receipts are not acceptable proof of title.
6. Therefore the cultivator is at the mercy of usurious moneylenders, who can manipulate cost of credit, interest, debt balance, monetary advances, and repayment patterns, with multiple legal institutions behind them.
7. The cultivator thus can make no improvements on his land to enable him to become a more productive farmer.
8. The cultivator also becomes involved in a pattern of debt that often is larger by far than his current annual productive return (though some of this debt cannot be laid at the door of agriculture).
9. Not only is long-term improvement of the land impossible, but the accumulation of permanent material wealth has also become impossible.
10. The debt becomes uncollectible, the land is foreclosed by the moneylender, bulwarked by a phalanx of legal institutions.
11. The landless peasant is thrown upon his own inadequate resources, and he often becomes a tenant, a situation from which there can be no escape. Here revolution is born.

What is there in this sequence of events, occurring again and again in the history of southern and eastern Asia, to recommend to the integral shifting cultivator the adoption of permanent-field cultivation on some one of the plots of ground he now occupies, particularly if he has had any contact with higher cultural groups and knows very well that he stands strong chances of being fleeced of everything he possesses? It is really no wonder that culture groups practicing integral shifting cultivation have tended to retreat in the face of advancing "civilization," for such groups have observed the historic trend of events and know full well that the institutional machinery of civilized societies works for the good of those societies.[31]

---

[30] FAO staff, 1957, p. 9.

[31] Anas (1958, p. 221), quoting from the *Annual Report of the Territory of New Guinea* (1956–57), says: "It is interesting to record the growing belief by responsible administrative officers that there is virtually little unclaimed native land." This statement suggests that in New Guinea a careful and intelligent approach to the problem of land control is not having the destructive effect that the European impact has had elsewhere. Here native groups can assert their proprietary interest in land formerly controlled by right of usufruct, and can have such claims recognized by Australian and Trust Territory administrative officers of the political state in a way not available to the hill peoples of Burma in the nineteenth century. There certainly are other recent instances of this enlightened approach to the problem of land control in other parts of southern and eastern Asia, but the general statement of the historic process stands.

In political states where both systems of land control were to be found until very recently, both systems were applied in a kind of tolerant, mixed pattern. Within the recognized ways of acquiring a proprietary control over lands noted for the pre-British Burmese Kingdom, it is evident that both systems of land control were operative. Taxes in such political administrations were not the inevitable thing they are in occidental societies. Government did not make a fetish of knowing what was happening to each and every plot of land. This led one British civil servant to remark that the Burmese government seems "to have been too listless and indifferent to determine" the precise conditions applying to continuance of occupancy of land.[32] It would seem that a different philosophy regarding land control, rather than listlessness and indifference, was in the minds of Burmese rulers and administrators.

Land Control under Partial Systems of Shifting Cultivation

Most of the previous discussion pertains to issues of land control among culture groups to whom shifting cultivation was an integral part of their way of life so long as they could maintain that way of life. Shifting cultivation as a cropping technique is carried on by many other kinds of people, and to distinguish these Conklin used the term "partial systems."[33] In partial systems the cropping procedure reflects only an economic concern, since other cultural customs reflect participation in many other ways of life. In a sense the term "partial systems" serves as a catch-all category for all those cases that clearly do not belong within the framework of integral systems. Conklin suggests that there were at least two major subtypes, supplementary and incipient, and I suggested earlier that there were others, but that the matter of classification would be postponed to a late chapter of this study.[34]

Although the total number of people who practice shifting cultivation as a partial system may be large, the subject must be approached in terms of individuals, single families, or relatively small working groups. The way of life adhered to, aside from the cropping procedure, may range from the very simple to the most complex of twentieth-century patterns. The cropping procedure followed may range from the very simple digging-stick gardening technique to the employment of a diesel bulldozer, and the produce may range from food for home use to totally marketed textile fibers. The present discussion is concerned with issues of land control rather than with cropping and disposal procedures. This part of the subject has been little studied, and it may be that the statements made here do not adequately cover the issues involved.

It is important to realize that the partial shifting cultivator is usually a person out of step, to some degree, with his society. Were he fully in step, a member of a homogeneous society, he either would be an integral shifting cultivator or he would not employ shifting cultivation at all, but would be totally engaged in some other kind of agriculture or some other occupational pattern. This distinction cannot be made absolute, but the concept is useful, as it indicates that shifting cultivation is being carried on as a means toward some other goal or situation, and that the

---

[32] Scott and Hardiman, 1900, 2:371.
[33] Conklin, 1957, pp. 2–3; see my quotation of Conklin's classification in chap. ii.
[34] Conklin, *loc. cit.*; see my chap. iv, section entitled "Evolution of Shifting Cultivation."

cropping practice itself is not engaged in as a whole and permanent procedure. Previously the point has been made that shifting cultivation can be an expedient procedure purposely adopted when the circumstances indicate its utility.

In terms of land control, partial shifting cultivators may be divided for the sake of simplicity into two broad categories. Either they are working within the framework of land control acceptable to the political system under which they live, or they are squatters temporarily occupying a sector of land without consideration of the prevalent system of land control operating in their territory, whether this be right of usufruct or private landownership.[35]

Considering first the issue of working within the framework of private landownership, perhaps the largest single number of partial shifting cultivators are those persons from regions of established agriculture where the range of opportunity is no longer attractive or persons who have become landless and migrate to a frontier zone where arable land is available, with the aim of becoming landholders. Often possessing little in the way of economic resources, such a person, family, or group of persons can devote only human labor to the task of clearing land for planting crops on which to subsist temporarily. Shifting cultivation is the normal cropping procedure for such people. They clear a little more of the wild vegetative cover during each planting season, with the hope that a given tract of land will eventually become an adequate and productive landholding. Such people today normally pay taxes on their landholding, and hope eventually to secure recognition of their rights of ownership. In most contemporary political states this eventual recognition is private ownership in the full sense of the term.[36]

Everywhere in southern and eastern Asia in the contemporary era, there are people who commence shifting cultivation on the frontiers, aiming to develop a farmstead on which they can eventually change to some form of permanent-field cropping system. This is the universal procedure of the frontiersmen who produce the permanent agricultural landscapes of the earth. A good technologist will turn into a good permanent farmer in time, a poor workman may end up by ruining the land, giving up his claim, and moving on. Occasionally there are the restless frontiersmen-at-heart (a breed sacred to and honored by many cultures), who cannot stand having too many near neighbors, who keep moving with the advancing frontier. There still are advancing frontiers in almost every political state in southern Asia, and the process is an ongoing one at the present time, involving large numbers of people.[37]

---

[35] This broad statement recognizes exceptional cases. In general, the first clause refers primarily to control by private ownership, though there are situations in contemporary political states where relaxation of tight colonial administration permits the continuance of customary law to an unusual extent.

[36] Conklin (1957, pp. 2–3) termed this category "incipient" with the implication that the homesteader, squatter, or resettler permanently carries on shifting cultivation as a full-time occupation without ever working toward a farm on which he could practice permanent-field cultivation. There undoubtedly are such instances, but I believe it a mistake to suggest the permanence of practice of shifting cultivation among the great majority of them. In the next text paragraph are indicated two kinds of people, the ne'er-do-well and the professional frontiersman, who probably do permanently carry on a resultant shifting cultivation.

[37] The frontier, in this context, is not a single front line stretching across half a continent (as in United States history) which advances as a ragged line through time, but the marginal and interior zones of hill country, poorer lands, or lands once occupied in the past but now again lightly occupied. Wet delta margins, interior swamplands, grass-covered tracts, and high mountain tracts are also included. In the island realm this often means the hilly interiors rather close to coastal littorals, and in zones of occupied hill country it sometimes means the higher hill country. In some regions it can mean localities beset with heavy malarial incidence, which formerly caused a mortality rate that restrained permanent occupation.

Working within the framework of private landownership is another large class of people. They are the members of former culture groups who practiced integral shifting cultivation. When a group culture beings to disintegrate in the contest between simple cultures and more complex invading cultures, some of its members will retreat "deeper into the forest," in a sense, to continue the old way of life. But some members, significantly affected by the other body of culture, will remain in the same area, slowly taking on traits and trait complexes of the other culture group until finally they merge with it. These people form a class of retreating frontiersmen who, now out of context with any group culture, carry on a complex of living practices taken from both cultures. They frequently continue their shifting cultivation for a period of time, though its precise technology may change, until they acquire the means to become permanent-field cultivators or until they lose their lands entirely and sink into the category of tenants practicing a permanent-field cropping system.[38]

Some persons and families who possess land by private ownership which they crop by permanent-field agriculture cannot support themselves on these permanent fields. A pattern of complementary shifting cultivation is engaged in by many such people on lands belonging to the controlled public domain or to the uncontrolled wastelands of unused territory. Sometimes these sites of shifting cultivation are near the permanent fields; other times they are located at considerable distances from the permanent fields and regular homesites. Private landownership, and all that goes with it, applies to the permanent-field lands, with varying patterns of land controls governing the lands cropped by shifting cultivation. In these cases shifting cultivation, as a cropping procedure, may be a regular part of the operating economy of such peoples, but the fields themselves may never become parts of permanent farms. This general pattern may be found in the rural economy in the dry zone of Ceylon, where cropping of crown land by shifting cultivation is rather

---

[38] Buchanan (1807, 2:384), referring to south Malabar, India, wrote of a depressed group identified as Malasir, who were in debt to commercial traders, also saying: "They cultivate some small spots in the woods after the *Cotu-cadu* fashion, both on their own account and on that of the neighboring farmers, who receive the produce and give the *Malasirs* hire." Forsyth (1889, p. 161), discussing Gond tribesmen of the central Indian highlands, noted that Gond shifting cultivators who came into contact with Hindu lowlanders in the end either became laborers on Hindu farms, or were set up as farmers by Hindus on loans at high interest which could then be foreclosed, with the Hindus acquiring going farmsteads. Majumdar (1958, pp. 138–139) discusses the breakdown of Santhal culture patterns, and (pp. 142–149) refers to the Khasa of the Himalayan foothills near Dehra Dun as agricultural serfs. Majumdar (1950, pp. 1–89) discusses the Ho people of Chota Nagpur. In the early nineteenth century they were still a hunting people who did a little fishing and gathering, and practiced some shifting cultivation. By the early 1940's when Majumdar studied the Ho, only a few old men could use the bow and arrow, and hunting and fishing had become recreational only. The agricultural calendar was attuned to wet rice culture, but traditional labor exchange and barter economy still prevailed, with most money wages being spent on liquor. Hinduization was changing the dietary taboos, and beef and certain game animals were taboo, though the Ho still raised pigs and ate pork; Majumdar considered the level of living to be declining, for the Ho had not become very efficient wet rice cultivators. C. and E. von Fürer-Haimendorf (1948, p. 33) describe the Kolam people of Hyderabad as being quite split in their culture patterns, with a few far back in the hill country still carrying on shifting cultivation, whereas most Kolam had become settled cultivators. The Gond are described (*ibid.*, pp. 323–343) as still, in the 1940's preserving planting rituals, and the trait of women doing the weeding, from their days as *podu* cultivators, but then carrying on dry rice cultivation on fields that were plowed just before the rains. In their study of the Reddis, C. and E. von Fürer-Haimendorf (1945) dealt extensively with the issue of tribal deculturation, resulting from contact with Telegu lowland farmers who had filtered into the edges of the hill country as far as plow culture could penetrate, and with the increasing tendency of the tribesmen on the outer margins of the area to take on the material economy of the lowlanders.

carefully controlled by annual permit in easily accessible sectors. Two sets of land practices are involved, but both lie well within the conceptual framework of control by private ownership, as that overall system operates.[39]

In parts of Indonesia, on the other hand, permanent-field agriculture may be supplemented by a freewill shifting cultivation entirely without control by land authorities. Here the "control" of such lands as are cropped by shifting cultivation is by the older system of right of usufruct only. If and when land control in terms of private ownership is brought into play locally, by agents of the state, such lands tend to gravitate toward the category of privately owned lands through the imposition of taxes, salable crops, and other economic forces.[40]

There are many other kinds of situations, involving small numbers of persons, in which shifting cultivation is practiced as a partial system. Picture a lumbering operation in a forest concession. Workmen with bulldozers, log haulers, and chain saws operate from a base camp at a permanent installation. Workmen pick out choice spots that are cleared in lumbering procedures, and use a bulldozer to clear the site of undergrowth and debris. Workmen will plant such sites once or twice on their days off and repeat the process on other sites in later years, never with an effort to develop permanent farms. This is a pure squatter operation in regard to land, but partial shifting cultivation in regard to cropping practice. Some workmen may decide to establish a permanent farm on such land. A fence is erected, a sleeping hut is built, a sign is posted, taxes are paid, parts of the land are planted each year, sometimes with long-term tree crops being planted on some plots. Never having much time to devote to the farm, the men do little more than shifting cultivation for years, but eventually the lumbering job is given up for permanent residence on the farm. Such a farm comes into permanent occupancy with the expectation of private land ownership. Sometimes, early in the procedure, a workman's family takes up residence at the site, the sleeping hut becomes a home, and the shifting cultivators range likely spots nearby as squatters until a kind of permanent cropping pattern gets established on the claimed land.[41]

Throughout the length and breadth of southern and eastern Asia there are innumerable variations and sequences in which shifting cultivation as a cropping system constitutes an expedient operation auxiliary to other economic activities, either taking advantage of or ignoring systems of land control. The general tendency is for control through right of usufruct to decline, for control through private landownership to increase, and for pure squatter activities to enter the scene and then decline. Many a clearing has been started under the concept of the right of usufruct by an innocent party ignorant of the intricacies of land control by legal institutions of the kind going with private ownership, only to find that someone else secured a title to the now productive land which is backed by the power of the political state. Oral statements by neighbors, actual residence on the

[39] See Farmer (1957) for a full discussion of the subject. Some of my own information is drawn from Wikkramatileke (1963). The chena of the dry zone of Ceylon is the classic illustration of nondestructive complementary shifting cultivation, but the same element of complementation can be found among other peoples and in other areas, much less well documented.

[40] See Ter Haar (1948) for discussion of the growth of such patterns.

[41] Patterns such as this were observed in 1957 in the Agusan Valley of Mindanao around corporate lumber camps, and along the east coast of northern Mindanao around smaller lumbering concessions. The latter illustration involved a trained forester who was about to quit work for the lumber concern.

land, clearing and cropping operations—all adequate proof of ownership by the concept of right of usufruct—are of no avail in the face of a legal title indicating private ownership backed by the power of the political state.[42] Even tax receipts are of no value as evidence in such cases, which exist in far greater numbers than is often supposed.

---

[42] I have personally authenticated data on cases of this sort occurring in different parts of Mindanao, in which poor and not well-educated Filipinos were taken advantage of by well-educated and watchful Filipinos who knew the legal procedures to follow, and there are references in the literature to something similar.

CHAPTER VI

CROPS, CROP SYSTEMS, AND COMPLEMENTARY ECONOMIES

THIS CHAPTER deals with the crop plants, wild plant products, aquatic life, birdlife, animal life, other biotic forms, and inanimate resources which any class of shifting cultivators utilizes in combining various economies. It seeks a route through a complex maze in the simplest manner possible, suggesting only the wealth of variety in the types and forms of economy by which shifting cultivators in southern Asia support themselves. As the information covers a considerable span of time, during which change has been going on fairly rapidly, some of the generalizations may no longer be true. And, as many culture groups practicing shifting cultivation in some form are almost literally omnivorous, with almost any material becoming a utilizable resource, the chapter faces the danger of becoming an encyclopedic cataloguing of commodities. Such a listing is not my objective.

Rather, my objective is to consider distributional variations, successional elements of change, evolutionary trends, rational groupings, patterns, systems, levels of use, and other combines that lead toward the understanding and recognition of regional typologies and hierarchical rankings. Appendixes D and E carry the main burden of the listings, complemented by maps showing particular regionalisms. The text of this chapter attempts interpretation, but insufficient data makes considerable sketchiness and theoretical construction of patterns inevitable. The conclusions are only tentative and suggestive, and need further testing both in the literature and in field studies.

CROPPING-DIETARY PATTERNS

Appendix D gives a simple listing of usages and distributions for crop plants that are reported in the regional literature dealing with shifting cultivation. The table is not complete, because few writers have been careful to inventory the plants that form the subsistence resource of shifting cultivators. Most reports mention from five to fifteen plants, whereas Conklin listed seventy-seven, giving specific usages, planting patterns, and other information. The total number of plants mentioned by Barrau is even larger, through he was dealing with both shifting-cultivation and permanent-field cropping technologies.[1]

Appendix D clarifies certain characteristics of regional variation in crops used in shifting cultivation. The nature of the crop assemblage in the highland fringes of the continental interior is clearly quite different from that of the Melanesian

---

[1] Sometimes the data are inadequate for any kind of crop interpretation. The following statement (whose source shall remain anonymous) indicates the nature of the problem: "Small holes, two or three fingers deep, were made in the interstices between the stones on the steepest declivities of hills, and in each hole were dropped ten or twelve seeds taken by chance from a promiscuous mixture, and the crops were reaped as they came month after month." This was the total comment as to crops and cropping procedures. The author failed to recognize an essential fact about planting procedures in shifting cultivation. Many shifting cultivators carefully mix their seeds in proportionate volume so that seeds taken from a "promiscuous mixture" in the planting sack will produce a desired frequency of plants growing in a garden, and thus yield a carefully planned proportion of many different kinds of foods (see Conklin, 1957, pp. 74–84, including table 9; Barrau, 1958, pp. 35–61, with textual but not tabular listing). Burkill (1935) has been used as an anchor post for identifications.

island zone. It is obvious from the crop list alone that shifting cultivation in the Himalayan uplands does not fit the conventional description given shifting cultivation as a system of the tropics. The listing of crops for the Indo-Burma-Ceylon region seems to carry many items that also appear in the Melanesian region; but the list by itself cannot distinguish the fact that some of the items today are almost relict, in most of the Indo-Burma-Ceylon region, whereas they are staples in Melanesia.

Closer examination of the table, however, reveals differences. Examination of the taro group, for example, indicates for Indo-Burma-Ceylon only five of the thirteen Asiatic species; three of the five seem to be restricted in area (see fig. 4). The literature from which the list was compiled indicates that in India today no one mentions the dozens of races and varieties of alocasias, amorphophalluses, colocasias, and cyrtospermas which are mentioned by writers on New Guinea.[2] Writers comment that the use of taro in India is declining steadily, that taros are now largely emergency foods, or that they are gathered only from wild sources during starvation periods. Historic evidence suggests a gradual substitution for taros in the whole of Ceylon, India, Burma, upper southeast Asia, and south China, first by the gradual adoption of pulses, millets, grams, beans, and other seeded crop plants, then by the adoption of rice as a basic crop. This change relegated taros to the role of a complementary, ritual, bad-year and emergency, or famine-season crop, or of a wild, gathered food supply. With the gradual substitution for taro as a staple, the abundance of wild taros found in the forest gradually declined, as their planting in gardens and their frequency of feral continuance on lands under vegetative regeneration had declined. The decline of feral taros accentuated the decline of taros as a famine food. The shrinkage through historic time of total land area on which shifting cultivation has been practiced, and the decline of taro as a crop among permanent-field cultivators in favor of millets, grams, beans, rice, and other seeded crop plants, have been instrumental in eliminating taro as a significant crop in Ceylon, India, Burma, south China, and other western parts of the region under discussion.

The distribution of yams in Appendix D suggests conclusions similar to those for taro (also see fig. 5). The original center of wild yam distribution must have been

[2] No complete bibliographic listing is given for these and related data, screened from my whole pattern of reading. However, compare the comments by C. and E. von Fürer-Haimendorf (1945) on the Reddi economy of south central India (taro and yam grown only in village kitchen gardens, both dug from wild sources in times of need, but both complementary to the staple grains grown in field patterns), and those by Hutton (1921a) on one Naga group in northeast India (rice dominant, Job's tears on cold uplands, millet used for beer and eaten only in extremes, a large number of seed-sown plants, one kind of taro mentioned, no reference to yams) with the comments by Williams (1928) on the Orokaiva of eastern New Guinea (taro basic, in seventeen varieties, sago a special-need complement with trees selected and transplanted to uncultivated swamps, yams, sweet potatoes, sugarcane, bananas, New Guinea asparagus, and coconut as regular complements), those by Hogbin (1951) on the Huon Gulf coast of eastern New Guinea (taro basic, eaten every day in the year with twelve types grown locally, sweet potatoes and yams complementary, but with manioc (in 1950) replacing both in popularity and also replacing sago in popularity), those by Todd (1934) on southwest New Britain (taro the staple in more than sixty varieties and eaten all year long, sweet potatoes ranking second and bananas third, breadfruit and almonds ranking most popular as auxiliary foods, but yams, sugarcane, and New Guinea asparagus being relied upon when needed), those by Hogbin (1938) on the economy of the Wogeo Islanders off the north coast of eastern New Guinea (taro in dozens of varieties more than fifty kinds of bananas the basic staples, complemented by coconut, and by breadfruit and canarium almonds in season, very few seed-planted foods used), and the discussion by Ivens (1927) on Malaita Island in the Solomons (staples are yams, with 80 varieties, taros, with 120 varieties, canarium almonds from wild trees, coconut, and bananas, with 23 varieties).

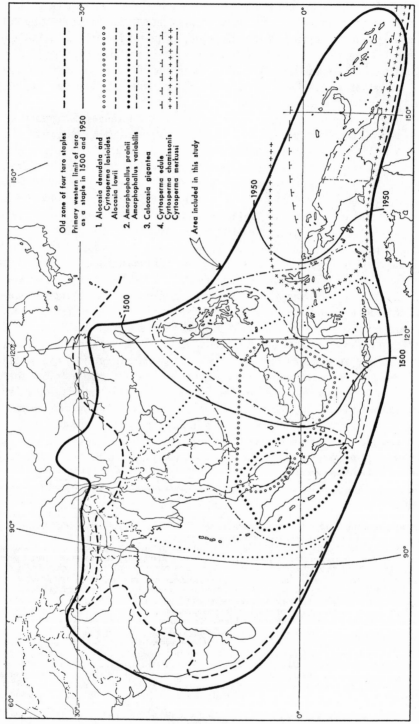

Old zone of four taro staples

Primary western limit of taro
as a staple in 1500 and 1950

1. Alocasia denudata and
   Cyrtosperma lasioides
   Alocasia lowii

2. Amorphophallus prainii
   Amorphophallus variabilis

3. Colocasia gigantea

4. Cyrtosperma edule
   Cyrtosperma chamissonis
   Cyrtosperma merkussi

Area included in this study

Fig. 4. Distribution and retreat of taros.

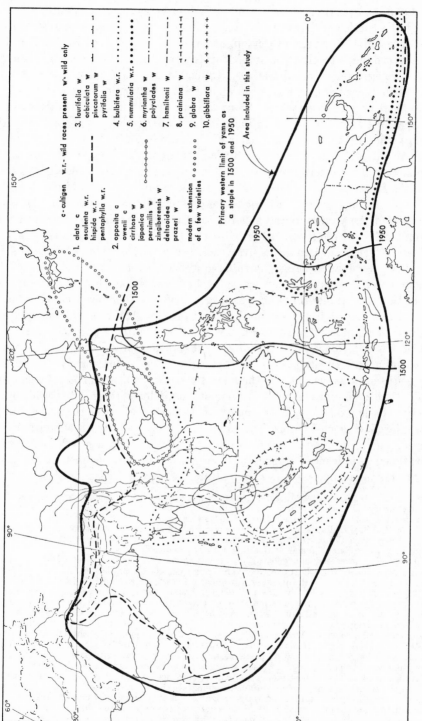

Fig. 5. Distribution and retreat of yams.

lowland and hilly portions of the mainland of Southeast Asia and Malaysia, where many of the species still are wild today, but the regional zone of distribution reaches into India, Burma, and Ceylon, and far out toward the open Pacific.[3] The historic record indicates that yams were formerly of far greater importance among the early crop growers of Southeast Asia, India, Burma, and Ceylon than they have been in recent centuries, and that there has been a pattern of substitution which has progressed steadily eastward. Yams are still a famine food among shifting cultivators in Ceylon, southern India, and lowland Bengal, among many of the Naga and other hill tribes of northeastern India, and in south China, but now fewer of them are found.[4] Among advanced agriculturists yams seldom are important as crop plants in this western area. In mainland southeastern Asia the same is true, though the frequency of retention as a crop plant and the availability as a wild food for use during starvation periods are greater. Toward eastern Malaysia the importance of the yam increases steadily, and it becomes the staple crop among many culture groups in lowland New Guinea, Melanesia, and Polynesia.

The ascendancy of grain crops over root, tuber, and rhizome crops needs far more acute investigation before its full evolutionary story will be clear. Such an ascendancy would seem to be part and parcel of the gradual shift from vegetative reproduction to seed planting as a cropping procedure. There are complications in the quick and casual judgment of this long process. The role of ritualism and sacredness of plants—ritualism with seasonal first plantings and the transfer of ritualism from one plant to another in the substitution for a former staple—needs acute examination.[5] In many areas where taro and yams were formerly staples, they bear vestiges of ritualism, though the main force of ritualism has been transferred to crops that have more recently become staples. This shift in ritualism applies not only to basic food crops, but to many of the ancient simples, the herbs, tubers, and seed-producing medicinals. The preservation of plants such as hydrocotyle, turmeric, and cordyline in the cultivated gardens of many a people today finds little rational significance, but such preservation is far more common among lower crop growers than among complex agriculturists. There is far less mention of many

---

[3] See Burkill (1935, 1:812–825) for a general discussion of the *Dioscorea* species, not all of which were recorded in Appendix D, and see Burkill (1951) for a discussion of the role of the yam in general in southeast Asian cropping-dietary usage.

[4] Not involved in this discussion, of course, is the modern rise of the sweet potato as an important staple in western China, among permanent-field cultivators. This is the sweet potato proper, *Ipomoea batatas,* and not a member of the *Dioscorea* group of tubers.

[5] "Ritualism" is here used as a general term covering all kinds and types of rites, ceremonies, ritualistic procedures, symbolic operations, and employments of magic designed to supplicate, placate, or render thanks to the gods, ensure good harvests, appease evil spirits, and ward off evil, and so on. In shifting cultivation as a whole, rituals, ceremonies, and magic are variably practiced from the time of plot selection through the postharvest activities. Such ritualism may attach to fields, to crops and animals, or to working groups. Greater significance normally is attached to the magic related to crop staples than to minor crops. The increasing importance of a particular crop may be accompanied by an increasing amount of planting-harvest ritual, whereas a crop declining in importance may gradually lose many of its former ritual activities. Many crops no longer of primary importance may, however, retain ritual activities now symbolic of the whole agricultural cycle. Some particular plant species having peculiar characteristics may attain sacred status, to become agents in the performance of rituals directed to crops now critical to the economy. Many secular-minded occidental scholars dismiss all ritual operations as evidence of primitiveness, whereas ritual operations often yield important clues to the ecological relationships of a cropping system to the local environment, indicate the changing nature of the cropping system, and yield evidence of important relationships between separate aspects of the whole culture. Conklin (1957) made particularly good use of the study of ritualism in unraveling many important relationships in his study of the Hanunóo.

of these in the commentaries on India, Burma, Ceylon, and parts of Southeast Asia today than in those on Melanesia and interior New Guinea.

The preservation of such vegetatively reproduced plants as the banana in the midst of grain cropping complicates the puzzle of succession in plant technology. And the casual references to bananas and plantains by observers almost obscure the issue.[6] In Appendix D no effort was made to distinguish between bananas eaten raw and those cooked before eating, or between finger (small) bananas and carabao (huge) bananas, as references in the literature are inadequate. The position of banana plants, however, suggests a possible clue toward unraveling the story among shifting cultivators. Among some peoples, bananas are planted only around houses, in villages, or in special spots, Among other peoples, bananas have become casually handled plants, chiefly used in field planting. They are harvested after the main cropping of the garden has been completed, and primary attention in gardening has shifted to a new site.

The planting sites for land cleared and cropped are one element of the shift in cropping systems and crop technology. Most of the taros and the yams prefer moist sites, though in the evolution of dozens of races and varieties within each species of each plant, there have been evolved yams and taros that will grow on drier ground. The wet field, the pit field, terracing, flat sites, hill-slope sites, and crest-of-ground sites are important to the whole issue of crop succession. A good site for some of the wet taros in aboriginal cropping systems may have been less suitable for growing a grain crop such as a millet, a gram, or an early variety of rice. New Guinea slope cultivators who grow a variety of crops often put their taros at the bottoms, their yams higher up, and some of the seeded plants near the tops of their fields. The gradual adoption of millets, grams, and rice among Indian shifting cultivators may well have led them out of the bottoms and the too-wet sites onto the slopes, which were more suitable for plants sown by seed. At this juncture it would seem better to dismiss this point as an interesting possibility rather than to generalize it into a causal factor.

Some yams are shallow tubered, the tubers being set near the surface of the ground under a crown of thorny roots which serve to protect them from wild pigs and other predators. Others are deep rooted, running to 10 feet in length of tuber.[7] Obviously, depth of soil on a planting site would have been a factor in cropping many of the deep-rooted tubers. Added to this rooting variance is the variable presence of the poison dioscorine in many of the species and races of both wild and cultivated yams.[8] Peoples living near the seacoast had in saltwater a ready means of removing the poison, but to peoples well inland with an inadequate supply of salt, removing the dioscorine was more troublesome. In very early periods, prior to the evolution of cultivated races of yams no longer thorny, deep rooted, or poison-

---

[6] Not only did I not attempt to distinguish, in Appendix D, the different bananas, but I declined to follow the older literatures in the attempt to distinguish between the banana and the plantain. See Simmonds (1959, pp. 54–63) for a comment on the advisability of abandoning the word "plantain."

[7] Many yams, especially the deep-rooted ones, are huge and very long. Burkill (1935, 1:815) noted 130 pounds for *D. alata*, and (p. 819) 77 pounds for a marketed tuber of *D. hispida*. Barrau (1958, p. 45) notes the old Melanesian technique of digging a pit around a growing large tuber and reinforcing the pit wall with sticks to permit enlargement of the tuber to 10 feet in length, and also mentions an 8.5-foot tuber seen in New Caledonia in 1953.

[8] Burkill, 1935, 1:813.

ous, the adoption of some other less troublesome crop may have been an avenue in the shift of cropping patterns in parts of southern Asia. We know very little about what motivated the early modern patterns of preferences in diet and crop growing, particularly in this part of the world.

SPECIFIC REGIONAL CROP-DIET PATTERNS

Several distinct, broad patterns of crop-dietary associations exist among shifting cultivators, and can be regionally segregated for the area from western India through the Solomon Island part of Melanesia.[9] This concern must temporarily be kept pre-Columbian to screen out the impact of American crop plants and European diet preferences on local agriculture. Overlaps, discontinuities, anomalies, and other problems prevent a neat and precise classification. The history of human movement, culture transfer, and human preferences in diet are about as complex here as anywhere else on earth. The suggested groupings can be extracted from the major table of crop listings, but the listing does not carry the notations of historic change which are integral elements in the regional zonation. Beginning with the Pacific region, these broad patterns can be distinguished, though this effort is rather speculative, owing to my own ignorance and the lack of data.

Western Melanesia, including New Guinea as a whole, was the region of taros, yams (or sweet potatoes in highland New Guinea), rhizomatic grasses, nuts, sagos, and minor greens. There was much local variation in the basic staple, with taros, yams, sweet potatoes, sagos, or even canarium nuts forming the locally important staple. Each of the basic species had a proliferated evolution of cultivated races, selected in time to suit taste preferences and ecologic environments. Locally there was a high degree of dependence upon essentially wild resources of a collecting pattern found among peoples dependent upon sago, canarium or terminalia almonds, even though planting had evolved preferred races and varieties. More significant, however, was the primary dependence upon tubers, rhizomes, rootstock sections, cuttings, and other forms of vegetative reproduction.[10] This region had few spice and flavor crops, and the diet was essentially bland, lacking a high degree of daily variety. There was a significant, steady dependence upon wild items the year around, even though for many groups there was little of a starvation period as-

---

[9] The identification of early and basic regional crop-dietary associations is not the primary basis for setting up a hierarchical ranking of systems of shifting cultivation, in terms of technological levels, but it is a key element in the recognition of fundamental differences in methods of shifting cultivation as kinds of cropping systems. If rice-dominant shifting cultivation in northeast India were to be equated with Kansas wheat farming of a generation ago, then New Guinea taro, banana, breadfruit, and canarium nut growing would have to be equated, at the very least, with the general mixed farming in parts of eastern United States a generation ago. The point is not the equivalence of the two Asian-American systems put together, but the dissimilarities in Asian land cropping systems. The simple object is to demonstrate that not all methods of shifting cultivation are sufficiently alike to be covered with a single casual general description which concentrates on the use of fire and the shifting of fields.

[10] Some crops, of course, are grown from seeds among all culture groups that can be observed today, but these are minor crops and it is likely that they are relatively recent acquisitions, even though the literal age of such seeding may run into centuries. The tree nuts cannot be held as true seed planting until the quite modern era, for the evidence indicates that most nut trees were wild, preserved rather than orchard planted, and claimed as private property by being found or as growing on claimed land. Some of the nut-tree distributional continuance has been accomplished through the action of birds. Guppy (1887, p. 85) noted that the fruit pigeons picked the canarium almonds, ate off the fleshy covers, and dropped the nuts to the ground, saving human picking, and that the pigeons chiefly were responsible for the dispersal of canarium nut trees.

sociated with the seasonality of grain cropping.[11] Some items, basic, staple, or highly significant here, were to be found as far as the west coast of India; for the most part, however, such items were of ancient tradition, often relict or relatively unimportant farther and farther west. The importance of cordyline in modern New Guinea is suggestive of this ancient role of a plant that has supplied food, flavoring, medicine, poison, and fiber, and has played an important religio-magic role. In India, on the other hand, the use of cordyline as food and dietary flavoring has long since declined to relict status. Perhaps, in its most basic and permanent elements, this whole eastern complex forms a plant-collecting, cropping-dietary combine that is the oldest in the Orient, preserved farther west only in fragmental form, or as religious and emergency residuals. This somewhat speculative conclusion needs further testing, but much of the evidence fits rather well with the conclusion.

Malaysia, as a whole, was a mixed zone with many local variations, where there was formerly much more of a graded pattern from west to east than can be seen in the modern period.[12] Yams, taros, nuts, sagos, and many of the older staples were being replaced by millets, grams, seeded vegetables, and coconut. The process of replacement required a long period of time and many different patterns of influences. The eastward movement of influences from India was complemented by southward-moving influences from the mainland of southeastern Asia. Even rice made partial inroads upon the planting-dietary pattern of western Malaysia at an early period. In this region many species of wild plants were endemic, as the present island pattern emerged and took its modern shape. Philippine patterns varied from those of Sumatra, and Sumatran patterns from those of Flores, Celebes, or the Moluccas.

Malaysia was a realm of many tropical fruits, of numerous leguminous plants, of many spicy, aromatic, and flavor-giving plants, of many fiber-producing plants, and of many plants carrying poisons of low to high potency.[13] Tuber, rhizome, root, shoot, and cutting propagation was combined with seed propagation in locally mixed proportions. The general trend of events, however, over a long period of time carried the seeded patterns and the grainlike food plants eastward. Rice showed this tendency quite clearly, and it was perhaps the last of the seed grains to expand at the expense of the tuber-root complex. The expansion of rice has continued since the arrival of the European in this region.

A third cropping-dietary combination was to be found in south central China,

[11] Many field reports refer to conscious wastage, failure to harvest the last products of gardens, the surplus of basic staple foods, and the general lack of a serious starvation period among the taro growers particularly. Such reports obviously refer to culture groups not suffering from shortage of land.

[12] Burkill (1935, 1:107) quotes Rumpf as saying for the late seventeenth century that the taro *Alocasia macrorrhiza* was "cultivated in the gardens of almost all of the islands of 'India aquosa,' especially in those toward the east, where rice is not abundant." Burkill (1935, 1:816), in commenting on the indigestibility of many of the yams, notes the replacement of the yam by the post-Columbian manioc and potato, and also reports Rumpf's comment that yams were used by inclination in Java but were used of necessity in Celebes and Boeton.

[13] Many of the leguminous plants of all parts of southern and eastern Asia have finally been bred into varieties producing seeds numerous enough, large enough, or sufficiently edible that they are now cultivated plants grown for the seeds, whereas in an earlier period they often were wild or tolerated but were used for their starchy roots, their tender leaves in vegetable cookery, or their value as medicine or poison. Both of the latter usages have often been discarded with the appearance and acceptance of seed-sown vegetables, supplying the "greens" purpose, and more useful medicinal plants.

Tonking, Laos, northern Thailand, and north Burma. This region was long dominated by seed-grain patterns in which a few of the millets, Job's tears, and early rices achieved dominance over the less numerous tubers, rhizomes, and roots native to China, and into which the winter cropping of wheats, barleys, buckwheat, and minor vegetables penetrated as far as they could be grown successfully. There are residual uses of a few of the yams, some of the taros, a few of the minor vegetables and varied subtropical fruits.[14] Some races of east Asian endemic plants like Chinese cabbages, soybeans, and oriental pears and plums were fitted into the regional pattern to add to the variation from the patterns found farther south. Extensions of this regional pattern to some extent penetrated into the Indian Himalayan foothill zone with the westward movement of people out of the foothill country of southwest China.[15]

The fourth cropping-dietary combination pertained to India and the eastern coastal zone of the Bay of Bengal. Here the ancient background usages of tubers, rhizomes, rootstock plantings, cuttings, and other aspects of vegetative reproduction became increasingly residual in normal shifting cultivation, except in occasional culture groups that preserved particular crops.[16] Only during starvation periods did resort to gathering of wild yams, taros, fruits, herbs, and vegetable foods show up strongly. In this region the elaboration of cropping-dietary patterns evolved a very large number of species and races of millets, grams, and other seed-grain crops commonly termed pulses. Throughout the Indian region this group of crop plants with its wealth of variety almost totally usurped the role of staple foods. Rice significantly entered the cropping-dietary combine of the shifting cultivator, but to a lesser degree than was true in Southeast Asia and western Malaysia. The pattern was augmented by a wide variety of fruits, minor vegetables, palms, brinjals, spice flavorings, and related items. The evolution of dietary preference for curry stuffs made this region the center of a spice-hot dietary that contrasted very sharply with the bland Melanesian diet.

A fifth, clear, cropping-dietary zone was to be found in the Tibetan border country, comprising the Himalayan foothill country of India, part of the north Burmese highlands, and the Chinese-Tibetan border zone. The regional crop pattern was based primarily on plants ecologically suited to cold winters and cool environments with highly seasonal growing periods. There seems to be no ancient tradition of a tuber-rhizome-root pattern in areas of higher elevation, though the lower foothill zone has such. The basic plant foods were wheat, barley, buckwheat, and the hardier races of millets and grams. The fruits were essentially the stone

---

[14] Taros were orginally cultivated somewhat farther north than the greater yam and, except for the species endemic to China, probably contributed more to an early food supply than did the general group of yams.

[15] Although the soybean recently has become commonly grown throughout India as a whole, under the pressure of modern agricultural science, it is only in the eastern Himalayan foothill country that there is an old tradition of growing soybeans.

[16] This does not mean that yams or taros are not to be found at all in the markets, or in the diets, of advanced agriculturists or urban dwellers of India. These crops are grown by permanent-field agriculturists, are found in markets, and are eaten by peoples of all levels and patterns of culture. In no sense, however, can any one of them be considered a staple crop or food. Similarly, advanced agriculturists use rootstock plantings for bananas and some other crops, use cuttings and vegetative methods of reproducing many decorative plants, and so on, but vegetative techniques now are being rejuvenated for particular purposes; in general, Indian agriculture as a whole may be described as a seed-sowing technology in increasing degree. The reference here is to a broad shift in the basic pattern over a long period of time.

fruits now familiar to Europeans; the nuts were those of cooler countries; and the vegetables were those now familiar to European.[17] Only in the lower fringes of this zone were any of the subtropicals to be found. As this was not a zone of tropical and subtropical tubers, it would seem to represent a late and marginal spread of shifting cultivation into the mountain environment, where grain and fruit food crops from a mid-latitude sequence eventually took over the roles of staple and complementary items.

Five early and fairly distinctive regional patterns have been described, but the Southeast Asian mainland core remains a region not closely identified with any of the five cropping-dietary patterns. The Southeast Asian mainland has a somewhat different pattern of crops and dietary combinations, but historic Chinese and Indian influence in this region is so mixed that the early picture is hard to determine.[18] Here variety is more emphatic than is regional uniformity in terms of ancient crop traditions, since there is more simple climatic seasonality, great variation from riverine lowland to high mountain shoulder, and very wet through seasonally wet to long dry-seasoned localities. Here was the home of many subtropical fruits and many tubers and vegetatively reproduced plants, as well as a very large number of leguminous plants which could be utilized for their starch-giving roots, their leaves, their young pods, and their mature seeds. There are today relict usages of legume roots, but modern usage is chiefly as greens or seed. Here rice growing may well have matured into the types and patterns we see throughout the Orient today. Out of this region may have come the red and cream-colored glutinous rices, the Asiatic black rices, the harder nonglutinous rices, the differentiation of dry-field and wet-field cropping patterns, the early spread of some of the millets, and the vegetable and fruit complements to rice as a staple. There were fewer of the old hot spices, aromatics, and piquant flavorings. But there remain islands of ancient patterns of several kinds. This area would seem to have certain characteristics of change through time, but not a crop-and-diet system that can now be differentiated as distinctive. It must have had such distinctness at an earlier period, but current knowledge is inadequate for full reconstruction of the picture.

RECENTLY EVOLUTIONARY TRENDS AND ANOMALIES

In recent centuries a number of basic changes have taken place in the cropping-dietary combines throughout the whole of southern and eastern Asia among shifting cultivators, but it is likely that the changes of the last few decades are even more significant. First in effect were the casual introductions of numerous American and European crop plants and a few African plants from the sixteenth to the early nineteenth century. Many of these have been adopted at varying times in the cropping systems of different peoples. Second, there has been the impact of the agricultural missionary and the government agricultural officer in recent decades,

---

[17] The Himalayan foothill-mountain front is a very significant zone for transmission of crop plants, as well as other culture traits, both eastward and westward between western and eastern Asia, and there are many puzzling and interesting aspects reflected in the localized presence of plants and technological practices. The present textual statement is intended only as a broad generalization.

[18] The textual paragraph is but a generalization. Far too little acute research has been done on many problems to afford a clear picture, and in my own reading for this study I have not tried to follow out many lines of inquiry which, if extended further, would provide a clearer statement.

who introduced both agricultural innovations and new patterns of living. Appendix D carries three different time references in this matter. In column 2, PC stands for a post-Columbian introduction to some part of the whole region. Shifting cultivators acquired many of these plants very promptly and spread their usage far ahead of the specific visits of the European. In the columns for regional distributions there are three time designations: PC suggests that the item reached the area prior to recent decades, but that it probably does not go back so far as the sixteenth century; RC means an introduction within recent decades only; X stands for present and past usage of the plant indicated, without suggestion of the time period during which introduction occurred.

The general trends may be described in two broad patterns. First has been the shrinkage of areas of shifting cultivation, the encroachment of permanent-field cultivation practices, and the introduction among the remaining shifting cultivators of both new crops and new cropping technologies. This has been brought about, sometimes, by government edict, but it also has been accomplished by the spontaneous spread of agricultural settlers or plantation operators on a spreading frontier. Though this pattern has led to a decline in shifting cultivation, it also has been a means of spreading new crop varieties and new crops among the remaining adherents to shifting cultivation. Under the second pattern, there has been the simple spread of crop items from culture group to culture group through the normal channels of interregional contact and trade. These broad patterns may be described as an acceleration of the long-term trend. Seed-planted crop plants recently have penetrated the interior of New Guinea at a rate and volume probably unprecedented in New Guinea agricultural history. The last three or four decades have seen a tremendous increase in the introduction of new plants. For example, wet rice cultivation, recently introduced by government officers and agricultural missionaries to many sections of New Guinea, illustrates the leapfrogging spread of a plant that was not successfully introduced into New Guinea during the whole early history of rice cultivation.

The impact of maize, lima bean, pumpkin, squash, and many other common garden vegetables, such as lettuce, carrots, cabbage, and parsnips, has been significant. These all are seed-planted items, and they are changing the traditional cropping-dietary patterns. It is true that some of them are used in ways no longer common in the West. For example, the blossoms and tender green leaves of pumpkin and squash are used as a vegetable green more commonly among shifting cultivators than are the mature fruits; and in New Guinea the maize tassel is often plucked very young, cooked, and eaten whole in the same way that the young inflorescences of some of the reeds and canelike grasses are used. The impact of such fruits as the custard apple, the papaya, passion fruit, guava, and pineapple on the dietary of many shifting cultivators has been very marked. Manioc, the white potato, and the American "taro," *Xanthosoma*, have had significant effects in localized regions, though manioc is more widely distributed than the other two. The peanut is having a substantial impact upon shifting cultivators, and, in New Guinea, peanut feasts sometimes take the place of the older yam feasts in intergroup obligational exchanges.

Though the general trend is to hasten the full distribution of all kinds of things grown by shifting cultivators and lessen the old contrasts between India and New Guinea, there remain a few anomalies, residuals, and regional persistences. Parts of New Guinea still lie outside the zone of rapid introduction of new plants and marked patterns of change. Tuber-root-rhizome propagators sometimes reject new plants of the seed-planted variety because they do not fit into any traditional pattern of garden operation or dietary complex. The reluctance of many Melanesian gardeners to take to rice growing is a prime example.[19] Though most of the Naga peoples of northeast India knew rice quite well by 1920, there were then marked differences in their use of the cereal.[20] The Angami, Khoirao, and Kacha were doing first-class wet-field terracing for rice, though some members of each tribe preferred to grow rice by shifting cultivation and all three groups continued to employ shifting cultivation for much of their crop growing. The Naked Rengma, Tangkul, and Maram were beginning to terrace for wet-field rice of their own accord, and the Zemi (Sema) were doing a little terracing under government persuasion. All four groups continued to use shifting cultivation at the same time. But though the Konyak held land good for rice growing, they were the only Naga group to cling to the staple taro crop *Colocasia esculenta*, using only shifting cultivation as their technology. Among all other Naga, taro had dropped to the level of an unimportant complement.

One other major anomalous regional pattern, that of highland New Guinea, must be mentioned. There the yam, taro, banana crop-diet staple was replaced by the sweet potato. At about 6,000 feet elevation, yams, taros, and bananas drop out of the garden-staple cropping pattern, and the sweet potato replaces them. By 8,000 feet the sweet potato is rather dominant, and few other crops can be grown as the upper limit of agriculture is approached at about 9,000 feet. Below 6,000 feet, and even as low as 2,500 feet, the sweet potato is occasionally a staple, but presumably these lower occurrences are either purely historical or are ecologically specialized developments. At median elevations it is common for yams, taros, and bananas to be grown as staples, with other plants as complements, in gardens sited at lower and more protected elevations. Sweet potato gardens, either staple or complementary, are sited on ridges and exposed sites at higher elevations.[21]

---

[19] Many Melanesians willingly accept polished rice, for dietary purposes, when issued as a part of their wage payments, but are disinclined, for various reasons, to grow rice themselves. Rice must be harvested, processed, and carefully stored within a very short time after the grain ripens, whereas yams can be left in the garden for a longer period, and most of the taros can be harvested as needed in the daily diet. Manioc, therefore, has been far more acceptable as a crop plant than has rice, because it can be handled in the traditional manner. Most peoples willingly accept the seeds of new plants, and know enough about seed-planting technology to use them, but they plant, grow, and use the products in their own localized ways.

[20] These statements were summarized from Hutton, 1922, pp. xxviii–xxix; Smith, 1925, pp. 147–149; Hutton, 1949, p. 26; and Leach, 1949, pp. 26–28.

[21] Elevations are given in round numbers. The forest limit varies from some 9,000 feet to about 12,000 feet; the upper limit of plant growth lies, variably, above those elevations; and some sweet potato gardens are planted above 9,000 feet. The upper limit of sweet potato production apparently has not been reached in many localities, but elsewhere the occurrence of frost is sufficiently frequent and severe to put a ceiling on the upward shift of gardens. Little can be said, reliably, for the upper limits of other domestic plants in highland New Guinea, or for the temperature patterns that control the common planting of such crops. Protected sites are utilized by shifting cultivators for particular crops from the lowlands into the higher highlands. See Williams (1928) for a coastal-piedmont plain pattern with taro and sago dominant; Lawrence (1955) for an inland locality between 1,500 and 3,000 feet, with taro dominant, yams, sweet potatoes, bananas, and sugarcane complementary; Williams (1940) for an inland area at about 2,600 feet, with sweet potatoes and taros the staples; Bjerre (1956) for a locality ranging upward

The anomaly lies in how and when the sweet potato became the staple crop-diet commodity at higher elevations. With the evolution of the crop-diet pattern has gone a marked change in the technology of cropping. Trenching for drainage, piling of dirt into raised beds, composting of plant materials, and other minor technological features of the highland cropping pattern are not typical of general shifting cultivation.[22] The whole cultural complex is so atypical of shifting cultivation that recently some students of the upland pattern have been seeking another framework for descriptive analysis which lies outside that normally employed for shifting cultivation.[23] If the sweet potato is considered solely a post-Columbian introduction, there is almost too short a time span remaining in which the evolution of the culture complex, and the populating of the most heavily inhabited part of New Guinea, could take place. Considering the sweet potato as a pre-Columbian, Pan-Pacific, tropic-littoral plant still does not explain its evolution as the basic staple of the New Guinean interior highlands.

The Annual Cropping Cycle and the Starvation Period

As suggested earlier, the seasonal control of cropping is chiefly a function of the timing of the dry season and the onset of rains in the main wet period. This working generalization, however, fails to apply around the Tibetan border, and begins to fail in the uppermost cropping zones in interior New Guinea.[24] The generalization also fails to be useful in the perennially wet areas where no significant dry season occurs, and in those unique spots so wet that burning cannot be done.

Most of the chief low mountain regions that have seasonal patterns are in the Northern Hemisphere, and the largest number of localities experience their dry season during the months from October to April. There is some correlation of cool season with dry season, though it is not very clear in regions where the hottest weather comes just before the rains. Classification of such data produces only a gross picture of climatic sequences, providing little more than a rough time chart for the annual cycle of operations and yielding little to any real analysis of the

---

from 4,000 feet, with the sweet potato a staple but taro, sugar cane, and bananas complements; Meggitt (1957) for a group resident at about 4,000 feet, with taro and yam gardens below that as complementary, sweet potato gardens above the villages producing the staple food, and sugarcane, pandanus, and bananas grown in the more protected sweet potato gardens as complements; Blackwood (1939) for a group resident between 4,000 and 6,000 feet, growing sweet potatoes as the staple, taro, yams, and sugarcane as subsidiaries, and European vegetables for occasional use or for sale to Europeans; Luzbetak (1958), Reay (1959a, b), and Gitlow (1947) for the main Wahgi Valley at about 5,000 feet, growing some sixty-five varieties of sweet potatoes as the staple, and bananas, sugarcane, pandanus, maize, and New Guinea asparagus as complementary; Meggitt (1956) for the upper Wahgi and surrounding areas up to 8,500 feet, with sweet potatoes the staple affected by frosts at upper levels, a little taro in protected spots, poor pandanus and sugarcane, and now taking to European cabbage and white potatoes as very applicable; Goodenough (1953) for a group living west of the upper Wahgi at 7,500-9,000 feet, growing sweet potatoes, a little sugarcane, and some cane grass.

[22] See Brass (1941), Nilles (1943, 1953), Gitlow (1947), Luzbetak (1958), Brown and Brookfield (1959), Brookfield and Brown (1963), and Salisbury (1962) for descriptions of upland garden technology and for comments on land control.

[23] Brown and Brookfield, 1959; Brookfield, 1962; Brookfield and Brown, 1963.

[24] Along the Tibetan border zone of India, Burma, and China, cropping becomes distinctly a seasonal matter through temperature controls, and the sequence is similar to that of the mid-latitudes to a considerable degree. For the higher elevations of New Guinea there are seasonal records of frosts, but the regional patterns of wet and dry seasons are complex, according to the local dominance of the southeast trades or the northern control of air masses. Double maxima occur in some areas, and generalized controls resemble those of tropical highlands more than those of the mid-latitudes (Brookfield, 1962).

annual cycle. Mapping the timing of regional variations in this annual climatic cycle produces far too many details for demonstration on a map to go with this study, besides being of doubtful utility.

Timing the annual cycle is useful in getting a picture of the activity pattern for a particular people. It helps to locate the pressure points of labor intensity— activity in cropping, hunting, fishing, and collecting wild commodities; relaxed intervals for feast giving, visiting neighbors, trip taking, and house building; periods of food scarcity; and the like. These data, however, are useful chiefly in comparing the life patterns of different cultures, and they do not contribute markedly to any critical evaluation of shifting cultivation within a culture beyond a certain point. Therefore, no detailed analysis of the annual cycle is made for different areas. Certain broad conclusions may be drawn from examination of the annual cycle, and these will be considered.

Common to all areas practicing shifting cultivation is the annual or periodic pattern of site selection, clearing, drying, burning, recleaning and second-burning, fencing, planting, weeding, watching, and selective harvest, with technological variations in the details and timing of these operations. In regions where the dry season is long, the timing may be stretched out for selection, clearing, drying, and burning, whereas in regions with a short and uncertain dry season, the whole task must be concentrated and is a pressure point for labor application. These variations are repeatedly dealt with in the literature on local areas.[25] There is a gross similarity in these patterns which does suggest that all shifting cultivation is alike, but such a conclusion is really no more justified than is the generalization that since American agriculture has a periodic cycle of ground preparation, fertilizing, planting, cultivating-weeding, and harvest, all American agriculture is essentially alike.

More effective distinctions of the annual cycle result from examination of the cropping patterns that accompany shifting cultivation. It is fairly clear that shifting cultivators who depend on taros as their staple food supply have an annual cycle of operations which is very different from that of those people who grow rice as their staple.[26] Among many taro growers, all the operations of the annual cycle

---

[25] For acute observations see Freeman (1955) for west central Borneo; Conklin (1957) for the central Philippines, where burning-planting periods are July–August and April–June, respectively; Judd (1964) for northern Thailand; and Watters (1960) for a general discussion of annual cropping cycles. Most of the references cited dealing with a specific people contain discussions of such cycles.

[26] Compare the annual cropping cycle on the Huon Gulf coast of northeastern New Guinea (with five or six taro gardens kept going the year around, taro eaten every day of the year, clearing and planting done off and on all year long, taro planted on marshy flat soils during the dry season from March to July, and on the sloping or sandy soils during the wet season; taro harvestable from the sixth to the tenth month after planting; about twenty minor crops, of which manioc and coconut are the chief ones, with manioc being fed to the pigs most of the year and eaten by humans only during the occasional bad years; normal steady surplus of food, with some taro spoiling in the gardens off and on all year; yams and sweet potatoes not liked and grown only as minor variety crops; see Hogbin, 1951), with that of the Land Dyak and the Iban of Sarawak, Borneo (clearing of new fields from June to early August, burning done in August or by early September, planting completed by early October, harvest completed between late March and mid-May; rice in a single seasonal planting the backbone of cropping, with eight or ten other crops minor and not even complementary; dietary based strongly on rice; in hunger period scavenging of the forest for anything edible; starvation periods of serious proportions infrequent, but common enough to be a threat and a constant worry; dietary sufficiency for the year also dependent upon the successful storage of rice yield throughout the year; see Freeman, 1955, and Geddes, 1954a). In 1947 the Huon Gulf coast was unusually wet, with no dry season, so that the

seem to be carried out during every month of the year, and the cycle, therefore, is one pertaining to a particular plot of ground only. Operations are so spaced that the harvest period reaches right around the calendar year. In good years, then, there is no really distinct cropping cycle, and there is no hunger period. Extraordinary natural calamities, tribal wars, and such phenomena are all that disturb the pattern of production and the harvest of food supply. This noncyclic planting and harvest around the year has become the stock description for tropical shifting cultivation.

The annual cycle for the growers of rice, pulses, seed-bearing legumes, and other seed-planted crops is much more specific. Seed-producing plants are far more responsive to delicate patterns of seasonlity than are tuber, rhizome, and rootstock crop plants. Cropping practice has concentrated upon the single planting period for seed-planted crops. This concentration has produced a single, specific annual cycle which requires that all clearing, burning, planting, weeding, watching, and harvesting be done within a relatively short period at their proper time during the year. This annual cycle correlates with climatic seasonality by concentrating upon the best dry period for burning, with planting occurring in the following rainy period. The Iban of Borneo have an annual cycle as closely timed as that of the spring wheat planters of Canada, and abnormal weather can disturb the one as severely as the other. This fact of seasonality has been overlooked in the normal description of shifting cultivation as a timeless phenomenon of the tropics.

To an extent, some tuber planters have produced an annual cropping cycle that is specific and is tied to fairly precise timing for the operational sequences.[27] Such are the yam planters of the Trobriands, who have selected their planting stock for storage qualities and have concentrated their cropping cycle into one annual planting of yams. Trobriand Islanders, however, also grew taro in largely noncyclic patterns; Malinowski has noted that clearing, burning, and planting go on in May–June, July–August, October–November, and February–March. He has also observed that taro was a more ancient staple crop than yams, thus indicating an increasing tendency toward a cyclic pattern in crop growing. In the Solomons on Malaita (Mala) Island, one crop a year with some eightly varieties of yams was the rule during the 1920's; and on the small island of Ulawa to the southeast, two crops, one primary and one early and small, were the rule. On Ulawa, plantings were some months later than on Malaita, a change to which yams seemingly had become adjusted.[28]

The primary conclusions concerning the annual cropping cycle are: (1) that tuber, root, rhizome, and rootstock planters in areas without strong climatic seasonality appear to have a repeating cycle of cropping operations staggered around the year so that harvesting is relatively continuous and there are no marked

---

lowland flats were too flooded for planting, and all planting had to be done on slope fields; there was, however, no real scarcity. In 1949 Borneo suffered an erratic season, with continuous rain from August 14 to Setpember 12, at what should have been the best dry period. Poor burning was done in desperation on September 15, planting was late, and the crop year was a mediocre one. No real starvation was in sight for the spring of 1950, but careful budgeting of rice dietary consumption was necessary to avoid such a period. See also the calendar sequence itemized in note 33, chapter 3, above, for the Lamet of Indochina, who have a distinctly cyclic single cropping pattern based primarily on rice as a staple. Judd (1964) presents an annual work Calendar for northern Thailand.

[27] See Malinowski, 1935, vol. 1.
[28] See Ivens, 1927.

periods of hunger or starvation; and (2) that shifting cultivators who have discarded tubers, roots, rhizomes, and rootstock crops in favor of seed-planted grains, pulses, grams, seed legumes, and seed-sown vegetables have become distinctly seasonal in their cropping cycle, and suffer periods of want, hunger, and starvation when the annual weather cycle is bad. Peoples who combine vegetative-planted and seed-planted crops have alternative sources of food and do not necessarily suffer a hunger period. Their cropping patterns as punctuated both by distinct seasonality and by more widely distributed operations. Peoples such as the canarium nut gatherers, who combine the gathering of wild nuts and fruits with cropping patterns, are seasonally dependent upon the ripening period of these items.[29] A larger and larger sector of shifting cultivation in this part of the world is taking on the specific seasonal operating, cycle, in that the seed-planted patterns of southern and eastern Asia have become more widespread than the vegetative-planted patterns.

The Gathering of Plant Products

No detailed discussion of plant gathering is presented here, either regionally or by culture groups, but certain generalizations and conclusions must be noted. It is obvious from the literature that every group of shifting cultivators draws a portion of its sustenance, tool materials, fibers, medicines, ritual materials, insecticides, and poisons from the wild plant world of the surrounding forest. Many groups also draw cash-sale products from this reservoir. There can be no finite measures for the proportionate shares of such materials, but they amount to an economically significant volume in the course of the year.[30] In times of strain, when cropping patterns go bad, the wild resource may be relied upon almost entirely for short or long periods of the year. In some groups, at lower levels of cropping ability, this dependence is close to balancing the amount of produce harvested from planting, whereas some groups more accomplished in planting rely on wild produce only for the trimmings of their economy, in the normal course of events.

The significance of one aspect of appropriation from the wild resource is seldom pointed out. This is the presence of feral plant stocks on lands undergoing vegetative regeneration where a repeating crop cycle is employed over the same lands at intervals of eight to fifty years. Very seldom is every root, tuber, banana, fruiting shrub, herb, or other economic plant removed from an old garden before the land is returned to regeneration, even though it may be the practice to let pigs scavenge the plot. Many of these items "go wild," or become feral, with some ease for a period of a few years and maintain themselves in a plant cover that has not yet reached multicanopied layers of small and large trees by the time the plot is again

[29] On Wogeo Island, in the eastern Schouten Islands, off the Sepik River mouth in northeastern New Guinea, at latitude about 3° S., the harvest season for canarium almonds normally runs from mid-April through June, with a lull in late May, (Hogbin, 1938, p. 131). In the Solomon Islands, less than 5 degrees further south, the harvest season falls in late July and August (Ivens, 1927, pp. 367–369). These differences in fruiting and harvest periods in the tropics are often overlooked in the matter of tropical planting. For a discussion of seasonality in fruiting patterns in the tropics which counters the general tone of nonseasonality, see Spencer (1959b).

[30] Under ordinary circumstances the observer of local life has no effective opportunity to measure the variety and the volume of food materials or of other resources gathered from the surrounding ranges, and I know of no study that has been able to arrive at such a measure. Fox (1952) did conclude that about 50 per cent of the subsistence of the Philippine Pinatubo Negrito was derived from the sweet potato, and about 14 per cent from maize, but that fishing, hunting, and gathering were still critical, that about 450 plants entered into Pinatubo usages, and that these Negrito, who had recently begun to grow plants, were not yet really crop producers.

cleared. Many items are purposely planted in regenerating ranges for the very purpose of providing reserve gathering resources.[31] People who gather "wild" products from the surrounding forest often are not gathering truly wild plants, but only the feral reproductions of domestic plants they themselves planted at an earlier time. Particularly is this true of vegetatively reproduced plants, but it also applies to fruit trees.

In the discussions of many vegetatively reproduced plants, it is hard to determine whether domestic plants become feral or whether nondomesticated plants are purposely grown in planted gardens. "Wild bananas" are frequently referred to as being gathered, but it is somewhat doubtful whether, in the whole of southern and eastern Asia and the island realm, there are many truly wild bananas that yield a fruit that can be eaten with any real profit.[32] In references to growing such plants as cane grass and New Guinea asparagus in gardens and gathering them from the forest, it is uncertain whether domesticated plants or wild ones are under discussion. When a young canarium almond tree, spared in the clearing of a garden site, profits from the increased growing opportunity, the ash leached into the soil, and the disruption of the surface soil around it, should it be thought of as a domesticated tree, a feral tree, a semidomesticate, or a wild tree? When it becomes privately owned and is protected from harm, has its status changed? Conklin wisely differentiates among cultigens, cultivates, domesticates, first-degree semidomesticates, second-degree semidomesticates, and nondomesticates in dealing with plant production and procurement on Mindoro Island in the Philippines.[33]

It is clear that almost all the seed-planted full domesticates, both those normally labeled cultigens and those that may be labeled cultivates, do not survive well in the vegetative growth on garden plots returned to the regenerative cycle. As the peoples of southern Asia have shifted their attention from vegetatively reproduced tubers, roots, rhizomes, and rootstock crop plants to seed-planted crop plants, there has been an eventual decline in volume and frequency of vegetatively reproduced plants in the forest and the appropriative reserves of uncropped lands.[34] In time this may affect the degree of support available from noncultivated areas, despite the fact that the ecological environment is one making for rapid plant growth. Therefore, it is reasonable to suggest that the peoples of many parts of New Guinea

---

[31] See the various indications of this in Conklin, 1957, pp. 86–87, 110, 123–126, 133–138, 152–153.

[32] Simmonds, 1959, pp. 66–71.

[33] Conklin, 1957, p. 44. Essentially his definitions were: *cultigen:* a plant fully dependent upon man for survival; *cultivate:* plant requiring special treatment but not necessarily artificial propagation; *domesticate:* any plant that at any time is artificially propagated rather than depending upon purely wild reproduction; *first-degree semidomesticate:* wild plant specifically preserved and protected when clearing for new cropping because of its utility to man; *second-degree semidomesticate:* wild plant not preserved or protected when clearing for new cropping, but not otherwise intentionally killed; *nondomesticate:* plant that is neither protected, saved, planted, nor specially considered in any way that would affect its reproduction rates. These terms are not always used as a botanist might use them, but the botanist seldom considers the degree of relationship to man so carefully as Conklin has. The recognition of these varying degrees of relationship to man is an important element in understanding the processes of plant domestication which too often have been discussed as a single operation.

[34] This conclusion is stated in broad, general terms for the long term. It is obvious that in the last century or two the Hanunóo (described by Conklin, 1957) have not let their wild plant environment decline markedly. Other peoples also are careful in these matters when their cultures are stable, but a group undergoing disintegration and cultural change may not be so efficient. It is the periods of culture change, particularly those related to cropping patterns, which permit the degrading of the plant environment.

and other parts of Melanesia have a richer reserve of wild plant growth upon which to draw than do some of the peoples of south China or India. No flat generalization is possible, therefore, concerning the degree to which any given people may depend upon the gathering of wild plant resources.

The degree of degrading in the wild vegetative range is a final factor to be taken into account in the amount of appropriative plant resources that can be drawn from the surrounding plant ranges. In regions where clearing of the land is sufficiently slow to allow land to return to mature, canopied forest, such forest probably supplies less usable plant resources than does the less mature vegetation. At the other extreme is the vegetative cover that has degraded into bamboo-and-grass thicket, grass and pyrophytic perennial trees and shrubs, or the grassland association that is dominated by cogon, alang-alang, and lalang grasses.[35] Though some of these grasslands may supply abundant animal resources, they yield but little edible plant food. Contrary to the impression given by many Occidentals that natives pay no attention to the spread of grasslands, most integral shifting-cultivator groups are very conscious of this threat. They fear it and attempt to restrain the spread of grass-dominant vegetational associations because they are aware that the spread threatens not only their own reuse of the land for cropping but the food yield available through gathering.

There are few data that are useful in comparing possible returns from plant appropriation activities today with those of any given period in the past. So little is known of the history of vegetative change that the definition of "forest primeval" is impossible. In no area of southeastern Asia below the upper altitudinal limit of agriculture can it be certainly stated that a forest primeval still exists in which to attempt an assessment of resources useful in a combination of shifting cultivation and range appropriation.[36] It is likely, in view of the whole effect of man upon the increasing productivity of plants from which the domesticates have been drawn, that the "rainforest primeval" was less productive than the third- or fourth-growth forests. In the present state of assessment of vegetative ranges, however, this must remain a matter of speculation. In some areas it is quite possible that the resources available today in regenerated forest ranges are greater than those of any earlier period, but it is certain that the resources to be culled from the degenerated forest ranges of some zones now are considerably less than the volume obtained in times past.

UTILIZATION OF ANIMAL, BIRD, AND AQUATIC RESOURCES

The information on animal, bird, and aquatic foods and materials is far more scarce, sporadic, and nonsystematic than that on plant foods. Although the discussion on utilization of wild resources should properly be separated from that on

---

[35] Several genera and species are involved, chiefly *Imperata* spp. *Saccharum* spp., and *Themeda* spp., but in particular localities other grasses and other kinds of plants have become similar pests.

[36] Because Australian observers feel that there is little unclaimed land in New Guinea, one might believe that most of the territory has been significantly altered as to its vegetative composition (see Australian Department of External Territories, 1958). Harrison, curator of the Sarawak Museum, has stated verbally that he believes the central interior of Borneo has never been worked over by shifting cultivators, and that only a thin scattering of sago-extracting collectors occupied the interior until at least the last thousand years. It may well be that some areas are not worked over sufficiently to alter the basic yield pattern of usable products, but for the broad range of territory covered in this study I stand by my textual statement.

domestic resources, the useful data are insufficient to support two separate discussions, and the subject is treated as a whole in this section. There is frequent mention of hunting, for example, but the comment too often turns out to be that special dogs are kept for hunting, that hunting is no longer so productive as it once was, or that hunting is done in the slack seasons. The comments on fishing frequently point out that the returns are meager, that certain kinds of nets or spears are used, or that fishing is an important complement to the economy. There often is mention of chickens around villages, but no comment as to why they are there, or whether the hens ever lay eggs. There are comments about pigs, that is, that wild pigs are numerous and require that gardens be fenced, that the village sows breed with wild boars in the forest, or that pork is eaten primarily during festival periods. There may be a detailed description of the religious rite accompanying the slaughter of a mithan bull, but no comments as to what was done with the carcass afterward.

It is clear that in the Australian life zone the wallaby, phalanger, cassowary, tree rat, and varied marsupials are sought, whereas in the island section of Melanesia the shark, palolo worm, turtles, and many localized fishes and shellfishes replace the bird and animal populations of the Australian zone. Similarly, in the Southeast Asian portion of the oriental life zone, various deer, bear, "wild cattle," jungle fowl, and pheasants are special forms sought. Groups that have an animal totem never eat their totem. Elderly people have fewer taboos than do younger people. Many groups are almost omnivorous (whatever that may mean), whereas some groups have specific taboos not common to neighboring groups. Every group utilizes wild animal, bird, and aquatic resources. The processes of acquiring wild foods range from casual activity to formal group hunting with fire, or with dogs, or with specific trap lines. The acquisitive process is primarily a male activity, except for the securing of relatively immobile forms of food such as colonies of grubs from rotten logs. Among some groups the regular hunting of larger animals is done primarily to restrict the population of animal predators who prey on gardens, the meat supply secured being a secondary consideration rather than a primary aim. The volume secured ranges from casual amounts at random periods to staple dependence upon such foods for significant periods by groups that regularly make crop growing their primary activity. For the less accomplished groups of crop growers, of course, the acquisition of animal foods may at all times provide a significant share of the dietary.

An interesting question, on which there is very little evidence at present, relates to the relative density of wildlife in regions little occupied by shifting cultivators, in regions where shifting cultivators never allow land to reach an old, mature state of vegetative regeneration before recropping it, and in occupied regions where hunting is a frequent complementary occupation. Was the primordial wildlife population heavy, and did man only reduce it? Did the presence of feral plant cultivates provide an enlarged food supply in the regenerating forest, and did the presence of gardens afford predators a food supply that tended to increase their numbers? There is reference in the literature to the slight need for fencing against predators in mature forest regions very scantily occupied by shifting cultivators, and to the increasing need for fencing and protective hunting when the human population increases. There also is reference to protective hunting, as mentioned above, and to the small yield of game in areas long occupied by a dense population that has overhunted the ranges. The historic significance of the above questions cannot be answered here, but the implications suggest a wide range in the volume of wild meat supply potentially available to a group of shifting cultivators.

The use of animal products from domestic animals is considerable among some groups and insignificant among others, depending upon two factors of control: (1) the number and variety of domestic animals normally kept by the group, and (2) the variety and seriousness of the religious rites that govern the use made of animal products. Many groups on the mainland and in some of the islands keep mithan cattle, but few use such cattle for purposes other than social status, religious rituals, or ceremonial eating. More groups keep chickens and dogs, for several purposes. There are widespread and numerous ritual uses of the chicken, but there is little evidence as to whether more chickens are expended upon ritualism (and not eaten afterward) than go directly into the domestic cooking pot, and there is little specific information on the use of eggs. The dog is trained as a watchdog by some groups and tolerated as an "announcer of strangers" by others. It is permitted scavenging rights and never fed by some groups, whereas others breed, train, feed, and give privileged household status to dogs. Some groups keep both scavenging dogs and hunting dogs. Dogs are very widely eaten, but little is known about how such dogs are maintained. Dogs enter into ritualism among some groups, but not among others. Some groups apparently raise dogs to sell to other groups for varied purposes.

Goats, sheep, and horses have sporadic distribution among the somewhat higher levels of shifting cultivators, and utilization of each is variable, ranging from ritualistic to commercial purposes. Some meat from one or more of these animals is eaten, but the picture in the literature is exceedingly spotty. In general, these animals are more common on the Asiatic mainland and in the Lesser Sunda Island zone than elsewhere. The keeping of cattle, in the ordinary sense of the term, is not practiced to any extent by integral shifting cultivators themselves, but cattle keeping is often present within the range of territory utilized by shifting cultivators.[37] This is particularly notable in parts of India, in the Philippines, and in the Lesser Sunda Islands, where landlords of permanent-field agriculture, local chiefs or rajahs, and modern "landed gentry" coming into frontier regions acquire and keep herds and sell off numbers of cattle that are run on the lands under regeneration for the later use of shifting cultivators.

The pig is the animal reported to be most commonly in use by shifting cultivators. The ritualism that surrounds this animal makes it exceedingly difficult to measure its significant contribution to the dietary. Some groups kill predatory will pigs, by various devices, and eat them as often as possible without ritualism. while

---

[37] The frequent comment that a people "keep cattle" is an indadequate indication of the role of cattle in the culture, and the loose generalization as to whether a group belongs to the "cattle people" or not is almost meaningless, in the economic sense. The ritualistic practice of keeping a few head of the specialized breed of cattle (known as "mithan" in East Asian anthropological literature) so that bulls may be sacrificed on appropriate occasions is a very different thing from keeping cattle for meat, for hides, for regular sale, and for simulation of the socioeconomic status pattern of true cattle raisers. Much study is needed on the full socioeconomic significance of cattle keeping, and the picture for much of southern and eastern Asia is very unclear. See Simoons (1961) for a general discussion of the uses of selected animal foodstuffs.

at the same time keeping domestic pigs which are eaten only at seasonal festivals. Elaborate ceremonies having economic exchange rationale, social significance, and traditional religious ritualism accompany the distribution and eating of pork at such times. Some groups apparently distinguish between wild and domestic pig stock only by the criterion that those that can be rounded up and returned to villages at night are domestic.[38] Suckling of wild shoats secured at a distance and later feeding and pampering the young pigs turns them into domestic stock. A contemporary gradation in the keeping, hunting, ritual use, and dietary significance of the pig from west to east has resulted from the impact of Hinduism Buddhism, and Mohammedanism upon the religious mores, economic habits, and ritual practices of shifting-cultivator groups in India, Ceylon, Burma, Thailand, Malaya, and the western sector of Malaysia. In India some groups no longer keep domestic pigs or eat domestic pork, but they hunt and eat wild pigs in hunger periods, at which time the social mores are temporarily waived. The complicated socioeconomic patterns of pig keeping, pig exchange, and pig festivals make a simple analysis in terms of occidental economics almost impossible on the basis of present information.

There is little merit in listing animal resources derived or utilized with the aim of extracting a conclusion therefrom as to the significance of animal foods or materials in the dietary or the economy. Nevertheless, an effort is made in Appendix E to indicate the regional variety that *is* reported as present in some way. The very sketchiness of the list serves to indicate the kind of record that is needed to produce an effective analysis of the role of animal husbandry and hunting and fishing in the livelihood patterns of shifting cultivators.

Several conclusions may be drawn from the literature. First, there is need for much closer examination of the role of animals in the culture of shifting cultivators. This requires not only careful ethnozoological fieldwork of a kind not done in the past, but also careful recognition of the distinctions between wild and domestic animal populations. It also presupposes the recognition that different hierarchies of shifting cultivators vary in their degree of dependence upon animals. Second, it is clear that in some areas wild animal resources have declined because of excessive exploitation without any balancing increase in domestic animal resources. Third, it is clear that religious patterns of control, reaction, and motivation very strongly affect utilization of animal products almost everywhere. Certain of these patterns are more strongly operative in the western than in the eastern part of the region, but other patterns today are more commonly present in the eastern zone, with no evidence of ever having been present farther west. Finally, it is apparent that animal resources play a much greater role in the total, economy

---

[38] The pig is listed in Appendix E under one species only. The attempt to further distinguish species and subspecies of old races and varieties of pigs, for a study at this level, is unnecessary. Various species are named for various localities, but identifications often are suspect. In some areas, no doubt, long breeding histories have produced distinct races. The introduction of new breeding stock from Europe and China has altered many of these patterns within recent periods. There is some question as to the taxonomic variety for all the old pig stock in southern Asia, and the issue is beyond the range of this study. The pig seems peculiarly susceptible to taming or domestication when secured young and fed and kept in or near human living quarters. Fresh research on southern Asian pigs seems called for. See Brookfield and Brown (1963, pp. 58–59, 63–64, 94–96) for a discussion of the pig ceremony, and Salisbury (1962), for a discussion of the economic role of the pig.

of many populations than studies have thus far documented. It would appear that animal resources form a significant complement to the dietary, to the total economy, and to the whole culture of many groups.

THE COMPLEMENTARY ECONOMY OF INTEGRAL SHIFTING CULTIVATORS

The literature on shifting-cultivator societies frequently refers to the sale, exchange, barter, or giving of items, commodities, products, and materials. These references are often casual, and sometimes are entered chiefly to record an interesting social practice rather than to assess economic significance. Integral shifting cultivators are supposed to operate a subsistence economy, self-contained, self-productive, and self-sufficient, apart from the surrounding economic world. To deny, however, that the Iban of Sarawak or the Tanga of the Bismark Archipelago have an "economics" of some regional significance is to ignore one of the elements of interregional exchange.

The fact that the Iban of Sarawak grows rubber to sell to Chinese traders who travel the rivers of the region as rubber buyers has economic repercussions. The Iban today buy shotguns and shells with which to reduce the predator population threatening their gardens. They also buy brass gongs, pottery jars, textiles, iron tools, and an occasional outboard motor, kerosene, and a wide variety of other products. They sell their rice surpluses, and they regularly harvest from the forest such items as jelutong, rattan, gutta-percha, illipe nuts, and various gum-resinous products, a large share of which they sell on the world market via itinerant traders. Iban families who are "wealthy" in pottery jars, brass manufactures, and similar accumulated capital will, in bad years, dispose of some of their wealth in return for rice, textiles, tools, medicines, and sundries. Even from offhand references to such subjects, it seems that the matter of "subsistence economy" is somewhat suspect.[39]

The recency of this contemporary trade pattern is seriously to be doubted if one reads the early history of oriental trade. Indian traders have frequented the waters of western Malaysia for more than 2,000 years, and Chinese traders have voyaged south for 1,500 years. The ranks of Polynesian, Melanesian, Micronesian, and other "sea-gypsy" voyagers in the waters of the Indian and South Pacific oceans reach back into prehistory. Products like false dragon's blood, gharuwood, sandalwood, beeswax, ivory, sapanwood, various camphors, dammar, and tortoise shell, to say nothing of the common spices, pepper, nutmeg, and cloves, have come from jungles and beach fronts into trading stations for scores of centuries.[40] Chiefly these have been the forest products that lie beyond the subsistence level of foods and medicine. They were secured from the appropriative ranges by shifting cultivators who disposed of them to traders who had ventured out from permanent towns, ports, and marts of trade into the hinterlands. Most of them have always been secured as wild products by groups of shifting cultivators who knew their own home ranges and

---

[39] In most descriptive studies of local regions or culture groups the notes on trade are scattered throughout the text, almost as incidental comments. Many such studies assert on one page that the group practices a subsistence economy, and on another page state that the production of a cash crop is important (see, for example, Freeman, 1955, pp. 103–108).

[40] See almost any account of a trading voyage to the East in the sixteenth, seventeenth, or eighteenth century for references to various of these products; see Wheatley (1959) for notations and distributional maps on some of them in earlier centuries.

produced items when the prices were favorable, when the buyers were traveling, and when there was something to be had in return.[41]

The very existence of cowrie-shell money among interior New Guinea folk, whose trading is sometimes described as ritual exchange focused upon the pig and the festival banquet, belies the fact of no other exchange. There is an old trade pattern in fish, salt, shell products, and lowland plant products which moves inward from productive New Guinea coasts and rivers. Islanders have been voyaging, and trading their surpluses for their scarcities. Out of the higher Himalayan country has long come a varied list of products scarce in the lowland to be exchanged for lowland items. Although the Lamet now sell bear gallbladders, rice, and other products for old city clothing, old bottles, and other things, they doubtless sold bear gallbladders for other products a thousand year ago. Pearls now are secured by European pearl buyers who pay cash money to Trobriand Islanders for their labor in what is termed "commercial pearling," but pearls are an old product here and flowed into trade patterns in this part of the world long before the European buyer arrived.[42]

The modern era, of course, has given a broader base to the complementary economy of shifting cultivators. Some of the best forestry employees, hired for cash wages by governments and by logging concessionaires, are shifting-cultivator folk who are well acquainted with the flora and its growing habits. Work on road construction, airfields, port facilities, building installations, and similar projects supplies a source of income; and growing vegetables for European settlements provides some groups a new source of support. Many such sources of income could be mentioned. Almost every good description of these cultures provides examples of exchange, trade, sale, barter, surplus, and scarcity, but the European conviction that such peoples are backward and self-subsistent has discouraged closer examination of this complementary aspect of their economy, thus providing readers with an incomplete analysis which reinforces the conviction of backwardness and total lack of exchange.

Every shifting-cultivator group possesses a pattern of exchange which complements its economy. Surpluses are disposed of; products, scarce or valuable elsewhere, are extracted from the resource range and traded; local scarcities are traded in when they can be had. Cultural mores being what they are, surpluses, capital, wealth, and property take various forms in different cultures, but all the higher-level hierarchies of integral shifting-cultivator groups have such patterns. The lower the level of culture and the closer it is to a hunting-gathering economy, the fewer the ranges and patterns of this sort; but even the simplest cultures possess some patterns of exchange which complement the economy and broaden the culture pattern of the group. The nature of the complementary elements depends largely

---

[41] The statistically minded geographer and economist may well continue to ignore the growing fact that contemporary customs returns are not compiled for goods moved by small craft, and that the international customs list compresses into the category "not elsewhere specified" a wide range of commodities; the bulk and dollar value data are somewhat concentrated, often into patterns that disguise the full flow of commodities. By choosing only the items with large numbers, the fascination for statistics seems to indicate that more and more of less and less is being traded, though this really is not true. To conclude that prior to the existence of statistical summaries there was no significant trade is equally faulty.

[42] See Austen (1945, pp. 45–46) for a review of modern pearling, ending in a comment that it is a local judgment that the natives, if they decline to produce pearls as desired by Europeans, are lazy.

upon the habitat, its productivity, and its location in relation to coastlines, trading routes, and commercial centers. It is true that the southern mainland of Asia and western Malaysia have lain within an old trade orbit of greater proportions than has interior New Guinea, and that Melanesian trade patterns have involved different patterns from those of the Malabar Coast of India. Nevertheless, the wide range of commodity production and trade is essentially a function of the complementary activities of the traditional shifting-cultivator societies throughout history.

CROP SYSTEMS AND COMPLEMENTARY ECONOMIES OF PARTIAL SHIFTING CULTIVATORS

My primary concern in this chapter has been to deal with integral shifting-cultivator societies and their patterns. There remains the issue of those shifting cultivators who do not form whole societies, as such, but population elements marginal and subordinate to the expansion of sedentary cultivators of permanent-field systems of agriculture. Although the lines of development may be suggested, the extreme variety to be found precludes neat summarization.

The most common aim of the marginal shifting cultivator is to establish a cropping system that will eventually bring him into harmony with the general nature of permanent-field agriculture in the region where he operates. Thus the Filipino who establishes a frontier caingin farm and engages in some version of partial shifting cultivation employs the crops, the tools, the procedures, and the marketing patterns common to his sector of the Philippines. The shifting cultivator in northern Thailand, establishing a frontier farm and using the *tamrai* system, follows the regional patterns for north Thailand; and the rural resident of Ceylon follows other Ceylonese when establishing a chena holding. The Filipino often hopes that he will eventually have a permanent farm with a regular production pattern producing food crops, which can either be eaten or sold, and commercial crops, which yield a monetary return. The Thai hopes eventually to produce a similar pattern of crops, correlated to his marketing zonation, whereas the Ceylonese may consider his chena as complementary to his permanent-field cropping system or to his non-farm job.

Marginal shifting cultivators engage in whatever income-producing activities they can, which are adaptable to their conditions of life. As they do not form integral culture groups with a uniform distribution, level of culture, or pattern of opportunity, the distribution of these activities ranges widely. Anywhere near an urban or marketing center, partial shifting cultivation may follow an almost wholly commercial crop pattern concentrated within a narrow range of crops. Distinctly commercialized shifting cultivation tends toward monocrop specialization, whether it be bananas, cotton, rice, fruits, or vegetables. Distant from urban and marketing centers, crop patterns may remain broad at the start, but often tend to narrow over a period of time as the permanent-field system comes into operation in the locality. Thus the southern Philippine farm shows a steady increase in coconut plantings; the western Malaysian farm increases in rubber tree coverage; the Indian farm may run to pulses, oil seeds, or cotton; and the Ceylon farm may produce curry stuffs, such vegetables as pumpkins and chillies, or such crops as cotton. In some foothill localities, widely distributed, such new crops as cacao, coffee, oil-yielding nut trees, or citrus fruits have recently become popular.

The range of complementary activities among marginal shifting cultivators is extremely broad. They may engage in wage labor on roads, in forests, in mines, or in industrial plants, or in clerical or marketing occupations. They may be associated with permanent-field agriculture on other lands, with wage labor on agricultural plantations, or with activities related to transport systems. They may also be involved in independent extraction of a limited number of forest products. Among many marginal shifting cultivators the annual income from the nonagricultural job away from home may be larger than that from partial shifting cultivation, in which event the partial shifting cultivation really is the complement. Often in this latter pattern there is a sliding-scale situation in which the income or commodity production of the shifting-cultivation farm is quite minor at the start; but as the farm becomes cleared to a greater degree, the income or production rises until finally it may bring a greater return than the original income mainstay. But if this happens, there is every chance that the farm becomes a permanent-field farm in fact, no longer operated in the shifting-cultivation pattern.

There are situations, and regional environmental ecologies, in which some form of partial shifting cultivation seems able to continue as a competitive form of land use. This may or may not be a conclusion derived from looking only at recent and present decades; viewed from long historical perspective, all partial shifting cultivation as herein defined may be temporary and evanescent. Some situational patterns seem to arise from the varied nature of local economy in which modern dollar economics is causally significant.[43] Most such situations either are fairly near urban concentrations, or marketing and shipping centers, or they are scattered along primary transport lines leading to such concentrations and centers. Perhaps Ceylon is the best-known example of that environmental ecology in the dry zone in which partial shifting cultivation seems a constant auxiliary to regular rural and village permanent-field agriculture. The very age and stability of partial shifting cultivation in the dry zone makes most of the textbook generalizations and the "campaign of abolition" allegations relatively untrue. There are other locations of this kind, but they are less well studied and identified.[44]

The hastening retreat of all forms of shifting cultivation in peninsular India has led most regional writers to describe shifting cultivation as residual. Partial shifting cultivation is more widely distributed in the hilly portions of peninsular India than often is recognized. It had become increasingly restricted in the eastern part of south central China, but remained very common in southwest China until

[43] The "market garden" type of agriculture around the urban and marketing centers of some southern Asian cities seems to exemplify these situational patterns. Particularly where rough and hilly areas are not far from market centers, or where tracts still covered by jungle vegetation exist, agriculture has not evolved into intensive and permanent land-use patterns to be equated with occidental patterns of truck and market gardening, but is quite unlike other local regional forms of agriculture. Transport is adequate and price patterns are good, but general land-use development has not yet caught up with the economic pattern. Certainly some of these patterns will prove to be evanescent.

[44] Although I cannot now document this assertion fully it seems likely that parts of the dry zone of Burma would show some resemblances to Ceylon, unless the development of irrigation has altered these patterns. Parts of peninsular India may well contain partial patterns somewhat like those of Ceylon. A few dry-coast areas in the Philippines have resemblances. The Lesser Sunda Islands certainly have localities with similarities. Eastern Java and Madura once had patterns very similar, and some of the older and looser uses of the term *tegal* point in this direction.

the introduction of the Communist pattern of control. On much of the mainland of Southeast Asia partial shifting cultivation is widely scattered around the margins of the lowlands, and extends into the hill country. Partial shifting cultivation also continues to be significant in much of the Philippines. In western Malaysia, outside Java, partial shifting cultivation is spotty but widely distributed, particularly along the coastal fringes of the larger islands. In eastern Malaysia the distribution of partial shifting cultivation is very wide, becoming integral in local patches and island interiors and situational and transitional along coasts and in well-developed islands. On New Guinea there is less partial shifting cultivation, for the integral pattern remains dominant; but with increasing culture change, the partial patterns will increase as the integral forms break down under governmental and missionary pressure to develop permanent-field agriculture. Outside New Guinea, partial shifting cultivation is widely scattered throughout Melanesia, marking a transition to varying forms of permanent-field agriculture; but there are many local variations in the Melanesian pattern.

CHAPTER VII

TECHNOLOGIES, TOOLS, AND SPECIFIC TYPOLOGIES

EARLIEST CROP-GROWING MAN, in any one ecological environment, had available to him a fair body of knowledge incorporated into a series of oral traditions, remembered experiences, concepts, tool systems, procedural methods, known results of things tried, known failures, and known successes. He was aware that environment sometimes fitfully altered its annual weather routine, often to his jeopardy. Living in uncertainty, he invoked the aid of his gods through magic rituals, and he occasionally ventured some new procedure. A few of these ventures paid off in some small improvement in a tool, a procedure, or a plant variety. In time, in different local environments, the cumulative efforts produced systems that were dissimilar. The dissimilarities increased through time as experienced crop growers gained headway and as simple appropriators began to take their first steps in crop growing. Despite the tendency toward equalization through borrowing, the basic variation can only have become greater with the passage of time, producing a wide and varied range of systems of shifting cultivation which does not permit a single simple descriptive analysis. This is why Pelzer sought the broad, inclusive definition and Conklin sought the minimal statement.[1] This is why in the present study I seek a multiple approach and the recognition of multiple levels and varieties of accomplishment through time.

THE ELEMENTS OF TYPOLOGY

In chapter II twenty-six different orders of operational observation are set down which in field examination and literature review appear to have had a bearing upon the full assessment of shifting cultivation. Not all these are, strictly speaking, elements of typology, and the itemization is separated into categories for clearer understanding. In glancing at the elements of morphology which have generally been considered when discussing the nature of shifting cultivation, one notices that only a few stand out in the literature. These may be listed as follows:

1. Site selection processes
2. Clearing procedures used to secure a "field"
3. Burning procedures used to eliminate vegetation
4. Planting procedures employed to get a crop down
5. Weeding procedures employed during the growing season
6. Harvest procedures employed in securing the crop
7. Fallowing system followed after cropping

Not all authors have dealt with these in the same detail, but the list represents the items normally discussed under technology.

There are obvious omissions in such a listing, because every people practicing shifting cultivation does something in the way of appropriative activities such as gathering, hunting, and fishing, and almost every people carries on some procedure designed to yield products that are sold or bartered. The assertion that these are

---

[1] See the two definitions quoted from Pelzer and Conklin in chapter ii.

not part of shifting cultivation per se can only be answered with the observation that shifting cultivation is an integral system that includes cropping, appropriation, and exchange, just as commercial grain farming cannot be fully comprehended without including the sale of the crop, the acquiring of dollars, and the exchange of dollars for consumption goods.

There are still other factors of importance to shifting cultivation which are variably omitted by economists, geographers, botanists, and some agronomists. Such is the factor of ritualism. If it be asserted that ritualism is not properly a typological element in shifting cultivation, the response again must be: Can commercial grain farming in the United States be dealt with effectively if ritualism is omitted? The answer is obvious, but this points out an important difference between contemporary American agriculture and integral shifting cultivation.[2] The secularity of American agriculture is notable in the twentieth century, as opposed to traditional crop growing in many other parts of the world. The very volume of religious ritualism employed in integral shifting cultivation is one of its outstanding characteristics. There are, however, significant variations in the application of ritualism among shifting cultivators, making the comparative study of ritual a very useful tool to the investigator. In much the same way several other features frequently omitted in the discussion of shifting cultivation are actually useful diagnostic tools in the comparative study of the system in general.

It appears reasonable, then, to suggest that the simple list of seven elements given above is inadequate for a full analysis of shifting cultivation, and that any full typological analysis of the whole system of shifting cultivation must involve at least the following elements if it is to be complete.

1. Site selection: topography, soil, drainage, and plant cover
2. Land clearing: cutting, lopping, grubbing, saving of trees
3. Burning: elimination of dried vegetation, disposal of ash
4. Fencing protection: fences, traps, snares, watch procedures
5. Planting: method, order, timing, sex division, siting
6. Weeding cultivation: frequency, degree, sex division, efficiency
7. Harvest: method, order, timing, storage, sex division, labor
8. Field shift: pattern, crop to follow, order, frequency, direction
9. Fallowing: timing, nature, control, maturity
10. Land control: nature, agency, control, taxation, time change
11. Residence: place, mobility, grouping, structure, time change
12. Dooryard garden: presence, use, nature, control over, change
13. Tools: number, kind, usage, change, specialization
14. Crop-animal complex: nature, numbers, kinds, use, time change
15. Appropriation: fish, animals, plants, extracts, degree, change
16. Labor: patterns, sex division, timing, payment, time change
17. Ritualism: presence, primary-secondary, control, impact
18. Avoidance-acceptance: taboo nature, type, sex, age, biotic
19. Exchange: nature, amount, kind, role, control, crop yield
20. Consumption: nature, control, commodity, change, degree

My studies of shifting cultivation originally began with a list approximating the standard list of seven items given above, and with the thought that a simple

[2] Although it is possible to make an analytical comparison of American agriculture and shifting cultivation, using American criteria, the full understanding of shifting cultivation necessarily depends on working from the viewpoint of the shifting cultivator, as the two systems are now so dissimilar.

comparative analysis of the crop-growing systems of numerous culture groups might yield a comprehensive understanding of the general system. Even when I began this particular study it seemed possible to construct a relatively simple hierarchical ranking of levels and stages of shifting cultivation. Gradually the significance of numerous other elements and factors became so obvious that the simple hierarchical ranking became a will-o'-the-wisp. Now the only possibility seems to be a series of hierarchical rankings for which culture-group examples could be found. Many culture groups, however, do not fit any single system of ranking. It has become evident that changes within individual systems, from the time of primordial crop growing to the present, have resulted in a mixture of elements of one system with those of another until the simple pattern of generalization now finds many contradictions and anomalies.

In a study such as this there is the danger of overclassifying, of separating related matters into too many categories. Classification for its own sake is not the objective of this study, and the separation of different levels of activity into different categories has the aim only of distinguishing clearly the wide variation that does exist. Fuller understanding of the significance of many of these features may make it possible to simplify the entire classification of shifting cultivation as an integral system.

EVOLUTION AND MIXTURE IN TYPOLOGICAL SYSTEMS

In discussing the evolution and intermixture of structural elements and cultural factors, not every single trait, process, and element can be dealt with fully; only preliminary generalizing can be done. As site selection and processing is a primary matter, this is the first generalization.

SITING, CLEARING AND BURNING

In early chapters I discussed factors influencing selection of sites, processes of clearing, and auxiliary activities carried on during clearing and burning. Here it should be sufficient to construct a hierarchical ranking of different levels of skill exhibited in the whole procedural complex, and to comment briefly on certain aspects of the complex. The following list begins with a very simple procedural aim, but later listings suggest an increasing level of sophistication.

1. Site chosen for pure convenience, being near at hand and possessing cover that can be reduced sufficiently to permit planting amid the debris, with little knowledge of what factors are important to good crop yields. No special tools or procedures employed at any stage.
2. Site chosen with some comprehension of gross situation and with some knowledge that soil, plant cover, and drainage are useful in producing a better yield. Simple burning done but primary clearing very poor, and almost no secondary clearing and cleaning done after burning. No fencing material saved. No special tools involved. Purely random location in reference to previous site.
3. Mature forest site chosen at random because here clearing and burning produce a "field" in which weed growth would be slower than on previously used sites, with "new" soil-ash volume giving improved yields. Clearing tools evolving slightly, but heavy-forest technology barely present. Fencing not preceded by planned selection and saving of material, but some simple fencing done.
4. Mature forest site chosen for its virtues, good clearing tools now present, improved clearing technology includes buttress-platform and key-tree felling. Fencing material selected and saved. Site sometimes contiguous to last location.

5. Mature forest site chosen, using all previous technology, but now using simple criteria of exposure, drainage, surface type, and, to some extent, soil quality.
6. Mature forest site chosen for a new clearing, using all above technology in higher level of sophistication, but reusing the preceding year's best area of clearing for a second cropping.
7. Regenerated site chosen for greater ease of clearing and burning, but now a different technology is used because sites lack mature tree growth. Burning procedure now careful, using cleaning and reburning. Fencing material carefully selected and saved for efficient fencing. Selection now considers differential soil quality of preceding clearing cycle, and makes careful selection based on exposure, drainage, and soil moisture.
8. Regenerated site chosen, using all above technology, and adding avoidance of previous poor sites, knowledge of problems of grasses, and clear recognition of chief factors making for good yields.
9. Site selection based on the criterion of new kind of crop to be grown. Involves recognition of new edaphic and ecologic factors as important to the new crop in site selection. Could involve continuance of older patterns of site selection for older crops still being depended upon.
10. Site selection limited to grass or scrublands, forest lands no longer being available. Experimental techniques for coping with turf, such as turning sod after burn, require development of new tools. Such older technology as proved applicable in selection-clearing processes is still in use.
11. Site selection is on limited area basis after recognition that natural regeneration will not reconstitute soil. Some working and management of the soil under crop is combined with conscious replanting of tree seedlings to assist regeneration.
12. Site selection is on limited area basis, as above, but plot construction by soil working, composting, and other features akin to soil management are also employed.

Although the above list is given in approximate evolutionary order, not all elements could have followed each other in strict sequence in any single area. It may well be that the above list can be better arranged after critical field checking of comparative systems. It is probably true that the borrowing of certain technologies, tools, and procedures by a culture group at one evolutionary stage from a nearby culture group at another stage could have occurred without a wholesale take-over of the whole system of site selection and processing. Although the Pinatubo Negrito of the Philippines use burning techniques in clearing their patches, the Tapiro of western New Guinea do not. Neither the Pinatubo nor the Tapiro use a site-selection and clearing process that can be equated to that of the Lamet of Indochina or the Wogeo Islanders. And the methods of site selection and processing employed by several groups in the Chimbu country of highland New Guinea are far more sophisticated than those of many other well-advanced New Guinea culture groups.

Uncritical site selection must be typical of relatively unskilled shifting cultivators. As shifting-cultivator societies continue their operations, they slowly began to appreciate the numerous criteria involved in site selection and to raise the level of the selective processes. It must be evident that the ancestral forbears of the Lamet, Angami Naga, Wogeo Islanders, and many others, once employed systems of site selection and processing far inferior to those now practiced by their descendants. Variation in these skills, either by means of slow evolution within the group itself, or by means of borrowing that rapidly enhances the home system, is significant in ranking the whole system of crop growing employed by a given people.

One must realize that today many shifting cultivators are no longer free to use all the lands formerly at their disposal; their choice of sites is often severely controlled by alien agencies such as forestry departments, or limited by the encroachment of sedentary cultivators. Such a culture group may well practice a system of expediency in the selection and preparation of sites for planting.

Present data, and my inability to interpret them, probably render the above hierarchical construct somewhat inadequate. A closer analysis of this aspect of the varying systems of shifting cultivation, however, should follow upon the recognition that there are such evolutionary stages represented in site-selection processes among shifting cultivators in the twentieth century, ranging from almost primordial patterns to sophisticated patterns rather close to modern soil management.

FENCING, PLANTING, WEEDING, AND HARVESTING

To many Europeans the procedures involved in planting, weeding, and harvesting have seemed to lack order, timing, rational cause, operational relationships, and considered technological processes. The apparent disorder of the fields has evoked from Occidentals (accustomed to neat, precise, formally arranged field patterns and crop-planting patterns) reactions of distaste which have led to qualitative judgments about shifting cultivation. The practice of mixed planting, with climbing vine-producing plants mixed among grain crops, tall herbs such as bananas, and low-growing herbs is too often taken as a mark of the lowest technological order and as an indication that such cultivators are ignorant of the developed skills of crop growing. Because a Negrito jungle patch is a helter-skelter thing looking little like a one-crop field landscape, and because it is somewhat similar to the mixed plantings of the Angami Naga, the occidental mind apparently assumes that crop growing among all shifting cultivators is of very low quality. The same reaction is elicited by an American vegetable garden in which the gardener has mixed his plantings profusely; in fact the term "tropical jungle" is sometimes applied to such a garden. The evident pleasure of Occidentals at seeing the neat checker boarded, trenched, and nearly monocultured fields of sweet potatoes in highland New Guinea leads them, from the visual impact alone, to the judgment that these gardeners must be of higher quality than most shifting cultivators.

Although many of the jungle patches are indeed primitive, the mixed plantings of many of the higher-level shifting cultivators have rational ecology behind them. Many tropical and subtropical crop plants in their native environments prefer some shade, protection, and "nurse-plant" relationships. Many of them are not adapted to growing in pure stands, fully exposed to the sun. Only selective breeding of special varieties has produced varieties and strains that can tolerate pure-stand plantings. Some such specialized breeding has gone into the development of the many varieties of taros, yams, sweet potatoes, and maniocs. To a more limited degree it is found among the native varieties of bananas and a few other plants. Specialized breeding has also developed varieties of seed-planted crop plants in the central and western sectors, such as the rices, beans, grams, and millets. It is, of course, quite untrue that all shifting cultivators always use mixed planting; many of the more expert groups approximate pure-stand plantings of selected crops.

Cropping technologies of shifting cultivators cannot be blanketed with a single generalization. The planting ecology as well as the production economics of the shifting cultivators of southern and eastern Asia varies widely. The Negrito who clear crude patches and plant a few crop plants to produce a portion of their annual sustenance understand little of cropping technology, and depend rather casually upon the bounty of nature; their cropping technology is of a low order, and they can do little to influence the bounty, or the vengeance, of nature. The Trobriand Islanders, the Wogeo Islanders, the Chimbu, and the Angami Naga operate on a much higher level of technology, using their skills to strive toward a predetermined goal; they must be placed in a very different category of cropping technology.

Fencing has often been described in some detail as an accompaniment of the shifting garden plot. The need for fences varies with the kind, variety, and population of predators, but there is a variability in the technology of fencing which seldom is considered. The fencing technology of the Negrito never becomes skillful, efficient, and really protective, regardless of the need, whereas among some of the advanced shifting cultivators fencing is planned, efficient, and protective, and is employed as an adjunct dveice in securing wild game when the need is present. Considering fencing as necessary, these rough patterns, at least, may be set up.

1. Fences crudely built from casually acquired materials of short durability, using a very simple technology, and achieving a low order of protection.
2. Fences crudely built from materials left after burning, using simple technology, and achieving a fair efficiency.
3. Fencing built of materials selected prior to burning, involving careful construction technology, and achieving rather efficient protection.
4. Fencing built of materials selected prior to burning, involving careful construction technology, achieving efficient protection, but with planned weak points around which game-securing devices are arranged.

Planting procedure varies widely in the purely technogical sense, but it also varies with the nature of the crop. Vegetative planting procedures form one sequence, and seed-planting procedures form quite a different sequence. The tools employed in vegetative planting, however, may be variably employed in seed planting. Seed-planting procedures usually involve some additional tools and may come to employ sets of tools seldom found among vegetative planters. Planting may be simply a matter of getting the roots or seeds into or onto the cleared ground, with little reference to the productive ecology of the site, and among the Raji, the Negrito, and many other groups it is this casual procedure. Among the Lamet, the Wogeo, the Chimbu, and many others, planting involves careful planning of the whole gardening operation with an eye to the ecologic and edaphic values of the precise planting sites.

A preliminary listing of procedural levels suggests the following:

A. Vegetative Planting
1. Random digging of holes into which bits of vegetable material are thrust, with little reference to edaphic considerations, and with fully mixed planting of different kinds of plants.
2. Random digging of holes for planting vegetative materials, with some recognition of need for spacing, provision of poles for climbing items, consideration of nurse-plant relationships, and very simple recognition of edaphic relationships.
3. Planned spacing of holes in which soil is loosened to a depth best for the particular variety of vegetative material, planned provision for any climbers, careful consideration of edaphic needs of variety, the whole garden being planned by edaphic needs of different kinds of plants.

4. Planned planting of particular sites in one-crop patterns, recognizing both kinds of crops and different varieties of each, with full provision for climbers, edaphic needs, soil quality, length of maturation period, and related features.
5. Planned planting on particular sites in one-crop patterns, after full working of soil to provide sites appropriate to particular kinds and varieties of plants.

B. Seed Planting by Dibbling

1. Dibbling of seed in random patterns, using digging stick, with no consideration of edaphic needs for kinds of plants or varieties, with mixed plantings on same general site in random proportions.
2. Dibbling of seed in random patterns, using digging stick, with no consideration of edaphic needs for kinds or varieties of plants, but employing mixed planting in some predetermined proportions.
3. Dibbling of seed in specific patterns determined by edaphic considerations within a general site, achieving mixed planting for the whole plot but separate, precise siting for kinds and varieties of plants.
4. Dibbling of seed in specific patterns resulting in one-crop planting for either or both kinds and varieties of plants, employing full consideration of edaphic needs, soil quality, maturity periods, and related issues.

C. Seed Planting by Broadcasting

1. Simple broadcast of mixed volumes of seed on cleared site prior to rains with no further treatment of soil surface.
2. Simple broadcast of seed on cleared site with casual brushing of surface by a tree branch or some simple device that accomplishes a kind of sweeping action.
3. Broadcast of seed in some predetermined distribution over the site, involving some recognition of edaphic conditions, with some sweeping of the soil surface.
4. Broadcast of seed in some predetermined distribution, approaching one-crop or single-variety plots, and involving careful recognition of edaphic conditions and variable raking with some set of tools specifically devised to improve upon sweeping.
5. Broadcast of seed in planned patterns on soil surfaces dug, worked, formed into beds, or otherwise treated, by hand methods, resulting in planned patterns of one-crop or interplanted sequences, soil raked in some formal manner after planting.
6. Broadcast of seed in planned patterns on fields prepared by plowing with animal-drawn equipment, achieving planned results, and involving some postplanting raking or dragging of the field with animal-drawn equipment.

D. Planting in Dooryard Gardens

1. Casual planting of vegetative materials in sites, beds, and plots with relatively little preparation prior to planting.
2. Careful planting of any materials in prepared beds formally processed prior to planting, with variably involved preparation according to kind and variety of material planted.

This listing of planting patterns has made no attempt to distinguish regional concentrations of the different systems. Until the advent of the European in New Guinea, seed-planting procedures were minimal and vegetative procedures were dominant. The introduction of seed planting of grainlike plants in the western sector may have marked the earliest use of dibbling procedures, but dibbling of seed-planted crops is now rather widespread. The use of broadcast seeding appears primarily in the western zones, as does the employment of animal-drawn equipment. The gradual eastward spread of seeded planting has resulted in a mixture of the planting technologies among certain culture groups; some groups employ several technologies for their garden plots and show various practices in their dooryard gardening. At the present time it is often difficult to judge the level of technology employed in planting procedures, owing to inadequate reporting. It is equally difficult at present to determine comparative advancement among the several technologies employing vegetative planting, seeding by dibbling, and broadcast seeding.

No attempt is made to established any formal ranking of weeding procedures, but there certainly are different technological levels of weeding and caring for the crop during the growing season. Weeding procedures range from casual wandering through the field and occasionally pulling and slashing weeds to regularized procedures carried out sequentially during the growing season. These procedures vary with the crop pattern, and good weeding for a solidly planted rice crop is different from that for a composted sweet-potato bed. Weeding done on the third cropping of a field when it is planted to yams varies markedly from the weeding done during the first cropping when it was planted to rice. Weeding in gardens afflicted with grass intrusion varies markedly from weeding given the first cropping of a plot cleared in mature forest. Since weed growth is one of the essential factors in fields shifting, closer observation is needed on the rates of weed growth, the reproduction of pyrophilous perennials, and the rates of intrusion of grasses and bamboos. The onset and rates of regeneration among wild plants appearing in gardens during the crop year, and during the first year after completion of cropping, is not well known.

Harvesting as a procedure depends significantly on the nature of the crop planting, of course, and the daily plucking of taro from the garden for the daily meal is a different procedure than is the seasonal digging of the yams for storage for the coming months. The tools and procedures of rice harvesting employed by some peoples have been minutely described, for they often exhibit both ritualism and culture-group specialization. The daily plucking of taros, however, receives little comment. The Negrito and other very simple crop growers eat their crops as they ripen, with little attempt at storage. Advanced shifting cultivators, particularly those who have developed seasonal harvest technologies, have very precise methods of harvesting, storage, and preservation, and they have procedures for budgeting the food supply throughout the following season. It cannot be said that grain planters possess a higher technological proficiency in harvesting than do vegetative plant growers, for the procedures of some of the yam growers in New Guinea and farther parts of Melanesia are of a very high order.

Many culture groups growing rice today use rather efficient reaping tools and threshing techniques, whereas others pluck the individual rice heads by hand. When planted rices are mixed as to maturation periods this means for some groups a prolonged harvest season and a rather simple operational procedure. The Iban of Borneo, on the other hand, purposely grow rices of varying maturation periods, being very careful to keep their rices of varying maturity solidly planted in separate fields, and following a precise harvest schedule. Their technology, however, employs women as the rice harvesters, and they pluck each head by hand, using a small knife to cut the stem; harvesting requires 14 to 20 woman-days per acre, which cannot be termed very high technological proficiency.[3]

In summary, it is evident that there are mixed technologies involved in actual crop production. Some producers of very ancient crops have, by today attained a

---

[3] Freeman, 1955, pp. 61–65.

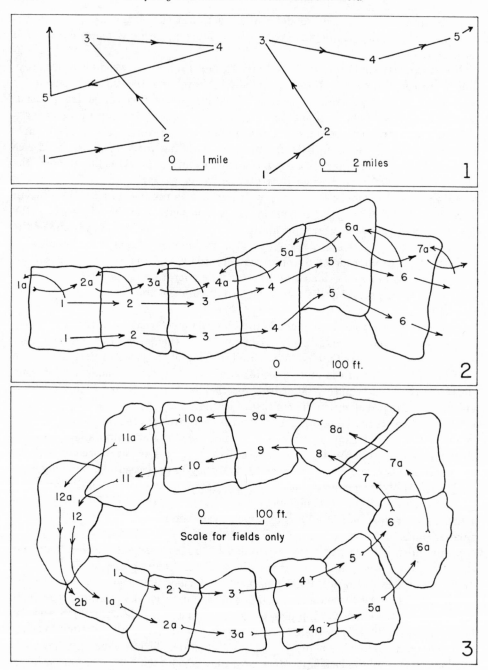

Fig. 6. Field-shift patterns.

rather high order of proficiency in many aspects of their technology, whereas other producers of the same crops have made very little technological progress. Technology originally applicable to ancient crops is being applied to crops of more recent age among the group in question, and low-level technology is being applied by the growers of many relatively young crop plants.

FIELD SHIFT, FALLOW, RESIDENCE, AND THE DOORYARD GARDEN

In the history of truly advanced agricultural practice the resting of a given field, by whatever means, is considered a virtue, a good thing, and a sign of the very advancement that is attributed to such practice. But when observers turn to the consideration of shifting cultivation, resting a field for regeneration of the soil becomes a fault that proves shifting cultivation a poor system that must be improved by making the cultivators crop the same ground every year.

As I stated previously, knowledgeable shifting cultivators do not consider field shifting "abandonment"; such practice is the regenerating, fallowing, and resting of the soil after a period of cropping. Primordial crop-growing man obviously did not know that he was regenerating his soil by moving his crop-plot to another site. It is doubtful that his first cropping efforts really exhaused the soil. It is doubtful that the Zambales Negrito, the Tapiro Pygmy, the Himalayan Raji, and others are sufficiently habituated to crop growing today that they could either truly exhaust the soil or that they could cope with weed growth on a once-cropped plot.

Field-shift patterns are of many kinds, but they may be grouped, conventionally, into the three basic patterns illustrated on the accompanying sketch (fig. 6).[4] First is the random pattern of shift found among the simplest of shifting cultivators, in which succeeding fields are picked by abstruse criteria consisting chiefly of omens and signs (fig. 6, 1). Succession of fields is separated by long distances, as illustrated in the two variations.

The second pattern of field shifting may be described as unidirectional, in that a people moves slowly through a landscape in one predominant direction. Clearing of new fields usually flanks the site of former fields. Such a pattern can be practiced by a considerable population, in company, strung out along an advancing front. This pattern of operation often reduces the forest as it moves, with a succession of parklands, grasslands, and relatively poor vegetative succession following in its wake. The movement may be a slow one, with recropping and sequential reuse of certain fields, or it may be relatively rapid with little reuse of fields. The accompanying sketch (fig. 6, 2) illustrates two possible variations. In the lower pattern all crops are grown in the same field, with a new field being cleared each year and last year's field being returned to regeneration. In the upper sequence the primary crop is planted in field 1, with secondary crops being put into field 1a, which was last year's primary field. During the next year a new field (field 2) is cleared for production of the primary crop, secondary crops being planted in last year's primary field (now field 2a). No field, in this pattern, is used a third year. A more complex pattern (not illustrated) would use a given field three years in a row with a succession of crops in each, there always being the new (primary)

---

[4] The sketches are illustrative only, and are representative of described patterns, simplified into three basic types. Multiple variations of field shift patterns are to be found in many different situations.

field, a secondary field (last year's primary field), and a third field that is being used for the last time.

A third kind of shift pattern is the circular system that moves through a given territorial orbit during an interval of time, returning again to repeat the cycle (fig. 6, 3). Repetition of the cycle may be fairly precise, or it may amount only to selective repetition of a pattern within a general territory, the precise site pattern varying considerably in time and order of use. The accompanying sketch suggests two full cycles, made precise here only for puposes of illustration. Variations exist both in preciseness and in the number of fields kept in the crop succession during any one year.[5] Such people can live in numbers in a region, and they are permanent residents of a territory.[6] Their sense of territoriality has developed, their concept of ownership of lands is maturing, and their institutional patterns of land control are being elaborated into a definite system.

Fallowing of once-used fields, whatever the duration of the specific cropping system, is essentially a process of letting the weeds grow until plant cover has become regenerated. It may involve the long-term growth of a heavy forest cover, or it may involve only the regeneration of sufficient vegetation to produce a good burn and an ash volume the next time the plot is cleared. In the wide variety of conditions found among shifting cultivators there is the full range of variation. In the first pattern of field shift described above (fig. 6, 1), it is rather obvious that heavy forest would take over the small clearing quite rapidly. Here the term "abandon" does have some meaning when describing the cessation of cropping. In the second pattern of field shift (fig. 6, 2), cropping for a single year and returning the land to regeneration in the second year would not prevent the rather rapid regeneration of full forest cover. In a slowly moving pattern of field shift, however, involving the use of a given plot for several years in first- to perhaps fourth-stage planting, regeneration might well be considerably slower, with a long-term impact on vegetational patterns. In the third pattern of field shift described (fig. 6, 3), regeneration can never produce a really heavy forest, so that some pattern of secondary growth association is the normal cover on regenerating lands. Here the term "abandon" has no real meaning, for the practicers of this system of field shift fully intend to return to a given site at the appropriate time. In situations where the fallow cycle is rather short and where tropical grasses get a start, territorial ranges can end up chiefly as grassland ranges.

When shifting-cultivator peoples have had plenty of room for maintaining long-term cycles of reuse, good growth patterns result. Restriction of the territorial range, however, from whatever cause, reduces the fallow interval and poses a permanent threat to the continuation of good vegetative cover on the whole range. At the upper levels of shifting cultivation, shifting cultivators strongly influence

[5] In a regionally circumscribed closed-cycle rotation system the precise patterns of fields in use may be quite complex. Three variables are involved: the local growth rate for wild plant growth, the length of the cycle permitted by the pressure of population upon land, and the cropping system employed. The third sketch indicates only a very simple closed cycle. For variations in practice see Williams (1928), Freeman (1955), and Conklin (1957).

[6] For a discussion of the possibilities of permanence of a people in a local region, dependent upon shifting cultivation, see Carneiro (1960), who demonstrates for a Brazilian situation the mathematical base for residential permanence. I am not aware that a similar illustration has been published in the literature for southeast Asia, though Conklin (1957) suggests stability of the Hanunóo for nearly a century as a minimum figure.

the patterns of vegetative growth, by planting selected types of trees when return-ing the land to regeneration. Perhaps the most notable instances of this occur in the New Guinea highland country, where planting of casuarina trees is rather common at the time of returning the land to regeneration. Among many culture groups an important consideration in the length of the fallow interval is the amount of wood needed for house construction, for fencing, and for climbing-poles used in the cultivation of such plants as yams and cucurbits.

It is evident that shifting cultivators at the lower levels are not fully aware of the various reasons for maintaining a long fallow interval. On the other hand, there is ample evidence that culture groups at higher levels of shifting cultivation deliberately stretch out the period, when this is at all possible, until in their con-sidered judgments, a plot has rested long enough, has sufficient cover to provide an ash volume, and has sufficient woody material to provide the requisite number of poles, logs, limbs, and other useful items.

Residence patterns conform to the field-shift system much of the time. In the first pattern of field shift (fig. 6, 1), residence follows the field location, population density is small, and the settlement pattern is one involving dispersal. The field-shift pattern illustrated in the second section of figure 6 involves the periodic shift of residence, with new dwelling sites every few years. This shift pattern is used by people who have truly become crop growers, whose dependence upon appropria-tion is no longer dominant, and whose sense of freedom and love of the wild have receded. Residence patterns may range from dispersed dwellings near the fields through a linear pattern of straggling clusters to small village clusters. In any variation of the third shift pattern the village is the normal residential pattern. Cultivators may still reside in the fields during the crop-watching periods, but the village system has developed as a part of their whole way of life. There are, of course, many variations in the sequence of maintaining a relatively closed shift cycle, and some peoples prefer a dispersed residence pattern in which dwellings are scattered throughout the territorial range. Some peoples prefer to live in house clusters and hamlets, whereas other culture groups seem to use all three locational patterns of residence.

The very nature of tropical housing among shifting-cultivator peoples is such that it is often easier to build a new house than to repair an old one. Although a whole village may move a few hundred yards this way or that over a century, it is still regarded as a permanent village. The Wogeo Islanders have lived in villages on their island for centuries, and there are many other instances of this kind.

The dooryard garden must be considered in relation to field shifting and resi-dence patterns. The true dooryard garden, by its very nature, suggests some degree of fixity in residential site occupance. If we return, conceptually, to the possible beginning of crop-growing activities—a planting patch close by a sleeping-hut and cooking-hearth site—we have suggested a dooryard garden of sorts. The relation-ship of the dooryard garden and the female presence at the hearth seems a very old one. If such early residence sites were periodically shifted a few dozen yards as a hut fell apart to avoid vermin, predators, and rampant jungle growth, and to permit the building of a new structure, a new garden could also be started at each new site. Long-term perennials such as fruit trees would not have been part of planting at this stage. Such early crop planting, it is suggested in chapter iv, was a minor endeavor barely complementing an operative living economy based on other resources. The dooryard garden probably never supplied the whole of a living economy, but always remained complementary. Before crops grown in garden plots became the main element of an economy, the dooryard garden would have been expanded into a crop field. Such an expansion would have taken the garden plot away from the dooryard.

Once field-plot crop growing began to produce food staples sufficient to supply primary economic support, the dooryard garden shows some kind of specialization and specific preferential choice. Once field-plot economic support has been achieved, dooryard gardens are not mandatory. The dooryard garden may be abandoned, or it may be retained merely for shade and privacy. It may become the place for growing sacred-magic plants, plants for special uses, plants of long-term maturity, and new kinds of plants. Dispersed residence patterns, in which residential sites are relatively near field plots, may disincline families toward maintaining dooryard gardens. Village dwelling, with field plots at some distance, invites the development of dooryard gardening but does not require it.

Whether the dooryard garden is useful in understanding the evolution of crop-growing systems and the varietal development of patterns of shifting cultivation is not at all clear. Information about the frequency and the nature of dooryard gardens among shifting cultivators is inadequate for the formulation of conclusions. The dooryard garden does not seem to have fixed relationships with either shifting cultivation or particular forms of social structure.[7]

TOOL PATTERNS

The scarcity and simplicity of tools employed in shifting cultivation is a recurrent theme in the literature on the subject, but too many writers have failed to observe carefully and to record accurately the numbers, types, and varieties of tools actually employed in all the cropping-harvesting procedures. Particularly where only a single tool is recorded, the observation is suspect. There has been almost no comparative study of tools used by different groups. Unquestionably the number of tools is small and they are simple in nature, but many groups possess and use more tools than have been reported. There are a few studies of localized tool patterns and an occasional generalization. A fairly notable exception to this is to be found in the studies by C. and E. von Fürer-Haimendorf, and to them should go some of the credit for certain concepts in this monograph. The following two sections from one of their volumes crystallize an amorphous line of thought.[8]

The traditional systems of agriculture of most aboriginal tribes, from the highly specialized rice-cultivation on irrigated terraces of the Angami Naga to the rough shifting cultivation of the Panyer in the western Ghats, have one feature in common: they are entirely dependent on human labour, unaided by the use of domestic animals. It is this feature which justifies their classification as systems of neolithic type in contrast to the plough-cultivation of later ages. Yet, in spite of this common element there is, not merely in secondary characteristics but also in degree of development, a wide disparity in the forms of agriculture practiced by the various tribal popu-

---

[7] See Terra, 1949, 1950, 1953. Terra (1953) presents an extensive tabulation of nearly 100 groups by several traits.
[8] C. and E. von Fürer-Haimendorf, 1945, pp. 4–5 (first two paragraphs), 335–336 (last two paragraphs).

lations and it would be erroneous to regard as one and the same all agricultural systems falling under the heading "shifting cultivation."

From the economic, though perhaps not the technological viewpoint, the chasm between the elaborate and extremely productive shifting cultivation of the Nagas and other hill-tribes of Assam and Burma and the Hill Reddis' crude methods of raising small quantities of grain with the help of no other implement than the digging stick, is as deep as between ploughing and the Nagas' hoe cultivation; and if the latter is rightly considered a very ancient form of agriculture, a far greater age must be attributed to the digging stick cultivation of such backward tribes as the Hill Reddis.

This digging-stick cultivation constitutes, no doubt, a far more ancient stage in agricultural development than hoe-cultivation, and in Peninsular India it seems to be a characteristic of a once widely distributed pre-Austrasiatic and pre-Dravidian population, standing between the primitive food gatherers, such as the Chenchus and certain jungle tribes of the southwest coast and the more advanced hoe-cultivators, such as the Marias, Bondos, Gadabas and Mundas. Hitherto the ethnological stratum of the digging-stick cultures has received little attention, and a great deal of confusion has been caused by the practice of regarding all aboriginal cultures based on "shifting cultivation" as of the same order and similar antiquity. Where the more advanced hoe-cultivators dominate the field, the last remnants of the older digging-stick cultivators were generally overlooked, and it is only in recent years that such tribes as the Baigas of the Central Provinces have been studied by the anthropologists. The Kolams in the rugged hills between the Godavari and the Penganga, today scattered amidst the more progressive Gonds, seem to belong to the same group of ancient jungle-folks and like the Reddis they cultivate on hill-slopes and dibble most of their crops.

These tribes have retained much of the heritage of the earlier races of food-gatherers and hunters. The chase and the collecting of wild jungle produce is still an essential factor in the economic system, villages are small and of no great permanency, though far less frequently shifted than the settlements of such tribes as the Chenchus; the land is common property of the village community, and no rigid social organization hampers the personal freedom of the individual, who may join now one and now another community. And in the field of material culture the bow and the digging stick are, as of old, the most important implements. Yet, beside all these links with the past, there are revolutionizing new elements. Man has broken the chains of his complete dependence on nature and freed himself from the inexorable necessity of spending every day of his life in the quest for food. The raising of crops secures a comparatively stable basis of diet and the possession of fields leads to a more settled mode of life, which in turn renders possible the construction of solid houses, the acquisition of more substantial household goods, and the domestication of pigs and fowls.

In the face of inadequate evidence on tools only a preliminary kind of hierarchical separation of tool patterns can be made. It is obvious that pre-cropgrowing man had tools of a fair variety. Chopping, excavating, prying, knocking, cutting, scraping, and pounding tools, either in complex or in varying combinations, all had been developed prior to the crop-growing era. The digging stick is a primary tool of such precropping economy. Since such activities continued as a part of the economy of the earliest crop growers, the digging stick would have continued in use among such people, and would have been a chief tool in the planting of vegetatively reproduced crop plants once an actual planting procedure became elaborated. The digging stick, therefore, may be placed as one of the very early tools in the simplest vegetative crop system.

The digging sticks of the Paleolithic peoples varied greatly in size and length, and so do those employed by crop growers. The digging stick varies in length from about 3 feet to more than 6 feet, and from less than an inch in diameter to more than 3 inches. Some are double ended. Many are private tools kept for years, but

some peoples fashion a new one for each planting season, discarding it when planting is finished. So far as I know, in southern Asia the only contemporary digging
sticks showing the spatulate form at the lower end are those used in the New
Guinea highlands. Spatulate-ended digging sticks are widely distributed eastward
from New Guinea as contemporary tools, though what the earlier distributions
were is uncertain.[9]

Other precropping tools came into use among the earliest crop growers in much
the same way. Either an axe or an adze for cutting heavy vegetation and a knife
for slashing lighter vegetation, cutting fruits loose, breaking open large, heavy
fruits or tubers, and for other uses certainly were on this earliest list. Further
development of crop-growing tools, as distinct from domestic tools and appropriative tools, depended upon inventions related to particular environmental ecologies,
crop sequences, and culture maturities.

Raking, as a procedure, can be done with a tree limb that retains its twigs, with
bamboo that retains its branchlets, by some broomlike device, or in other ways.
Sometimes the term "raking" obviously does mean the use of a specific tool properly
termed a rake; sometimes a broad-bladed tool without teeth is described as a hoe
and sometimes as a rake. There are references to all forms of "raking," which
sometimes becomes as far afield from proper raking as slicing back and forth with
the digging stick or heavy knife to disturb the surface soil after broadcast planting.
Sometimes something akin to raking is done even after dibbling seed with a digging
stick. This phase of activity is very poorly reported in most of the literature. Hoes
vary greatly in shape, form, material, and working action.[10]

Harvesting procedures among shifting cultivators and permanent-field cultivators are mixed. Three specific techniques are: hand plucking of grain heads, hand-
knife cutting of grain heads, and sickle cutting of stalks. The use of the sickle is
found chiefly in China and India, the hand knife is widely distributed west of New
Guinea, and hand plucking is to be found almost everywhere. Shifting cultivators
in the western zone do use the sickle somewhat, but permanent-field cultivators
use all three procedures.

In India the general decline of vegetative planting and the rise of seed-planted
cropping patterns find the balance of techniques among shifting cultivators on the
side of broadcast seeding. The more primitive cropping systems retain the digging
stick and planting by dibbling and also show little variety in tools. Predominantly
seed planters, who use the broadcast seeding technique, have a variety of hoes,
rakes, brushing devices, harvesting tools, and all-purpose tools. Those in contact
with permanent-field cultivation systems may also be taking on the use of animal-
powered agricultural tools.

In mainland Southeast Asia tool patterns are mixed. Rice planting among shifting cultivators is normally done by dibbling with the digging stick. The use of
hoes, rakes, harvest knives, and other tools is a recent development among shifting
cultivators, though the use of the small, curved hand knife in clipping rice heads
seems to be indigenous where rice is a major crop. Western Malaysia shows these
same mixed patterns, but in eastern Malaysia broadcast planting of seed almost

---

[9] See Barrau, 1958.
[10] Compare the Assamese hoe of the Naga with the hoe of the New Guinea Kuman (see Balfour,
1917, for the former; Nilles, 1942, for the latter).

totally disappears and the digging stick becomes supreme. In New Guinea and other eastern islands the lowlanders continue the simple tool complex of the axe-adze, knife, and digging stick, but highland New Guinea displays more numerous tools. Spatulate digging sticks approaching spades, the hoe, trenching tools, and a variety of knives indicate an isolated region of pre-European tool specialization.

In general reference such terms as "digging-stick culture," "digging-stick cultivators," "hoe culture," "hoe cultivators," and the like have very loose patterns of application, and they are often applied indiscriminantly to any cropping system or technology that is clearly not "plow culture." The term "hoe culture" is also often applied to permanent-field cultivation in southeastern Asia; in this usage it is not truly indicative of a generic system, for most permanent-field cultivators know about the use of animals and animal-powered equipment whether or not they can afford to use them. In Indian application there is a trend to restrict the term "hoe cultivator" to the shifting cultivators who use broadcast seeding and a variety of hand tools. In indicating a generic system this is a step in the right direction. Much remains to be done, however, in deciphering the development of tool systems among different culture groups and the history of diffusion with regard to tools and tool systems.

Speculatively, at this point, it appears that the following tool systems can be identified for shifting cultivators.

A. Digging-Stick Systems (Digging-Stick Cultivation)
  1. Digging stick, axe-adze, knife complex, with the bushbeater a declining tool as the axe-adze and the knife improve. Minor use of other domestic tools in the cropping system, which is essentially vegetative planting.
  2. Digging stick, axe-adze, knife complex, augmented by small hand knives employed in grain-head clipping. Planting by dibbling with the digging stick. Domestic tools perhaps being modified to process seeds and grains.
B. Hoe Systems (Hoe Cultivation, or Hoe Culture)
  1. Axe-adze, knife, hoe, rake, harvest knife-sickle complex, with the digging stick retained but declining in importance, and with seed broadcasting dominant.
  2. Axe-adze, knife, hoe, trenching tool, digging stick in spatulate form for turning turf and soil. Vegetative planting primary, using digging stick and hoe. This pattern refers only to highland New Guinea.
  3. Axe-adze, knife, hoe, rake, sickle complex, and well-developed varieties of each, with broadcast seeding primary to dominant in use, and with the digging stick relict in cropping.
C. Transitional Plow System (Incipient Plow Culture)
  1. Plow, roller, clod breaker, rake, and animal power in use but not dominant and not used on all plots cultivated. Hand tools including axe-adze, knives, knife-sickle, hoe, rake, flail, and modified domestic tools. Primarily a seed-planting cropping system patterning itself on some permanent-field system but not applying it to all areas cultivated. Digging stick relict in cropping procedures.

CROP COMPLEXES, APPROPRIATION, AND LABOR PATTERNS

Regional differentiation in cropping patterns and regional appropriation are discussed in the preceding chapter; here only the conclusions are presented, in terms of typologies. In this study, I contend that aboriginal cropping systems of lowland southern and eastern Asia employed vegetatively reproduced crop plants that were not significantly different from many of the wild plants appropriated from the forest and jungle ranges. There was, of course, regional centering of species, varieties, and assemblages. If a single crop staple can be indicated it may well have been taro in one of its various forms. There is indication that yams replace taros in some regions.[11]

The introduction of seed-planted crops represented a later evolution of crop patterns on a wholesale scale, perhaps associated with human migration. Starting somewhere west of the Indian humid zone, these crop patterns have spread slowly southward and eastward.[12] Gradually, and regionally quite variably, the use of many native leguminous plants (both appropriative and semidomesticated at first) shifted from the fleshy or nodular root to the seed pods and tender green leaves. At some median point in this process the subtropical wild rices entered domestication and were evolved into a multiple-raced complex of even greater value as a seed-planted staple, adding to the eastward trend of seed planting. The introduction of seed-planted crop plants and their extensive adoption as crop staples produced a decline of the older crop plants, which became feral in regenerating ranges and could be gathered as "wild jungle produce" and affected the patterns of plant appropriation that could take place in complementing the crop economy.[13] Very few of the well-domesticated seed-planted grain and grainlike crop staples can hold their own in the jungle, so that occasional crop failures introduced a new level of intensity to the now seasonalized hunger periods.

The advent of a long series of American crop plants in the post-Columbian period set off a new wave of substitution and decline. Vegetatively reproduced American plants reached a far higher degree of use in the eastern sector and in those outpost islands of old patterns in the central and west central sectors. The seed-planted American plants, on the other hand, found their most significant usage in the western sector, which was already acquainted with seed planting. Within the past century an intensification of this dispersion of non-Asian crop plants has included many European cool-climate plants that Europeans carried into the cooler hill-country zones to grow around the summer resorts and hill stations. In quite recent times such alien plant patterns have penetrated deeply into New Guinea.

In establishing levels of operation, a listing of plant-crop systems becomes more a chronological list than one specifying precise technology, but the following is suggestive.

1. Vegetatively reproduced crop plants useful for food, fiber, dye, poison, medicant, ritual potion, and sacred value. Food economy augmented by appropriated wild greens, fruits, nuts, snack foods, and other items. Vegetative plants used chiefly for fleshy root portions, tubers, rhizomes, or bulbs, though some used for fruits, fibers, dyes, and poisons.
2. Vegetatively reproduced crop complex, with added numbers of semidomesticates. Appropriation significantly augments economy, as above. Utility of some vegetatively reproduced plants increased by selective breeding of special varieties, and primary interest in some vegetatively reproduced plants shifted to seeds, fruits, leaves, and other parts not used earlier.
3. Vegetatively reproduced crop complex now augmented by seed planting with entry of grain and grainlike plants. Other elements continuing as above.
4. Balanced dependence upon vegetative planting and seed planting, but with some vegetatively

---

[11] Malinowski (1935, vol. 1) specifically comments on this shift.

[12] I refer here to the drier parts of India and the country west of India, recognizing that at the time of initiation of seed cropping much of northwest India may have been more moist than it is today.

[13] See pp. 125–127, above.

reproduced plants declining in importance, frequency, and distribution as seed-planted crop plants increase in numbers through diffusion or domestication and increase in importance through increasing dependence. Perhaps at this level rice becomes one of the significant crop plants in mainland Southeast Asia and in eastern India, and the beans, grains, oil seeds, and others become significant in central and western India.

5. Seed-planted crop plants form the primary crop sequence, with vegetatively reproduced plants declining in the crop system. Appropriation still draws significantly upon "wild" vegetatively reproduced plant series. Rices, millets, sorghums, beans, and others are now dominant.

6. Dependence upon seed-planted crop series, with vegetatively reproduced plants grown only in dooryard gardens for ritual, first-eating, ceremonial, or minor crop value. Vegetatively reproduced plants are still culled from the forest and jungle, but dependence upon such appropriation is during hunger periods, and the volume is declining.

Although a formal listing is not spelled out, we can see a similar ranking chronology in operation for domestic animals.[14] The earliest grouping might find only the dog in significant position. Somewhat later groupings would find the pig dominant, the dog important, fowls regionally variable, and cattle absent. Late groupings would find the pig and the dog in positions of decreased importance, cattle present in a ceremonial or sacred role, and the economy increasingly dependent upon plant-crop systems.

The role of labor is a difficult subject, and my own knowledge of the historical and hierarchical patterns of the division of labor is insufficient to produce a clear analysis. I admit to confusion over the arguments of matriarchy and patriarchy and their significance to the operations of shifting cultivation. In the modern period both men and women work at crop production. Men do most of the heavy work in plot clearing, women do much of the cleanup; men carry on the important magic and symbolic planting, but both sexes do bulk planting. Women do most of what weeding is done, men hunt the big animals; women do most of the plant gathering, both sexes share fishing activities. Men, women, and children take care of dooryard gardens; both sexes harvest (though women do more reaping and men more transporting); both sexes watch crops; and women process most of the crops into victuals or products. It does appear that where taro is a staple, women do most of the planting and almost all of the daily harvesting for the day's cookery. Among the most advanced seed-planting peoples, men have taken on a larger part of the planting and harvesting chores. If the dooryard garden was once almost exclusively a woman's domain, the situation is no longer so clear cut, for now men also take care of such plantings.

RITUALISM AND ACCEPTANCE-AVOIDANCE

Ceremonial, ritual, and magic connected with crop growing, and issues of taboo and acceptance-avoidance of food products in southeastern Asia, evoke varied reactions from European observers. The anthropologist accepts such culture complexes at their face value, whereas others usually react negatively and categorize elaborate magic ceremonials as merely evidence of primitive culture. There are,

---

[14] There is a regional variation in animal-keeping patterns, as well as the variable level contrast. The dog and the pig were once used throughout the whole range of southern Asia and the island world, whereas the large animals were not to be found eastward of the Lesser Sunda islands in pre-Columbian time. The keeping of sacred animals such as mithan by integral shifting cultivators does not at all indicate the onset of any element of plow culture. The adoption of animal-powered tools, on the other hand, appears to be a first step toward permanent-field cultivation.

however, varying levels of application of both magic and taboo, and analysis of these different patterns of application may yield significant clues in tracing the development of cropping systems. The effective data on agricultural ceremonials have not been studied in a manner that will permit the clear-cut isolation of regional and typologic patterns, but some suggestions may be made toward this end. Among hunting, gathering, and fishing peoples ceremonial observances, rituals, and magical incantations normally precede the acquisitive operations; they are performed to ensure good hunting conditions, good luck in the actual hunt, or the presence of ample game to be hunted, but these ceremonies have nothing to do with the propagation or the production of large populations of game. Among agricultural peoples, on the other hand, such ceremonies, rituals, and magical incantations are concentrated upon the actual growth process by which large yields of high quality are ensured. These ceremonies enlist the aid of the gods on the side of production and attempt to ward off the destructive effects of evil spirits and malignant forces. The degree of application of such ritualism varies and there is marked variety in the association of ritualism with specific crops.

It appears that the simplest crop growers, who still appropriate much of their food from the wild, have very few rituals surrounding their crop-producing activities. Among confirmed agricultural peoples, whole lives seem to be dominated by their crop-growing routines, ritualism related to production seems at a maximum. As a particular crop plant achieves status as a staple, the strongest magic and ritualism centers upon it. As culture groups shift emphasis from one crop to another, the focus of magic ceremonials shifts to the new primary crop. Many of the oldest plant cultigens in southern Asia are attributed with magical power, which enters the ritualism surrounding the planting and harvesting of staple crop plants.[15] Culture groups possessing large numbers of crop plants may use many plants in the magic rituals, but they seem to attach no particular importance to the performance of magic ceremonies for many of the minor crops. In general, the fruit crops seem to have little magic associated with them. Ritualism and ceremonial magic associated with crop production appears to decline in significance at the higher levels of land, cropping, and tool systems, suggesting that as culture groups develop permanent-field agricultural systems there is greater reliance upon the accumulated knowledge concerning agricultural production and less significance attached to ceremonial rituals in which magic contributes to the production process.

There is very rough geographic correlation in the distribution of ritualism. ceremonial, and the use of magic in southeastern Asia and the island world, but

---

[15] Perhaps the most significant of these plants are tumeric (*Curcuma longa*), cordyline (*Cordyline* spp.) croton (*Croton tiglium*), ginger (*Zingiber officinale*), hydrocotyle (*Centella asiaticas*), gandarusa (*Justicia gendarusa*), holy basil (*Ocimum sanctum*), and various of the andropogon grasses (*Andropogon* spp.), but there are many others, with regional concentrations. In general, peculiar colors, dye contents, odd shapes, particular aromas, and other specific properties may give rise to use in making magic. Normally rather specific acts, repeating of specific language, particular kinds of motions, and a specific order of operation of the activities compose particular ritualisms, and these may involve symbolic cutting, scattering, planting, and gathering motions or actions. Often the precise pattern varies the situation, or is developed to suit a specific objective. Normally the precise composition of materials, the formulas, and the specific actions are matters kept secret to the maker of the magic, but others are rather stylized symbolic actions. Conklin (1957) discusses the various specific procedures related to the seasonal work cycle; Lambrecht (1932) describes in considerable detail the ceremonies connected with shifting cultivation as well as with wet-field rice growing.

there is a great deal of variation in this distribution, and the present generalization disregards the local regional variation in technological level of crop-growing. Eastern New Guinea and the islands north and east of New Guinea appear to be in some respects the zone of most highly developed, comprehensive, and dominant agricultural ritualism in all of Southeast Asia and the island world. Here ritualism is highly developed both for plant crops and for animal production. Western Malaysia and the eastern sector of the mainland show less comprehensive patterns of ritualism which are often concentrated upon a single staple crop. In India and Burma most of the ritualism seems to refer to older, and perhaps very old, crops in which the ritualism is largely symbolic and not very active. The above statements are too generalized and too sweeping, but they suggest inferences worth checking and field testing.

Agricultural ceremony and ritualism attaches to the employment of supposedly magical properties of plant materials and to the human activities by which the ceremonies are carried out. Such ritualism has the combined purposes of supplicating the gods, warding off evil spirits and forces, and instituting a positive magical bond between the crops planted and the forces making for high productivity. The employment of magic ceremonials begins before clearing the plots of vegetated ground chosen for planting, and it continues through the seasonal cycle to the postharvest period. Evidence is lacking regarding the evaluation of such ceremonial ritualism, but there seems ground for suggesting that the practices surround particular kinds of plants having peculiar attributes, qualities, and effects. It also seems probable that such ritualism was first practiced by the master magician-priest, or shaman, within each culture group, for some groups still retain this pattern. Among some groups, and in some situations, the cultivators of garden plots began to prepare the materials and administer the ceremonies by themselves. In the latter stages of agricultural ritualism, the practices are symbolic only, pertain to fewer crops, employ fewer magic materials, may be irregular in application, and may be performed only by the more conservative members of a culture group. In such groups many of the plants formerly grown for their magical powers became only decorative plants kept because of tradition or their attractiveness.

Specific situations illustrate many of the above contentions. Those discussions relating to the very simplest crop growers, who are still close to hunting and gathering, do not mention ceremonialism.[16] The strongest patterns of ceremonial ritualism appear to exist among the yam- and taro-producing peoples of the islands off eastern New Guinea. In the 1930's when no virgin forest was left in the Trobriand Islands and little hunting and gathering could be done, a master magician would choose, by his own procedures, the locality to be cleared. He supervised the clearing, allocated the family plots, and carried out both preclearing and preburning ceremonies. The master magician performed the elaborate ceremonies preceding the planting of yams, the chief staple, but individual planters performed the lesser ceremonies for the planting of taro. Malinowski thought the yam ceremony was adapted from an older taro-planting ceremony. The master magician continued his activities during the growing season and conducted the harvest ceremonies. Upon harvest, the yams were first placed on exhibition in garden

---

[16] See Fox, 1952; Bijlmer, 1939, p. 125.

arbors, with accompanying rituals. Transport to the permanent village storehouses took time, but its completion was accompanied by another exhibition and more ceremonial activities.[17]

In the d'Entrecasteaux Islands, Fortune noted that once the communal clearing was completed, the crop garden became totally private and completely sacred, with trespass by non–family members forbidden. Magic was carried out privately, chiefly employing leaves of the croton plant *Cordyline terminalis.*[18] On Tanga Island in the Bismarck Archipelago, once the garden plot was planted some member of the cultivating family had to be present at all times until after harvest to prevent trespassers from breaking the operative continuity of the garden magic. The ceremonials were privately administered and were continuous during the growing season. The magic did not apply to the soil itself, but to the function of crop growth, and the entry of an intruder could interrupt the continuity and destroy the effect of the magic upon the growing plants.[19] On Tanga such ceremonial growth magic, was also applied by each family to raising pigs. The magic was carried to the point that no family ever ate its own pig, but bestowed it upon others in a series of elaborate ceremonies aimed at raising social status and demonstrating the effectiveness of the magic applied by the raiser of the pig.[20]

Much has been made of the elaborate ceremonial exchanges involving pigs, food staples, tools, and other valuables, which have been observed throughout much of New Guinea. Ceremonialism here, of course, extends well beyond agricultural production into the realm of trade, interregional relations, and other aspects of regional culture, but such ceremonialism is often quite complex in the realm of agricultural production alone. Several New Guinea culture groups were known to catch young wild pigs and cassowary chicks and raise them to maturity, applying varieties of magic during the growing periods.[21] In some groups among which the yams were crop staples not only did much magic attend plot preparation and planting, but men always planted on the ground of others, as they did not eat yams from their own plots.[22]

In contrast with these strong patterns of comprehensive ceremonial ritualism are the patterns to be seen in the Philippines, western Malaysia, and the eastern sector of the Southeast Asia mainland. Rice is normally the dominant food staple, and yams and taros have been relegated to a minor position. Of the crop plants, rice is the center of ceremonial magic, taboo, and ritualism. A variety of complementary plants may be grown, many of them without any ceremonial ritualism at all. Also a variety of crop plants may be grown in small quantities, the leaves, roots, stems, or seeds of which enter the ceremonial magic applied to rice. Second-year cropping on old rice plots may be devoted to wide variety of crop plants without any ceremonial observances at all.[23] Only among a few groups do yam and taro require ceremonial applications of magic. The pig has lost most of its status as a ceremonial animal, although when pigs are killed for food there is

---

[17] Malinowski, 1935, 1:64–68, 81, 459–470.
[18] Fortune, 1932, pp. 114–115.
[19] Bell, 1954, pp. 34–35.
[20] Bell, 1947, pp. 36–59.
[21] Nilles, 1944, pp. 3–4; Williams, 1936, pp. 224–225; Williams, 1930, pp. 60–62.
[22] Whiting and Reed, 1938, pp. 179–181.
[23] Vanoverbergh, 1941, and Scott, 1958, are typical accounts.

some ceremonial practice. Water buffalo, zebu cattle, and mithan cattle have been added to the list of animals employed in ceremonials. Conklin has clearly documented the pattern found among the Philippine Hanunóo. Rituals, ceremonies, and taboos are only active when applied to rice. There appears to be no ritualism for taros and yams; there are a number of crop plants grown purely for their magic powers, but cordyline is no longer such a magic plant, and maize has just begun to enter the ritual stage.[24] Freeman also has clearly documented the observation that rice ritualism so dominates the agricultural pattern of the Borneo Iban that no other crop plant receives significant ceremonial attention and there seem to be no surviving rituals surrounding any other crop plant.[25] Among the Lamet of northern Indochina, ceremonial ritualism in crop growing has declined to that surrounding the clearing of rice plots and to the planting, growing, and harvesting of rice. Buffalo and zebu cattle are ceremonial animals, and the pig retains no ceremonial status at all.[26]

In peninsular India the decline of agricultural ritualism among shifting cultivators stands in contrast to patterns evident in New Guinea. Gond peoples who once had full and formal patterns of agricultural ritualism applicable to old sets of crop plants and cropping practices still preserve the rituals as elements of oral literature-drama but apply them only spasmodically when growing dry rice planted on shifting plots plowed with oxen. The very preservation points to an era during which vegetatively planted crop plants were staples, and it also points to the decline of agricultural ritualism. In 1940 the Reddis preserved a seasonal taro first-eating ceremony for field-grown vegetables in general, but most of the small volume of taro grown by the Reddis was raised in dooryard gardens and eaten without any ceremony.[27]

Rituals relating to the pig, the chicken, and the dog are found in various forms throughout the zone of discussion, though dog sacrifice and ritualism are relatively unimportant today. Rituals involving mithan cattle have penetrated only as far eastward as Malaysia. Those surrounding the goat have spread slightly farther eastward in Malaysia than have those for the mithan. Ritual employment of the zebu and taurus cattle breeds, the water buffalo, the horse, the sheep, and the donkey find restricted usage only.

The issue of avoidance-acceptance among shifting-cultivator peoples indicates great variation in the patterns, and there are many changes in practice that seem to relate to the penetration of organized religion into the realm of animism. It is frequently remarked that both appropriative and crop-growing cultures are omnivorous, but this must be seen as relative to the degree of omnivorousness of the observer, that is, in relation to his own patterns of avoidance-acceptance of food items. Total omnivorousness does not exist, and every people has developed avoidance of something. There often are separations among a whole culture group, with particular avoidances found only among segments of the group. Such segmenting of avoidance taboos often follows clan lines or some related line of cleavage in the social structure.

---

[24] Conklin, 1957.
[25] Freeman, 1955.
[26] Izikowitz, 1951.
[27] See C. and E. von Fürer-Haimendorf, 1945, 1948.

Acceptance of plants for food usage usually rules out only strongly poisonous or toxic plants. The magic master who is the specialist in the making of magic with ritual plants may be the chief user of certain nonedible plants. I cannot discern any outstanding regional or evolutionary practices in the avoidance-acceptance issue other than those covered by the general observations that such uses are remnantal in the west for the old vegetative crops, are lacking for seed-planted crops in the east, and have rough correlation with the general crop distribution map.

In the realm of animal foods and products the issue of taboo is far more highly developed.[28] Peoples having an animal totem will almost never eat that totem, even in hunger periods. They have no compunctions, however, about eating the animal totem of a neighboring clan, even though the two clans occupy a single village. This accounts for some of the irregularities in reports of eating habits. Taboos against particular animal foods are culturally developed through historic time, and the broad regional generalization is harder to state. For example, bear is generally eaten along the Himalayan foothill zone from western India around to north China and clear down to Malaya. Within this zone, however, there are a number of specific avoidances of bear by particular culture groups. Monkeys are eaten almost everywhere in the whole region under discussion, yet there are numerous groups that do not eat a particular species of monkey, and the specific rationale for such avoidances finds no standard explanation.

It may be stated that, in general, the use of animal foods is determined more by the stocks available than by the issues of acceptance-avoidance. This becomes a matter of regional human population density, local environmental ecology, the regional necessity for appropriation, and the level of development of shifting cultivation toward a higher form of agriculture. Scantily populated regions sometimes have rich animal resources, whereas in regions of greater population density the volume of appropriation may keep the faunal population at a low level. It does appear that the historical impact of the Hindu and Moslem religions on issues of animal food acceptance-avoidance among shifting cultivators is strong in India, weak in southeast Asia and western Malaysia, and lacking in eastern and northern Malaysia and in the whole of Melanesia. This impact is particularly notable in reference to the pig, both as a domestic and a wild animal, but it also has wider application.

EXCHANGE AND CONSUMPTION

Shifting cultivation is usually considered subsistence agriculture, largely inadequate as a consumption economy, both quantitatively and in terms of differential malnutrition. The terms "subsistence" and "self-subsistent" as applied to the economy are used vaguely, and the concepts mean quite different things to different users. Often there is the failure to distinguish between the crop-growing system and food-consumption pattern on the one hand and the whole economy and living pattern on the other. This results in the generalization of the concept "subsistent" from the crop-growing and food-consuming sector to the whole economy. Because integral shifting cultivation always involves some range of complementary appropriative activities, this generalization of the concept "subsistent" frequently introduces a degree of error.

---

[28] For a general discussion of the use and avoidance of animal foods see Simoons, 1961.

If the definition of subsistence be taken to mean "self-contained," there must be no exchange of any sort in any commodity, whether it be a cultivated crop, an appropriated jungle product, or a handicraft manufacture. When applied to crop growing and food consumption the term "self-subsistent" is often taken to mean the consumption on the farm of all, or nearly all, the yield of the farm, but this dictionary definition itself contains an undefined variable. "Subsistence" and "commercial" frequently appear as two levels of operation at either end of a scale, and neither term fits the economic activity of the great majority of integral shifting cultivators.

Extremely few culture groups possess a whole economy that practices subsistence in the true sense. The indications are that many groups do practice a subsistent crop-growing and food-consuming system within the framework of a whole economy that cannot be labeled subsistent, in as much as they exchange appropriated commodities and some handicraft products for outside products. Some groups regularly exchange some portion of their food-crop production and much of their appropriated commodity volume for a wide range of consumer goods, tools, and other items. Small and weak culture groups may limit their patterns of exchange to casual or opportunistic barter, or to the exchange of special products only. Within large culture groups occupying dissimilar ecological niches in given environments, exchange may be only local and limited chiefly to particular surplus-scarcity contrasts.

There is a significant east-west differential in the patterns of trade, barter, and exchange. The evolutionary process of exchange economies is a very old one in southern and eastern Asia. The mainland, western sector shows a pronounced acceptance of formal trade, professional traders, monetary exchange, manufactured goods, and other elements. In the western sector it is only the small, weak and simple culture groups that are not significantly involved in some aspect of trade or exchange economy, either for their crop-growing and food-consumption systems or for their appropriative and handicraft systems. Where appropriative resources have declined in the landscape, exchange of crop products and handicrafts has increased. The eastern sector has maintained what may be Neolithic systems of exchange. The seasonal trading expedition, the complex and ritualistic gift giving, the cowrie media, the absence of professional traders, along with the participation in exchange of whole villages or whole culture units, all are features not now present in the western sector.[29] The eastern systems are such highly institutionalized patterns and are overlaid with such complex ritual that they barely appear to be forms of economic trade.[30] But their function as procedural patterns by which

[29] Contemporary studies no longer mention cowrie shell money as being common, though older ethnographic studies report its use and it is mentioned in travel accounts of previous centuries. Here and there in interior New Guinea cowrie shell money is still referred to, occasionally with value rates for little to big shells, and shells against pigs, chickens, and other items (see Pospisil, 1958*b*).

[30] Mauss (1954) considers the basic elements of gift exchange to be the continuation of normal Neolithic trading patterns. Hoebel (1958, chap. 26) summarizes the kula ring of the southwest Pacific from Malinowski, a highly stylized context in which two specific kinds of items kept moving constantly in circles of opposite directional movement, to establish the traffic flow under whose cover significant amounts of trade were carried on in entirely mundane products. The New Guinea highlander, of old, used to go on trading expeditions among neighboring peoples under a less highly stylized cover pattern. These old patterns are disappearing now, since product circulation is more frequent and free from the regional hostilities that inhibited trade but made the circular ritual exchange cover so necessary (see Nilles, 1953, pp. 8–9; Gitlow, 1947, pp. 68–81).

to arrange commodity exchange is that of economic trade, and the varied practices serve as the formal machinery by which exchange occurs.

The hunger period, which has been described so frequently and is sometimes termed the starvation period, during which food consumption is dependent upon appropriation of wild plant, animal, or aquatic resources, does indeed suggest that shifting cultivation may be an inadequate system. Seasonal weather calamities probably are more serious in causing such inadequacy than the systems of crop production themselves; they are similar to the calamity periods that result in crop failures in other agricultural systems. Formerly, militant invasion of a territory by another people was a factor in producing hunger periods. Excessive sale of crop staples may unduly liquidate supplies of the food staple in a calculated procedure by which a group will sell off supplies and knowingly accept a later hunger period. It is important to recognize that the shift from vegetatively produced plants to seed-planted crop plants is a factor in producing hunger periods. Hunger periods are more frequent among rice planters than among taro planters, for taro planters often have surpluses that are allowed to rot in the fields. Hunger periods are more common in the whole western sector of southern Asia than in the eastern zone.

In a situation that ranges from an economy that is somewhat adjusted to the twentieth century to another that is almost Neolithic, two classifications of exchange patterns are insufficient to label the economies of all culture groups practicing integral shifting cultivation. Although some culture groups engage in a pattern of exchange that may gross no more than a percentage point or two of their annual production, other culture groups practicing a regular form of shifting cultivation may engage in exchange patterns that gross almost half the value of their annual production. An annual exchange figure of 10 to 20 per cent of the annual production is fairly common among the higher levels of integral shifting cultivators. It is fairly clear that many shifting-cultivator societies would be better described under the heading of commodity exchange economies rather than under the heading of subsistence economy.

The following list of patterns can only suggest the variation in the whole economy of the shifting cultivator.

1. Full subsistence economy in the ordinary sense, combining collecting and cropping, with exchange limited to random acquisition of foods or goods through scavenging, beachcombing, pilferage, silent barter, or begged gratuity. Exchange volume no more than a fraction of 1 per cent of annual production. The Pinatubo Negrito of the Philippines would fit this category in most respects.[31]

2. Full subsistence economy with crop growing and jungle appropriation supplying food; regular barter in appropriated forest products supplying a wide variety of consumer goods and serving to maintain the supply of such goods. Exchange reaching perhaps as high as 5 per cent of total annual production. The Orokaiva of eastern New Guinea seem exemplary of this level.[32]

3. Primarily a subsistence economy as to food supply, but with seasonal or periodic acquisition of particular food supluses either from a nearby region or produced specifically for barter in a nearby region; appropriated forest products or local monopolies in animal or mineral products produced for barter being used in exchange. Augmented by barter in forest products for a wide variety of nonedible consumer goods. Exchange volume reaching 5 to 10 per cent

---

[31] Fox, 1952. See Bijlmer, 1939, for comment on the Tapiro, who probably exemplify this level also.

[32] Williams, 1928, 1930.

of annual production and possibly involving some use of medium of exchange. The Wogeo Islanders off northeast New Guinea would seem a fair example.[33]

4. Primarily a subsistence economy as to food supply, but involving regular production of crop products for sale in addition to production of the staple crop. Purchase of a wide variety of consumer goods by some kind of barter-sale. Forest products regularly produced for the same purpose augmented the exchange, which may reach 15 per cent of annual production, and may involve some medium of exchange. The Lamet of Indochina seem to exemplify this pattern.[34]

5. Chiefly a home production economy as to food supply, but involving price-determined barter of crop volumes and forest products for food items complementing the dietary, and involving production of non-food-crop commodities and forest products for price-determined barter in exchange for consumer goods. Exchange volume now reaching as much as 20 per cent of total annual production and perhaps 5 per cent of annual food-crop production. Medium of exchange may be money or some other recognized medium. Perhaps the Iban of Borneo exemplify this level of operation, and the northern Thai represent a variant of this pattern.[35]

6. Primarily a subsistence economy as to food supply, but involving a gathered and concentrated volume of food products that are tendered by host group to a neighboring guest group in a ceremonial feast the pattern being reversed in due time. Barter of varied commodities accompanying ceremonial exchange of gifts in many commodities, such barter often supplying primary source of consumer goods in particular lines. Exchange volume perhaps equaling 5 to 10 per cent of annual production. Many of the New Guinea highland groups fit this pattern.[36]

7. Chiefly a subsistence economy as to food, but involving formalized circular exchange of valuable or sacred items. The circular exchange routine serves to maintain trading relations with groups that, at the formal transmittal of the valuable or sacred items, engage in secular barter for all kinds of goods, including food commodities. Exchange is perhaps not more than 5 to 6 per cent of annual production, but the pattern is so formalized that barter forms an integral element in the economy. The Trobriand Islanders are the standard example of this pattern.[37]

8. Balanced economy with home production of staple and some appropriation of complements, involving production of specialty crops for sale to regular markets. Money is used to purchase food specialties and complements on the regular pattern, as well as a wide range of consumer goods. Exchange volume may reach as much as 30 to 40 per cent of annual production. The mixed permanent-field and shifting cultivation of southeast Ceylon may exemplify this kind of operation.[38]

In conceptual terms the first of the above systems is the only one that can be properly labeled a subsistence economy. In practical terms the first two patterns may be accepted as subsistence economies. The third pattern is marked by a specific intent upon exchange, and can no longer be termed a subsistence system, either conceptually or practically.

THE POSITION OF PARTIAL SHIFTING CULTIVATION

Partial shifting cultivation, by its very nature, is a hybrid practice and is less conducive to analysis than is integral shifting cultivation. It uses the procedures, technologies, and patterns of traditional shifting cultivation as a means to an objective formally part of another cultural milieu. Partial shifting cultivation also tends to use more advanced technologies whenever possible, technologies ap-

---

[33] Hogbin, 1934b, 1938, 1939a.
[34] Izikowitz, 1951.
[35] Freeman, 1955, for the Iban; Judd, 1964, for northern Thailand.
[36] For a summary discussion see Brookfield and Brown, 1963.
[37] Malinowski, 1935.
[38] Wikkramatileke, 1963.

propriate to its other cultural elements. As stated earlier, partial shifting cultivation in any one region bears relationships to local cultural and crop-growing
patterns. Among the Filipinos it resembles both integral shifting cultivation and
permanent-field agriculture, and in Ceylon it remains within the context of
Ceylon's traditional practice in both basic crop-growing systems. Wherever permanent-field agriculture has been deployed against a system of land use of lesser
technological maturity, partial shifting cultivation appears along the zone of
contact and conflict. It ranges the full breadth of hierarchical patterns for both
systems in the contemporary era, for now Negrito who have not yet become full-
time crop growers using shifting cultivation sometimes become wage earners and
turn their simple cropping sequence into a partial, or part-time, sequence only.
Occidental plantation operators and skilled modern agriculturists turn to partial
shifting cultivation in the search for increased money profits, both using the best
of modern technology.

If a successful hierarchical construct could be elaborated for integral shifting
cultivation, partial systems of shifting cultivation could probably match almost
every step in the construct. There has been too little examination of partial shifting
cultivation for itself to permit the independent development of such a series of
pattern levels, but there is ground for suggesting that such could be arranged.
Conklin's construct of major subtypes suggests two varieties, supplementary and
incipient. Certainly there are more varieties than these two; my classification at
the end of this chapter proposes six different varieties. Conklin was concerned with
partial systems among the simpler cultures only, whereas my concern has been
with varieties of shifting cultivation per se, regardless of the cultural level of the
population practicing the technologies.

INDICATIONS TOWARD A PATTERN OF HIERARCHIES

In chapter ii the classification proposed by Watters was set down as a significant
listing, useful in distinguishing the nature of the economy of a culture group or
regional population.[39] His classification distinguishes the role of shifting cultivation
in mixed economies, each of which also utilizes some other form of support besides
shifting cultivation. The degree of distinction is subjectively quantitative, using
such terms as "to a small extent," "some," and "almost entirely." As a classification
it is quite satisfactory for the purpose of separating numerous mixed economies
into different groups. The primary aim of this study, however, is not the separation of varying kinds of mixed economies, but rather the analysis of the evolutionary development of integral shifting cultivation. In pursuing that aim it has been
necessary to focus on shifting cultivation itself, rather than on the degree of
mixture to be found in varying economies. In that all integral shifting cultivators
do some fishing, hunting, and gathering—activities that I have termed appropriation—these activities do form a significant item of analysis in the qualitative
ranking of different levels of shifting cultivation. To the degree that some of the
higher forms of integral shifting cultivation do take on such traits as animal raising or land systems approaching private ownership, these higher forms show a
trend toward becoming mixed economies. This trend toward a mixed economy must

---

[39] Watters, 1960, p. 65.

be taken into account. The systematic ordering of different forms of shifting cultivation as such, however, must focus primarily on the qualitative level of shifting cultivation rather than on the quantitative degree of mixture to be found in any single economy. Watters remarks that the first three types itemized in his classification may stand in evolutionary sequence, as they all include a variable amount of hunting, fishing, and gathering. He also remarks that it is dangerous to attempt generalizations about evolution based on a few selected culture traits taken out of their ecological context.[40] For this very reason the present study presents a long list of culture traits that need to be examined, it indulges in almost too much classification of operational levels for these traits, and it also separates integral from partial systems of shifting cultivation.

I have not sought a single classification that separates different kinds of economies according to the contributory importance of shifting cultivation. I have sought to distinguish different forms of shifting cultivation within the framework of a single integral pattern of economy. What I have achieved, therefore, is not properly a classification of shifting cultivation, but a series of hierarchical rankings of different qualitative and technological levels of shifting cultivation. There is no thought that a culture group engaging in one level of shifting cultivation will, in any time sequence, develop its particular pattern so as to evolve into any other level. It is obvious that when a culture group does improve its crop-growing system, a process of growth is occurring, but it may well achieve this by borrowing new techniques and not through internal evolutionary growth. Certainly, the uppermost level of shifting cultivation has grown out of lower levels, but no sequence can be prescribed by which any one people will develop its cropping system.

Earlier in this chapter qualitative and procedural subtypologies involved in integral shifting cultivation are enumerated so far as is practical. A total of more than fifty separate qualitative varieties is set down. These range from almost primordial to highly sophisticated; they include chronologically ancient and relatively modern procedural elements, and they include several ranges of crop combinations. It is evident from an examination of these numerous subtypologies that it is not possible to construct a single, simple, and abbreviated classification of the qualitative patterns of shifting cultivation, since the fifty subtypologies may be grouped into a great many different combinations. It is not possible to construct a unilinear progression of typological patterns. Instead, the construct must be a multilinear series that provides for different patterns of groupings. Initially, the construct must differentiate between the integral and the partial practice of shifting cultivation. Second, the construct must provide for the differentiation of integral typologies by primary cropping combinations, since these are matters of historical evolution of shifting cultivation. Third, the construct must distinguish different qualitative levels of typological patterns within any one major category. Stripped to its basic features the hierarchical construct attempts to distinguish six different levels of skill complexes in three different major categories of integral shifting cultivation. A fourth major category is established for the assignment of different varieties of partial shifting cultivation, but the basis of this assignment

---

[40] *Ibid.*, pp. 61–62.

must be different from that of integral practice, since partial shifting cultivation is quite a different category.

In the accompanying list of hierarchies the three major divisions of integral practice are designated as vegetative cropping, transitional vegetative and seed cropping, and seed planting. These three major divisions, themselves, are placed in what does appear to be an order of historical development. The fourth major division lists partial systems. Within each of the integral divisions, specific typologies are arranged in order of complexity. No real attempt is made to place the partial typologies in order of rank or complexity. In setting down a multilinear system of hierarchies it becomes necessary to employ a variety of conventional and shorthand names for identifying groups of procedures that enter into the different typologies at different levels. Not every significant criterion can be included under the label given any one major typology. In the accompanying classification four primary criteria have been employed: the pattern of field shift, the pattern of residential mobility, the major aspect of the tool technology, and the primary grouping of the crop complex. Items common to all typologies may be omitted from designation of the typologies as such, though the degree of application may be significant in establishing the level of a typology. Certain problem sectors, such as the dooryard garden, are not made the primary elements in naming typology, though practices in such sectors may be significant to the establishment of particular levels of typology. The construct is presented in two forms. The accompanying list presents only named typologies, grouped into primary categories. In Appendix F, an extension of the list supplies analytical descriptive notations under each typology. This extended treatment attempts to consider secondary characteristics, both as to kind as to degree of importance, which suggested separation of the major typologies. The extended treatment also suggests culture groups that appear, from data available, to fit the typology in question.

The classification is presented with a keen awareness of the danger of error posed by the interpretation of data and a similar awareness of the danger inherent in the classification of a particular group in the face of incomplete data. Appendix F is presented as an initial effort for purposes of examination, review, critical revision, and reconstruction. Although I feel confident in suggesting that not all shifting cultivation is equivalent, I am only tentatively certain of many of the conclusions implied, owing to incomplete data and my own inadequate command of the data. As an exploratory study, perhaps this effort will prove most useful as a challenge to further examination of shifting cultivation in all its ramifications, examinaiton that can lead toward a better understanding of the whole history of tropical agriculture. I should again warn that although the typologies are set down in order of increasing complexity from 1 through 18, this is not intended to suggest any pattern of evolutionary development at this point of study.

SUGGESTIVE CLASSIFICATION OF HIERARCHIES OF SHIFTING CULTIVATION
INTEGRAL, VEGETATIVE CROPPING SYSTEMS: THE OLDEST TRADITIONAL SERIES

1. Random shift, seasonally resident, digging stick, vegetative cropping
2. Random shift, periodically resident, digging stick, vegetative cropping
3. Linear shift, periodically resident, digging stick, vegetative cropping
4. Cyclic shift, periodically resident, digging stick, vegetative cropping

5. Cyclic shift, sedentarily resident, digging stick, vegetative cropping
6. Declining shift, sedentarily resident, digging stick-hoe culture, vegetative cropping

INTEGRAL, VEGETATIVE AND SEED-PLANTING CROPPING SYSTEMS: A YOUNGER TRANSITIONAL SERIES
EVOLVED IN THE WESTERN SECTOR

7. Random shift, seasonally resident, digging stick, vegetative and seed planting
8. Random shift, periodically resident, digging stick, vegetative and seed planting
9. Linear shift, periodically resident, digging stick, vegetative and seed planting
10. Cyclic shift, periodically resident, digging stick, vegetative and seed planting
11. Cyclic shift, sedentarily resident, digging stick–hoe culture, vegetative and seed planting
12. Declining shift, sedentarily resident, hoe culture–plow culture, vegetative and seed planting

INTEGRAL SEED-PLANTING CROPPING SYSTEMS: A YOUNGER WESTERN SERIES

13. Random shift, seasonally resident, digging stick, seed planting
14. Random shift, periodically resident, digging stick, seed planting
15. Linear shift, periodically resident, digging stick, seed planting
16. Cyclic shift, periodically resident, digging stick, seed planting
17. Cyclic shift, sedentarily resident, digging stick–hoe culture, seed planting
18. Declining shift, sedentarily resident, hoe culture–plow culture, seed planting

PARTIAL SYSTEMS: COLLATERAL SYSTEMS BY GROSS GROUPINGS ONLY

19. Temporary chance patterns, continued without evolutionary elements
20. Frontier migrant settler, evolutionary toward permanent-field farming
21. Frontier zone, declining practice by former intregral shifting cultivator
22. Permanently complementary; subsistence complement to permanent-field farming
23. Permanently complementary; commercial complement to permanent-field farming
24. Urban fringe commercial, market production
25. Sedentary farmer with private land control, shifting cultivation permanently complementary inside farm holding

Chapter VIII

SUMMARY AND CONCLUSIONS

THROUGHOUT MUCH of the analytical literature dealing with shifting cultivation there is evident a search for a system of definition, for a pattern of classification, and for some means by which to effectively compare shifting cultivation with other kinds of cropping systems. Some of these attempts have used simplistic approaches, seeking a single most effective operation, such as fire, which could characterize all of shifting cultivation. Other attempts have sought inclusive, qualitative descriptions. Still others have sought, by concentration on quantitative approaches, to differentiate shifting cultivation from other forms of crop growing. Almost all such attempts have sought a single or unilinear answer, and they have refrained from multiple classification in order to arrive at the simply stated generalization. Many such studies have thereby excluded from consideration significant elements of the whole system. Even the search for a new term by which to refer to shifting cultivation has sought the single generalization and an escape from the difficulties of past patterns of study. Almost all such studies have limited their examinations of shifting cultivation to specific peoples who practice a particular version of the cropping systems, and this has posed problems of making generalizations fit the particular system studied. Studies not tied to specific peoples have often made certain basic assumptions that have required acceptance of environmental or cultural determinism in some degree to account for elements or expressions of practice not examined.

This study seeks a broadly comparative set of results, which requires that we take into account the widest possible range of criteria and refrain from becoming tied to the features of any one system practiced by a particular group of people. In so doing this study runs the risk of becoming theoretical at times, but it has proceeded from no set of a priori conclusions. The names attached to the system as a whole suggest that any single name is only a convenient handle and not an analytically descriptive definition. The wide and long-term distribution of shifting cultivation suggests that the practice has been almost worldwide, that it ranges from sea level to the highest possible elevation at which crop growing is possible, and that all kinds of peoples at all levels of general culture practice some form of shifting cultivation when the circumstances suggest its applicability. The study attempts to clarify the point that shifting cultivation is not a relict pattern of crop growing expressive of very primitive culture, but that its practice continues in southeastern Asia because no substitute has been accepted, or learned, by the peoples in many parts of the region. It is very clear from the evidence presented that shifting cultivation finds so many expressions among different peoples that no simple, short list of criteria can effectively encompass the whole system. An attempt has been made to distinguish between the whole practice, termed integral shifting cultivation, and the part-time practice termed partial shifting cultivation, in which peoples use only the cropping technique. It seems evident that shifting cultivation, as an integral operation by a culture group, may be regarded as Neolithic in origin and technological pattern, in opposition to contemporary agriculture as practiced in parts of Anglo-America and Europe.

There is evidence that shifting cultivators have worked all kinds of physical landscapes, and that there is no essential causal relationship between cultivation and hilly to mountainous regions. Similarly, there is ample evidence that shifting cultivation is not merely a phenomenon related to tropical climates where a non-seasonal pattern of operations seems normal or causal. Soil studies clearly indicate that shifting cultivation does not in itself ruin soils and produce destructive erosion. Such consequences most commonly indicate some maladjustment in the entire socioeconomic and political situation of a particular people which prevents them from practicing shifting cultivation the way they would prefer to do. It is quite clear that many shifting-cultivator peoples develop a fine sense of the regional and qualitative variations in the soils they cultivate. Such awareness is indicative of a people who are far advanced technologically from the very beginnings of crop-growing practice. It should be amply clear from evidence presented that there is a wide range of attitude toward wild vegetation and marked variation between the attitudes of local residents of a region and those of outsiders who come from regions of different culture. There is ample evidence that advanced shifting cultivators attach very high values to the maintenance of an effective vegetative cover in their home territories, in contrast with the mild concern shown for vegetation by beginning practitioners of crop growing by shifting cultivation. It is clear that almost every culture group practicing shifting cultivation depends rather emphatically upon appropriative activities, which results in the utilization of wild biota to complement both their cropping activities and their economic system. Confusion between the cropping system and the economic system has led many students to overgeneralize shifting cultivators as participants in self-subsistent economies.

Many studies of shifting-cultivator populations have made various specific assumptions with regard to the patterns of culture exhibited by these populations. Whereas anthropologists have related aspects of the crop-growing system to many attributes of culture, most of the studies and generalizations by students of other disciplines have neglected the examination of general culture, thereby not taking into account factors of causal relationships. This failure to examine general culture has often resulted in some of the causal relationships being attributed to environmental determinism. The present study has ranged widely through culture complexes, finding ample evidence that points to numerous ways in which aspects of culture, in the hands of specific peoples, alter the generalized operations of the cropping systems. Such evidence throws much doubt upon the simple deterministic conclusions often advanced for the practice of shifting cultivation.

It is clearly indicated that permanent-field agriculture has been expanding into regions where peoples formerly carried on shifting cultivation. Accompanying such agricultural practice have been patterns of private landownership by which shifting-cultivator peoples have been dispossessed of their former territorial ranges. The process can be seen as a very old one, predating the coming of the European. It is evident, however, that since the coming of the European the procedures of political administration he introduced have also greatly restricted the practice of shifting cultivation, often producing further maladjustments of both a sociopolitical and an economic nature among culture groups practicing shifting cultivation. Because European administration reinforced and extended the systems of private ownership of land and state control of the public domain, the incompatibilities between the loosely administered pre-European land systems and shifting-cultivator land systems were greatly increased and made more emphatic. The result has often been the restriction of territorial ranges of shifting-cultivator societies to the point where maladjustments have become severe and shifting cultivation has begun to exhibit all the faults that commonly are ascribed to it as a system.

The specific examination of criteria and criteria complexes indicates emphatically that there are not merely a few ways in which shifting cultivation differs as to specific pattern among different peoples; there are a larger number of significant factors continuously operative over a long period of time. It is evident that shifting cultivation in the hands of a people just beginning to plant crops and still gathering most of their subsistence from the jungle is but an elementary subpattern in a large group of patterns; it differs in almost every respect from the advanced crop-growing subpattern of a people who have achieved a high technological level of shifting cultivation, have developed a high density of population and a social structure that affords land and labor controls, and have begun to alter their system of land control toward permanent-field cultivation and private ownership of land. This examination of specific criteria threatened overclassification of specific items, but it permitted us to set down the variety of items that enter into the combination of practices. The wide range of possible combinations indicates clearly why almost no two culture groups practicing shifting cultivation operate fully comparable and identical subpatterns.

The overall consideration of the many subpatterns in shifting cultivation suggests that it is possible to rank them into groups ranging from the very elementary and beginning subpatterns practiced by peoples who are just beginning to grow crops to the advanced and relatively complex subpatterns of peoples who have been long resident on given territorial ranges, who depend upon periodic vegetative regeneration of land for recropping operations, who employ different cultural practices to speed that regeneration and to preserve the quality of the land, and who support relatively high densities of population on those territorial ranges. Such ranking can be accomplished by using different critical elements as keys to whole cultural practices. Our abbreviated list of diagnostic elements considers the shift patterns, the residence systems, the tool systems, and the cropping practices; and a brief list of ranked hierarchies is presented in chapter vii on this basis. Our elaboration of the collective group practices, under varying combinations of the primary elements, yields a more complete tabulation of typological hierarchies. Such a tabulation is schematic only and is subject to critical appraisal under field study when specific data on all aspects reviewed can be marshaled for comparative analysis. Such a system of ranking hierarchies or typologies is useful in several respects as a means of understanding, but it is not an end in itself. It neither suggests a specific evolutionary sequence nor does it suggest causal factors involved in the growth of one subpattern into another.

The general development of crop growing from earliest times to the contemporary period does indicate evolutionary growth in many of the techniques and procedures and in the nature and productivity of the crop plants themselves; it also indicates the elaboration of many patterns containing almost innumerable subpatterns within each major hierarchy. Shifting cultivation is one such system belonging to an early set of formulations of techniques, procedures, and crops. But just as there is no single descriptive analysis applicable to the whole of twentieth-century American agriculture, there is no single descriptive analysis applicable to shifting cultivation. The ranking of subpatterns of shifting cultivation has about the same utility as the ranking and classification of subpatterns of contemporary American agriculture. The procedure of ranking and classifying subpatterns serves chiefly to demonstrate that shifting cultivation is not a single, simple system of crop growing, but a congeries of very specific subpatterns containing different aspects of significant variation.

A secondary result of this study of shifting cultivation in southeastern Asia is the recognition of a broad pattern of historical shift from vegetative cropping toward seed-plant cropping. It is clear that seed planting has been advancing eastward and replacing the older pattern of vegetative planting. Within southeastern Asia it is clear that the westernmost practitioners of shifting cultivation have almost totally discarded vegetative cropping practices, whereas there are many culture groups in the eastern, island sector which did not use seed-planting practices until these were introduced in recent decades. Between western India and the Solomon Islands there is almost every combination of the two forms of planting practice, with the consequent variation in crop staples. The eastward spread of seed planting is not uniform, and there are numerous groups that retain specific crops of vegetative habit, employing them in different economic roles within their particular subpatterns of cropping practice. The distributional aspects of this eastward shift in planting practices disclose remnant islands of older practice scattered as far west as the Naga territories. Accompanying this eastward spread of planting practice is the spread of tool patterns, involving the proliferation of hand tools and the gradual decline of the digging stick. These distributions, also, are not uniform, but show remnantal preservations in western localities.

This study assesses technological operations of shifting cultivation to the end that a tentative classification of different levels of operation has been developed. This classification is not to be thought of as an evolutionary sequence per se but as the categorizing of different technological levels of crop growing. Such a classification may have obvious utility in trying to place different culture groups in particular rankings, but it must be recognized that the broad growth patterns of crop-growing skills may be considered evolutionary only in the broadest sense. Within the growth patterns, direct evolutionary development moves very slowly, where as diffusionary movements of technological and cultural practices may alter the sequence of developments very drastically, as they have in New Guinea during the last three decades.

Numerous questions arise as a result of the changing distribution of shifting cultivation, the changes in cropping practices, and the collateral changes in cultural features. At this stage of the examination of culture groups in the whole of southeastern Asia few of these questions can be answered. Perhaps the first question concerns the very origin of crop growing itself. It has been suggested in this study that vegetative cropping practice indicates an autonomous origin of plant domestication and the development of a subpattern of crop growing. The replacement of vegetative cropping by seed planting is suggestive. The ability of a culture group to accumulate the high densities of population shown in highland New Guinea raises problems concerning the technologic and systemic margin between shifting cultivation and more advanced agriculture. The interlinkage of socioeconomic organization and land control through cropping practice raises questions as to how best to improve the cropping systems of the remaining shifting cultivators of southeastern Asia, and it throws grave doubt on the probable outcome of merely prohibiting further use of the cropping practice as such. The continuance of shifting cultivation by peoples who already have developed permanent-field cropping systems raises questions regarding the future administrative systems of control over the public domain in every country adopting legal concepts of private property in land. The very fact that shifting cultivation continues as an integral socioeconomic system among many different peoples of southeastern Asia raises questions in itself. Why such practices should continue in tropical lands when other systems have long been available for adoption raises questions concerning the best ways to use tropical soils, to develop utilization of rugged hill country, and to pattern future systems of economic development.

A significant question surrounds the problem of the size of the territorial range needed to allow a given population to continue the permanent practice of shifting cultivation in their home territory, although almost no data are available to make the answer explicit. Certainly the area must vary with the level of the practice and the quality of the local environment. In areas of expanding population, even at a low density, to what degree has population growth resulted from increased efficiency of shifting cultivation, and to what degree has the expansion of population been compensated for by enlargement of the territorial range? If we do view shifting cultivation as a Neolithic technology, what is the upper limit of the technology, both as to achievement and as to population density? Numerous studies of the highland New Guinea peoples raise questions in this matter, but these are phrased most explicitly by Brookfield (1961, 1962) and Brookfield and Brown (1963), who obviously feel that highland New Guinea does not fit the standard definitions of shifting cultivation.

Finally, there is real doubt as to whether there is yet sufficient understanding of the very relationships of cultural attributes, in the hands of a given people, to the particular attributes of the given physical environments occupied, at present or in the past, to answer the crucial question as to why a particular set of practices is followed. It is not sufficient to partially describe each practice or to make assumptions as to the causal relationships involved. Although this study is not able to answer this question, it attempts to show that the answers do not lie in considering shifting cultivation a simple, single, remnantal, and primitive system of crop growing. Rather, this study suggests that the answers lie in the recognition of shifting cultivation as an early, broad and general system of crop growing, perhaps referable to the Neolithic, within which each subpattern constitutes an effort to match elements of culture to particular attributes of a physical environment that is ecologically different from any other environment. C. and E. von Fürer-Haimendorf (1945) recognized the historic relations of tools and technologies to ethnic strains and cultures, and they recognized the broad diversity of specific operational levels in specific places. There is manifest need for much more critical study of shifting cultivation, study that will involve critical assessment of the relative level of cultural expertise in all cultural elements having a bearing upon the occupation of a specific environment at a specific time.

APPENDIXES

APPENDIX A

FAMILIES AND LAND AREAS UTILIZED IN SHIFTING CULTIVATION [a]

(In thousands)

Area	Number of families	Acreage of land cleared annually	Acreage of land still harvesting	Acreage of fallow land	Total acreage
Pakistan.........	750	2,600	500	16,900	20,000
India............	3,100	12,000	2,000	41,000	55,000
Nepal-Bhutan.....	200	750	100	4,150	5,000
Ceylon..........	40	100	25	475	600
Burma...........	700	2,850	750	18,450	22,000
Thailand........	400	1,000	200	8,800	10,000
Laos............	350	650	100	7,250	8,000
Cambodia........	2	10	2	38	50
South Vietnam....	35	85	20	545	650
North Vietnam[b]..	50	100	30	670	800
China[b]..........	1,200	4,500	500	20,000	25,000
Formosa..........	85	300	50	1,650	2,000
Philippines.......	400	1,800	500	9,700	12,000
Indonesia.........	3,800	13,000	4,000	68,000	85,000
British Borneo....	175	750	600	4,150	5,500
New Guinea......	500	1,600	1,000	9,900	12,500
Total..........	12,000	42,095	10,377	212,628	264,100

[a] Estimates here given do not agree with census data or other official statistics for any country involved. The data here are derived from widely scattered statistics, and at best represent only an arbitrary estimate. Totals in the first four columns are approximate.
[b] Estimates applicable to precollectivist period.

APPENDIX B

1. NATIVE LANGUAGE TERMS

(As they occur in the literature on agriculture; English spellings only are listed)

India-Pakistan-Nepal:

bendar	Korku tribal term used in Berar area of Central Provinces.
beora	Central Indian term, involving lopping branches, but not felling big trees, and using digging-stick planting.
bewar	Used in the Central Provinces. Variant spellings: *beora, niwar.* Primarily a Baiga tribal term.
bharti	Modified version of *Kumri* formerly used in Nilgiri Hills of South India.
bimra	Old Gond and Bhumia term from Mandla District, Central India.
bodaga	Older term from southern India now little used.
chelka podu	South Indian variant of regular *podu* involving plowing between stumps before planting. See *podu.*
cotu-cadu	Older term from the Malabar coast.
culumbi	North Kanara term from near Goa.
dadh	Old Bhil tribal term from eastern Gujerat applicable to cultivation on flatlands and involving broadcast seeding of grains. See *jhimta.*
dahya	General term in central India. Perhaps originally a Bhutia tribal term. Variant spellings: *dahi, dahia, daho, dhaya, dhai-ya, daya, dabi, dhya.*
dale	Used in the Western Ghats.
dippa	Used in central India by the Hill Maria and others; properly applies to flatlands only. Variant spelling: *deppa.*
erka	Used in Central India. *Mudur erka* refers to use of forest lands and *marram erka* applies to scrublands only.
guhad	Central Indian term applied to bamboo cover cut, burned, and cropped.
ijran	Used in the Kumaon Himalaya. Properly a term for lands being temporarily cropped by shifting cultivation but destined eventually for permanent-field use. Is in contrast with the permanently terraced, dry-farmed lands covered by the term *upraon,* and the wet terrace lands covered by the term *talaon.* Both *upraon* and *talaon* lands are cropped annually.
jara	Used in central India.
jhimta	Old Bhil tribal term from eastern Gujerat applicable to cultivation on sloping lands. See *dadh.*
jhum	General term used in much of north and northeastern India, originally a Bengali-language term. Variant spellings: *jhoom, jum, jumea, joom, djum, zuhm.*
kalabanjar	Used in Kumaon Himalaya.

kandala	Used in Kumaon and Garhwal Himalaya. Sometimes applied in same way as term *ijran*, sometimes loosely used.
khil	Bhotia tribal term used in Himalayas west of Nepal. Variant spelling: *katil*.
komon	Used in northern Orissa and central Himalaya. Properly applied, refers to the lopping-transport-burning described under the term *rab*. Often used loosely. Variant spelling: *koman*.
korali	Used in the northwest provinces and south to Gujerat.
kurao	Used in the central east coast–Eastern Ghats.
kumri	General term applied in much of peninsular India, said to have originated in Kanara on the west coast. Variant spellings: *cumrie, coomrie, kumeri, kumari*.
marhan	Central Indian term applied to cutting-burning of flat, forest-covered lands.
pam	Used in the north Bengal plains and the Bhutan terai; refers to flat lowlands seasonally flooded.
parka	Old term once widely used in central India. Originally applied to system involving clearing-burning of seed beds and transplanting to plowed fields. Variant spelling: *pharka*.
podu	General term used in east central and southeastern India, said to have been a Telegu-language term. See *chelka podu*. Variant spellings: *podhu, pothu, pode, poduar*.
ponna	Used along Malabar coast.
penda	Used in Bastar sector of central India. Properly applies to sloping lands only. Variant spelling: *prenda*.
punahad	Used in the Shevari Hills of central India.
punam	Used along the Malabar coast and in the Nilgiri Plateau.
rab	Used in the Western Ghats and the interior sectors of the west coast. Term originally meant only cultivation, but by loose extension it has been applied to whole system of crop growing in any shifting sequence. Properly used today it refers to the lopping of branches (*tahal* or *shindad*) and gathering of grass and leaves from territory surrounding and near the land to be cropped (kumaki), and burning them in heaps on the land prior to planting. In this usage it may refer either to permanently cropped fields or to fields cropped intermittently.
walra	Used in northwest peninsular India. Variant spelling: *wolar*.

Ceylon:

chena	General term applied to any sequence of shifting cultivation. The ancient term was *hena*, singular, or *hen*, plural, then properly referring to the class of brushwood and small jungle-grown lands used for cropping, as opposed to *mucalaan*, the mature-growth forest lands used for cropping. The decline in extent of heavy forest-grown lands led to disuse of the distinguishing term, with *chena* being used as the general term. Variant spelling: *chemass*, occasionally used old term.

Andaman-Nicobar Islands:

ya   Used as the general term for all shifting cultivation.

Burma:

hai   Shan Plateau general-use term.

hkaibang   Kachin term for modified *taungya* in which rice is grown on hoe-cultivated grassland.

lepok   Upper Burmese term for a dry-soil, short-crop, long-fallow system.

taungya   General term widely used. *Ya* properly used in former times as general term for class of lands used in shifting cultivation. Variant spelling: *toungya*.

yi   Kachin term in general use.

Thailand:

napa   Properly used to distinguish rice grown by shifting cultivation, as opposed to *nadam*, rice grown by wet-field methods on permanent fields.

tamrai   General-use term.

Indochina:

hai   Term used by several tribal groups of Laos.

miir   Mon-khmer linguistic term used by some tribal groups of upland southern Laos and Annam.

ray   General use term normally used by French writers. Variant spelling: *rai*.

Malaya:

ladang   General Malay term used in English.

padi huma   Malay term applied to Sakai shifting cultivation when rice is cropped.

tenggala   Malay term properly referring to rice growing by plow-culture shifting cultivation, using multiple cropping of field and long fallow.

Indonesia:

ladang   General term normally used by occidental writers, said to be of late Malay-language origin. Variant spelling: *laddang*, in older literature.

joema   General term often used by local populations, probably from early Malay-language origin, derivative from old genetic term *uma*. Variant spellings: *umah, humah, oemah, omo, juma, kjoema*.

tegal   Used in eastern Java, Madoera, and nearby areas. Strictly used, appears to refer to a sequence that resembles the *rab* of southern India, but term is now loosely used by many authors. Variant spelling: *tagal*.

Eastern New Guinea:

kep pene Highland term for land often cultivated, fallowed between cultivations, used for sweet potatoes.

pene Highland term for land not cultivated in memory of present generation.

Philippines:

caingin General term for all kinds of shifting cultivation, and sometimes for application to rural sites less carefully handled than permanent, wet rice fields. Variant spellings: *caingan, kaingin, kaingan, kaiyingan.*

uma Used by Manobo tribal peoples of Mindanao.

fo-ag Used by Bontoc Igorot of north Luzon as a term for any field cultivated in the manner of shifting cultivation.

China:

k'ai-huang, k'ai'keng, k'ai-shan Terms, with other variants, meaning to open up lands not previously cultivated.

keng-huang, keng-shan, keng-ti With other variants, meaning to newly cultivate or to reclaim lands once cultivated.

miao-nung, miao-tien With variants, meaning primitive or tribal cultivation, usually involving shifting cultivation.

shan-nung, shan-tien With other variants, meaning hill and mountain cultivation.

The above Chinese terms, with numerous others, refer to the opening of new lands, hill cultivation, or something related. In some instances this is not truly shifting cultivation, whereas in others, it may be only a version of shifting cultivation, particularly when mountain (*shan*) or tribal (*miao* or *man*) reference is indicated.

Korea:

hwajon Generally used in English for fire-field cultivation.

kaden *Hwajon* is Korean for fire-field cultivation. *Kaden* is the Japanese term.

Japan:

kaden Generally used in English for fire-field cultivation. Sometimes spelled in English as *karen.*

Fiji:

teitei General term, but English version uses several terms.

American tropics:

coamile Southern Mexico.

conuco Widely applied in the Caribbean and northern South America.

degras Used in Martinique.

ichale Term used in earlier time in Guadalupe.

kekchi Guatemala.

milpa	Guatemalan Maya-language term now widely used by writers in all parts of the American tropics.
roça	Brazilian term.

African tropics:

chitemene	General term more often used in Africa. Properly refers to system of lopping branches and burning them on field to be planted, and is comparable to Indian term *rab*.
fang	An old term sometimes used in the Congo.
lougan	From the Ivory Coast.
masole	From the Belgian Congo.
shamba	Central African.
tavy	Chiefly applied to Madagascar.
uma	Old term sometimes applied in Madagascar and eastern coastal zone, but now little used.
zande	Central African term for a specific system.

Unlocated:

ku	Used in literature as a synonym.

2. NON-ENGLISH EUROPEAN-LANGUAGE TERMS
(As they occur in the literature on agriculture)

assart	Early English. Originally taken from Old French. Early English usages involved more grubbing than burning. Sometimes originally used in variant *essart*.
Brandkultur	German. Used in various ways in German, but applied as English term in general application.
Brandrodungsbau	German.
Brandwirtschaft	German origin, abbreviated from *Brandlandwirtschaft* and *Brandrodungslandwirtschaft*. The abbreviation applied in English as general term for shifting cultivation.
brûlis	French. Commonly used in French as a general term, and by English writers adapting the French term.
burnbeat	English, late seventeenth-century term meaning to pare off and burn sod or turf to improve a field for cultivation. Sometimes used as the equivalent of *denshire*.
denshire	Early seventeenth-century English term meaning to clear or improve land by burning the turf, stubble, and so on, and spreading the ashes. Early spellings had variants *denshare* and *densher*. From Devonshire.
écobuage	French. Seldom adapted in English writing.
essartage	French. Sometimes used as *essart*, or as a form of *sartage*. Originally probably implied more grubbing than burning.
Haubergwirtschaft	German.
nomadism agricole	French.
raubban	Dutch term applied to shifting cultivation in Indies.

roturacion   Spanish. Also used as *roturas*. Both also carry meaning of simple rotation of fields and crops.

Reutbergschaft   German. Originally implied more grubbing than burning.
svedjebruk   Swedish.
swidden   Derived from medieval English "swithen," itself derived and originally adapted from Scandinavian root. In English originally used properly for "a place on a moor which has been cleared by fire." Has numerous spelling variants. Not now contained in modern English dictionaries.

3. COMMON ENGLISH TECHNICAL TERMS
(As they occur in the literature on agriculture)

axe cultivation	nomadic agriculture
brand tillage	nomadic cultivation
bush fallowing	patch agriculture
bush gardening	patch cultivation
cut and burn agriculture	predatory cultivation
digging-stick agriculture	primitive horticulture
digging-stick cultivation	roving agriculture
field-forest rotation	shifting agriculture
fire farming	shifting cultivation
fire-field agriculture	shifting axe cultivation
fire-field cultivation	shifting crop agriculture
fire-field horticulture	shifting dibble cultivation
fire economy	shifting-field agriculture
fluctuating agriculture	shifting-field-forest cultivation
fluctuating cultivation	shifting horticulture
hill culture	shifting seasonal cultivation
land-rotation agriculture	slash and burn agriculture
land-rotation cropping	slash and burn cultivation
land-rotation cultivation	slash and burn farming
long-fallow cultivation	slash and dibble agriculture
long-term bush fallow	slash and dibble planting
migratory agriculture	transient agriculture
migratory cultivation	transient cultivation
migratory hoe tillage	transient horticulture

APPENDIX C

Diagnostic Criteria Significant to an Analysis of Shifting Cultivation

The following list of subjects and diagnostic variations, as an index of typologic elements, indicates the range of elements that make up the whole of shifting cultivation. The subjects are arranged sequentially.

1. Nature of the land surface chosen for cropping
   a. Flatter and level surfaces primarily
   b. Steeper slopes primarily
   c. Mixed patterns of surfaces, comprising steep, flatter, rocky surfaces
   d. Stream-bottom sites
   e. Wet lands that naturally remain damp during a growing season
   f. Drained to dry lands
   g. Sunny to shaded exposures sites for particular cropping
2. Vegetation patterns of lands chosen for cropping
   a. Virgin or very old forest, frequently termed virgin forest
   b. Maturely regenerated forest, but not yet approaching a local climax; commonly termed secondary forest, but perhaps this term includes forest regenerated many times
   c. Immature regenerated forest growth fully covering ground
   d. Immature regenerated tree growth not yet fully covering ground
   e. Scrub tree growth fully covering ground
   f. Scrub tree growth not yet fully covering ground
   g. Grass parkland to straight grassland
   h. Recognition that composition, luxuriance, size of trees, and other vegetative criteria yield diagnostic clues as to fertility of soil or readiness of soil for another cropping
3. Clearing and burning procedures employed
   a. Random clearing and burning, with stumps and felled trunks left intact, and with girdled but dead trees left standing
   b. Random clearing and burning, live trees left standing
   c. Full clearing and full burning resulting in clean field surface
   d. Secondary clearing subsequently carried out
   e. Careful burning, escape fires insignificant
   f. Careless, poor burning, with escape fires common
4. Field-shift patterns intended or unintentional
   a. Random "ill-omen" desertion during season prior to harvest
   b. No real sequence, patch choice dependent upon chance events of year
   c. Random shift to distant site, by magical and ritual controls.
   d. Annual crop-season shift with full reversion of cropped land
   e. Periodic shift with full reversion after final cropping
   f. Linear shift onto full quota newly cleared adjoining lands, which results in steady and progressive clearing of mature forest
   g. Cyclic shift involving rotation of crops on land not yet reverting, plus some pattern of annual new clearance; cyclic shifting often follows extremely

complex patterns, and involves multiple cropping sequence on oldest lands, plus annual reversion quota of final nature

5. Planting procedures
    a. Scattering of grain seed which remain uncovered
    b. Scattering and covering of grain seed by some technique
    c. Dibbling of seed in hole planting, by tool making of holes
    d. Digging of holes or hills for tubers
    e. Pushing vegetative plant stock into soil
    f. Ritual procedures for most crops planted
    g. Ritual procedure for particular crops only, common for a traditional "sacred" crop, but seldom for newly acquired or minor crop plants
6. Treatment of soils prior to, during, and after planting
    a. No recognizeable soil-treating procedures
    b. Casual disturbance of soil surfaces in clearing and planting
    c. Raking of ashes and surface soil after planting
    d. Preparation of soil in holes only, in which planting is done
    e. Piling of soil into hills as growth begins
    f. Soil fully turned prior to planting
    g. Soil turned a second time prior to planting
    h. Raised beds created by digging and piling of soil from drainage ditches
7. Weeding and care during growing period
    a. No weeding performed during growing period
    b. Single early weeding by pulling and slashing weed growth
    c. Continuous weeding by pulling and slashing weed growth until harvest
    d. Weeding repeated selectively for successive crops
    e. Provision of poles for climbers
    f. Arranging of plants for nurse-plant purposes during season
    g. Constant ritualism, using symbolic magic
    h. Casual or occasional ritualism per omens, desecration, and so on
    i. Preharvest ritualism
8. Harvest patterns and customs
    a. Single crop followed by field reversion
    b. Randon gleaning of left-over items during later seasons
    c. Successive harvest of long-term maturing crops through several growing seasons, resulting from planned planting practices which include quick-growing items, long-term fruit timings, crops left in ground until needed, and so on
    d. Harvest of "owned" planting stock on once-cropped lands
    e. Harvest of "owned" trees in perpetuity, with no recultivation for annual crop
    f. Harvest rituals of varying types
9. Fallow techniques intended
    a. Natural regeneration only
    b. Planting of wild trees as simple vegetative cover for soil regeneration
    c. Random scattering of seedstock, chiefly tree growing
    d. Planting of domesticated tree stock intended as later full-land crop pattern
    e. Regeneration standards as to what constitutes regenerated vegetative cover are many and involved, with many control factors

10. Land tenure system
    a. Control held by group in common by traditional customary law; selection of land next to be cleared by many systems, ranging from open forum to selection by shaman, land master, or government agent
    b. Control held by clan, subclan, or a major social group by traditional customary law
    c. Control by lineage grouping by traditional customary law
    d. Control by family units by traditional customary law
    e. Control by area-occupance units by traditional customary law
    f. Land under private ownership in modern legal sense
    g. Government land forming public domain, occupance by simple squatter cropping
    h. Government land forming public domain, occupance by squatter cropping, paying taxes, and later establishing private legal ownership
    i. Government land forming public domain, cropping controlled by permit of government agent, as annual or seasonal practice
11. Maintenance procedures during and after clearing
    a. No recognizable procedures of any kind
    b. Casual procedures as required seasonally
    c. Logs oriented on slopes to prevent erosion
    d. Casual terracing by crude leveling procedures
    e. Regular and formal terraces for dry fields only
    f. Formal terracing for wet fields, with water control
    g. Pit development on lowland sites making for wet fields
12. Fencing procedures
    a. No fencing procedures used
    b. No fencing procedures in normal times, but in emergencies
    c. Casual and spasmodic
    d. Impromptu, produced when need arises, but effective building
    e. Regular, planned for when clearing, built after planting
    g. Fencing with stiles for human transit, and/or set with trap devices
13. Tools employed
    a. Beating club, axe, knife only
    b. Digging stick, knife, axe-adze group of traditional tools; may involve significant use of only small number of types, or may employ full range of six or eight specific tools
    c. Beating club additional tool to digging-stick group
    d. Hoe, adze-hoe, protospade, footed digging stick, hand plow, and so on, added to digging-stick group
    e. Recognition of added tools used in turning soil or raising beds in different ways
    f. Plows and added animal-powered tools
    g. Mechanized tools
14. Grasslands resultant from field reversion
    a. Insignificant development
    b. Steady appearance with reversion by normal reversion schedule

    c. Appearance by virtue of shortened regeneration cycle

    d. Related to burning for cattle grazing rather than cropland reversion to regeneration

    e. Related to overuse of land from multiple sources

15. Soil erosion produced

    a. Insignificant because of flat surfaces cropped

    b. Insignificant on slopes by virtue of excellent cropping practices

    c. Regularly result from poor cropping practices

    d. Resulting from overshortening of regeneration cycle but not from cropping practices per se

    e. Occasional result of local catastrophic events

    f. Inherent in nature of surface rather than produced by cropping techniques

    g. Produced by rooting-digging action of fauna

16. Crop patterns employed

    a. Tubers primary (or at least grainless crop series)

    b. Wet taro primary, other crops accessory

    c. Mixed patterns, grains and tubers both significant

    d. Grains expanding their role, tubers declining

    e. Grain crops dominant to exclusive

    f. Wet rice expanding, still accessory to other patterns

    g. Wet rice important to dominant

    h. Mixed patterns, but tree crops incidental to important

    i. Tree crops significant element

    j. Vegetables critical elements

17. Dooryard and village gardens

    a. Dooryard gardens lacking

    b. Small, casual, few to single item cropped

    c. Permanent, regular, and multicropped, significant in volume

    d. Tree crops chiefly, with shade, shelter, protection factor

    e. Ritual crops primary

18. Nonagricultural economic gathering functions

    a. Gathering major to dominant

    b. Gathering significant at all times

    c. Gathering incidental in volume, but particular in selection

    d. Gathering significant only during starvation periods

    e. Particularized pattern of gathering

    f. Fishing important in overall economy

    g. Fishing casual, incidental, or significant only as sport

    h. No fishing done at all

    i. Hunting of game important in overall economy

    j. Hunting casual, incidental, or significant chiefly as sport

    k. Hunting with dogs as formal style

    l. Gathering in any form insignificant to absent

19. Status of cattle among culture group

    a. Maintained chiefly for ceremonial purposes

    b. Utilized regularly for meat

  c. Utilized chiefly for milk

  d. Raised primarily for cash sale

  e. Totally absent

20. Status of the pig among culture group

  a. Maintained chiefly for ceremonial purposes

  b. Raised primarily for festival consumption

  c. Utilized regularly as food

  d. Raised for use in trading-gift-ceremonial-festival pattern

  e. Banned owing to taboo, religion, and so on

  f. Status as sacred animal

  g. Not raised at all, without taboos being present

21. Other animals and fowls

  a. Chickens

  b. Other fowls

  c. Dogs, raised for food

  d. Dogs, kept as pets or for hunting purposes

  e. Dogs, tolerated as watchdogs or scavengers

  f. Dogs raised and kept primarily as watchdogs

  g. Goats

  h. Sheep

  i. Horses

  j. Water buffalo

  k. Miscellaneous other animals

22. Status of housing among culture group

  a. No real housing as such, campsite shelters only

  b. New house built at every annual or seasonal field shift

  c. New house built at each periodic field shift

  d. New houses built or rebuilt with shifts in migration cycle

  e. Housing permanent

  f. Permanent housing, but temporary housing occupied on crop plot during late growing and harvest seasons

  g. Housing permanent, with field-watch shelter an accessory

  h. Housing permanent, but relocated at irregular intervals

23. Distribution of population in village or dispersed patterns

  a. Population migratory, with no permanent residence sites

  b. Dispersed residence normal to whole group

  c. Population resident in hamlets, clusters, and nonvillage groupings, with lineage groups sometimes living more or less together in clustered homes not constituting villages

  d. Permanent villages occupied, with seasonal dispersal to cropped localities

  e. Population village resident, but villages random, straggling

  f. Population resident in reguar and permanent villages

  g. Villages located primarily on ridges, spurs, and other high defensive sites

  h. Villages located primarily in cropland locality

  i. Villages located primarily by streams, lakes, seashores

  j. Both village and dispersed residence patterns utilized

24. Social structure of the group
    a. Organization by matriarchal patterns
    b. Organization by patriarchal patterns
    c. Lack of dominance by one organizational system, with several systems present
    d. Little or no control of economy through social structure
25. Participation in trade, exchange, and sale of products of the economy
    a. Insignificant development of exchange
    b. Particular product exchange
    c. Significant degree of exchange rather general
    d. Role of gift-exchange pattern
    e. Cash sale a primary function
26. Climate, as expressed in wet and dry seasons of the year
    a. General problem of seasonality
    b. Regularity of seasonal pattern
    c. Length of cropping season without irrigation
    d. Number of dry months
    e. Lack of dry season a problem

Some explanatory remarks are in order regarding certain aspects of the above presentation. Because my concern is to analyze and compare shifting cultivation as a functioning system of crop growing, some category patterns lump together certain criteria that do not intrinsically form integral elements of culture. When listing planting procedures, for example, the actual mechanics of getting the seed-stock into the ground do not involve ritualism. But rituals either are a significant part of the whole planting procedure, or are neglected. It was felt at the outset that the presence or absence of rituals as concerned certain crops might yield a clue to certain aspects of the evolution of the agricultural system.

Similarly, both fencing and terracing may at first glance seem rather unimportant criteria, as their practice is not highly critical to the mechanics of crop growing as such. Both proved to be very useful in the overall process of evaluating and differentiating the agricultural system. Dooryard and village gardens are not, in themselves, a part of shifting cultivation. Few authors have reported carefully on this subject, but the presence of these gardens is an important clue to the evolutional level of shifting cultivation as practiced by particular peoples. Concern for the issue of social structure, stated vaguely in the outline of criteria, is only a partial concern which many anthropologists will feel is both poorly assessed and inadequately considered. It is included largely because of the persistent theme among some anthropologists and sociologists that "the cattle people, who are patriarchal," do this and that, and that "the pepole without cattle, who are matriarchal," do otherwise.

Scattered throughout the list are a number of items that do not pertain at all to shifting cultivation, but belong instead to permanent-field agriculture. These are included because a number of culture groups today practice both shifting-field and permanent-field crop growing, and the assessment would be incomplete for such groups were the criteria omitted from the list.

APPENDIX D

DISTRIBUTION AND USAGE PATTERNS OF CROP PLANTS CULTIVATED BY SHIFTING CULTIVATORS IN SOUTHERN AND EASTERN ASIA

In the following list the record has been taken from the sampled literature and resolved as accurately as possible. The list makes no claim to total accuracy and certainly is incomplete, because it was complied from the surveyed literature dealing specifically with shifting cultivation. About 230 crops are listed, sometimes involving differentiation of species and sometimes not. Burkill's *A Dictionary of the Economic Products of the Malay Peninsula* (1935) and Bailey's *Hortus Second,* (1941) were used as guides, but a crop not reported in the literature surveyed as actually being cultivated by shifting cultivators was not included just because it was in Burkill or Bailey, even though these are comprehensive sources.

When a term such as "leafy vegetable" was encountered, it was recorded only under "Greens." If sufficient description was given that reasonable identification could be made, the item was recorded under its proper common and botanical name. Canarium nut, for example, was recorded under "Almond, canarium," without separate listing by species, because few reports made further identification possible; whereas cowpea and yard-long bean were recorded under "Gram" and sublisted under *Vigna catiang* when the report seemed accurate enough to warrant such specific recording. Although this was done as carefully and as guardedly as possible, only a reasonable degree of accuracy may be assumed for the list.

The following is a guide to the symbols used in the list:

N	Northern sector	BE	Beverage usage
E	Eastern sector	CH	Chewing usage
S	Southern sector	F	Fencing
W	Western sector	FA	Famine food
C	Coastal zone	LI	Lighting oil
H	Upland locality	ME	Medicinal, as such
DR	Dry climate zone	NA	Narcotic, as such
WE	Wet climate zone	OI	Used as an oil
?	Uncertainty	P	Used in perfumery
X	General usage under the	RO	Resin, gum usage
	heading given, or present in	SM	Smoking usage
	the region indicated without	PC	Post-Columbian time, general
	a specific time	RC	Recent in time
	reference		

The second column, Post-Columbian, is used broadly to indicate a plant of non-oriental origin, introduced to southeastern Asia since 1500, with no further indications as to time of arrival. In the regional distributional columns, two time factors are carried further than the recording by a X indication of the presence. PC indicates an arrival prior to recent time but probably later than the seventeenth century, whereas RC suggests introduction within only recent decades, including World War II introduction for parts of New Guinea.

English name and synonyms	Post-Columbian or recent	Botanical names	Major patterns of usage								Regional distribution					
			Staple item	Vegetables-greens	Flavor in cooking	Snack-fruit-beverage	Fiber-technology	Medicine-poison	Dye coloring	Religio-magic	Indo-Burma-Ceylon	Highland fringe	Central South China	Southeast Asia	Malaysia	Pacific
Abaca		*Musa textilis*					X								N	
Achuete	PC	*Biza orellana*							X			X		X	X	X
Almond		*Prunus amygdalus*														
Almond, canarium; pili		*Canarium album, commune, polyphyllum, ovatum, salmonense, nungi and spp.*	X			X	X				X			X	X	X
Almond, Indian; tauga		*Terminalia catappa, chebula, edulis, okari and spp.*				X		X	X		X			X	X	X
Amaranth		*Amaranthus caudatus, frumentaceus and spp.*		X				X	X					X	X	X
Apple		*Malus spp.*				X						X	X		X	
Apple, custard	PC	*Annona reticulata*				X		X				X				
Apple, Malay, Macopa, South Sea		*Syzygium malaccensis, Eugenia malaccensis*				X					X					
Apple, rose		*Eugenia jambos, Syzgium jambos*				X										
Apricot		*Prunus armeniaca*				X							X			
Areca		*See Palm, betel*				X				X	X			X	X	
Arrow grass		*Miscanthus floridulus*												X		
Arrowroot		*Tacca pinnatifida leonpetaloides*	X									X		X		
Asparagus, New Guinea		*Andropogon spp.*		X											N	X
Asparagus bean		*See Bean, asparagus*		X											X	X
Asparagus pea		*See Pea, asparagus*														
Bajra		*See Millet, Pennisetum typhoideum*														

Balimbing	Averrhoa bilimbi carambola													X		X
Bamboo	Bambusa spp., Dendrocalamus spp., Gigantochloa spp., and other genera		X X			X X			X X	X X	X X		X	X X	X X	X X
Banana, plantain	Musa spp. See textual note	X		X				X				X			X	
Barley	Hordeum vulgare and agriocrithon	X	X X	X			X	X		X X				X	X	
Barringtonia	Barringtonia edulis and spp.		X X			X	X X X				X X	X		X X X	X X X X X	X X X X
Basil, sweet	Ocimum basilicum	X	X X	X		X X X			X X	X X X	X X X X X	X X X X	X X X	X X X X	X X X X X	X X X X X
Basil, holy	Ocimum sanctum	X		X		X X X				X	X X X	X X	X X	X X X	X X X X	X X X X
"Beans"	Loosely used, no ident.																
Bean, asparagus	Vigna sesquipedalis	X	X X X	X	X	X X X	X X X			X X	X X X	X N X X	X N X	X N X X	X X X X X	X X X X X
Bean, broad	Vicia faba	X X	X X X	X	X					X	X X	X X X	X	X X X	X X	X	X
Bean, Goa	Psophocarpus tetragonolobus									X X	X X X	X X	X X	X X X X	X X X X X	X X X X
Bean, hyacinth; lablab	Dolichos lablab (Lablab vulgaris)		X X X X	X X X	X	X X	X X X X			X X	X X X	X X X X	X	X–H	X	X X	X X
Bean, lima PC	Phaseolus lunatus		X X X	X			X X X										
Bean, Lyon's	Mucuna cochinchinensis		X X X	X	X X	X X X	X X X				X	X	X	X	X X X		
Bean, rice	Phaseolus calcaratus		X X X	X X			X X X				X	X	X X				
Bean, St. Thomas'	Entada gigas, phaseoloides (scandens)		X X X	X X	X X	X X X	X X X				X X	X X	X X		X X C	X X C C	X X C
Bean, sea	Vigna marina	X	X X X		X	X X X	X X X			C	X X	X N X	X	C N	X C	X C C	X C
Bean, soy	Glycine soja	X	X X X	X	X X	X X X	X X X			X	X X	X X X	X	X X X	X X X X	X X X X	X X X
Bean, sword	Canavalia gladiata	X	X X X	X			X X X			X	X X	X X X	X	X X X	X X X X	X X X X	X X X
Bean, Urd	Phaseolus mungo	X	X X X		X	X X	X X X			X	X X	X X	X	X X X	X X	X X X	X X X
Bean, yam PC	Pachyrhizus trilobus, erosus		X X X	X			X X X				X	X X					
Bean, yard-long	See Bean, asparagus; Gram, cowpea																	
Belinjau, tulip	Gnetum gnemon		X	X		X	X				X		X	E	X		X X
Betel	Piper belle				X					CH		X		X			
Bireh, birah	See Taro, Alocasia sp.																
Bottle gourd	See Gourd, bottle																
Breadfruit	Artocarpus altilis, communis, incisis	X	X		X					X	X	X	X	X	X	X	X X
Brinjal	Solanum spp.				X						X			X			
Broomcorn	See Millet, Panicum miliare																
Buckwheat	Fagopyrum esculentum, tataricum, cymosum	X		X							X		X	X	X	X	X

English name and synonyms	Post-Columbian or recent	Botanical names	Staple item	Vegetables-greens	Flavor in cooking	Snack-fruit-beverage	Fiber-technology	Medicine-poison	Dye coloring	Religio-magic	Indo-Burma-Ceylon	Highland fringe	Central South China	Southeast Asia	Malaysia	Pacific
Bullock's heart		See Apple, custard														
"Cabbage"		Loosely used, no ident.														
Cabbage	PC	Brassica oleracea var.		×							×	×	×	×	×	×
Cacao	PC	Theobroma cacao						BE			H		H	H	H	HRC
Calabash Gourd		See Gourd, calabash									×		×	×	×	RC
Calamondin		Citrus microcarpa, mitis			×							RC			W	×
Cane grass; Pitpit		Saccharum edule, robustum		×				BE			×				E	RC
Canna		Canna spp.				×					×				×	
Cardamom		Elettaria cardamomum			×			×			×		×	×	×	×
Carrot	PC	Daucus carota		×	×						×	×	×	×	×	
Cashew	PC	Anacardium occidentale				×		×			×		×	×	×	H
Castor bean		Ricinis communis					LI	×			×				×	×
Casuarina		Casuarina spp.					×				×				×	×
Cauliflower	PC	Brassica oleracea var.		×							H	×	H	H	H	HRC
Changkok		Sauropus androgynus, albicans		×							×				×	
Chempedak		Artocarpus champeden				×				×	×				×	
Chenopodium		Chenopodium murale		×				×			×	×	×	×	×	×
Chestnut, Otaheite, Tahitian		Inocarpus edulis	×			×									E	×
Chickpea		See Gram														
Chilies		See Pepper, chili														
Cinnamon		Cinnamomum spp.			×	×	×	×			×	×	×	×	×	×
Citron		Citrus medica						×			×		×	×	×	×
Clove		Eugenia aromatica		×	×											
Cockscomb		Celosia cristata		×												
Coconut		See Palm, coconut														
Coffee	PC	Coffea spp.						BE			×		×	×	×	RC
Cola		See Kola nut														

Common name	Scientific name / note	1	2	3	4	5	6	7	8	9	10	11	12	13	14
Cordyline, ti, dracene..	*Cordyline fruticosa, terminalis* and var..........						E	E	×					×	×
Croton..................	*Croton tiglium*..........	×			×		×	×	×	×		×	×	×	×
Cotton..................	*Gossypium* spp..........	×	×					×	×	×		×	×	×	
Cowpea.................	*See* Gram														
"Cucumber"..........	Loosely used, no ident......		×	×	×			×	×	×		×	×	×	×
Cucumber.............	*Cucumis sativas*.........	×	×	×	×			×	×	×		×	×	×	PC
Custard apple.........	*See* Apple, custard														
Cycad..................	*Cycas circinalis, media, rumphii*..........	×	×	×	×				×	×	×	C		C	C
Dal. *See* Gram															
Derris..................	*Derris* spp..........	×	×	×	×					×		?		C	C
Dracene...............	*See* Cordyline	×		×										×	×
Duku...................	*See* Lanzone														
Durian.................	*Durio zibethinus*.........	×	×	×	×				×	×		×	×	×	×
Eggplant...............	*Solanum melongena* and spp..	×	×	×	×				×	×		×	×	×	×
"Fern tips"............	Loosely used, no ident......	×	×	×					×	×		×	×	×	×
Fern....................	*Marattia fraxinea, Nephrolipis biserrata*..........	×	×	×	×				×	×		×	×	×	×
Fig, chiefly wild.......	*Ficus* spp..........	×	×	×	×		RE		×	×		×	×	×	×
Flemingia..............	*Flemingia vestita* and spp...	×	×						×			×		W	×
Galangal, greater......	*Languas pyramidata (galanga)*		×	×					× × ×	× × × × ×		× × ×	× × ×	× × ×	× × ×
Gambier...............	*Uncaria gambir*.........					CH				×					
Gandarusa.............	*Justicia gandarusa*														
Garlic..................	*Allium sativum*.........		×	×					×	×		×	×	×	×
Gingelly...............	*See* Sesamum														
Ginger.................	*Zingiber* spp. and related....	×	×						×	×		×	×	×	×
Goa bean..............	*See* Bean, Goa									×					
Goldthread, Huanglien.	*Coptis teeta*..........							×	×	×		× × ×	× × × ×	× × ×	× × ×
"Gourds"..............	Loosely used, no ident......	×	×	×	×			×	×	×		×	×	×	×
Gourd, calabash.......	*Lagenaria ciceraria*.........	×	×						×	×		×	×	×	×
Gourd, dishcloth.......	*Luffa acutangula* and spp....	×	×						×	×		×	×	×	×
"Gram"................	Used loosely, no ident.......	×							×	×		×	×	×	
Gram		×	×												
Chickpea, Bengal.....	*Cicer arienatum*..........	×	×						×	×		×	×	×	
Pigeon pea, chick pea, red gram......	*Cajanus cajan (indicus)*.......	× ×	×			?			× ×	× ×		× ×	× ×	× ×	
Mung, green gram.....	*Phaseolus aureus*..........	×							×	×		× ×	× ×	DR ×	×

English name and synonyms	Post-Columbian or recent	Botanical names	Staple item	Vegetables-greens	Flavor in cooking	Snack-fruit-beverage	Fiber-technology	Medicine-poison	Dye coloring	Religio-magic	Indo-Burma-Ceylon	Highland fringe	Central South China	Southeast Asia	Malaysia	Pacific
Black gram		*Phaseolus mungo*	×	×							×	×	×	×	DR	
Horse gram		*Dolichos biflorus*	×	×							×	×		×		×
Cowpea, yard-long bean		*Vigna catiang*	×	×							×	×	×	×		×
Grass pea		*Lathyrus sativus*	×	×							×		DR	N		H
Lentil, masur		*Lens esculenta*	×	×							DR ×		×	×		
Pea, garden		*Pisum sativum*	×	×							×	×	×	×		
Pea, field, matur.		*Pisum arvense*	×	×							×	×	×	×		
Green gram		*Phaseolus radiatus*	×	×							×	×	×	×		
"Green plum"		Loosely used, no ident				×										
"Greens"		Loosely used for leafy vegetables		×												
Guava and guavano	PC	*Psidium guavaja* and spp				×		×			×	×	×	×	×	×
Hemp		*Cannabis sativa*					×	×	×		×	×	×	×	DR	×
"Herbs"		Used loosely to refer to such items as vegetables, spices, medicines, etc.						×			×			×		
Hibiscus		*Hibiscus* spp		×			×	×		×	×	×	×	×	×	×
Hyacinth bean		*See* Bean, lablab														
Hydrocotyle, Indian		*Centella asiaticas*		×	×			×	×		×	×	×	×	×	×
Indigo		*Indigofera* spp					×	×	×		×	×	×	×	×	
Jackfruit, jak		*Artocarpus integra, integrifolia*	×	×		×					×	×	×	×	×	
Jalu, Lolo		*Eppiprenum* spp	×	×				×			×	×		×	×	?
Jambo		*See* Apple, Malay	×	×											×	?
Jhangora		*Oplismenus frumentaceus*		×			×	×			×	×	×	×	×	×
Job's tears		*Coix lachryma*		×						×	×					×
Jowar		*See* Millet	×	×			×	×		×	×	×	×	×	×	×

Common name	Scientific name													
Kanari nut	*See* Almond, canarium													
Kapok	*Ceiba pentandra*			CH	BE		X	X	X	X		X	X	X	
Kava	*Piper methysticum*							X	X	X		X	X	X	
Keladi	*See* Taro														
Kola nut	*Cola acuminata*			CH	CH		X X	X X	X X	X X		X	X X	X X X	X
Kondol	*Benicasa cerifera, hispida*		X	X			X			X X			X	X N	
Kuchoi	*Allium tuberosa*		X X	X			X			X	N		X	X	X
Kudzu vine	*Pueraria lobata, thunbergia*		X			X		X	X	X			X	X	
Kunai grass	*Imperata arundinacea*														
Kurakan	*See* Millet, *Eleusine coracana*														
Kutki	*See* Millet														
Kuwei, musk-mallow	*Abelmoschus manihot*		X			X	X	X	X	X		X	X	X	X
Lablab bean	*See* Bean, lablab														
Lanzone, langsat	*Lansium domesticum*			X				X	X	X		X X	X	X	
Lemon	*Citrus limon*			X			X X	X X	X X	X X X		X X	X X	X X X X	
Lemon grass	*Cymbopogon* spp.			BE	BE		X	X	X	X X		X	X	X X	X
Lentil	*See* Gram	PC	X			X		X	X X	X X		X	X	X X	RC
Lettuce	*Lactuca sativa*		X					X	X	X		X	X	X	
Life plant	*Kalanchoe integra*			X	X			X X	X	X			X	X	
Lime, juice	*Citrus aurantifolia*			BE	BE			X X	X	X		X	X	X	RC
Lime, sour	*Citrus hystrix*			X	X			X X	X	X			X	X	
Lotus	*Nelumbo nucifera*		X	X			X			X X		X	X	X	
Mabolo	*Diospyros discolor*		X	X X	X		X	X	X	X X X			X	X X	
Maize	*Zea mays*	PC	X	X X	X		X	X	X	X	N		X X	X X	PC
Malay apple	*See* Apple, Malay		X	X	X		X	X	X	X			X	X	X
Mango	*Mangifera* spp.		X	X	X			X	X	X			X	X	X
Mangrove seed	*Brugeira, Rhizophora, Mucronata,* and other genera		X		X			X							X
Manioc, cassava, tapioca	*Manihot dulcis, esculenta, ultissima*	PC	X	X	X			X		X			X	X	X
"Melon"	Loosely used for many different items		X X	X X	X X			X X	?	X X		X	X X	X X X	X ?
Melon	*Cucumis melo*	PC	X X					X		X			X X	X X	?
Milk bush	*Euphorbia tirucalli*		X				X	X	X	X			X	X	?
"Millet"	Used loosely, no ident		X			X			X	X				X	
Millet															
Great millet, sorghum, jowar	*Sorghum vulgare*		X	BE			X	X	X	X		X	X	X	

English name and synonyms	Post-Columbian or recent	Botanical names	Staple item	Vegetables-greens	Flavor in cooking	Snack-fruit-beverage	Fiber-technology	Medicine-poison	Dye coloring	Religio-magic	Indo-Burma-Ceylon	Highland fringe	Central South China	Southeast Asia	Malaysia	Pacific
Little millet, shayan, shamay, kutki, broomcorn		*Panicum miliare*	×	×							×	×	×	×	×	
Proso millet, barai		*Panicum miliaceum*	×	×							×	×	×	×	×	
Pearl millet, bajra		*Pennisetum typhoideum*	×	×							×	×	×	×	×	
Italian, foxtail millet		*Setaria italica*	×	×							×	×	×	×	×	
Finger millet, ragi kurakan		*Eleusine coracana, Cynosurus coracana*	×	×							×	×	×	×	×	
Barnyard millet		*Echinochloa frumentacea, Panicum crus-galli*	×	×							×	×	×	×	×	
Kodo millet		*Paspalum scrobiculatum, Paspalum sanguinale, Digitaria spp.*	×								× E			W ×		
Mulberry, bush		*Morus alba* in bush var.					×				× E					
Mulberry, tree		*Morus alba* in tree var., *Morus indica*			× ×	BE	× ×				× E	×	×	×	×	×
Mulberry, paper		*Broussonetia papyrifera*					×						×	×	×	×
Mushroom		*Agaricus* spp.		×	× ×	×		×		×			×	×	×	×
Mustard		*Brassica juncea, nigra*	×	×							×	×	×	×	×	
Nipa palm		See Palm, nipa														
"Nuts"		Loosely used, no ident.				×										
Nutmeg		*Myristica fragrans* and var.			× ×			× ×	×	×	×				× E	×
Oilseed		Term used agriculturally to cover small-seeded oil-producing plants, mainly *Brassicas, Sesamum, Linums, Arachis,* but includes many others		×	OI		×	×			×	×	×	×	×	

Common name	Scientific name	Code
Okra	*Hibiscus esculenta, Abelmoschus esculenta*	
Onion	*Allium cepa* and var	
Orange	*Citrus sinensis* and var., and other spp.	
"Palm"	Used loosely, no ident.	
Palm, Australian nut	*Cycas media*	
Palm, betel, areca	*Areca catechu*	
Palm, coconut	*Cocos nucifera*	
Palm, fishtail	*Caryota* spp.	
Palm, nipa	*Nipa fructicans*	
Palm, Palmyra	*Borassus flabellifer*	
Palm, sago	*Metroxylon bougainvillense, oxybracteatum, rumphii, sagu, salmonense, vitiense, warburgii*	
Palm, sugar	*Arenga saccharifera (pinnata)*	
Palm, wine	*Caryota urens*	
Palm, grass, kru bilong	*Setaria palmifolia*	
Pandanus, screwpine, pandan	*Pandanus brosimos, conoides, houletti, julianetti, lerum, odorus, tectoris* and spp.	
Papaya	*Carica papaya*	PC
Para cress	*Spilanthes acmella*	
Parsnip	*Pastinaca sativa*	PC
Passion fruit	*Passiflora edulis* and sp.	PC
"Peas"	Used loosely, no ident.	
Pea, cow. *See also* Gram	*Vigna sinensis (catiang)*	
Peach	*Prunus persica* var	
Peanut, groundnut. *See also* Oilseed	*Arachis hypogaea*	PC
Pear, European	*Prunus communis* and var.	
Pear, oriental	*Pyrus pyrifolia* and var. (*sinensis*)	
Pepper, black	*Piper nigrum*	
Pepper, chili	*Capsicum annuum*	PC
Perilla	*Perilla ocimoides*	
Pigeon pea	*See* Gram, *Cajanus cajan*	

English name and synonyms	Post-Columbian or recent	Botanical names	Staple item	Vegetables-greens	Flavor in cooking	Snack-fruit-beverage	Fiber-technology	Medicine-poison	Dye coloring	Religio-magic	Indo-Burma-Ceylon	Highland fringe	Central South China	Southeast Asia	Malaysia	Pacific
Pili		*See* Almond, canarium														
Pitpit	PC	*See* Cane grass														
Pineapple		*Ananus sativas, comosa*			×	×	×	×			×		×	×	×	PC
Plaintain		*See* Banana. Seldom used properly				×						×				
"Plum"		Used loosely to refer to varied fruits not ident			×	×					×		×	×	×	×
Plum, European		*Prunus domestica* and var				×										
Plum, hog	PC	*Spondia* spp. Some spp. are ancient, others are post-Columbian			×	×					×			×	×	×
Plum, Jambo		*See* Apple, rose														
Pomegranate		*Punica granatum*			×	×		×			×	×	×	×	×	RC
Pomelo		*Citrus maxima*			×	×		× ME			×		×	×	×	
Poppy, opium		*Papaver sonniferum*						× NA		×	×	×	×	×		
Potato, sweet		*Ipomoea batatas*	×	×		×					×	×	×	×	×	× RC
Potato, white	PC	*Solanum tuberosum* var	×	×	×						×	×	×	×	×	RC
"Pulse"		Loosely used for some grain-like crop. *See* Gram														
"Pumpkin"	PC	Often loosely used to refer to some *Cucurbita*														
Pumpkin		*Cucurbita pepo* var		×	×	×		×			×	×	×	×	×	PC
Radish		*Raphanus sativus* var		×	×						×	×	×	× RC	× RC	RH
Ragi		*See* Millet, finger														
Ranti, terong		*Solanum nigrum*		×							×	×	×	× H	×	
Rape		*Brassica napus*		×	OL						× H	×	×	× H	×	×
Raspberry, northern		*Rubus idaeus?*			×	×					H	×		H		

Common name	Scientific name	PC												
Raspberry, Malaysian..	*Rubus sorbifolius?*					X	X	X	X	X		X	X	
Reed, edible..	*Arundinaria* spp.			X		X	X	X	X	X		X	X	
Rice..	*Oryza sativa* and spp. Rarely identified as to species, variety, type.	PC	X			X	X	X	X	X	X	X	X	RC
Rose apple..	See Apple, rose			X		X	X	X		X		X	X	X
Roselle..	*Hibiscus sabdariffa*	PC		X	X X (P)	X	X X	X	X	X	X	X X	X X	X
Rubber..	*Hevea brasiliensis*	PC												
Sago..	See Palm, sago			X	X	X X	X	X	S	X	X	X X	X	X
Sandalwood..	*Santalum album* and spp.				X	X	X							
Santol..	*Sandoricum koetjape (indicum)*					X	X			?	X	X X X	X X	X
Scutelleria..	*Scutellaria* spp.			X X (OL)	X X	X	X		?	X X	X X X	X X X	X
Sesamum, gingelly, til..	*Sesamum indicum, orientale*								X	X				
Shallot..	*Allium ascalonium*													
Shavan..	See Millet, little													
Soap nut..	*Sapindus* spp.			X X (BE)	X	X	X	X	X	X	X	X	X	X
Sorghum..	See Millet, great													RC
Soursop..	*Annona muricata*	PC												
South Sea apple..	See Apple, Malay													
Spinach, New Zealand..	*Tetragonia expansa*			X X (F)	X X	X X X	X X	X X X	X X X	X X X	X X X	X X X	?
Spurge, slipper..	*Pedilanthus tithymaloides, Euphorbia tirucalli*	PC												
"Squash"..	Loosely used, no ident.													RC
Squash..	*Cucurbita maxima* var.	PC												
Sugarcane..	*Saccharum officinarum*, spp. and var.			X (SU)	X	X	X	X	X	X	X	X	X	X
Sugar palm..	See Palm, sugar													
Sweet potato..	See Potato, sweet													
Tahitian chestnut..	See Chestnut, Tahitian													
Tamarind..	*Tamarindus indica*				X	X X	X	X X	X X	X	X	X X	RC
Tangerine..	*Citrus nobilis* and spp.				X	X	X	X	X	X	X	X	X
Tapioca..	See Manioc													
"Taro"..	Loosely used, no ident.		X			X	X	X	X	E			X X
Taro, keladi, bireh, birah, gabi, etc..	*Alocasia cucullata*		X	X	X	X X X X X	X	X	E		X X	X X
	denudata		X	X				S					
	indica		X	X									
	macrorrhiza		X	X			X X X X X		X X	X X X	X X X X X	X X
	sanderiana						N						

English name and synonyms	Post-Columbian or recent	Botanical names	Major patterns of usage								Regional distribution					
			Staple item	Vegetables-greens	Flavor in cooking	Snack-fruit-beverage	Fiber-technology	Medicine-poison	Dye coloring	Religio-magic	Indo-Burma-Ceylon	Highland fringe	Central South China	Southeast Asia	Malaysia	Pacific
Taro, etc. (continued)																
		Amorphophallus campanulatus prainii (poirou)	X	X				X			X		X	X	X	X
		variabilis	X	X				X							X	
		Colocasia esculenta (antiquorum)	X	X							X		X	X	X	X
		Cyrtosperma edule	X	X				X							E	X
		chamissonis	X	X											E	X
		lasioides	X	X											X	X
		merkusii	X	X				X							X	E
	PC	*Xanthosoma atrovirens*	X	X											X	X
		sagitifolium	X	X											X	X
		violaceum	X	X											X	
Tauga nut		See Almond, Indian														
Tea		*Camelia assamica, sinensis*			X	BE					X		X	X	X	RC
Ti		See Cordyline														
Til		See Sesamum														
Tobacco	PC	*Nicotiana tabacum*				SM		X			X	X	X	X	X	X
Tomato, tree	PC	*Cyphomandra betacea?*			X	X		X			X	X	X	X	?	
Tomato, vine	PC	*Lycospericon esculentum*			X	X		X			X	X	X	X	X	RC
"Tree leaves"		Loosely used, no ident.		X	X		X	X			X	X	X	X	X	X
Turmeric		*Curcuma longa (domestica)*			X			X	X	X	X	X	X	X	X	X
Turnip		*Brassica rapa*		X	X				X	X	X	X		X	X	H
Ubi		See Yam, *D. bulbifera*		X												
Vegetable marrow		Used loosely for varied *Cucurbita* and *Luffa* spp.	X	X												
"Vetch"		Used loosely, no ident.									X					
Vetiver		*Vetiveria zizanioides*					X	X			X	X	X	X	X	X
Walnut		*Juglans regia* and spp.		X	X	X	X		X		X	X	X H		X	

Common name	Botanical name	Symbols (left → right)
Watermelon	*Citrullus vulgaris*	× × × × ×
Wheat	*Triticum sativum* and spp.	× × × RC × × × × H × ×
"Yams"	Loosely used, no ident.	× ×
Yam, ubi, hubi, kemil, tugi, etc.		
Greater yam	*Dioscorea alata*	× × × × × S × S × × × ×
	bulbifera (sativa)	× × × × × × × × S × ×
	esculenta (aculeata)	FN × E E DR ×
	hispida	× × × × × × ×
	laurifolia	× × × S × × S × ×
	mummularia	× × ×
Chinese yam	*opposita (batatas)*	× × × × × × × N W ×
	orbiculata	× × × × × ? S ? ×
	pentaphylla	× × × × × × S × ×
	piscatorum	FA × × × S × ×
	pyrifolia	× × ×
Yam bean	See Bean, yam	
Zedoary	*Curcuma zedoaria*	E × × × E ×

APPENDIX E

In the following list the record has been taken from the sampled literature and resolved where possible. The list certainly is incomplete and is relatively uninformative, as ethnozoology is a meagerly developed science. Terms in quotation marks were taken as reported and are not identifiable in greater degree. Where a reference seemed specific, a genus and species reference was supplied when possible. A better regional list could have been compiled from Carter, Hill, and Tate (1945), Tate (1947), Loveridge (1945), and similar volumes, but these sources do not verify that all items have been utilized by shifting cultivators.

The following is a guide to the symbols used in the table:

N   Northern sector   ?   Uncertainty of data
E   Eastern sector   X   Usage by pattern recorded among
C   Coastal locations   some of regions noted

Table of animal terms, usage, and regional distribution.

Common term	Zoological identification	Hunted wild	Pet	Use uncertain	Kept	Eaten	Sale product	Technical usage	Ritualism	Indo-Burma-Ceylon	Highland fringe	Central South China	Southeast Asia	Malaysia	Pacific
1. "Ants"	?	X		X		X				NE					X
2. "Bandicoot"	?	X				X				N					X
3. "Bats"	?	X		X		X	X			N					
4. "Bear"	Selenarctos thibetanus, Helarctus malayanus					X	X		X	X	X	X	X	X	X
5. "Birds"	?	X	X		X	X	X	X	X	X	X	X	X	X	X
6. Cassowary	Casuarius spp.	X	X	X	X	X	X	X	X	N	X	X	X		X
7. Cat	Felis domestica races	X			X	X				X	X	X	X	X	X
8. Catfish	?					X									X
9. "Cattle"	?	X			X	X	X	X	X	X	X	X	X	X	X
10. Chicken	Gallus sp. breeds	X			X	X	X			X	X	X	X	X	X
11. Cockatoo	Psittacidae fam.					X									X
12. Crocodile	Crocodylus spp. and Tomistoma spp.	X		X		X	X	X	X						
13. "Crustaceans"	?	X				X				X	X	X	X	X	X
14. "Deer"	?	X			X	X	X			X	X	X	X	X	X
15. "Dog"	Canis familiaris in varied breeds	X			X	X	X	X	X		X	X		X	
16. "Dolphin"	?	X	X	X		X		X				X		X	X
17. Donkey	Equus asinus					X		X				X			
18. "Duck"	?					X									
19. Dugong	Dugong dugong	X		X		X	X		X						X
20. "Eel"	?	X			X	X	X			X	X	X	X	X	X
21. "Fish"	?	X			X	X	X								X
22. Fish, Flying	?	X				X									X
23. "Frogs"	?	X				X								X	
24. Goat	Capra hircus breeds	X		X		X	X		X		X	X	X	X	
25. Goose	Anser spp. in variety					X									
26. Goral	Naemorhedus goral spp.	X		X	X	X	X			X	X		X		
27. "Grubs"	?	X		X	X	X				X	X		X		
28. Honey (bee) and wax	—	X			X	X	X	X	X	X	X	X	X	X	X
29. Horses	Equus caballus breeds	X		X	X	X	X	X		X	X	X	X	X	X
30. Iguana	Varanus spp.	?		X	X	?	X	X			X	X	X	X	?

32.	Kangaroo	*Macropus* spp.
33.	"Kangaroo bear"	?
34.	"Land crabs"	?
35.	"Lizards"	?
36.	"Locusts"	?
37.	"Marsupials"	?
38.	Megapod and eggs	*Megapodius* spp.
39.	Mithan	*Bos frontalis* breeds
40.	"Monkeys"	?
41.	Mule	Ass-horse hybrid
42.	"Opossum"b	?
43.	Palolo worm	*Eunice viridis*
44.	"Parrots"	?
45.	Peacock	*Pavo cristatus*
46.	"Phalanger"	*Phalanger maculatus* and spp.
47.	"Pheasants"	*Phasianus* spp.
48.	Pig	*Sus* spp., not differentiated
49.	Pigeon, wild	*Carpophaga* spp.? *Ducula bicola*?
50.	Pigeon, domestic	*Columba* spp. ?
51.	Porcupine	*Atherurus macrourus* ?
		Acanthion klossi ?
52.	Python	*Pythoninae molurus* ?
53.	Rail	Rallidae family
54.	"Rats"	*Rattus* spp. or ?
55.	Rhinoceros	*Rhinoceros sumatrensis*
		unicornis
		sondaicus
56.	Serow	*Capricornis* spp.
57.	"Shark"	?
58.	Sheep	*Ovis aries* in breeds
59.	"Shellfish"	?
60.	Silkworm	*Bombyx mori* ?
61.	"Snakes"	?
62.	Python (not boa constrictor)	Pythonidae family
63.	"Squirrels"	?
64.	Tree kangaroo	*Dendrologus* spp.
65.	"Tree rat"	*Melomys* spp. or ?
66.	Water buffalo	*Bos bubalus* breeds

a The animal referred to as "iguana" is properly termed "monitor lizard," of which there are numerous species. Australian usage of the term "iguana" has become fairly common.

b The opossum is normally referred to in Australian-Pacific literature as "possum," of which there are numerous genera and species.

APPENDIX F

A. INTEGRAL, VEGETATIVE CROPPING SYSTEMS—THE OLDEST TRADITIONAL SERIES

1. Random shift, seasonally resident, digging stick, vegetative cropping

   Crop site shifted seasonally or annually by random ritual choice; residence by single families, bands, or lineage groups on or near site, with marked temporary mobility during year; clearing system poor and casual, occasionally lacking burning; simplest range of tools in digging-stick complex; vegetative cropping complex of rudimentary variety, with random planting procedures; cropping ritualism simple; social structure simple, lineage groups, band and working groups; territoriality vaguely defined, land control absent to very loose, tenure system absent; food appropriation strong to dominantly contributory, extractive appropriation chiefly subsistent, with very slight exchange component.

   Subtypes would show variation in clearing procedures, social structure, gardening skills, territorial mobility, and dependence upon appropriation.

   Examples: Tapiro Negrito, Nassau Mountains, Dutch New Guinea (Bijlmer, 1939).

2. Random shift, periodically resident, digging stick, vegetative cropping

   Crop site shifted seasonally or annually by ritual choice within limited territory; residence by family, band, and lineage groups on sites chosen for utility and moved only at intervals; simple range of tools in digging-stick complex; clearing system simple and inefficient but related to site and cover; vegetative crop complex with fair variety but little specialization; cropping ritualism simple but with some crop focus; social structure simple with variable family, band, and lineage group working patterns; territoriality loose but vaguely specified, land control loose but evolving, tenure system absent to minimal; food appropriation vitally contributory, extractive appropriation minimal beyond subsistent but evolving.

   Subtypes would show variation particularly in siting and clearing, gardening skills, territoriality, and social structure.

   Examples: Ayom Negrito, Ramu River Valley, northeast New Guinea (Gusinde, 1958).

3. Linear shift, periodically resident, digging stick, vegetative cropping (a theoretical stage)

   New crop site cleared seasonally or annually on some flank of previous clearing, with some reuse of previous site, little ritualism in site selection; residence periodically moved nearer to current crop site and located per some utility, residence by single families, lineage groups, or working groups in semidispersed, hamlet, or cluster pattern; simple range of tools in digging-stick complex but quality good; clearing procedures well organized per sites and cover, burning and secondary clearing fairly efficient, fencing from unburned timber or selective sources; vegetative cropping complex with fair range and some varietal specialization; planting procedures systematic by recognition of choice sites; ritualism involving seasonal controls of cropping routine, somewhat focused on a primary crop; social structure fairly organized, working groups variable, division of labor in cropping routines present; territoriality fairly specific, land control loose to inefficient, tenure system temporarily effective only, food appropriation continuous and significantly complementary, extractive appropriation selective but not significantly pointed to exchange commodities.

Subtypes would show variation particularly in clearing and sequential cropping routines, residential mobility, social structure, and territoriality complex.

Examples: No clear examples can be identified in the literature, and I have not seen an example.

4. Cyclic shift, periodically resident, digging stick, vegetative cropping

New crop garden cleared seasonally, by intervals, with annual routine by selective choice from regenerated sites per local criteria, with some application of productive criteria; residence periodically moved nearer to current crop gardens and sited by local utility, residence by single families, hamlet clusters, or small villages; simple range of digging-stick tools expertly made and used; clearing procedures careful and adjusted to local vegetative patterns, secondary clearing and burning carefully done, fencing materials culled out, productive fruit trees saved in clearing; dooryard gardens variably present; vegetative cropping complex; planting procedures recognizing productive criteria for specific crops; social structure well organized but not highly involved, working groups variable, division of labor fairly well developed; ritualism important in planting-harvesting routines and focused on staple crop; territoriality specific, land control effective, tenure system relatively simple but organized for permanency; food appropriation complementary and growing for exchange commodities.

Subtypes would show variation particularly in cyclic shift routines, in residential mobility, in clearing-cropping routines, in social structure, and in land control and tenure systems.

Examples: Abelam, above Sepik River Valley, northeast New Guinea (Kaberry, 1940); Kukukuku, eastern New Guinea (?) (Bjerre, 1956); Ipili, Porgera Valley, eastern highland New Guinea (?) (Meggitt, 1957); Garia, southwest of Madang, northeast New Guinea (?) (Lawrence, 1955); Malaita-Ulawa in Solomon Islands (Ivens, 1927; Hogbin, 1934a, 1939b).

5. Cyclic shift, sedentarily resident, digging stick, vegetative cropping

New crop gardens cleared periodically during annual cycle, with routine selective choice from regenerated vegetative ranges and regular consideration of many productivity factors; dispersed, cluster, hamlet, or village residence in sedentary patterns, some crop-season shift to garden sites; digging-stick tool complex well developed and carefully used; clearing procedures involving careful routines per predetermined objectives, with careful control over fires, culling of fencing, poles, and construction woods; vegetative cropping complex, complemented by tree crops, dooryard gardens, planting procedures carefully developed per crops and many varieties;

ritualism important in formalized planting-harvesting routine but is applied purpose rather than controlling; social structure involved, formalized, and structured, with division of labor marked and integrated with other culture elements; territoriality specific, land control and tenure system well developed; food appropriation restricted to complementary role but well developed, per environment, in extractive exchange commodities.

Subtypes would show qualitative variation in many elements, with maturity aspect of varied elements significantly varied.

Examples: Orokaiva, of eastern Papua (Williams, 1928, 1930); Wogeo, of eastern Schouten Islands, northeast New Guinea (Hogbin, 1934*b*, 1938, 1939*a*); Keraki-Semarji of Fly River, southwest Papua (Williams, 1936); Trobriand Islanders (Malinowski, 1935; Austen, 1945); Tanga-Boieng of Bismarck Archipelago (Bell, 1946–1948, 1954); Dobu of d'Entrecasteaux Islands (Fortune, 1932).

6. Decining shift, sedentarily resident, digging stick-hoe culture, vegetative cropping

Some new garden space cleared seasonally or annually, but with well-developed replanting routines on previously cleared plots involving several-year use of any given site, careful consideration of new sites per vegetative regeneration and ecologic-edaphic criteria; dispersed, hamlet, cluster or village residence per culture-group choice-pattern, residence sedentary when in villages; tool systems showing evolution of digging-stick complex into hoe-culture complex to some degree; clearing procedures involving careful and predetermined routines; vegetative cropping complex, with strong development of specialized varieties for particular season length and ecologic-edaphic situations; dooryard gardening variably developed per culture-group custom; preparation of soil prior to planting according to vegetative and edaphic needs of garden sites; ritualism symbolic to declining in control over cropping procedures; postcropping stimulation of vegetative regeneration; social structure involved and structured; with division of labor marked and integrated into many facets of culture; territoriality highly specific, land-control system specific, and tenure system highly developed with controls tending to perpetuate holdings in given lines of inheritance leading toward concepts of private ownership; site selection, soil preparation, and tenure system becoming integrated into land-management concept; appropriation declining into barely complementary role in food economy but selectively developed, per environment, in extractive lines for exchange economy.

Subtypes would show wide range of variation in many aspects but most notable in degree of integration of the land-management complex of procedures.

Examples: Chimbu and Kuma of Wahgi Valley, highlands of eastern New Guinea (Brown and Brookfield, 1959; Nilles, 1942, 1943, 1953); Dani of Baliem Valley, highland New Guinea (Archbold, Rand, and Brass, 1942; Brass, 1941; Brookfield, 1962); Konyak Naga of northeast India (Hutton, 1922).

B. INTEGRAL, VEGETATIVE-SEED PLANTING CROPPING SYSTEMS— A YOUNGER
TRANSITIONAL SERIES MOVING EASTWARD.

7. Random shift, seasonally resident, digging stick, vegetative-seed planting

Crop sites shifted annually or seasonally by random ritual choice; residence by single families or small working group or band on or near crop site, considerable temporary mobility; very simple range of digging-stick tool complex; clearing system poor with casual execution; vegetative and grainlike seed crops planted by digging stick in random patterns; cropping ritualism simple but controlling; social structure simple with working groups small; territoriality vaguely defined, and control absent to loose, tenure system absent to vague; appropriation strong to dominantly contributory.

Subtypes would show variation particularly in siting patterns, clearing systems, social structure, gardening skills, and in cropping combinations.

Examples: Ple Senoi, Temoq Jakun, and a few other Senoi and Jakun groups, plus possibly Jehai and Lanoh Negrito, all of Malaya (Williams-Hunt, 1952); Subanun of Mindanao (Finley, 1913; Frake, 1960); Manobo of eastern Mindanao (Garvan, 1941); Pinatubo Negrito of Zambales, Luzon (Reed, 1904; Fox, 1952).

8. Random shift, periodically resident, digging stick, vegetative-seed planting

Crop site shifted annually or seasonally by ritual choice within limited orbit-area; residence by single families or small groups on sites chosen for utility and moved at intervals; simple range of digging-stick tools; clearing systems adapted to site and cover; vegetative and seed-planted crops planted by digging-stick routines in minimal patterns; cropping ritualism simple but focused on vegetative crop series, with only minor focus on seed-planted series; social structure simple with variable working group patterns; territoriality loose but forming, land control very loose, tenure system absent to minimal; appropriation strong to vitally contributory.

Subtypes would show variation particularly in siting-clearing systems, cropping combinations, gardening skills, and territoriality.

Examples: Some Senoi and Jakun groups of Malaya, particularly some Temiar Senoi (Williams-Hunt, 1952; Slimming, 1958).

9. Linear shift, periodically resident, digging stick, vegetative-seed planting.

New crop site cleared annually on some flank of previous clearing, tendency to seed planting of new site and reuse of previous year's site in vegetative planting, little ritualism in site selection; residence periodically moved nearer to current sites and located per some utility, residence by single families, lineage, or working groups living in clusters or hamlets; simple range of digging-stick tools used for all purposes; clearing procedures well organized, burning and secondary clearing fairly efficient; vegetative crop complex providing staples, seed-planted crops minor to complementary; cropping ritualism involving seasonal controls, focused chiefly on vegetative crops; social structure fairly organized, working groups variable, division of labor becoming marked per vegetative–seed-planted crops; territorality fairly specific, land control loose to minimal evolvement, tenure system temporarily applicable; appropriation continuous and significant but chiefly complementary.

Subtypes would show variation particularly in clearing and sequential cropping routines, residential mobility, social structure, cropping combinations, ritual applications, and social structure.

Examples: Many Temiar Senoi, some Semai Senoi, and a few Jakun groups of Malaya (Williams-Hunt, 1952); Magahat of southern Negros, Philippines (?) (Oracion, 1955); Bukidnon of northern Mindanao (Cole, 1956).

10. Cyclic shift, periodically resident, digging stick, vegetative-seed planting

New crop gardens cleared annually, by selective choice system from regenerated ranges per local criteria, with some application of productive criteria; residence periodically moved nearer to current crop gardens and sited by some utility, residence by single families, hamlets, lineage clusters, or small villages; simple range of digging stick tools expertly used; clearing procedures careful and related to local vegetative patterns, secondary clearing and burning carefully done, fencing materials culled out, productive fruit trees saved in clearing; dooryard gardens present in variable degree; vegetative-crop complex showing decline in importance, grainlike legumes and some grains in ascending importance, with number of plant species planted increasing significantly; planting procedures recognizing productive ecologic-edaphic criteria per crop patterns; social structure well organized but not highly involved, working groups variable, division of labor significant per vegetative–seed-planted crops and cropping routines; ritualism symbolic in planting and harvesting routines, sometimes still attached to vegetative crops, but tendency for order of importance to shift slowly to seed-planted crops; territoriality specific, land control effective, tenure system simple but organized for permanency and taking into account vegetative–seed-planting variation in cropping system; food appropriation complementary but seasonally varied per harvest productivity, and growing selective for extractive exchange commodities.

Subtypes would show variation particularly in cyclic shift routines, in clearing-cropping routines per vegetative-seed planting, in patterns of ritualism in social structure, and in land control and tenure systems.

Examples: Southern groups of Bison Hills Reddi of Eastern Ghats of India (C. and E. von Fürer-Haimendorf, 1945); Kolam of southern India in their traditional patterns (C. and E. von Fürer-Haimendorf, 1948); Tinguian of Luzon (Cole, 1922).

11. Cyclic shift, sedentarily resident, digging stick-hoe culture, vegetative-seed planting

New crop gardens cleared annually with routine selective choice from regenerated vegetative ranges, organized consideration of numerous productivity factors for particular crop combination; dispersed to hamlet residence present, but with medium to large villages dominant, and with residence sedentary; digging-stick tool complex selectively used, hoe complex increasing in importance for seed-planted crop series; clearing procedures predetermined per objective, with careful control over fires, culling of fencing, poles, construction, and other woods; vegetative-cropping complex declining to minor position, often as dooryard gardens, the seed-planted crop complex strongly ascendant and supplying staples, planting procedures specialized per crop patterns with grain crops often in pure stands, numbers of species and varieties of seed-planted crops increasing markedly but some specialization on staples normal; ritualism declining and sometimes adherent to selective vegetative plants in symbolic patterns but sometimes showing transfer to grain plants; social structure involved and structured, working groups variable but smaller, division of labor marked in certain routines and not in others; territoriality specific, land control well developed, and tenure system well developed and becoming very complex; food appropriation restricted to minor complementary role except in hunger period when it even becomes dominant, selective in extractive resources for exchange economy.

Subtypes would show variation in many elements per level of culture and territorial resources, and not all examples clearly are evolving hoe complex of tools.

Examples: Kolam of southern India in their more advanced patterns (C. and E. von Fürer-Haimendorf, 1948); Gond of southern India in their traditional patterns (C. and E. von Fürer-Haimendorf, 1948); a few Semai Senoi and several Jakun groups of Malaya, chiefly when breaking tribal traditions (Williams-Hunt, 1952); Isneg of northern Luzon (Vanovergbergh, 1932, 1941); some peoples of Mountain Province, northern Luzon (Scott, 1958a); Hanunóo of Mindoro, Philippines (Conklin, 1957).

12. Declining shift, sedentarily resident, hoe culture-plow culture, vegetative-seed planting

Some new garden space cleared seasonally or annually by selective choice from regenerated vegetative ranges, organized consideration of productivity features for particular crop combination, but with tendency for longer planting routines on hoe-cultured sites and larger and smoother sites toward annual cropping routine with soil preparation by plowing; dispersed, hamlet, cluster, or village residence per culture-group choices, residence sedentary when in villages; digging-stick tool complex declining and selectively used, tendency to become relict in favor of hoe complex of tools, with plow complex ascendant, but selective use of tools related to sites and particular crops; vegetative crop sequence declining in overall importance but with selective retention of particular crops, seed-planted crops ascendant in field use, both vegetative and seed-panted crops found in dooryard gardens, seed-planted crops increasing in variety; ritualism symbolic with traditional crops and fragmentary with primary crops; social structure involved and structured, working groups variable but declining in importance, division of labor marked in some routines but not in others; territoriality specific, land control well developed, traditional tenure system complex, but the whole pattern of territoriality, land control, and tenure changing under impact of political state, with private ownership ascendant; appropriation restricted and selective except in hunger periods for food economy, selective of extractive resources per environment for exchange and cash-sale commodities.

Subtypes would show variation in many respects, particularly in degree to which plow culture, seed planting, and private ownership are bringing about decline of traditional systems.

Examples: Gond of southern India in their more advanced patterns (C. and E. von Fürer-Haimendorf, 1948); Kalinga of eastern Mountain Province north Luzon (Scott, 1958*b*).

C. INTEGRAL SEED-PLANTING CROPPING SYSTEMS—A YOUNGER WESTERN SERIES

113. Random shift, seasonally resident, digging stick, seed planting

Crop site shifted annually or seasonally by random ritual choice; residence by bands or lineage groups on or near site for seasonal periods, with marked temporary mobility; clearing system poor and casual, but using fire; simplest range of digging-stick complex of tools; seed-planting crop complex in small range of varieties, with random planting procedures; cropping ritualism very simple; social structure simple, with lineage and band structure; territoriality vaguely defined, land control absent to loose, tenure system absent; appropriation for food economy strong much of the year, appropriation for exchange commodities limited in range but present.

Subtypes would show variation particularly in social structure, gardening skills, territorial mobility, and dependence upon appropriation for both food and exchange patterns.

Examples: Himalayan Raji, just west of Nepal (Pant, 1935; Majumdar, 1958); some Dafla of Assam Himalaya (?) (von Fürer-Haimendorf, 1955); some Lepcha of Bhutan in mid-nineteenth century (Dalton, 1872).

14. Random shift, periodically resident, digging stick, seed planting

Crop site shifted annually or seasonally by ritual choice within limited territorial range; residence by single family–band groups on sites chosen for some utility and moved only at intervals; simple range of digging-stick tools; clearing system related to site and cover; seed-planting cropping compex in limited range of crops; cropping ritualism simple but related to crop staple; social structure simple with variable family, band, and lineage working patterns; territoriality loose but vaguely specified, land control loose but evolving, tenure system absent to minimal; food appropriation strong and vitaily contributory, but least at crop harvest, greatest in hunger periods, extractive appropriation selective for exchange items.

Subtypes would show variation particularly in siting-clearing procedures, gardening skills, territoriality, and appropriative patterns.

Examples: Some Lepcha of Sikkim in mid-nineteenth century (?) (Hooker, 1854; Dalton, 1872); Plains Miri of Assam (Dalton, 1872).

15. Linear shift, periodically resident, digging stick, seed planting

New crop site cleared annually on some flank of previous clearing, with some reuse of previous clearing for other than staple crop, but little ritualism in site selection; residence periodically moved nearer to current crop site and located by some utility, residence by single family, lineage group, working-group hamlet patterns; digging-stick tool complex well developed in good quality; clearing procedures well organized to site patterns, secondary clearing fairly efficient; seed-planting crop complex in wide variety but concentrated on a grain staple; planting involving some pure stands, with recognition of choice sites for particular crops; ritualism developed around crop staple in seasonal pattern but not life controlling; social structure fairly organized, working groups variable, division of labor in working routines present; territoriality fairly specific, land control loose but operative, tenure system temporarily effective and developing; food appropriation significant in complementary pattern most of year but vital during any hunger period, and involving chiefly wild products not eaten in normal pattern, extractive appropriation selective for exchange commodities.

Subtypes would show considerable variation dependent upon contact with neighbors of higher culture.

Examples: No clear examples can be identified in the literature. Iban of Borneo show tendency to move primarily in one direction in major terms, but may be cyclic in local terms (Freeman, 1955).

16. Cyclic shift, periodically resident, digging stick, seed planting

New crop garden cleared annually, with systematic selective choice from regenerated sites per local criteria, with significant application of productive criteria; residence moved periodically nearer to current cropping sites and located by utility, residence by hamlets and lineage clusters operating from long houses that form villages; simple range of digging-stick tools expertly made and used; clearing procedures careful and adjusted to local vegetative patterns, secondary clearing and burning carefully done to produce clear field plots, fencing materials culled when needed; dooryard gardens for selective vegetable and fruit crops in casual manner; seed-planted cropping complex rich in variety but locally selective and concentrated upon a grain staple; planting procedures recognizing productive criteria for specific crops and rather well developed; ritualism focused on crop staple almost entirely; social structure well developed but not intricately structured, with variable working group patterns, division of labor developed; territoriality specific, land control effective, tenure system relatively well organized, the whole complex subject to inroads of permanent-field farmers; food appropriation complementary in minor way except for hunger periods, extractive appropriation quite selective to fit exchange markets.

Subtypes would show considerable variation dependent upon contact with neighbors of higher or different culture.

Examples: Hill Miri of Assam Himalaya (Dalton, 1872); Iban of west Borneo (Freeman, 1955).

17. Cyclic shift, sedentarily resident, digging stick-hoe culture, seed planting

New crop gardens cleared annually, with routine selective choice from regenerated vegetative ranges, regular consideration of many factors making for productivity; dispersed, cluster, hamlet, or village residence in sedentary patterns; digging-stick tool complex declining in use with hoe complex ascendant and common though primitive; clearing routines fitted to sites but according to predetermined objectives, with careful control of fires and selective culling of useful woods; seed-planting crop complex in rich variety but concentrated on particular staples for culinary specialization, planting procedures selective for crops, crop ritualism slight to relict symbolism, dooryard gardens not fully functional but selective homestead, hamlet, or village scattering of shrub and tree items; social structure involved and formalized, with selective division of labor and structure integrated into noncropping culture; territoriality and specific land control well developed, tenure system well developed; food appropriation highly selective in complementary sense except during hunger periods, extractive appropriation selective per environment for exchange and sale markets.

Subtypes would show wide range of qualitative variation in many elements, with relation to neighboring cultures.

Examples: Baiga of Maikal Hills, central India (Nag, 1958); Ho of Chota Nagpur in nineteenth century (Majumdar, 1950) (?); Lepcha of Sikkim in twentieth century (Gorer, 1938); Abor of Assam (Dalton, 1872); some Bhutan Dafla (Bower, 1953); Hill Maria Gond of central India (Grigson, 1949); such Naga groups as Lhota and Sema (Zemi) (Mills, 1922).

18. Declining shift, sedentarily resident, hoe culture-plow culture, seed planting

Some new garden space cleared annually for particular cropping sequences, but with well-developed replanting routines on previously cleared plots, and with plowed lands tending to become permanent fields, less careful consideration of new sites per vegetative regeneration in favor of siting on plowable lands; dispersed, hamlet, cluster, or village residence per culture-group choice, residence tending to become more sedentary with village locations; tool systems show decline of digging stick to relict use and declining use of other digging-stick complex tools, use of hoe-tool complex common, and increasing use of plow-complex tools; clearing procedures on new lands tending toward expediency; vegetative-cropping complex declining into dooryard gardening, with many former crops now relict, seed-planted grain crops dominant and specialized on smaller number of crops; preparation of soil varied per site and procedure in use, expedient preparation on shifting sites, hoe-culture procedures common, with plowing of primary fields becoming standardized in pattern followed locally by permanent-field farmers; ritualism declining to symbolic or relict patterns and most commonly applied only to traditional crops; territoriality specific but suffering inroads of permanent-field farmers backed by legal institutions, land control subject to increasing disruption, traditional tenure system breaking down as land is lost to permanent-field farmers, moneylenders, and others, but tending to private ownership otherwise; food appropriation declining in regularity but significant in hunger periods, appropriation quite specific as to extractive resources for commodity exchange or cash sale.

Subtypes would show wide variation in many aspects as to the relict status of traditional shifting-cultivation routine and the acceptance of plow-culture routines.

Examples: Hill Garo of Assam, India (Nakane, 1958; Das, 1960; Burling, 1960); Khasi of Assam Khasi Hills (Majumdar, 1958); Bhotiya, Himalayas west of Nepal (Pant, 1935); Pauri Bhuiyan of Chota Nagpur (Mahapatra, 1955); such northeast Indian Naga groups as Angami, Khoirao, Kacha, Ao, Tangkhul, Maram, and Naked Rengma (Bower, 1950*b;* Hodson, 1911; Hutton, 1921, 1922; Mills, 1922; Smith, 1925).

BIBLIOGRAPHY

BIBLIOGRAPHY

The following bibliography, numbering about 455 items, includes all the useful works surveyed in the course of this study, both those serving as background and those contributing descriptive material on shifting cultivation in southern and eastern Asia. Items marked with an asterisk are background studies or studies used in support of some point of view, theory, fact, or historical reference. Such items do not contain factual material contributing directly to the analysis of shifting cultivation in southern and eastern Asia in the modern period. A general and worldwide bibliography of more than 1,200 items on the subject of shifting cultivation, as such, may be found in Conklin, 1961, and an annotated worldwide bibliography on fire, primitive agriculture, and grazing may be found in Bartlett, 1955–1961. When a title contains only a restricted place-name, a more general geographic reference is added immediately after the bibliographical data.

Aiyappan, A. 1948. *Report on the Socio-Economic Conditions of the Aboriginal Tribes in the Province of Madras.* Madras: Government Printer. Southeastern India.

Allen, G. C., and A. G. Donnithorne. 1957. *Western Enterprise in Indonesia and Malaya.* London: George Allen & Unwin.

Allison, W. W. 1963. "A Compound System of Swidden ("Kaingin") Agriculture," *Philippine Geographical Journal,* 7:159–172.

Allsop, F. 1953. "Shifting Cultivation in Burma: Its Practice, Effects and Controls, and Its Use to Make Forest Plantations," *Proceedings of the Seventh Pacific Science Congress, 1949,* 6: 277–285.

Anas, M. 1958. "Australian New Guinea: A Geographical Survey." Unpublished Ph.D. dissertation. Australian National University, Canberra.

Andrus, J. R. 1947. *Burmese Economic Life.* Stanford: Stanford University Press.

Archbold, R., A. L. Rand, and L. J. Brass. 1942. "Results of the Archbold Expeditions, No. 41. Summary of the 1938–1939 New Guinea Expedition," *Bulletin of the American Museum of Natural History,* 79:197–288.

Armstrong, W. E. 1928. *Rossel Island: An Ethnological Study.* London: Cambridge University Press. Louisade Archipelago off eastern New Guinea.

Arnold, G. 1957. "The Usun Apan Plateau," *Geographical Journal,* 123:167–178. Interior British Borneo.

Assam Secretariat. 1896. *Physical and Political Geography of the Province of Assam.* Shillong: Assam Secretariat Printing Office. Northeastern India.

Aufenanger, H. 1961. "The Cordyline Plant in the Central Highlands of New Guinea," *Anthropos,* 56:393–408.

Aufenanger, H., and G. Höltker. 1940. *Die Gende in Zentralneuguinea, von Leben und Denken eines Papua-stammes in Bismarckgebirge.* Vienna: Missionsdruckerei St. Gabriel. Central New Guinea.

Aung, M. H. 1953. "Customary Law in Burma," in P. W. Thayer, *Southeast Asia in the Coming World.* Baltimore: Johns Hopkins Press. Pp. 203–216.

Austen, L. 1945. "Cultural Changes in Kiriwina," *Oceania,* 16:15–60. Trobriand Islands, off eastern New Guinea.

Australian Department of External Territories. 1958. *Report on the Administration of New Guinea, 1956–1957.* Canberra: Government Printer.

Baden-Powell, B. H. 1892. *The Land Systems of British India.* Oxford: Clarendon Press. 3 vols.

*Bagby, P. 1959. *Culture and History: Prolegomena to the Comparative Study of Civilizations,* Berkeley and Los Angeles: University of California Press.

*Bailey, L. H., and E. Z. Bailey. 1930, 1941. *Hortus Second: A Concise Dictionary of Gardening, General Horticulture and Cultivated Plants in North America.* New York: Macmillan.

Baldwin, M., *et al.* 1948, 1952. *Soil Conservation: An International Study.* FAO Agricultural Studies, no. 4. Rome.

Balfour, H. 1917. "Some Types of Native Hoes, Naga Hills," *Man,* 17 (sec. 74):105–107. Northeast India.

Banks, E. 1949. *A Naturalist in Sarawak*. Kuching Press. British Borneo.

Barrau, J. 1953. "Taro," *South Pacific Commission Quarterly Bulletin*, 3(4):31–32.

———. 1954. "Traditional Subsistence Economy and Agriculture Progress in Melanesia," *South Pacific Commission Quarterly Bulletin*, 4(3):2–7. Southwest Pacific.

———. 1956. *Polynesian and Micronesian Subsistence Agriculture*. Nouméa: South Pacific Commission.

———. 1958. *Subsistence Agriculture in Melanesia*. Honolulu. Bernice P. Bishop Bulletin 219. Southwest Pacific.

———. 1959. "The 'Bush Fallowing' System of Cultivation in the Continental Islands of Melanesia," *Proceedings of the Ninth Pacific Science Congress*, 1957, 7:53–55. Southwest Pacific.

———. 1960. "Plant Introduction in the Tropical Pacific: Its Role in Economic Development," *Pacific Viewpoint*, 1(1):1–10.

Barrett, C. 1954. *Isles of the Sun*. London: Heinemann. Eastern New Guinea.

Bartlett, H. H. 1919. "The Manufacture of Sugar from *Arenga saccharifera* in Asahan, on the East Coast of Sumatra," in *Twenty-first Report, Michigan Academy of Science*. Pp. 157–158.

———. 1956. "Fire, Primitive Agriculture, and Grazing in the Tropics," in W. L. Thomas, Jr., *Man's Role in Changing the Face of the Earth*. Chicago: University of Chicago Press. Pp. 692–720.

———. 1956, 1957, 1961. *Fire in Relation to Primitive Agriculture and Grazing in the Tropics*. Vol. 1. Ann Arbor: Botanical Gardens. Vols. 2, 3. Ann Arbor: University of Michigan, Department of Botany. Bibliography annotated particularly as to the role of fire.

Barton, R. F. 1949. *The Kalingas: Their Institutions and Custom Law*. Chicago: University of Chicago Press. Northern Philippines.

Baudesson, H. 1919. *Indochina and Its Primitive People*. New York: Dutton.

*Beals, R. L., and H. Hoijer. 1953, 1959. *An Introduction to Anthropology*. New York: Macmillan.

Beauclair, I. de. 1956. "Culture Traits of Non-Chinese Tribes in Kweichow Province, Southwest China," *Sinologica*, 5:23–35.

Bell, F. L. S. 1946, 1947, 1948. "The Place of Food in the Social Life of the Tanga," *Oceania*, 17:139–172; 310–326; 18:36–59, 233–247; 19:51–74. Bismark Archipelago, off eastern New Guinea.

———. 1954. "Land Tenure in Tanga," *Oceania*, 24:28–57. Bismark Archipelago, off eastern New Guinea.

Belshaw, C. S. 1955. *In Search of Wealth; A Study of the Emergence of Commercial Operations in the Melanesian Society of Southeast Papua*. American Anthropological Society Memoir no. 80. Eastern New Guinea.

———. 1957. *The Great Village: The Economic and Social Welfare of Hanuabada, an Urban Community in Papua*. London: Routledge & Kegan Paul. Eastern New Guinea.

Bernatzik, H. A. 1936. *Owa Raha*. Vienna: Buchergilde Gutenberg. Solomon Islands, Southwest Pacific.

Berndt, R. M. 1962. *Excess and Restraint: Social Control among a New Guinea Mountain People*. Chicago: University of Chicago Press.

Bertrand, G. 1959. *The Jungle People*. London: Hale. Upland Indochina.

Beukering, J. A. van. 1947. *Het Ladangvraagstuk, een Bedrijfs—en Sociaal Economisch Probleem*. Batavia: Mededeelingen van het Department van Economische Zaken. No. 9. Indonesia.

Bijlmer, H. J. T. 1939. "Tapiro Pygmies and Pania Mountain-Papuans," *Nova Guinea*, n.s., 3: 113–184. Western New Guinea.

Birch, H. F. 1960. "Soil Drying and Soil Fertility," *Tropical Agriculture*, 37:3–10.

Bjerre, J. 1956. *The Last Cannibals*. London: Joseph. New Guinea.

Blackwood, B. 1931. "Report on Field Work in Buka and Bougainville," *Oceania*, 2:199–219. Solomon Islands, Southwest Pacific.

———. 1939. "Life on the Upper Watut, New Guinea," *Geographical Journal*, 94:11–28. Eastern New Guinea.

Blalock, J. S. 1954. "A Short Study of Pepper Culture with Special Reference to Sarawak," *Tropical Agriculture*, 31:40–56. British Borneo.

Blanchard, W., ed. 1958. *Thailand: Its People, Its Society, Its Culture.* New Haven: Human Relations Area Files.

Bogesi, G. 1947. "Santa Isobel, Solomon Islands," *Oceania,* 18:208–232.

Bower, U. G. 1950a. *Drums behind the Hill.* New York: Morrow. Northeast India.

———. 1950b. *Naga Path.* London: John Murray. Northeast India.

———. 1953. *The Hidden Land.* London: John Murray. Northeast India.

*Braidwood, R. J. 1960. "The Agricultural Revolution," *Scientific American,* 203:130–152. Middle East.

*Braidwood, R. J., and B. Howe. 1960. *Prehistoric Investigations in Iraqui Kuristan.* Oriental Institute for Studies in Ancient Oriental Civilization no. 31. Chicago: University of Chicago Press. Middle East.

Brass, L. J. 1941. "Stone Age Agriculture in New Guinea," *Geographical Review,* 31:555–569.

Brookfield, H. C. 1960. "Population Distribution and Labor Migration in New Guinea," *Australian Geographer,* 7:233–242.

———. 1961. "The Highland Peoples of New Guinea; A Study of Distribution and Localization," *Geographical Journal,* 127:436–448.

———. 1962. "Local Study and Comparative Method: An Example from Central New Guinea," *Annals,* Association of American Geographers, 52:242–254.

Brookfield, H. C., and P. Brown. 1963. *Struggle for Land, Agriculture and Group Territories among the Chimbu of the New Guinea Highlands.* Melbourne: Oxford University Press.

*Brown, D. M. 1953. *The White Umbrella: Indian Political Thought from Manu to Ghandi.* Berkeley and Los Angeles: University of California Press.

Brown, G. 1910. *Melanesians and Polynesians: Their Life Histories Described and Compared.* London: Macmillan.

Brown, P., 1960. "Chimbu Tribes: Political Organization in the Eastern Highlands of New Guinea," *Southwestern Journal of Anthropology,* 16:22–35.

Brown, P., and H. C. Brookfield. 1959. "Chimbu Land and Society," *Oceania,* 30:1–75. Highland eastern New Guinea.

Buchanan, F. 1807. *A Journey from Madras through the Countries of Mysore, Canara, and Malabar.* London: Cadell & Davies. 3 vols. Southern India.

Buck, E. 1915. "Rab: A Unique System of Cultivating Rice in Western India," *International Institute of Agriculture, Monthly Bulletin of the Bureau of Agricultural Intelligence and Plant Diseases,* 6:1011–1117.

Bulmer, R. 1960. "Political Aspects of the Moka Ceremonial Exchange System among the Kyaka People of the Western Highlands of New Guinea," *Oceania,* 31:1–31.

Burbridge, F. W. 1880. *Gardens of the Sun.* London: John Murray. Borneo and Sulu.

*Burkill, I. H. 1935. *A Dictionary of the Economic Products of the Malay Peninsula.* London: Crown Agents for the Colonies. 2 vols.

*———. 1951. "The Rise and Decline of the Greater Yam in the Service of Man," *Advancement of Science,* 7:443–448. Southeast Asia.

*———. 1953. "Habits of Man and the Origins of the Cultivated Plants of the Old World," *Proceedings of the Linnean Society of London,* 164:12–42.

Burling, R. 1960. "An Incipient Caste Organization in the Garo Hills," *Man in India,* 40:283–298. Northeast India.

*Bushnell, G. H. S. 1956. "Slash-and-Burn Cultivation," *Man,* 56 (sec. 59):64. Terminological note.

Buttinger, J. 1958. *The Smaller Dragon: A Political History of Vietnam.* New York: Praeger. Indochina.

Cameron, J. 1865. *Our Tropical Possessions in Malayan India.* London: Smith, Elder & Co. Malaya.

Campbell, J. 1864. *A Personal Narrative of Thirteen Years Service amongst the Wild Tribes of Khondistan for the Supression of Human Sacrifice,* London: Hurst & Blackett. Northwest India.

Capell, A. 1943. "Peoples and Languages of Timor," *Oceania,* 14:160–219. Lesser Sunda zone of Indonesia.

————. 1948. "Distribution of Languages in the Central Highlands of New Guinea," *Oceania,* 19:104–129, 234–253.

————. 1954. *A Linguistic Survey of the Southwestern Pacific.* Nouméa: South Pacific Commission.

Carey, B. S., and H. N. Tuck. 1896. *The Chin Hills: A History of the People, Our Dealings with Them, Their Customs and Manners, and a Gazetteer of Their Country.* Rangoon: Government Printer. 2 vols. Eastern India-Burma border.

*Carneiro, R. L. 1960. "Slash-and-Burn Agriculture: A Closer Look at Its Implications for Settlement Patterns," in A. F. C. Wallace, *Men and Cultures,* being Selected Papers of the Fifth International Congress of Anthropological and Ethnological Sciences, 1956. Philadelphia: University of Pennsylvania Press. Pp. 229–234. Deals with an example in Brazil.

Carter, T. D., J. E. Hill, and G. H. H. Tate. 1945. *Mammals of the Pacific World.* New York: Macmillan Company.

Cassidy, N. G., and S. D. Pahalad. "The Maintenance of Soil Fertility in Fiji," *Agricultural Journal of the Colony of Fiji,* 24:82–86. South Pacific.

Ceylon, Government of. 1951. *Report of the Kandyan Peasantry Commission.* Sessional Paper 18, 1951. Colombo: Government Press. Ceylon.

Chalmers, J., and W. W. Gill. 1885. *Work and Adventure in New Guinea, 1877–1885.* London: Religious Tract Society.

Chattopadhyay, K. P. 1949. "The Tribal Problem and Its Solution," *Eastern Anthropologist,* 3: 15–21. India.

————. 1957. *Study of Changes in Traditional Culture.* Calcutta: University of Calcutta Press. India.

Chaturvedi, M. D., and B. N. Uppal. 1953. *A Study of Shifting Cultivation of Assam.* New Delhi: Indian Council of Agricultural Research. 20 pp. Northeast India.

Chaudhuri, H. N. 1903. *The Cooch Behar State and Its Land Revenue Settlements.* Cooch Behar: Cooch Behar State Press. North India.

Chemin-Dupontes, P. 1909. "La question forestière en Indo-Chine," *Bulletin du Comité de l'Asie Française,* 9(101):340–348. Indochina.

*Cheng, T. K. 1959. *Prehistoric China.* Cambridge: Heffer.

*————. 1960. *Shang China.* Cambridge: Heffer.

*Childe, V. G. 1936, 1941, 1951. *Man Makes Himself.* London: Oxford University Press. Different publishers for later editions.

*————. 1957. *The Dawn of European Civilization.* London: Routledge & Kegan Paul.

Colbourne, M. J., W. H. Heuhne, and F. de S. Lachance. 1960. "The Sarawak Anti-Malarial Project," *Sarawak Museum Journal,* n.s., 9:215–248. On seasonal field houses among the Iban, British Borneo.

Cole, F-C. 1922. "The Tinguian: Social, Religious, and Economic Life of a Philippine Tribe," *Field Museum of Natural History, No. 209, Anthropological Series,* 14:230–493. Northern Philippines.

————. 1945. *The Peoples of Malaysia.* New York: Van Nostrand.

————. 1956. *The Bukidnon of Mindanao.* Fieldiana; Anthropology, vol. 46. Southern Philippines.

*Colonial Office, 1952. *An Annotated Bibliography on Land Tenure in the British and British Protected Territories in South East Asia and the Pacific.* London: Her Majesty's Stationery Office.

Condominas, G. 1957. *Nous avons mangé la forêt.* Paris: Mercure de France. Southern upland Indochina.

————. 1960. "Les Muong Gar du Centre Viet-Nam," in G. P. Murdoch, *Social Structure in Southeast Asia.* New York: Viking. Wenner-Gren Foundation. Viking Fund Publication no. 29. Pp. 15–24. Indochina.

*Conklin, H. C. 1954. "An Ethnoecological Approach to Shifting Cultivation," *Transactions of the New York Academy of Sciences,* ser. 2, 17:133–142.

————. 1957. *Hanunóo Agriculture; A Report on an Integral System of Shifting Cultivation in the Philippines.* FAO Forestry Development Papers, no. 12. Rome.

————. 1959. "Shifting Cultivation and Succession to Grassland Climax," *Proceedings of the Ninth Pacific Science Congress, 1957,* 7:60–62.

*————. 1961. "The Study of Shifting Cultivation," *Current Anthropology,* 2:27–61. General bibliography.

Conroy, W. L. 1953. "Notes on Some Land Use Problems in Papua and New Guinea," *Australian Geographer,* 6:25–30.

Conroy, W. L., and L. A. Bridgland. 1950. "Native Agriculture in Papua–New Guinea," in *Report of the New Guinea Nutrition Survey Expedition, 1947.* Sydney: Government Printer. Pp. 72–91.

Cordiner, J. 1807. *A Description of Ceylon, Containing an Account of the Country, Inhabitants, and Natural Productions.* London: Longman, Hurst, Rees, and Orme. 2 vols.

*Coster, N. 1953. "An Evaluation of Tropical Pulse Crops," *Agricultural Journal of the Colony of Fiji,* 24:30–31.

Crawfurd, J. 1820. *History of the Indian Archipelago.* London: Constable. 3 vols.

Credner, W. 1935. *Siam, Das Land der Tai: eine Landeskunde auf Grund eigener Reisen under Forschungen.* Stuttgart: Engelhorn.

Cuisiner, J. 1946. *Les Muong: Géographie Humaine et Sociologie.* Paris: Institute d'Ethnologie. Upland Indochina.

Dalton, E. T. 1872. *Descriptive Ethnology of Bengal.* Calcutta: Government Printer. Eastern India.

*Darby, H. C. 1956. "The Clearing of the Woodland in Europe," in W. L. Thomas, Jr., *Man's Role in Changing the Face of the Earth.* Chicago: University of Chicago Press. Pp. 183–216.

*Darlington, P. J. 1957. *Zoogeography.* New York: Wiley.

Das, B. M. 1937. "Some Notes on the Economic and Agricultural Life of a Little Known Tribe on the Eastern Frontier of India," *Anthropos,* 32:440–449.

————. 1960. "Somatic Variations among the Hill and Plains Garo of Assam," *Man in India,* 40:128–148. Northeast India.

Das, T. C. 1945. *The Purums: An Old Kuki Tribe of Manipur.* Calcutta: University of Calcutta Press. Eastern India.

Davenport, W. 1962. "Red Feather Money," *Scientific American,* 206:94–104. Southwest Pacific.

Davies, H. R. 1909. *Yun-nan: The Link between India and the Yangtze.* Cambridge: Cambridge University Press.

De la Rue, E. A. F. Bourliere, and J–P. Harroy. 1957. *The Tropics.* London: Harrap.

Delgado, J. J. 1892. *Historia general sacro-profana, politica, y natural de las Islas del Poniente Llamadas Filipinas.* Manila: Juan Atayde. A manuscript written in 1751–1754, Philippines.

Department of External Affairs, Australia. 1958. *Report to the General Assembly of the United Nations on the Administration of the Territory of New Guinea, 1956–1957.* Canberra: Government Printer. The latest of a series of annual reports available to me.

Deshpande, C. D. 1948. *Western India: A Regional Geography.* Dharwar: Students Own Book Depot.

De Young, J. E. 1955. *Village Life in Modern Thailand.* Berkeley and Los Angeles: University of California Press.

Dobby, E. H. G. 1950. *Southeast Asia.* London: University of London Press.

————. 1953. "Food and the Changing Function of Southeast Asia," in P. W. Thayer, *Southeast Asia in the Coming World.* Baltimore: Johns Hopkins Press.

Dube, S. C. 1951. *The Kamar.* Lucknow. Universal Publishers. Peninsular India.

Dubois, C. A. 1944, 1960. *The People of Alor.* Minneapolis: University of Minnesota Press. Lesser Sunda zone of Indonesia.

Dumont, R. 1957. *Types of Rural Economy: Studies in World Agriculture.* London: Methuen. French ed.: Paris, 1954.

Dundas, J. 1944. "Bush Burning in Tropical Africa," *Empire Forestry Journal,* 23:122–125.

Dupeyrat, A. 1955. *Festive Papua.* London: Staples. Eastern New Guinea.

Durrad, W. J. 1939. "Notes on the Torres Islands," *Oceania,* 10:389–403. Northern New Hebrides, southwest Pacific.

*Dutt, R. 1950. *Economic History of India under Early British Rule.* London: Routledge & Kegan Paul.

Dutta, P. 1959. *The Tangsas of the Namchick and Tirap Valleys.* Shillong: Northeast Frontier Agency. Northeastern India.

*Eberhard, W. 1950, 1960. *A History of China.* Berkeley and Los Angeles: University of California Press.

Eggan, F. 1960. "The Sagada Igorots of Northern Luzon," in G. P. Murdoch, *Social Structure in Southeast Asia.* New York: Viking. Wenner-Gren Foundation. Viking Fund Publication no. 29. Northern Philippines.

*Ehrenfels, U. R. 1957. "Slash-and-Burn," *Man,* 57 (sec. 55):48. Terminological note.

*Ekwall, E. 1955. "Slash-and-Burn Cultivation: A Contribution to Anthropological Terminology," *Man,* 55 (sec. 144):135–136.

Elmberg, J. E. 1955. "Field Notes on the Mejbrat People in the Ajamaru District of the Bird's Head (Vogelkop), Western New Guinea," *Ethnos,* 20:1–102.

Embree, J. F., and W. L. Thomas, Jr., 1950. *Ethnic Groups of Northern Southeast Asia.* New Haven: Yale University Southeast Asia Studies.

Endle, S. 1911. *The Kacharis.* London: Macmillan. Northeast India.

*Evans, E. E. 1956. "The Ecology of Peasant Life in Western Europe," in W. L. Thomas, Jr., *Man's Role in Changing the Face of the Earth.* Chicago: University of Chicago Press. Pp. 217–239.

Evans, I. H. N. 1922. *Among Primitive Peoples in Borneo.* London: Seeley, Service & Co.

FAO staff. 1957. "Shifting Cultivation," *Unasylva,* 11:9–11.

Farmer, B. H. 1954. "Problems of Land Use in the Dry Zone of Celyon," *Geographical Journal,* 120:21–33.

————. 1957. *Pioneer Peasant Colonization in Ceylon: A Study in Asian Agrarian Problems.* London: Oxford University Press.

*Faucher, D. 1949. *Géographie Agraire: Types des Cultures.* Paris: Librarie de Medicis.

*Fautereau, E. de. 1956. "Slash-and-Burn," *Man,* 56, (sec. 171):148. Terminological note.

Finley, J. P. 1913. *The Subanu: Studies of a Sub-Visayan Mountain Folk of Mindanao.* Carnegie Institution of Washington, Publication no. 184, Part I. Southern Philippines.

Forbes, H. O. 1885. *A Naturalist's Wanderings in the Eastern Archipelago: A Narrative of Travel and Exploration from 1878 to 1883.* New York: Harper and Brothers. Southeast Asia and the Indies.

*Forde, C. D. 1934, 1952. *Habitat, Economy and Society: A Geographical Introduction to Ethnology.* London: Methuen.

Forsyth, J. 1889. *The Highlands of Central India: Notes on Their Forests and Wild Tribes, Natural History and Sports.* Rev. ed. London: Chapman, Hall.

Fortune, R. F. 1932. *The Sorcerers of Dobu: The Social Anthropology of the Dobu Islanders of the Western Pacific.* London: George Routledge & Sons.

Fosberg, F. R., ed. 1958. "Symposium on Climate, Vegetation, and Rational Land Utilization in the Humid Tropics," *Proceedings of the Ninth Pacific Science Congress, 1957,* 20:1–169.

Fox, R. B. 1952. "The Pinatubo Negritos: Their Useful Plants and Material Culture," *Philippine Journal of Science,* 81:173–414. Western Luzon, northern Philippines.

Frake, C. O. 1960. "The Eastern Subanun of Mindanao," in G. P. Murdoch, *Social Structure in Southeast Asia.* New York: Viking. Wenner-Gren Foundation. Viking Fund Publication no. 29. Pp. 51–64. Southern Philippines.

Frake, C. O., and W. H. Goodenough. 1956. "Malayo-Polynesian Land Tenure," *American Anthropologist,* 58:170–176. An exchange of correspondence under common title, relating to Indonesia and southwest Pacific.

Freeman, J. D. 1955. *Iban Agriculture: A Report on the Shifting Agriculture of Hill Rice by the Iban of Sarawak.* London: Her Majesty's Stationery Office. British Borneo.

Fuchs, S. 1960. *The Gond and Bhumia of Eastern Mandla.* London: Asia Publishing House. Central India.

Fürer-Haimendorf, C. von. 1951. Foreword to S. C. Dube, *The Kamar*. Lucknow: Universal Publishers. General statement on varying levels of primitive agriculturists, as exemplified by the Kamar.

———. 1955. *Himalayan Barbary*. London: Murray. Northeastern India.

Fürer-Haimendorf, C. and E. von. 1945. *The Reddis of the Bison Hills: A Study in Acculturation*. London: Macmillan. Peninsular India.

———. 1948. *The Raj Gonds of Adilabad*. London: Macmillan. Peninsular India.

Furness, W. H. 1902. *The Home Life of the Borneo Head Hunters*. Philadelphia: Lippincott.

Furnivall, J. S. 1948, 1956. *Colonial Policy and Practice: A Comparative Study of Burma and Netherlands India*. Cambridge: Campridge University Press.

Gardi, R. 1958. "Yamskult in Neuguinea," *Kosmos*, 54:9–17.

Garvan, J. M. 1441. *The Manobos of Mindanao*. Memoirs of the National Academy of Sciences, vol. 23. Washington: Government Printing Office. Southern Philippines.

Geddes, W. R. 1954a. *The Land Dyaks of Sarawak*. London: Her Majesty's Stationery Office. British Borneo.

———. 1954b. "Land Tenure of Land Dyaks," *Sarawak Museum Journal*, 6:42–51. British Borneo.

Geertz, C. 1963. *Agricultural Involution: The Process of Ecological Change in Indonesia*. Berkeley and Los Angeles: University of California Press.

Ginsburg, N., ed. 1955. *Area Handbook on Laos*. Chicago: University of Chicago Press. Upland Indochina.

Ginsburg, N., and C. F. Roberts. 1958. *Malaya*. Seattle: University of Washington Press.

Gitlow, A. L. 1947. *The Economics of the Mount Hagen Tribes, New Guinea*. American Ethnological Society Monograph no. 12. New York: Augustin. Eastern New Guinea.

Godden, G. M. 1898. "On the Naga and Other Frontier Tribes of Northeastern India," *Journal of the Royal Anthropological Institute of Great Britain and Ireland*, 26:161–201; 27:2–51.

Gonggrip, J. W. 1938. "Soil Management and Density of Population in the Netherlands Indies," *Comptes Rendus du Cong. Int. de Géographic*, 2 (sec. 3C):397–404.

Goodenough, W. H. 1953. "Ethnographic Notes on the Mae People of New Guinea's Western Highlands," *Southwestern Journal of Anthropology*, 9:29–44.

Gorer, S. 1938. *Himalayan Village: An Account of the Lepchas of Sikkim*. London: Michael Joseph. Himalayan India.

Gorrie, R. M. 1938. "The Relationship between Density of Population and the Method of Land Utilization in British India," *Comptes Rendus du Cong. Int. de Géographie*, 2 (sec. 3C):405–416.

Gourou, P. 1936. *Les Paysans du Delta Tonkinois*. Paris: Ed. d'Art et d'Histoire. Trans. into English by Richard Miller: *The Peasants of the Tonkin Delta: A Study of Human Geography* (New Haven: Human Relations Area Files, 1955). 2 vols. Northern Indochina.

———. 1940. *L'utilization du sol en Indochine Française*. Paris: Hartman. Indochina.

———. 1947. *Les Pays Tropicaux: Principes d'une Géographie Humaine et économique*. Paris: Presses Universitaires de France. Trans. into English by E. D. Laborde: *The Tropical World: Its Social and Economic Conditions and Its Future Status*. (London: Longmans, Green, 1953).

———. 1951. "Land Utilization in Upland Areas of Indochina," in *The Development of Upland Areas in the Far East*. Vol. 2. New York: Institute of Pacific Relations. Pp. 25–42.

———. 1956. "The Quality of Land Use of Tropical Cultivators," in W. L. Thomas, Jr., *Man's Role in Changing the Face of the Earth*. Chicago: University of Chicago Press. Pp. 336–349. General tropics.

Graham, D. C. 1942. "The Customs of the Ch'iang," *Journal of the West China Border Research Society*, Ser. A, 14:69–100. West China.

———. 1954. *Songs and Stories of the Ch'una Miao*. Smithsonian Miscellaneous Collections, vol. 123, no. 1, publication 4139. Washington: Government Printing Office. Southwest China.

———. 1958. *The Customs and Religion of the Ch'iang*. Smithsonian Miscellaneous Collections, vol. 135, no. 1. Washington: Government Printing Office. West China.

Graham, W. A. 1924. *Siam.* London: Moring. 2 vols.

*Greenaway, R. D. 1956. "Slash-and-Burn Cultivation," *Man,* 56 (sec. 22):16. Terminological note.

Grigson, W. 1938, 1949. *The Maria Gonds of Bastar.* London: Oxford University Press. Central India.

Grover, J. C. 1957. "Some Geographical Aspects of the British Solomon Islands in the Western Pacific," *Geographical Journal,* 123:298–317.

Groves, W. C. 1932. "Report on Field Work in New Ireland," *Oceania,* 3:324–361. Bismarck Archipelago, off eastern New Guinea.

———. 1934. "Tabar Today: A Study of a Melanesian Community in Contact with Alien Non-Primitive Cultural Forces," *Oceania,* 5:224–260, 346–360. Southwest Pacific.

Guppy, H. B. 1887. *The Solomon Islands and Their Natives.* London: Swan Sonnenschein, Lowrey.

———. 1903–1906. *Observations of a Naturalist in the Pacific between 1875 and 1879.* London: Macmillan. 2 vols.

Gurdon, P. R. T. 1914. *The Khasis.* London: Macmillan. Northeastern India.

Gusinde, M. 1958. "Die Ayom-Pygmaen auf Neu-Guinea," *Anthropos,* 53:497–574. New Guinea.

Haan, J. H. de. 1950. "Progress in Shifting Cultivation in Indonesia," *Transactions of the Fourth International Congress of Soil Science, 1950,* 1:314–320.

*Hahn, E. 1890. *Die Enstehung der Pflugkultur.* Heidelberg: Winter.

*Hallowell, A. I. 1943. "The Nature and Function of Property as a Social Institution," *Journal of Political and Legal Sociology,* 1:1–9.

Halpern, J. H. 1958. *Aspects of Village Life and Cultural-Change in Laos.* New York: Council on Economic Aid and Cultural Affairs.

Hamilton, A. P. F. 1948. "The Problem of Shifting Cultivation," *Indian Forester,* 74:2–6. North India.

Harrison, T. 1954. "Outside Influences on the Upland Culture of the Kelabits of North Central Borneo," *Sarawak Museum Journal,* 6:104–125.

Harroy, J-P. 1957. "Man and the Tropical Environment," in E. A. de la Rue, F. Bourliere, and J-P Harroy, *The Tropics.* London: Harrap. Pp. 157–192.

Harwood, L. W. 1950. "Observations on Indigenous Systems of Agriculture," *Agricultural Journal of the Colony of Fiji,* 21:3–9. South Pacific.

Held, G. J. 1947. *Papoea's van Waropen.* Leiden: Brill. English trans. *The Papuas of Waropen* (The Hague: Nijhoff, 1957). Eastern New Guinea.

*Herskovits, M. J. 1948, 1960. *Man and His Works.* New York: Knopf.

Hodson, T. C. 1911. *The Naga Tribes of Manipur.* London: Macmillan. Eastern India.

*Hoebel, E. A. 1949, 1958. *Man in the Primitive World.* New York: McGraw-Hill.

Hoffet, J. H. 1933. "Les Mois de la Châine Annamitique," *La Géographie,* 59:1–43. Upland Indochina.

Hogbin, H. I. 1934a. "Cultural Change in the Solomon Islands," *Oceania,* 4:233–267.

———. 1934b. "Native Culture of Wogeo: Report of Field Work in New Guinea," *Oceania,* 5:308–337. Schouten Islands, off northeastern New Guinea.

———. 1937. "The Hill People of Northeastern Guadalcanal," *Oceania,* 8:62–89. Solomon Islands, southwest Pacific.

———. 1938. "Tillage and Collection: A New Guinea Economy," *Oceania,* 9:127–151, 286–325.

———. 1939a. "Native Land Tenure in New Guinea," *Oceania,* 10:113–165.

———. 1939b. *Experiments in Civilization: The Effects of European Culture on a Native Community of the Solomon Islands.* London: Routledge & Sons. Southwest Pacific.

———. 1951. *Transformation Scene: The Changing Culture of a New Guinea Village.* London: Routledge & Kegan Paul.

Holman, D. 1958. *Noone of the Ulu.* London: Travel Book Club. Central Malaya.

*Honigmann, J. J. 1959. *The World of Man.* New York: Harper.

Hooker, J. D. 1854. *Himalayan Journals, or Notes of a Naturalist in Bengal, the Sikkim, and Nepal Himalayas, the Khasia Hills, etc.* London: John Murray. Northern India.

Hose, C. 1926. *Natural Man: A Record from Borneo.* London: Macmillan.

Hose, C., and W. Mcdougall. 1912. *The Pagan Tribes of Borneo.* London: Macmillan. 2 vols.

Howes, P. 1960. "Why Some of the Best People Aren't Christian," *Sarawak Museum Journal,* 9:488–495. British Borneo.

Hsia, E. C. H. 1957. *Land Use Conditions in Taiwan.* Chinese-American Joint Commission on Rural Reconstruction. Forest Series no. 5. Taipei.

*Hsü, C. S. 1952a. "The Well-Field System in Shang and Chou," in E. T. Z. Sun and J. De Francis, *Chinese Social History: Translations of Selected Studies.* Washington: American Council of Learned Societies. Pp. 3–17. Ancient North China.

*———. 1952b. "Some Agricultural Implements of the Early Chinese," in E. T. Z. Sun and J. De Francis, *Chinese Social History: Translations of Selected Studies.* Washington: American Council of Learned Societies. Pp. 18–20. Ancient North China.

Hutton, J. H. 1921a. *The Sema Nagas.* London: Macmillan. Northeast India.

———. 1921b. *The Angami Nagas.* London: Macmillan. Northeast India.

———. 1922. Introduction to J. P. Mills, *The Lhota Nagas.* London: Macmillan. Pp. xviii–xxix. Northeast India.

———. 1949. "A Brief Comparison between the Economics of Dry and Irrigated Cultivation in the Naga Hills," *Advancement of Science* (London), 6:26. Northeast India.

Imperial Gazetteer of India. 1907. *The Indian Empire.* New ed. Oxford: Clarendon Press. Vol. 3, *Economic,* in particular and scattered references in the other 24 volumes.

Ingram, J. C. 1955. *Economic Change in Thailand since 1850.* Stanford: Stanford University Press.

International Labour Office. 1953. *Indigenous Peoples: Living and Working Conditions of Aboriginal Populations in Independent Countries.* Studies and Reports, n. s., no. 35. Geneva.

Ishii, S. 1916. "The Island of Formosa and Its Primitive Inhabitants," *Transactions and Proceedings of the Japan Society* (London), 14:38–60.

Ivens, W. G. 1927. *Melanesians of the Southeast Solomon Islands.* London: Kegan Paul, Trench & Trubner.

Izikowitz, K. G. 1951. *Lamet: Hill Peasants in French Indochina.* Ethologiska Studier, no. 17. Göteborg: Etnografiska Museet.

Janaki Ammal, E. K. 1956. "Introduction to the Subsistence Economy of India," in W. L. Thomas, Jr., *Man's Role in Changing the Face of the Earth.* Chicago: University of Chicago Press. Pp. 324–335.

———. 1958. "Report on the Humid Regions of South Asia," in *Problems of Humid Tropical Regions.* Paris: UNESCO. Pp. 43–52.

Joachim, A. W. R., and S. Kandiah. 1948. "The Effect of Shifting (Chena) Cultivation and Subsequent Regeneration of Vegetation on Soil Composition and Structure," *Tropical Agriculturist,* 104:3–11. Ceylon.

Judd, L. C. 1964. *Dry Rice Agriculture in Northern Thailand.* Southeast Asia Program Data Paper, no. 52. Ithaca: Cornell University Press.

Kaberry, P. M. 1940. "The Abelam Tribe, Sepik District, New Guinea," *Oceania,* 11:233–258, 345–367. Northeast New Guinea.

Kano, T., and K. Segawa. 1956. *An Illustrated Ethnography of Formosan Aborigines.* Vol. 1: *The Yami.* Rev. ed. Tokyo: Maruzen.

Karan, P. P. 1960. *Nepal: A Cultural and Physical Geography.* Lexington: University of Kentucky Press.

Kauffmann, H. E. 1935. "Landwirtshcaft bei den Bergvölkern von Assam und Nord-Burma," *Zeitschrift für Ethnologie,* 66:15–111. Northeast Indies and Northwest Burma.

Keesing, F. M. 1938. "Population and Land Utilization among the Lepanto, Northern Philippines," *Comptes Rendus du Cong. Int. de Géographie,* 2 (sec. 3C):458–464.

———. 1962. *The Ethnohistory of Northern Luzon.* Stanford: Stanford University Press.

*Kihara, H., ed. 1956. *Land and Crops of Nepal Himalaya.* Vol. 2 of *Scientific Results of the Japanese Expedition to Nepal Himalaya, 1952–1953.* Kyoto: Fauna & Flora Research Society. Northern India.

*———. 1957. *Peoples of Nepal Himalaya.* Vol. 3 of *Scientific Results of the Japanese Expedition to Nepal Himalaya, 1952–1953.* Kyoto: Fauna & Flora Research Society. Northern India.

Kivekas, J. 1941. "Influence of Shifting Cultivation with Burning upon Some Properties of the Soil," *Soils and Fertilizers,* 4:194. Ceylon: Imperial Bureau of Soil Science.

Kloss, C. B. 1903. *In the Andamans and Nicobars.* New York: Dutton.

Kolb, A. 1942. *Die Philippinen.* Leipzig: Koehler.

Kooijman, S. 1955. "Population Study of the Marind-Anam," *South Pacific Commission Quarterly Bulletin,* 5 (1):21–23. Western New Guinea.

———. 1960. "Papuan Lunar 'Calendar': The Reckoning of Moons and Seasons by the Marind-Anam of Netherlands New Guinea," *Man,* 60 (sec. 211):164–168.

*Kroeber, A. L. 1923, 1948. *Anthropology.* New York: Harcourt Brace.

*Kuhnholtz-Lordat, C. 1939. *La Terre Incendiée: Essai d'Agronomie Comparée.* Nîmes: Maison Carrée.

Kunst, J. 1946. *The Peoples of the Indian Archipelago.* Leiden: Brill.

Lafont, P. B. 1959. "The 'Slash-and-Burn' (Ray) Agricultural System of the Mountain Populations of Central Vietnam," *Proceedings of the Ninth Pacific Science Congress, 1957,* 7:56–59. Upland Indochina.

Lambrecht, F. 1932. "The Mayawyaw Ritual," *Publications of the Catholic Anthropological Conference,* 4:1–167. Northern Philippines.

Langley, D. 1950. "Food Consumption and Dietary Levels," in *Report of the New Guinea Nutrition Survey Expedition, 1947.* Sydney: Government Printer. Pp. 92–142. Eastern New Guinea.

*Laurie, E. M. L., and J. E. Hill. and 1954. *List of Land Mammals of New Guinea, Celebes, and Adjacent Islands.* London: British Museum.

Lawrence, P. 1955. *Land Tenure among the Garia: The Traditional System of a New Guinea People.* Social Science Monograph no. 4. Canberra: Australian National University. Eastern New Guinea.

Leach, E. R. 1949. "Some Aspects of Dry Rice Cultivation in North Burma and British Borneo," *Advancement of Science,* 6:26–28.

———. 1950. *Social Science Research in Sarawak.* Colonial Research Studies, no. 1. London: Her Majesty's Stationery Office. British Borneo.

———. 1954. *Political Systems of Highland Burma: A Study of Kachin Social Structure.* London: London School of Economics and Political Science, G. Bell and Sons. North Burma.

———. 1959. "Some Economic Advantages of Shifting Cultivation," *Proceedings of the Ninth Pacific Science Congress, 1957,* 7:64–65. Northeast India and North Burma.

———. 1960. "The Frontiers of Burma," *Comparative Studies in Society and History,* 3:49–68.

Lee, Y. L. 1958. "Settlement and House Types in North Borneo." Unpublished M.A. Thesis. University of Malaya, Singapore.

———. 1961a. "Land Settlement for Agriculture in North Borneo," *Tijdschrift voor Econ. en Soc. Geografie,* 52:184–191.

———. 1961b. "Some Aspects of Shifting Cultivation in British Borneo," *Malayan Forester,* 24:102–109.

———. 1962. "The Long House and Dayak Settlements in British Borneo," *Oriental Geographer,* 6:39–60. Sarawak and North Borneo.

Legge, J. D. 1956. *Australian Colonial Policy: A Survey of Native Administration and European Development in Papua.* Sydney: Angus & Robertson. Southeastern New Guinea.

Lehman, F. K. 1963. *The Structure of Chin Society: A Tribal People of Burma Adapted to a Non-Western Civilization.* Urbana: University of Illinois Press.

LeRoux, C. C. F. M. 1948–1950. *De Bergpapoea's van Nieuw-Guinea en Hun Woongebied.* Leiden: Brill. 3 vols. Western New Guinea.

Lett, L. 1935. *Knights Errant of Papua.* Edinburgh: Blackwood & Sons. Eastern New Guinea.

Lewin, T. H. 1870. *The Wild Races of Southeastern India.* London: Allen & Co.

*Linton, R. 1955. *The Tree of Culture.* New York: Knopf.

Livera, E. J. 1947. "Agriculture and Erosion in Ceylon," *Tropical Agriculturist,* 103:234–239.

———. 1954. "Productive Land Use in Ceylon," *Tropical Agriculture,* 31:188–198.

Loeb, E. M., and J. O. M. Broek. 1947. "Social Organization and the Long House in Southeast Asia," *American Anthropologist,* 49:414–425.

Loeb, E. M., and R. Heine-Geldern. 1935. *Sumatra: Its History and People.* Vienna: Institut für Völkerkunde.

Loetsch, F. 1958. "Der Einfluss des Brandrodungsbaus auf das Gefüge des Tropenwaldes und die Wasserführung der Ströme, untersucht am Beispiel Nordthailands," *Erdkunde,* 12:182–205. North Thailand.

Loveridge, A. 1945. *Reptiles of the Pacific World.* New York: Macmillan Company.

Lundquist, E. 1955. *In Eastern Forests.* English ed. London: Hale. Eastern New Guinea.

Luzbetak, L. J. 1958. "The Middle Wahgi Culture: A Study of First Contacts and Initial Selectivity," *Anthropos,* 53:51–87. Highland Eastern New Guinea.

Maass, A. 1902. *Bei liebens wurdigen Wilden: Ein Beitrag zur Kenntnis der Mentawei-Insulaner.* Berlin: Susserott. Mentawei Islands off western Sumatra.

Mabuchi, T. 1951. "The Social Organization of the Central Tribes of Formosa," *Journal of East Asiatic Studies* (Manila), 1:43–69.

———. 1960. "The Aboriginal Peoples of Formosa," in G. P. Murdoch, *Social Structure in Southeast Asia.* New York: Viking. Wenner-Gren Foundation. Viking Fund Publication no. 29. Pp. 127–140.

*McClure, F. A. 1956. "Bamboo in the Economy of Oriental Peoples," *Economic Botany,* 10:335–361.

McKay, C. G. R. 1953. "The Rising of the Palolo," *South Pacific Commission Quarterly Bulletin,* 3(3):35. Southwest Pacific.

Mahapatra, L. K. 1955. "Food Quest among the Pauri Bhuiyan," *Eastern Anthropologist,* 9:48–52. Chota Nagpur zone of eastern India.

Majumdar, D. N. 1944. *Fortunes of Primitive Tribes.* Lucknow: Lucknow University Press. General India.

———. 1944, 1958. *Races and Cultures of India.* Bombay: Asia Publishing House.

———. 1950. *The Affairs of a Tribe: A Study in Tribal Dynamics.* Lucknow: Universal Publications. Chota Nagpur section of eastern India.

Majumdar, D. N., and T. N. Madan. 1956. *An Introduction to Social Anthropology.* Bombay: Asia Publishing House. A social Anthropology using chiefly Indian examples, for Indian student use.

*Majumdar, R. C., and A. D. Pusalker. 1951. *The Vedic Age.* London: Allen & Unwin. Earliest history of India.

*———. 1951, 1953. *The Age of Imperial Unity.* Bombay: Bhavan. Early history of India.

Malcolm, S., and J. Barrau. 1954. "Yams," *South Pacific Commission Quarterly Bulletin,* 4(3):28–31.

Malinowski, B. 1935. *Coral Gardens and Their Magic: A Study of the Methods of Tilling the Soil and of Agricultural Rites in the Trobriand Islands.* London: George Allen & Unwin. 2 vols. Off eastern New Guinea.

Marsden, W. 1783–1811. *The History of Sumatra.* London: privately printed.

*Masefield, G. B. 1949. *A Handbook of Tropical Agriculture.* Oxford: Clarendon Press.

Massal, E., and J. Barrau. 1954. "Breadfruit," *South Pacific Commission Quarterly Bulletin,* 4(4):24–26.

———. 1955a. "Sago," *South Pacific Commission Quarterly Bulletin,* 5(1):15–17.

———. 1955b. "Taros," *South Pacific Commission Quarterly Bulletin,* 5(2):17–21.

———. 1955c. "Sweet Potato," *South Pacific Commission Quarterly Bulletin,* 5 (3):10–13.

———. 1955d. "Cassava," *South Pacific Commission Quarterly Bulletin,* 5(4):15–18.

———. 1956a. "The Banana," *South Pacific Commission Quarterly Bulletin,* 6(1):10–14.

———. 1956b. "Some Lesser Known Pacific Plant Foods," *South Pacific Commission Quarterly Bulletin,* 6(3):17–18.

———. 1956c. *Food Plants of the South Sea Islanders.* South Pacific Commission Technical Paper no. 94. Nouméa.

Maurice A., and G. M. Proux. 1954. "L'Âme du Riz," *Bulletin de la Société des Études Indochinoises,* 29:125–258. Indochina.

*Mauss, M. 1954. *The Gift, Forms and Functions of Exchange in Archaic Societies.* English ed. London: Cohen & West. French ed. published in 1950.

Meggitt, M. G. 1956. "The Valleys of the Upper Wage and Lai Rivers, Western Highlands, New Guinea," *Oceania*, 27:90–135.

———. 1957. "The Ipili of the Porgera Valley, Western Highlands District, Territory of New Guinea," *Oceania*, 28:31–55.

———. 1958. "The Enga of the New Guinea Highlands: Some Preliminary Observations," *Oceania*, 28:253–330.

Mendez Correa, A. A. 1944. *Timor Portugues: Contribuicoes para o seu Estudo Anthropologico.* Lisbon: Imprensa nacional de Lisboa.

*Merrill, E. D. 1945. *Plant Life of the Pacific World.* New York: Macmillan.

*Michael, F. 1942. *The Origin of Manchu Rule in China.* Baltimore: Johns Hopkins Press.

Miller, C. D., M. Murai, and F. Pen. 1956. "The Use of Pandanus Fruit as Food in Micronesia," *Pacific Science*, 10:3–16.

Millon, R. F. 1955. "Trade, Tree Cultivation and the Development of Private Property in Land," *American Anthropologist*, 57:698–712.

Mills, J. P. 1922. *The Lhota Nagas.* London: Macmillan. Northeast India.

Milne, L. 1924. *The Home of an Eastern Clan: A Study of the Palaungs of the Shan States.* Oxford: Clarendon Press. Northeast Burma.

*Montagu, A. 1957. *Man: His First Million Years.* New York: World Publishing Co.

Morris, C. J. 1935. "A Journey in Bhutan," *Geographical Journal*, 86:207–227. Central Himalayan India.

Morris, H. S. 1953. *Report on a Melanau Sago Producing Community in Sarawak.* London: Her Majesty's Stationery Office. British Borneo.

Moubray, G. A. de C. 1931. *Matriarchy in the Malay Peninsula and Neighboring Countries.* London: Routledge & Sons.

*Mumford, L. 1956. "The Natural History of Urbanization," in W. L. Thomas, Jr., *Man's Role in Changing the Face of the Earth.* Chicago: University of Chicago Press. Pp. 382–398.

Murphey, R. 1957. "The Ruin of Ancient Ceylon," *Journal of Asian Studies*, 16:181–200.

Nag, D. S. 1958. *Tribal Economy: An Economic Study of the Baiga.* Delhi: Sevak Sangh. Northern peninsular India.

Naik, T. B. 1950. "Aboriginals of Gujarat," *Eastern Anthropologist*, 4:42–51. Northwest peninsular India.

Nakane, C. 1958. "Cross-Cousin Marriage among the Garo of Assam," *Man*, 108:7–12. Northeast India.

*Nakao, S. 1957. "Transmittance of Cultivated Plants through the Sino-Himalayan Route," in H. Kihara, ed., *Peoples of Nepal Himalaya.* Vol. 3 of *Scientific Results of the Japanese Expedition to Nepal Himalaya, 1952–1953.* Kyoto: Fauna & Flora Research Society. Pp. 397–420. Northern India.

*Narr, K. J. 1956. "Early Food Producing Populations," in W. L. Thomas, Jr., *Man's Role in Changing the Face of the Earth.* Chicago: University of Chicago Press. Pp. 134–151.

Nilles, J. 1942. "Digging Sticks, Spades, Hoes, Axes and Adzes of the Kuman People in the Bismarck Mountains of East Central New Guinea," *Anthropos*, 37:205–212.

———. 1943, 1944. "Natives of the Bismarck Mountains, New Guinea," *Oceania*, 14:104–123; 15:1–18.

———. 1953. "The Kuman People: A Study of Cultural Change in a Primitive Society in the Central Highlands of New Guinea," *Oceania*, 24:1–27, 119–131.

Norodom, K. 1956. "Comments on the Law and Practice in Cambodia," in *Studies in the Law of the Far East and Southeast Asia.* Washington: Washington Foreign Law Society and George Washington University Law School. Pp. 70–74.

Nye, P. H. and D. J. Greenland. 1960. *The Soil under Shifting Cultivation.* Technical Communication no. 51. Farnham Royal, England: Commonwealth Agricultural Bureaux.

O'Neill, T. 1961. *And We, the People.* London: Geoffrey Chapman. Eastern New Britain in Bismarck Archipelago.

Ooi, J. B. 1958. "The Distribution of Present Day Man in the Tropics: Historical and Ecological Perspective," *Proceedings of the Ninth Pacific Science Congress, 1957*, 20:111–124.

———. 1959. "Rural Development in Tropical Areas, with Special Reference to Malaya," *Journal of Tropical Geography*, 12:1–222.

Oomen, H. A. P. C. 1959. "Poor-Food Patterns in New Guinea," *Nieuw Guinea Studien*, 3:35–46.

Oosterwal, G. 1961. *People of the Tor*. Assen: Van Gorcum. Northeast New Guinea.

Oracion, T. S. 195. "Ceremonial Customs and Beliefs Connected with Magahat Kaingin Agriculture," *Silliman Journal* (Philippines), 2:222–236. Central Philippines.

Orleans, H. d'. 1898. *From Tonkin to India, by the Sources of the Irawadi, January '95 to January '96*. English ed. London: Methuen.

Ormeling, F. J. 1956. *The Timor Problem*. Groningen: Wolters. Lesser Sunda sector of Indonesia.

Pant, S. D. 1935. *Social Economy of the Himalayans*. London: Allen & Unwin. Northern India.

Parry, N. E. 1932. *The Lakhers*. London: Macmillan. Lushai Hills of eastern India.

Pascoe, E. A. C. 1955. "Aspects of Planning for Agricultural Development in Northern Borneo," *Tropical Agriculture*, 32:170–185.

Paul, W. R. C. 1949. "Roving Agriculture and the Problem of Dry Farming," *Tropical Agriculturist*, 105:4–13. Ceylon.

Pelzer, K. J. 1945. *Pioneer Settlement in the Asiatic Tropics*. American Geographical Society Special Publications, no. 29. New York.

———. 1958. "Land Utilization in the Humid Tropics: Agriculture," *Proceedings of the Ninth Pacific Science Congress, 1957*, 20:124–143. Chiefly southeast Asia.

Pendleton, R. L. 1939. "Some Interrelations between Agriculture and Forestry, Particularly in Thailand," *Journal of the Thailand Research Soicety, Natural History Supplement*, 12:33–52.

———. 1940. "Soil Erosion as Related to Land Utilization in the Humid Tropics," *Proceedings of the Sixth Pacific Science Congress, 1939*, 4:905–920.

———. 1942. "Land Utilization and Agriculture of Mindanao, Philippine Islands," *Geographical Review*, 32:180–210.

*———. 1954. "The Place of Tropical Soils in Feeding the World," *Annual Report, Smithsonian Institution, 1955*. Pub. no. 4232. Pp. 441–458.

Perron, P. C. du. 1954. "Étude d'un Peuplement Man Xanth-Y," *Bulletin de la Société des Études Indochinoises*, n.s., 29:23–42. Upland Indochina.

Phelan, J. L. 1959. *The Hispanization of the Philippines*. Madison: University of Wisconsin Press.

Pieris, R. 1956. *Sinhalese Social Organization: The Kandyan Period*. Colombo: Ceylon University Press. Ceylon.

Pospisil, L. 1958a. "Kapauku Papuan Political Structure," in V. F. Ray, *System of Political Control and Bureaucracy in Human Societies*. Proceedings of the 1958 Annual Spring Meeting of the American Ethnological Society. Seattle: University of Washington Press. Western New Guinea.

———. 1958b. *Kapauku Papuans and Their Law*. Yale University Publications in Anthropology, no. 54. New Haven: Yale University Press. Western New Guinea.

———. 1963. *The Kapauku Papuans of West New Guinea*. New York: Holt, Rhinehart and Winston.

Postmus, S., and A. G. van Veen. 1949. "Dietary Surveys in Java and East Indonesia, III," *Chronica Naturae*, 105:316–323.

Powell, W. 1883. *Wanderings in a Wild Country; or Three Years among the Cannibals of New Britain*. London: Sampson, Low, Marston, Searle & Rivington. Bismarck Archipelago, off eastern New Guinea.

Provinse, J. H. 1937. "Cooperative Ricefield Cultivation among the Siang Dyaks of Central Borneo," *American Anthropologist*, 39:77–102.

*Radin, P. 1953. *The World of Primitive Man*. New York: Schuman.

Rahman, R., and M. N. Maceda. 1958. "Some Notes on the Negritos of Iloilo, Island of Panay, Philippines," *Anthropos*, 53:864–876.

Rao, S. M. 1949, 1952. *Among the Gonds of Adilabad*. Bombay: Popular Book Depot. Peninsular India.

Raven, H. C. 1935. "Wallace's Line and the Distribution of Indo-Australian Mammals," *Bulletin of the American Museum of Natural History*, 48:179–293.

Read, K. E. 1954. "Cultures of the Central Highlands, New Guinea," *Southwestern Journal of Anthropology*, 10:1–43.

Reay, M. 1959*a*. "Individual Ownership and Transfer of Land among the Kuma," *Man*, 59 (sec. 108):78–82. Eastern New Guinea.

———. 1959*b*. *The Kuma: Freedom and Conformity in the New Guinea Highlands.* Melbourne: Melbourne University Press. Eastern New Guinea.

Reed, S. W. 1943. *The Making of Modern New Guinea.* Philadelphia: American Philosophical Society. Eastern New Guinea.

Reed, W. A. 1904. *Negritos of Zambales.* Department of the Interior Ethnological Survey Publications. Vol. 2, no. 1. Manila: Bureau of Printing. Western Luzon sector of the northern Philippines.

*Richards, P. W. 1952. *The Tropical Rainforest: An Ecological Study.* Cambridge: The University Press.

Robequain, C. 1946. *Le Monde Malais.* Paris: Payot. Trans. into English by E. D. Laborde: *Malaya, Indonesia, Borneo and the Philippines* (London: Longmans, Green, 1954).

Rosayro, R. A. de. 1947. "Forests and Erosion—with Special Reference to Ceylon," *Tropical Agriculturist*, 103:246–252.

Ross, W. 1936. "Ethnological Notes on the Mount Hagen Tribes," *Anthropos*, 31:341–363. Eastern New Guinea.

Roth, H. L. 1896. *The Natives of Sarawak and British North Borneo.* London: Truslove and Hanson.

Ryan, B., C. Arulpragasam, and C. Bibile. 1955. "The Agricultural System of a Ceylon Jungle Village," *Eastern Anthropologist*, 8:151–160.

Sahlins, M. D. 1960. "Political Power and the Economy in Primitive Society," in G. E. Dole, and R. L. Carneiro, eds., *Essays in the Science of Culture in Honor of Leslie A. White.* New York: Crowell. Pp. 390–415.

St. John, S. 1862, 1863. *Life in the Forests of the Far East.* London: Smith, Elder.

Salisbury, R. F. 1962. *From Stone to Steel: Economic Consequences of a Technological Change in New Guinea.* Melbourne: Melbourne University Press.

*Sauer, C. O. 1948. "Environment and Culture during the Last Deglaciation," *Proceedings of the American Philosophical Society*, 92:65–77.

*———. 1950. "Grassland Climax: Fire and Man," *Journal of Range Management*, 3:16–21.

*———. 1952. *Agricultural Origins and Dispersals.* New York: American Geographical Society.

*———. 1956. "The Agency of Man on the Earth," in W. L. Thomas, Jr., *Man's Role in Changing the Face of the Earth.* Chicago: University of Chicago Press.

*———. 1961. "Sedentary and Mobile Bents in Early Societies," in S. L. Washburn, *Social Life of Early Man.* New York: Viking. Wenner-Gren Foundation. Viking Fund Publication no. 31. Pp. 256–266.

Savage-Landor, A. H. 1904. *The Gems of the East: Sixteen Thousand Miles of Research Travel among the Wild and Tame Tribes of Enchanting Islands.* New York: Harper and Brothers. Island southeast Asia.

Scott, J. G. 1910. *The Burman: His Life and Notions by Shway Yoe, Subject of the Great Queen.* 3d ed. London: Macmillan. 2 vols.

Scott, J. G., and J. P. Hardiman. 1900. *Gazetteer of Upper Burma and the Shan States.* Rangoon: Government Printing Office. 5 vols.

Scott, W. H. 1958*a*. "A Preliminary Report on Upland Rice in Northern Luzon," *Southwestern Journal of Anthropology*, 14:87–105. Northern Philippines.

———. 1958*b*. "Economic and Material Culture of the Kalingas of Madukayan," *Southwestern Journal of Anthropology*, 14:318–337. Northern Luzon Sector of Philippines.

Seidenfaden, E. 1958. *The Thai Peoples.* Bangkok: Siam Society.

Seligmann, C. G. 1910. *The Melanesians of British New Guinea.* Cambridge: The University Press.

Shakespear, L. S. 1914. *History of Upper Assam, Upper Burmah, and the Northeastern Frontier.* London: Macmillan. Northeast India and northern Burma.

Shukla, B. K. 1959. *The Daflas of the Subansiri Region.* Shillong: Northeast Frontier Agency. Northeast India.

*Simmonds, N. W. 1959. *Bananas.* London: Longmans, Green.

*Simoons, F. J. 1961. *Eat Not This Flesh.* Madison: University of Wisconsin Press. Food taboos and acceptances of the Old World.

Sladen, E. B., and H. Browne. 1876. *Mandalay to Momein: A Narrative of the Two Expeditions to Western China of 1868 and 1875.* London: Macmillan.

Slimming, J. 1958. *Temiar Jungle.* London: Murray. Central Malaya.

Smedts, M. 1955. *No Tobacco, No Hallelujah.* London: Kimber. Eastern New Guinea.

Smith, W. C. 1925. *The Ao Naga Tribe of Assam: A Study in Ethnology and Sociology.* London: Macmillan. Northeastern India.

Smits, M. B. 1938. "Population Density and Soil Utilization in the Netherlands Indies," *Comptes Rendus du Cong. Int. de Géographie,* 2 (sec. 3C) :500–506.

Spate, O. H. K. 1945. "The Burmese Village," *Geographical Review,* 35:523–543.

———. 1953. "Changing Agriculture in New Guinea," *Geographical Review,* 43:151–172.

———. 1954. *India and Pakistan.* London: Methuen.

———. 1956. "Problems of Development in New Guinea," *Geographical Journal,* 122:430–436.

Spencer, J. E. 1949. "Land Use in the Upland Philippines," in *The Development of Upland Areas in the Far East.* New York: Institute of Pacific Relations. Vol. 1, pp. 26–57.

———. 1952. *Land and People in the Philippines: Geographic Problems in Rural Economy.* Berkeley and Los Angeles: University of California Press.

*———. 1954. *Asia East by South: A Cultural Geography.* New York: Wiley.

———. 1958. "Preliminary Notes on Shifting Cultivation in Southeastern Asia," *Yearbook, Association of Pacific Coast Geographers,* 20:49–51.

———. 1959a. Introduction to the Symposium on Effects of Shifting Cultivation on Natural Resources with Special Reference to Problems in Southeast Asia, *Proceedings of the Ninth Pacific Science Congress, 1957,* 7:51–52.

*———. 1959b. "Seasonality in the Tropics: The Supply of Fruit to Singapore," *Geographical Review.* 49:475–484.

*Spier, R. F. G. 1951. "Some Notes on the Origin of Taro," *Southwestern Journal of Anthropology,* 7:69–76.

*Stamp, L. D. 1925. *The Vegetation of Burma from an Ecological Standpoint.* Calcutta: Thacker & Spink.

Stebbing, E. P. 1922–1926. *The Forests of India.* London: John Lane. 3 vols.

Steen, C. 1944. *The Hill Peoples of Burma.* Calcutta: Longmans, Green.

———. 1948. "Material Culture of the Langsing Nagas, Northern Burma," *Southwestern Journal of Anthropology,* 4:263–298.

Steinberg, D. J., *et al.* 1957. *Cambodia: Its People, Its Society, Its Culture.* New Haven: Human Relations Area Files.

Stevenson, H. N. C. 1943. *The Economics of the Central Chin Tribes.* Bombay: Times of India Press. Burma.

Swann, N. 1950. *Food and Money in Ancient China.* Princeton: Princeton University Press. Ancient North China.

Tamesis, F. 1963. "Problems of Shifting Agriculture in the Asian Area," *Philippine Geographical Journal,* 7:84–97.

Tate, G. H. H. 1947. *Mammals of Eastern Asia.* New York: Macmillan Company.

Taylor, G. D. 1953. "Some Crop Distributions by Tribes in Upland Southeast Asia," *Southwestern Journal of Anthropology,* 9:296–308.

*Tempany, H., and D. H. Grist. 1958. *An Introduction to Tropical Agriculture.* New York: Longmans, Green.

Tennent, J. E. 1859. *Ceylon: An Account of the Island, Physical, Historical, and Topographical.* London: Longman, Green, Longman and Roberts. 2 vols.

Tergast, G. C. and W. C., and E. de Vires. 1951. "Utilization of Upland Areas in Indonesia and Western New Guinea," in *The Development of Upland Areas in the Far East.* New York: Institute of Pacific Relations. Vol. 2, pp. 43–100.

Ter Haar, B. 1948. *Adat Law in Indonesia*. New York: Institute of Pacific Relations.

Terra, G. J. A. 1949. "The Ethnological Affinities of the Type of Horticulture in Indonesia," *Chronica Naturae*, 105:323–326.

———. 1950. "Further Ethnological Affinities in Indonesian Agriculture," *Chronica Naturae*, 106:463–466.

———. 1953. "Some Sociological Aspects of Agriculture in Southeast Asia," *Indonesie*, 6:297–316, 439–463.

Thurnwald, R. C. 1934. "Pigs and Currency in Buin," *Oceania*, 5:119–141. Bougainville Island in the northern Solomon Islands.

Todd, J. A. 1934. "Research Work in Southwest New Britain," *Oceania*, 5:70–101, 193–213. Bismarck Archipelago, off eastern New Guinea.

*Troughton, E. 1957. *Furred Animals of Australia*. 6th ed. Sydney: Angus and Robertson.

Tubb, J. A. 1959. "Shifting Cultivation and Inland Fisheries," *Proceedings of the Ninth Pacific Science Congress, 1957*, 7:68–70. Southeast Asian mainland.

UNESCO. 1958. *Study of Tropical Vegetation: Proceedings of the Kandy Symposium, 1956*. Paris: UNESCO.

Vanoverbergh, M. 1932. "The Isneg," *Publications of the Catholic Anthropological Conference*, 3:1–80. Northern Philippines.

———. 1941. "The Isneg Farmer," *Publications of the Catholic Anthropological Conference*, 3:281–386. Northern Philippines.

Verhoeff, H. G. 1957. "Overheid en Grond in Nederlands-Nieuw-Guinea: Beginselen van Agrarisch Beleid," *Nieuw Guinea Studien*, 1:31–58, 129–146, 224–256. Western New Guinea.

Verma, B. B. 1956. *Agriculture and Land Ownership System among the Primitive People of Assam*. Delhi: Udyogshala Press. Northeast India.

Vidal, J. 1959. "Noms vernaculaires de plantes (Lao, Meo, Kha) en usage au Laos," *Bulletin de l'École Française D'Extrême-Orient*, 49:435–608. Upland Indochina.

*Wagner, P. L. 1960. *The Human Use of the Earth*. Glencoe: Free Press.

Wake, W. H. 1961. "The Relations between Transportation Improvements and Agricultural Changes in Madhya Pradesh, India, 1854–1954." Unpublished Ph.D. dissertation. University of California, Los Angeles. North Central Peninsular India.

*Wales, H. G. Q. 1934. *Ancient Siamese Government and Administration*. London: Quaritch.

Ward, F. K. 1946. *About This Earth*. London: Cape. Southeast Asia.

———. 1949. *Burma's Icy Mountains*. London: Cape.

Watt, G. 1889–1896. *Dictionary of the Economic Products of India*. Calcutta: Government Printer. 7 vols.

Watters, R. F. 1960. "The Nature of Shifting Cultivation," *Pacific Viewpoint*, 1:59–99. Methodological systematic study.

Watterson, G. 1958. "Fire and Axe Farming on the Way Out," *Unesco Courier*, 11:17.

Webber, T. W. 1902. *The Forests of Upper India, and Their Inhabitants*. London: Edward Arnold.

*Werth, E. 1954. *Grabstock, Hacke Und Pflug*. Ludwigsburg: Ulmer.

*West, R. C. 1957. *The Pacific Lowlands of Colombia: A Negroid Area of the American Tropics*. Social Science Series, no. 8. Baton Rouge: Louisiana State University Press.

*Wheatley, P. 1959. "Geographical Notes on Some Commodities Involved in Sung Maritime Trade," *Journal of the Malayan Branch Royal Asiatic Society*, 39(pt. 2):1–140.

*White, L. 1949. *The Science of Culture*. New York: Farrar, Straus, & Young.

Whiting, J. W. M., and S. W. Reed. 1938. "Report on Field Work in the Mandated Territory of New Guinea," *Oceania*, 9:170–216.

Whittlesey, D. 1937a. "Shifting Cultivation," *Economic Geography*, 13:35–52.

———. 1937b. "The Fixation of Shifting Cultivation," *Economic Geography*, 13:139–154.

*Whyte, R. O., G. Nilsson-Leissner, H. C. Trumble. 1953. *Legumes in Agriculture*. FAO Agricultural Studies, no. 21. Rome.

Wiens, H. J. 1954. *China's March toward the Tropics*. Hamden, Conn: Shoestring Press. Central and south China.

————. 1962. "Some of China's Thirty-Five Million Non-Chinese," *Journal of the Hongkong Branch of the Royal Asiatic Society*, 2:1–21. Notes on non-Chinese groups in southwest China under communism.

Wikkramatileke, W. A. R. 1955. "The Southeast Quadrant of Ceylon: A Study of the Geographical Aspects of Land Use." Unpublished Ph.D. dissertation. University of London.

————. 1957a. "Whither Chena? The Problem of an Alternative to Shifting Cultivation in the Dry Zone of Ceylon," *Geographical Studies*, 4:81–89.

————. 1957b. "Hambegamuwa Village: An Example of Rural Settlement in Ceylon's Dry Zone," *Economic Geography*, 33:362–373.

————. 1963. *Southeast Ceylon: Trends and Problems in Agricultural Settlement*. Chicago: Department of Geography Research Paper no. 83, University of Chicago.

Williams, F. E. 1928. *Orokaiva Magic*. London: Oxford University Press. Northeastern New Guinea.

————. 1930. *Orokaiva Society*. London: Oxford University Press. Northeastern New Guinea.

————. 1936. *Papuans of the Trans-Fly*. London: Oxford University Press. Southeastern New Guinea.

————. 1940–1941. "Natives of Lake Kutubu, Papua," *Oceania*, 11:121–157, 259–294, 374–401; 12:49–74, 134–154. Reprinted as Oceania Monograph no. 6. Eastern New Guinea.

————. 1944. "Mission Influence amongst the Keveri of Southeast Papua," *Oceania*, 15:89–141. Southeastern New Guinea.

Williams-Hunt, P. D. R. 1952. *An Introduction to the Malayan Aborigines*. Kuala Lumpur: Government Press.

Williamson, R. W. 1912. *The Mafulu, Mountain People of British New Guinea*. London: Macmillan.

Willis, J. C. 1907. *Ceylon: A Handbook for the Resident and the Traveler*. Colombo: Colombo Apothecaries.

Winnington, A. 1959. *The Slaves of the Cool Mountains*. London: Lawrence & Wishart. Non-Chinese culture groups in far southwest China under communism.

*Winstedt, R. 1951. *The Malay Magician*. London: Routledge & Kegan Paul.

*Wissmann, H. von. 1957. "Ursprunge und Ausbreitungswege von Pflanzen und Tierzucht und ihre Abhangigkeit von der Klimageschichte," *Erdkunde*, 11:81–94, 175–192.

Wyatt-Smith, J. 1954a. "Storm Forest in Kelantan," *Malayan Forester*, 17:5–11. Northeastern Malaya.

————. 1954b. "Survival of Isolated Seedbearers," *Malayan Forester*, 17: 30–32. Malaya.

*————. 1954c. "Suggested Definitions of Field Characters," *Malayan Forester*, 17:170–183. Discussion of types and terminology for varying kinds of forest.

*Yang, L. S. 1950. "Notes on Dr. Swann's Food and Money in Ancient China," *Harvard Journal of Asiatic Studies*, 13:524–557. Ancient North China.

PLATES

This plot was cleared and only lightly burned without adequate drying in mid-August, 1957. It is located west of the Agusan River in Agusan Province, Mindanao, Philippines. The rolling lowland plot had already been cropped once in rice and was ready for planting a second time, after which the plot would be planted to lumbang (*Aleurites moluccana*) for oil production. The zone had been logged in 1954 for clean timber over 28 inches in diameter. This is the kind of clearing often done by a partial shifting cultivator, aiming at a permanent farmholding of tree crops.

A flat lowland site containing termite mounds had been collectively cleared and burned, with clean-up reburning, early in July, 1958, in old regenerated forest north of Kuala Trengganu, Trengganu State, northeast Malaya. Intended cropping was a two-year sequence of rice, with regeneration after second cropping.

This view includes a multiple series of plots in different stages, photographed early in August, 1957, south of Butuan, east of the Agusan River, in Agusan Province, Philippines. Plot in foreground had been cropped in rice once and harvested in 1956, and the surface had become weed-covered. The middle section had been burned two weeks before the photo was taken, and patches of ashes litter the surface. Rice is the intended crop. The large plot in the middle distance had been cropped in rice once in 1954, and was in the process of regeneration. The whole region had been logged in 1950. The crest section, in background, and the far-left section have not been cleared for cropping. The site is medium-elevation rolling hill country.

A cleared and clean-burned rolling lowland plot is in process of planting to rice by digging stick, south of Khaki Buket, Perlis State, northern Malaya, in early July, 1958.

Young upland rice growing on a gently sloping plot in medium-elevation hill country. This is a first cropping on a well-cleared plot southeast of Mangalore, on the west coast of India, in early June, 1958. In the right center is a long, narrow strip of freshly cut vegetation which will dry until late in the year. The strip will then be burned and readied for a first planting the following May, at which time the present foreground plot will be planted a second (and probably last) time. In the background is maturely regenerated forest ready for clearing as the clearing-cropping sequence proceeds in a linear direction.

Subsistence chena plot in mid-mature growth on a flat lowland in late May, 1958. The plot, located in fairly well regenerated forest south of Wellawaya, inland southern Ceylon, is in the first year of a two-year sequence. It is being cropped in a very mixed planting containing pumpkin, bottle gourd, vegetable bitter gourd, maize, egg plant, bananas, chillies, citron, tomato, bitter cucumber, and manioc (being harvested).

Regeneration in process late in July, 1957, on a flat lowland north of Mamburao, on the west coast of Mindoro Island, Philippines. The foreground plot was cleared in January, 1956, burned in April, and cropped once in rice in the summer of 1956, with harvest being completed in early October. The single cropping had not killed all the roots and stumps, nor had it permitted an appreciable degree of soil leaching. No sector of this area had been cropped in many decades. The photo was taken from the top of a car, looking over the thickly regenerating cover that had reached an average height of almost 8 feet in ten months. In the background is the scab timber cover left after loose selective logging some years previously.

View of the grass cover that may result from a too-short cycle of recropping. The photograph was taken in rough, medium-elevation hill country near Upi, south of Cotabato, southwest Mindanao, Philippines, in October, 1948. On the hill at right center are two new clearings, indicated by felled timber on both flanks of the hill. Much of the ground cover was already in grass prior to the current clearing, and the two plots are the only cropped areas shown in the photo. There are but few tree species left in this landscape, and the regeneration after the current cropping of the two clearings is certain to extend the grass cover, offering little chance for forest regeneration.

INDEX

INDEX

Abandonment: of field, misuse of term, 10; of land, 87; error in reference, 144; inapplicable term, 146
Abelam: hierarchical status of, 204
Abor: hierarchical status of, 211
Adze, 150
Amaranthus, 36
American crop plants: introduction of, 120, 152
Andropogon grasses, 154
Angami, 121; size of villages, 68; hierarchical status of, 212
Angami Naga, 22, 139, 148
Animal keeping, 153
Animal resources, 127–131
Animals: distribution and uses of, 200–202
Animal totem: not eaten, 128
Annual cropping cycle, 122; timing of, 123; for taros, 123–124; for yams, 123–124
Antelope, 50
Ao: hierarchical status of, 212
Appropriation, 137, 151–152; significance of plant gathering, 50–51; decreased returns from, 52; early importance of, 62; early pattern, 64; rights of, 88, 91–92; of wild food, 116–117; of plant products, 125; from degrading regions, 127; of products for sale, 131; nonagricultural, 184
Aquatic resources, 127–131
Avoidance: of foods, customs of, 157–158
Axe, 150, 151
Ayom Negrito: hierarchical position of, 203

Baiga: hierarchical status of, 211
Bananas, 21, 30, 35, 36, 47, 111, 121, 122, 133, 140; inclusion of plantains, 115; planting sites, 115
Barleys, 118
Beans, 111, 140, 153
Bear, 128
Bear gallbladders, 132
Bees, 48
Beeswax, 131
Bhotiya: hierarchical status of, 212
Bhutan Dafla: hierarchical status of, 211
Biotic environment, 47–49
Bird life, 50
Bird resources, 127–131
Bismarck Archipelago, 16, 44, 131, 156
Bison Hills Reddi: hierarchical status of, 207
Bondos, 149
Borneo, 14, 15, 36, 44, 45, 69, 72, 78, 123, 124, 127, 143, 157
Brass gongs, 131
Broadcasting, 142
Buckwheat, 118
Buddhism, 130
Buffalo, 48
Bukidnon: hierarchical status of, 207

Burma, 15, 43, 44, 78, 98, 100, 104, 111, 114, 118, 122, 130, 134, 155; land system in, 97, 105
Burning, 136, 137, 138; effect on soils, 32–33; of grasslands, 34; by hunters, 41; in dry period, 44; in moist regions, 44; of fields, 70; in annual cropping cycles, 123; procedures of, 138–139, 181

Cabbage, 118, 120, 122
Cacao, 134
Calendar, planting: timing of, by stars, 44
Cambodia, 36, 97, 98, 99
Camphors, 131
Canarium almonds, 126; dispersal of, 116; harvest period, 125
Cane grass, 122, 126
Carrots, 120
Cassowary, 128, 156
Casuarina trees: planting of, 147
Cattle, 129; status of, 184
Celebes, 117
Ceremonial magic, 153; per crop staple, 154
Ceylon, 14, 15, 20, 81, 108, 111, 114, 130, 133, 134, 161, 162; chena system, 21; crop watching, 69; partial system, 107
Chenchus, 149
Chickens, 48, 128, 129; presence of, 185
Chillies, 133
Chimbu, 141; population density for, 15; hierarchical status of, 205
Chin, 96
China, 15, 16, 29, 43, 44, 64, 97, 99, 111, 114, 118, 122, 127, 130, 150, 158; as a crop region, 117
Chota Nagpur, 11
Chronology of crop staples, 152
Citrus fruits, 134
City clothing, 132
Civilization rights, 91
Classification of hierarchies: detailed, 203–212
Clearing, 136; of fields, 25; of forests, effects on vegetation, 40; procedures, 138–139, 181
Climate: causality relation to shifting cultivation, 42–44; significant elements, 186
Clod breaker, 151
Cloves, 131
Coconut, 111, 117, 123
Coffee, 134
Collecting: of wild foods, by Lamet, 49; seasonality of, 49; significance of plant gathering, 50–51; decreased returns from, 52; of plant products, 125
Commercial shifting cultivation: crops grown, 133
Commodity exchange: items traded, 131
Complementary economy: of integral shifting cultivators, 131
Configuration of slope: importance of, 30

Consumption, 137, 158

Cordyline, 114, 154; importance of, in New Guinea, 117; status in west, 157

Cotton, 133

Cowrie shell money: use in New Guinea, 159

Crop complexes, 151–152

Crop patterns: regional, notes on, 116; recent changes in, 119–120; variation in, 184

Cropping sites: shift in, from roots to rice, 115

Cropping systems, 65, 110; chronology of, 152–153

Crop plants: differentiation in stage of domestication, 126; American, 152; European, 152; use in ritualism, 154; distribution of, 187–199; list of, 187–199; uses for, 187–199

Crop region: Melanesia, 116; Malaysia, 117; South China, Indochina, Thailand, Burma, 117; Himalayas, 118

Crops: multiple varieties of, 111

Crop watching, 62, 147, 153; seasonal need for, 68–69

Crop yields: decline of, 21; range of, 22

Crop zones: elevation limits of, in New Guinea, 121; frost problem, 121–122

Croton, 154, 156

Cultigens: as crop plants, 126; defined, 126

Cultivation: as term, meaning of, 10; of soil, 141–142

Culture: defined, 54; axioms of, and corollaries, 54–55; ecological equilibrium, 56; as an agent, 57; as style or configuration, 63

Culture groups: preference for hill country, 30; differentiation, 64

Custard apple, 120

Dafla: hierarchical status of, 209

Dammar, 131

Dani: hierarchical status of, 205

Deer, 50, 128

D'Entrecasteaux Islands, 44, 156

Diagnostic criteria: useful in analysis of shifting cultivation, 181–186

Dibbling: description of, 142; use in New Guinea, 142

Dietary patterns, 116

Diffusion, 63; role of, 55

Digging stick, 61, 151; use in planting, 142; description of, 149–150; as early tool, 149; spatulate-ended, distribution of, 150

Dispersed settlement: use of, 67

Dobu: hierarchical status of, 205

Dogs, 48, 153; as hunting animals, 128; in ritualism, 129; as pets, 129; as human food, 129; as watchdogs, 129; presence of, 185

Domestic animals: as food sources, 129; chronology of, 153

Domesticates: defined, 126; as crop plants, 126

Domestication of plants: conditions for, 58–61; timing of, 59

Donkey, 157

Dooryard gardens, 25, 137, 144; use by Lamet,

35, 48; origins of, 62; Reddi, 111; planting of, 142; related to field shift, 147–148; and village residence, 148; as women's domain, 153; men caring for, 153; variation in, 184

Dyak: and Christianity, 79

Economic factor: role of, 70–74

Environmental determinism, 57

Erosion: nature of, 33; agencies causing, 33–34, 184

Ethnic patterns: map of, 18

European crop plants: introduction of, 152

Exchange, 137, 158; systems of, 186

Exchange patterns: institutionalized patterns, eastern sector, 159; obligational aspects of, 159; regional variation in, 159; role of gift giving in, 159; analysis of, 160–161

Exchange system: ubiquity of, 132–133

Fallowing, 136, 144; techniques, variation in, 182

False dragon's blood, 131

Feast pattern: economic impact of, 71

Fencing, 62, 137, 138, 140; need for, 141; timing of, 141; procedural systems, 183

Feral crop plants, 128; decline in, 111; importance of, 125–126; collection of, 126

Fertilizer: ashes as, 39

Festival: eating of pigs, 130

Field shift, 137; systems of, 144; diagrams of patterns, 145; variations in, 181

Field shifting: and residence patterns, 147

Filipinos: following timbermen, 21

Fire: role in vegetative change, 39–40; escape of, 41; uses in hunting, 128

Fishing, 128; among Lamet, 49; decreased returns from, 51–52

Flail, 151

Flatlands: preemption of, by sedentary cultivators, 27–29; preference for, by shifting cultivators, 27–29; problems of, for shifting cultivators, 27–29

Forest reserves: effect on wild game, 51

Forests, 39–40

Fowls, 153

Frontiersman: role of, 106

Fruits, 133

Fuyughe, 71

Gadabas, 149

Gandarusa, 154

Gardens: siting of, 75

Garia, 16, 90; hierarchical status of, 204

Garo, 13, 82

Gathering: significance of plant gathering, 50–51; decreased returns from, 52; of plant products, 125

Gharuwood, 131

Gift giving: commodity as exchange, 159

Ginger, 154

Glutinous rice: location of, 119

Goats, 129; presence of, 185

Gond, 19, 82; settlement pattern, 66; displacement from lands, 107; taking on permanent-field cultivation, 107; hierarchical status of, 208, 209
Grain crops: ascendancy over root crops, 114
Grams, 111, 115, 117, 118, 140
Grasslands: burning of, 34; agencies causing, 40; growth of, 40; spread of, 127; resultant from clearing, 183
Grubs, 51
Guava, 120
Gutta-percha, 131

Hamlets: siting of, 65–66
Hanunóo, 30, 35, 42, 114, 126; seasonal residence among, 69; plant environment, 127; stability of, 146; ceremonial ritual among, 157; hierarchical status of, 208
Harvest, 136, 137; ceremonials, 155; patterns, 182
Harvesting, 140; description of, 143; labor required, for rice, 143; method of, 150
Harvest period: of canarium almonds, 125
Hierarchical systems, 162
Hierarchies of systems: descriptions of, 203–212
Hill Garo: hierarchical status of, 212
Hill Maria Gond: hierarchical status of, 211
Himalayas, 8, 19, 36, 38, 62, 76, 107, 111, 158; as a crop region, 118; crop transmission zone, 119
Hinduism, 130
Hinduization: of tribal people, 107
History: defined, 54
Ho: displacement of, from lands, 107; taking on permanent-field cultivation, 107; hierarchical status of, 211
Hoes, 150, 151
Holy basil, 154
Horses, 129, 157; presence of, 185
Housing: siting of, 67; replacement of, 147; status of, 185
House site: right to, 92
Hunger period, 71, 122, 160
Hunting: use of fire in, 41; by Lamet, 49; seasonality of, 49; by shifting cultivators, 50; decreased returns from, 51–52; comment on, 128; dogs, 128
Hydrocotyle, 114, 154

Iban, 22, 44, 47, 123, 124, 131, 143; seasonal residence among, 69; wealth of, 72; economic exchange among, 72; rice ceremonial, 157; hierarchical status of, 210
Illipe nuts, 131
Incipient shifting cultivation: residence pattern of, 68
India, 13, 15, 19, 22, 29, 43, 44, 64, 66, 69, 73, 76, 78, 94, 96, 97, 98, 100, 107, 114, 116, 117, 121, 122, 127, 129, 130, 133, 152, 155, 158; decline of taros and yams, 111; as crop re-

gion, 118; retreat of shifting cultivation, 134; tool uses, 150; decline of ceremonial magic, 157
Indicator plant: in forest regeneration, 42
Indochina, 14, 15, 29, 35, 36, 44, 64, 72, 78, 98, 118, 161
Indonesia, 15, 33, 42, 86, 97, 100, 108
Inheritance: of land, 80; of land rights, 91
Integral shifting cultivation: definition of, 23; economic system of, 72
Integral shifting cultivators: complementary economy of, 131
Ipili: hierarchical status of, 204
Iron tools, 131
Islam, 130
Isneg: hierarchical status of, 208
Ivory, 131

Jakun: hierarchical status of, 206, 207, 208
Japan, 43
Java, 99
Jehai: hierarchical status of, 206
Jelutong, 131
Job's tears, 35, 118
Jungle fowl, 128

Kacha, 121; hierarchical status of, 212
Kachari, 95; land claiming, 100
Kachin, 36
Kalinga: hierarchical status of, 209
Kelabit, 45
Keraki-Semarji: hierarchical status of, 205
Kerosene, 131
Keveri, 82
Khasa, 107
Khasi, 95; hierarchical status of, 212
Khoirao, 121; hierarchical status of, 212
Kingship: concept of, 96–97
Kiriwina: settlement pattern of, 66
Knife, 150, 151
Kolma, 19, 149; taking on permanent-field cultivation, 107; displacement of, from lands, 107; hierarchical status of, 207, 208
Konyak Naga: retention of taro as staple, 121; hierarchical status of, 205
Korea, 43
Kuki, 68, 76; replacement of Zemi, 20
Kukukuku: hierarchical status of, 204
Kula ring, 159
Kuma, 93; hierarchical status of, 205
Kuman, 42, 82

Labor, 137; patterns of, 151–152
Lamet, 22, 139, 141; soils, knowledge of, 35; exchange pattern of, 48–49; annual calendar, 49; economic exchange among, 72; exchange system of, 132; exchange volume of, 161
Land: ownership, 86; abandonment, 87; inheritance, 87; alienation, 88; used for secondary purposes, 88; tenure, 88–90; occupance cycle, 89; privacy of tenure, 89; re-

version of private tenure, 90; inheritance of rights in, 90–91; transfer of rights to, 90–91; survey and title, 102; displacement, 107–108

Land clearing, 137

Land control, 137; among shifting cultivators, 85; conceptual principles of, 86; evolutionary aspects of, 93–96; changing systems of, 99

Land Dyak, 123

Landforms, 28

Landownership: private, growth of, 95–96; among Naga, 96

Land system, 77; disturbance of by European, 78; relation to social organization, 85; controls over, 86; introduction of European, 100; problems of, 101–104

Land tenure: and kingship, 96; impact of political state on, 96; Burmese, 97; Cambodian, 97; Thailand, 97; replacement of native, 98; under partial systems, 105; controls over, 183

Lanoh Negrito: heirarchical status of, 206

Lepcha, 82; hierarchical status of, 209, 211

Lesser Sunda Islands, 129, 153

Lettuce, 120

Levies: on lands cultivated, 93

Lhota: hierarchical status of, 211

Lima bean, 120

Lizards, 51

Long house: as settlement form, 66

Magahat: hierarchical status of, 207

Magic, 153; role of, 69–70. *See also* Ritualism

Maintenance procedures, 183

Maize, 35, 36, 120, 125

Malaita, 124

Malaita-Ulawa: hierarchical status of, 204

Malasir, 107

Malaya, 14, 15, 20, 99, 130, 158

Malaysia, 114, 118, 130, 131, 133, 135, 155, 156, 157, 158; as crop region, 117; tool uses, 150

Manioc, 35, 36, 120, 121, 123

Manoko, 16, 40, 82; hierarchical status of, 206

Maram, 121; hierarchical status of, 212

Marginal shifting cultivators: commercial cropping among, 133; income-producing activities of, 133

Marias, 149

Market gardening: by shifting cultivators, 134

Massim, 68

Master-magician, 155

Mech, 13, 82

Melanesia, 111, 114, 118, 121, 127, 128, 143, 158; as crop region, 116

Mentawei Island, 44

Mesolithic: timing of, 59

Miao: migration of, 29; tradition-bound culture of, 29

Millets, 35, 60, 111, 115, 117, 118, 140, 153

Mithan, 128, 129, 157

Mohammedanism, 130

Moluccas, 117

Morphology: of settlements, 66–67

Mundas, 149

Naga, 64, 76, 94, 95, 96, 111, 114, 121, 149

Naga groups: general shift to rice staple, 121; increase in wet-field rice cropping, 121

Naikpods, 19

Naked Rengma, 121; hierarchical status of, 212

Negrito, 36, 42, 62, 141, 143, 144

Negrito, Philippine: economy described, 36

New Caledonia, 115

New Guinea, 5, 13, 15, 20, 22, 29, 35, 36, 43, 64, 69, 78, 82, 90, 93, 94, 95, 111, 114, 115, 116, 117, 121, 123, 125, 126, 127, 132, 133, 135, 139, 142, 143, 147, 150, 155, 156, 159, 160, 161, 170, 187; lands claimed, 104; anomaly of sweet potato highland crop, 122; tool systems, 151

New Guinea asparagus, 111, 126

Nutmeg, 131

Obligational exchange: economic function of, 71–72

Obligational patterns: of land cultivator, 93

Oil seeds, 133

Omnivorousness: of shifting cultivators, 51; as culture trait, 157

Orokaiva, 16, 111; exchange volume, 160; hierarchical status of, 205

Outboard motor, 131

Ownership of land: private, change to, 98

Pakistan, 13, 29

Palolo worm, 128

Pandanus, 122

Panyer, 148

Papaya, 120

Papua, 71, 82

Parsnips, 120

Partial shifting cultivation: definition of, 23; complementary economics of, 133; crop systems of, 133; distribution of, 135; comparative economic analysis of, 161–162; Ceylon pattern of, 162

Partial systems, 101; land tenure, 105

Passion fruit, 120

Pauri Bhuiyan: hierarchical status of, 212

Peanut, 120

Pearls, 132

Pears, 118

Peasants, 128

Pepper, 131

Permanent-field agriculture: expansion of, 167

Philippines, 11, 14, 15, 20, 22, 23, 33, 38, 40, 42, 67, 68, 69, 78, 82, 83, 97, 99, 100, 108, 109, 123, 125, 129, 133, 135, 139, 156, 157, 160; pioneer settlement of, 21

Pigs, 48, 71, 128, 153; distribution of, 50; as food, 129; in ritualism, 129; wild, as food source and as predator, 129; domestication routine, 130; species listing of, 130; loss of ceremonial status in west, 156; status of, 185

Pinatubo, 42, 139; as crop growers, 125; share of food collected, 125

Pinatubo Negrito: exchange volume of, 160; hierarchical status of, 206

Pineapple, 120

Pioneer: settlement, 106

Pioneering system: shifting cultivation as, 5

Plains Miri: hierarchical status of, 209

Plantain. *See* Bananas

Plant domestication: conditions for, 58–61

Plant environment: maintenance of, 126

Planting, 136, 137, 140; of trees, 147

Planting calendar: timing of, by stars, 44

Planting period: for taros, 123; for yams, 123; for seed-planted crops, 124–125; for vegetatively reproduced crops, 124–125

Planting procedure: seed mixing, 110; variation in, 141, 182

Planting season: for rice, 47; in Solomon Islands, 47; for taros, 47; for yams, 47

Ple Senoi: hierarchical status of, 206

Plow, 151

Plums, 118

Political administration: in shifting-cultivator society, 77

Political factor: role of, 74–75

Political state: impact of, on land tenure, 96, 97

Political structure, 64

Polynesia, 114

Population distribution: resulting from settlement patterns, 185

Post-Columbian introductions: crop plants, 120

Potatoes, 122

Pottery jars, 131

Precipitation regime: effect of, on cropping cycle, 44

Public domain: nature of, 91; impact on, by European, 99–100

Pulses, 124, 133

Pumpkins, 120, 133

Pyrophytic Vegetation: durability of, 39–40

Rainy season: problem of, 45; cyclic factors of, in planting, 45–46

Raj Gonds, 19

Raji, 36, 62, 72, 76, 141, 144; economy described, 19–20; hierarchical status of, 209

Rake, 150, 151

Raking: as procedure in planting, 150

Rat bandicoots, 50

Rats, 51

Rattan, 131

Reddi, 149, 157; displacement of, from lands, 107; taking on permanent-field cultivation, 107; dooryard gardens, 111

Regeneration: of forests, 42; of vegetation, by planting, 147

Rejection of new plants, 121

Religion: effect of, on settlement pattern, 67; role of, 69–70; impact of, on field shift, 70; planting ritual of, 114; animals in, 130

Residence, 137, 144

Residence patterns: related to field shifting, 147

Rice, 22, 35, 36, 48, 49, 107, 111, 115, 117, 118, 121, 123, 131, 132, 133, 140, 143, 150, 153, 156; planting season of, 47; replacing yams and taros, 60; planting periods for, 124; as chief ceremonial object among Iban, 157

Rice yields: range of, 21, 22

Ritual: role of, 69–70

Ritualism, 137; shift in, 114: significance of, 114; use of pig in, 129; with domestic animals, 129; in commodity exchange, 130; and acceptance-avoidance and taboo, 153; among crop growers, 154; among hunters, 154; crop plants used in, 154; maximum occurrence of, 154; per crop staple, 154; distribution of, 154–155; decline of, in west, 155; New Guinea as dominant region of, 155; animal magic in, 156; garden magic in, 156

Rodents, 51

Roller, 151

Root crops: dominance in eastern sector, 117

Rotational cycle: effect of shortening, 34

Rubber, 131

Sago, 111, 116, 117

Sandalwood, 131

Santal, 19, 107

Sapanwood, 131

Sarawak, 22, 44, 123, 131

Schouten Islands, 125

Sea gypsies, 131

Seasonality: tropical, detailed aspects of, 45; of planting staple crops, 123–124; overlooked aspects of, 124

Seasonal residence: for crop watching, 69; of Iban, 69

Sedentary residence: beginning of, 65

Seed mixing: prior to planting, 110

Seed planting: as origin of plant domestication, 60; by broadcasting, 142; by dibbling, 147, description of, 142; eastward spread of, 142; younger sequence, 153

Self-subsistence: inaccuracy of concept of, 158; possible cases of, 160

Semai Senoi: hierarchical status of, 207

Semidomesticates: as crop plants, 126; defined, 126

Senoi: hierarchical status of, 206, 208

Settlement morphology, 66; effect of Christianity upon, 67–68

Settlement patterns: brief listing of, for different peoples, 16; role of, 64; variation in, 185

Settlements: size of, 67–68

Shaman, 155

Shark, 128

Sheep, 129, 157; presence of, 185

Shifting: as term, meaning of, 7; of fields, systems for, 144

Shifting cultivation: descriptive notation of, 2; as rotation system, 3; court and government rulings on, 3; families employing, 3; reactions to, 3; destructiveness of, 4, 33–34; importance of, 4; historical role of, 4–5, 53, 58; last frontier of, 5; decline of, 6, 53, 120, 134; future of, 6; replacement of 6, 82; terminology, 6–7, 8, 175–180; disciplines interested in, 10; map of, 12; distribution of, 13, 17; elevation limits of, 13; acreage of, 14; populations using, 15, 16; economics and, 19, 70–74; definition of, 22; structure of, 22; integral systems of, 23; partial systems of, 23, 80–83, 135; classification of, 23–25; gross characteristics of, 25; relationship of, to landforms, 26–30, 39; cultural history and, 29; attitude toward soil in, 35; wet-mulching system in, 44; hunting in, 50; plant gathering in, 50–51; origins of, 61–62; differentiation of, 63–64; settlement patterns in, 64, 65–67; residence patterns in, 68; religion in, 69–70, 79; political factor in, 74–75; incipient system of, 80, 81, 82, 106; opportunistic system of, 80, 81; land systems of, 84–85; commercial aspects of, 133; restrictions on, 139–140; disorderliness of, 140; vegetative planting in, 141; fencing in, 141; hierarchies of, 149, 162, 164–165, 203–212; typologies of, 162; as neolithic system, 170; diagnostic criteria significant to, 181–186

Shotguns, 131

Sickle, 151

Site selection, 136, 137; factors in, 26, 139

Siting: as procedures, 138–139

Sloping lands: use of, by shifting cultivators, 29–30

Snakes, 51

Social organization: impact of, on land systems, 85

Social structure: early growth of, 65; systems of, 186

Social system: role of the, 78–80

Soil cultivation practice: by shifting cultivators, 31; in tropics, 31

Soil erosion: agencies causing, 33–34, 184; degree of, 33–35

Soil fertility, 61

Soils: effect of cultivation on, in tropics, 31; tropical, characteristics of, 32; conditioning of, by forest cover, 39; treatment of, 182

Solomon Islands, 44, 46, 116

Sorghums, 153

Soybeans, 118

Spice crops, 116

Spices, 131

Splintering-off: of living groups, 62

Squash, 120

Starvation period, 71, 122, 160; New Guinea, 123; impact of irregular rainy season, 123–

124; lack of, among taro planters, 125; and shift to seed planting, 160. *See also* Hunger period

Subanu: economy described, 67; residence pattern of, 67; adoption of permanent-field system of, 83; hierarchical status of, 206

Subsistence economy, 71; invalidity of, 131

Sugarcane, 36, 111, 122

Sumatra, 117

Survival training: for early man, 57

Sweet potato, 35, 111, 114, 116, 122, 125; yields, range of, 22; as highland crop in New Guinea, 121

Swidden: terminology, 9

Taboo, 137, on totem, 128

Tai, 29

Tanga, 16, 131

Tanga-Boieng: hierarchical status of, 205

Tanga Island, 156

Tangkhul, 121; hierarchical status of, 212

Tapiro, 139, 144; exchange volume, 160; hierarchical position of, 203

Taro, 22, 29, 30, 44, 121, 122, 152, 155; varieties of, 35–36; planting season, 46–47; replacement by rice, 60; decline of feral, 111; distribution, 111; map of distribution of, by species, 112; site preference, 115; wastage of surplus of, 117; current use of in western zone, 118; planting period, 123–124; as older than yams, 124; daily harvest of, 143; first-eating ceremony, 157

Taro ceremony: age of, 155

Taro yields: range of, 122

Taurus cattle, 157

Taxation: absence of, among shifting cultivators, 77

Taxes: as levies on exercise of tenure, 93

Tea, 49

Technologies, 136

Temiar Senoi: hierarchical status of, 206, 207

Temoq Jakun: hierarchical status of, 206

Tenure: land, 88–90; secondary usage, 92; evolutionary aspects of, 93–96; changing in New Guinea, 94; change among Naga, 94–95

Terminology: native language terms for shifting cultivation, 175–179; European language terms for shifting cultivation, 179–180; English synonyms for shifting cultivation, 180

Territoriality, 84; development of, 75; external controls on, 75–76; internal controls on, 76–77; European change in, 77; outside impacts upon, 77

Textiles, 131

Thailand, 14, 29, 40, 44, 97, 118, 123, 130, 133

Thievery: pattern of, 69

Tibetan Highland, 43

Timber: mining of, 138

Tinguian: hierarchical status of, 207

Tobacco, 36

Tools, 36, 136, 137; patterns of, 148, 183
Tool systems: range in, 149; classification of, 151
Tortoise shell, 131
Totem: avoidance of, 158
Trade: commodities involved in, 131; systems of, 186
Trade patterns: analysis of, 160–161
Trading expeditions: New Guinea, 159
Trapping, 49, 62
Tree-felling systems: descriptions of, 26–27
Tree rat, 128
Trees: ownership of, 88–89, 95; planting of, 147
Trenching tool, 151
Trespass: prohibition of, 92
Trial by fire: use of, in field burning, 70
Tribal chief: becoming king, 97
Tribal wars: effect on cropping cycle, 124
Trobriand Islanders, 47, 82, 124; pearling, 132; exchange volume of, 161; hierarchical status of, 205
Trobriand Islands, 66
Tubers, 21
Turmeric, 114, 154
Turtles, 128
Typological systems: mixture in, 138; evolution of, 138
Typology: elements of, 136; criteria of, 136–137
Typology of cropping, 63

Ulawa, 124

Vegetables, 21, 35, 133
Vegetation: effect of burning, on soils, 33; attitudes toward, 36–38; values of, to different culture levels, 36–38
Vegetation patterns of land chosen for cropping: variation in, 181
Vegetative associations: Hanunóo system of, 42
Vegetative cover: degrading of, 127
Vegetative origin: of plant domestication, 58
Vegetative planting: description of, 141

Vegetative reproduction: oldest pattern of, 152
Village dwelling: and dooryard gardens, 148
Village residence: beginning of, 65
Villages: siting of, 65–66; morphology of, 66–67; size of, 67–68; location of, 68

Wa, 17
Wage labor, 132; varieties of, among shifting cultivators, 134
Wallabies, 50, 128
Wastage: of surplus taros, 117
Water buffalo, 157; presence of, 185
Wealth: accumulation of, 72–73; discussion of, 131
Weeding, 136, 137, 140, 143; variation in, 182
Weeds, 61
Wheats, 118
White potato, 120
Wild bananas: gathering of, 126; inaccuracy of reference, 126
Wild cattle, 128
Wild game: comparative volume of, 50; regional variation of, 50; decrease in volume of, 51
Wild plant resource: variation in, 127
Wogeo, 35, 42, 61, 139, 141, 147; economy described, 20; exchange volume of, 161; hierarchical status of, 205
Wogeo Island, 125
Wood: for fencing, 138–139

Yam ceremony: age of, 155
Yams, 22, 30, 35, 116, 117, 118, 121, 122, 152, 155, 156; planting season for, 46–47; replacement of, by rice, 60; distribution of, 111; map of distribution, by species, 113; cooking of, 115; growing habit of, 115; site preference of, 115; size of, 115; planting period for, 123–124
Yields, crop: decline of, after initial cropping, 31

Zebu cattle, 48, 157
Zemi, 121; economy described, 20; village pattern of, 68; hierarchical status of, 211